George Whitefield

The Works of the Reverend George Whitefield, M.A.

With a select collection of letter

George Whitefield

The Works of the Reverend George Whitefield, M.A.
With a select collection of letter

ISBN/EAN: 9783337159900

Printed in Europe, USA, Canada, Australia, Japan

Cover: Foto ©Thomas Meinert / pixelio.de

More available books at **www.hansebooks.com**

GEORGE WHITEFIELD, M. A.

Late of PEMBROKE-COLLEGE, OXFORD,
And Chaplain to the Rt. Hon. the Countefs of HUNTINGDON.

CONTAINING

All his SERMONS and TRACTS
Which have been already publifhed:

WITH

A SELECT COLLECTION of LETTERS,
Written to his moft intimate Friends, and Perfons of Diftinction, in *England, Scotland, Ireland*, and *America*, from the Year 1734, to 1770, including the whole Period of his Miniftry.

ALSO

Some other PIECES on IMPORTANT SUBJECTS, never before printed; prepared by Himfelf for the Prefs.

To which is prefixed,

An ACCOUNT of his LIFE,
Compiled from his Original PAPERS and LETTERS.

VOL. VI.

LONDON:
Printed for EDWARD and CHARLES DILLY, in the Poultry; and Meffrs. KINCAID and CREECH, at Edinburgh.
MDCCLXXII.

CONTENTS.*

SERMON XXXII. A Penitent Heart, the best New Year's Gift.

LUKE xiii. 3. *Except ye repent, ye shall all likewise perish.*
Page 3

SERM. XXXIII. The Gospel Supper.

LUKE xiv. 22, 23, 24. *And the servant said, Lord, it is done as thou hast commanded, and yet there is room. And the lord said unto the servant, Go out into the highways, and hedges, and compel them to come in, that my house may be filled. For I say unto you, that none of those men which were bidden, shall taste of my supper.* p. 20.

SERM. XXXIV. The Pharisee and Publican.

LUKE xviii. 14. *I tell you, this man went down to his house justified rather than the other: For every one that exalteth himself, shall be abased; and he that humbleth himself, shall be exalted.* p. 36

SERM. XXXV. The Conversion of Zaccheus.

LUKE xix. 9, 10. *And Jesus said unto him, This day is salvation come to this house; forasmuch as he also is the Son of Abraham. For the Son of man is come to seek and to save that which was lost.* — — — p. 49

SERM. XXXVI. The Marriage of Cana.

JOHN ii. 11. *This beginning of miracles did Jesus in Cana of Galilee, and manifested forth his glory; and his disciples believed on him.* — — p. 64

---

* The Sermons marked with a *, are now first published from the Author's own Manuscripts.

[iv]

SERM. XXXVII. The Duty of searching the Scriptures.

JOHN v. 39. *Search the Scriptures.* — — p. 79

SERM. XXXVIII. The Indwelling of the Spirit, the common Privilege of all Believers.

JOHN vii. 37, 38, 39. *In the last day, that great day of the feast, Jesus stood and cried, saying, If any man thirst, let him come unto me and drink. He that believeth on me, as the scripture hath said, out of his belly shall flow rivers of living water. But this spake he of the Spirit, which they that believe on him should receive.* — — — p. 89

SERM. XXXIX. The Resurrection of Lazarus.

JOHN xi. 43, 44. *And when he had thus spoken, he cried with a loud voice, Lazarus come forth. And he that was dead, came forth, bound hand and foot with grave-cloaths: and his face was bound about with a napkin. Jesus saith unto them, Loose him, and let him go.* — — p. 103

SERM. XL. The Holy Spirit convincing the World of Sin, Righteousness, and Judgment.

JOHN xvi. 8. *And when he is come, he will reprove the world of sin, and of righteousness, and of judgment.* p. 127

SERM. XLI. Saul's Conversion.

ACTS ix. 22. *But Saul increased the more in strength, and confounded the Jews which dwelt at Damascus, proving that this is very Christ.* — — — p. 143

SERM. XLII. Marks of having received the Holy Ghost.

ACTS xix. 2. *Have ye received the Holy Ghost since ye believed?* — — — p. 161

SERM. XLIII. The Almost Christian.

ACTS xxvi. 28. *Almost thou persuadest me to be a christian.*
p. 174

SERM.

SERM. XLIV. Chrift, the Believer's Wifdom, Righteoufnefs, Sanctification, and Redemption.

1 Cor. i. 30. *But of him are ye in Chrift Jefus, who of God is made unto us, wifdom, righteoufnefs, fanctification, and redemption.* — — — p. 187

SERM. XLV. The Knowledge of Jefus Chrift the beft Knowledge.

1 Cor. ii. 2. *I determined not to know any thing among you, fave Jefus Chrift, and him crucified.* — p. 203

SERM. XLVI. Of Juftification by Chrift.

1 Cor. vi. 11. *But ye are juftified.* The whole verfe is: *And fuch were fome of you; but ye are wafhed, but ye are fanctified, but ye are juftified in the name of our Lord Jefus Chrift, and by the Spirit of our God.* — — p. 214

SERM. XLVII. The great Duty of Charity recommended.

1 Cor. xiii. 8. *Charity never faileth.* — p. 227

SERM. XLVIII. Satan's Devices.

1 Cor. ii. 11. *Left Satan fhould get an advantage over us; for we are not ignorant of his devices.* — p. 241

SERM. XLIX. On Regeneration.

2 Cor. v. 17. *If any man be in Chrift, he is a new creature.* p. 257

*SERM. L. Chriftians, Temples of the living God.

2 Cor. vi. 16. *Ye are the Temple of the living God.* p. 273

SERM. LI. Chrift the only Prefervative againft a Reprobate Spirit.

2 Cor. xiii. 5. *Know ye not your ownfelves, how that Jefus Chrift is in you, except ye be Reprobates.* — p. 287

SERM. LII. The heinous Sin of Drunkennefs.

Ephesians v. 18. *Be not drunk with wine, wherein is excefs; but be filled with the Spirit.* — — p. 303

SERM. LIII. The Power of Chrift's Refurrection.

PHILIP. iii. 10. *That I may know him, and the power of his refurrection.* — — — p. 317

SERM. LIV. Interceffion every Chriftian's Duty.

1 THESS. v. 25. *Brethren, pray for us.* — p. 331

SERM. LV. Perfecution every Chriftian's Lot.

2 TIM. iii. 12. *Yea, and all that will live godly in Chrift Jefus, fhall fuffer perfecution.* — — p. 345

SERM. LVI. An Exhortation to the People of God not to be difcouraged in their Way, by the Scoffs and Contempt of wicked Men.

HEBREWS iv. 9. *There remaineth therefore a reft to the people of God.* — — — p. 361

*SERM. LVII. Preached before the Governor and Council, and the Houfe of Affembly, in Georgia, on January 28, 1770.

ZECH. iv. 10. *For who hath defpifed the day of fmall things.*
p. 369

SERMON

SERMON XXXII.

A Penitent Heart, the beſt *New Year's Gift.*

LUKE xiii. 3.
Except ye repent, ye ſhall all likewiſe periſh.

WHEN we conſider how heinous and aggravating our offences are, in the ſight of a juſt and holy GOD, that they bring down his wrath upon our heads, and occaſion us to live under his indignation; how ought we thereby to be deterred from evil, or at leaſt engaged to ſtudy to repent thereof, and not commit the ſame again; but man is ſo thoughtleſs of an eternal ſtate, and has ſo little conſideration of the welfare of his immortal ſoul, that he can ſin without any thought that he muſt give an account of his actions at the day of judgment; or if he, at times, has any reflections on his behaviour, they do not drive him to true repentance: he may, for a ſhort time, refrain from falling into ſome groſs ſins which he had lately committed; but then, when the temptation comes again with power, he is carried away with the luſt; and thus he goes on promiſing and reſolving, and in breaking both his reſolutions and his promiſes, as faſt almoſt as he has made them. This is highly offenſive to GOD, it is mocking of him. My brethren, when grace is given us to repent truly, we ſhall turn wholly unto GOD; and let me beſeech you to repent of your ſins, for the time is haſtening when you will have neither time nor call to repent; there is none in the grave, whither we are going; but do not be afraid, for GOD often receives the greateſt ſinner to mercy through the merits of CHRIST JESUS; this magnifies the riches of his free grace; and ſhould be an encouragement for you, who are great and notorious ſinners, to repent, for he will have mercy upon you, if you through CHRIST return unto him.

St. *Paul*

St. *Paul* was an eminent instance of this; he speaks of himself as "the chief of sinners," and he declareth how GOD shewed mercy unto him. CHRIST loves to shew mercy unto sinners, and if you repent, he will have mercy upon you. But as no word is more mistaken than that of repentance, I shall

I. Shew you what the nature of repentance is.

II. Consider the several parts and causes of repentance.

III. I shall give you some reasons, why repentance is necessary to salvation. And

IV. Exhort all of you, high and low, rich and poor, one with another, to endeavour after repentance.

I. Repentance, my brethren, in the first place, as to its nature, is the carnal and corrupt disposition of men being changed into a renewed and sanctified disposition. A man that has truly repented, is truly regenerated: it is a different word for one and the same thing; the motley mixture of the beast and devil is gone; there is, as it were, a new creation wrought in your hearts. If your repentance is true, you are renewed throughout, both in soul and body; your understandings are enlightened with the knowledge of GOD, and of the LORD JESUS CHRIST; and your wills, which were stubborn, obstinate, and hated all good, are obedient and conformable to the will of GOD. Indeed, our deists tell us, that man now has a free will to do good, to love GOD, and to repent when he will; but indeed, there is no free will in any of you, but to sin; nay, your free-will leads you so far, that you would, if possible, pull GOD from his throne. This may, perhaps, offend the Pharisees; but (it is the truth in CHRIST which I speak, I lie not) every man by his own natural will hates GOD; but when he is turned unto the LORD, by evangelical repentance, then his will is changed; then your consciences, now hardened and benumbed, shall be quickened and awakened; then your hard hearts shall be melted, and your unruly affections shall be crucified. Thus, by that repentance, the whole soul will be changed, you will have new inclinations, new desires, and new habits.

You may see how vile we are by nature, that it requires so great a change to be made upon us, to recover us from this state of sin, and therefore the consideration of our dreadful state should make us earnest with GOD to change our condition, and that change, true repentance implies; therefore, my brethren, consider how hateful your ways are to GOD, while you continue in sin; how abominable you are unto him, while you run into evil: you cannot be said to be christians while you are hating CHRIST, and his people; true repentance will entirely change you, the bias of your souls will be changed, then you will delight in GOD, in CHRIST, in his law, and in his people; you will then believe that there is such a thing as inward feeling, though now you may esteem it madness and enthusiasm; you will not then be ashamed of becoming fools for CHRIST's sake; you will not regard being scoffed at; it is not then their pointing after you and crying, "Here comes another troop of his followers," will dismay you; no, your soul will abhor such proceedings, the ways of CHRIST and his people will be your whole delight.

It is the nature of such repentance to make a change, and the greatest change as can be made here in the soul. Thus you see what repentance implies in its own nature; it denotes an abhorrence of all evil, and a forsaking of it. I shall now proceed

Secondly, To shew you the parts of it, and the causes concurring thereto.

The parts are, sorrow, hatred, and an entire forsaking of sin.

Our sorrow and grief for sin, must not spring merely from a fear of wrath; for if we have no other ground but that, it proceeds from self-love, and not from any love to GOD; and if love to GOD is not the chief motive of your repentance, your repentance is in vain, and not to be esteemed true.

Many, in our days, think their crying, GOD forgive me! or, LORD have mercy upon me! or, I am sorry for it! is repentance, and that GOD will esteem it as such; but, indeed, they are mistaken; it is not the drawing near to GOD with our lips, while our hearts are far from him, which he regards. Repentance does not come by fits and starts; no, it is one

A 3   continued

continued act of our lives; for as we daily commit sin, so we need a daily repentance before GOD, to obtain forgiveness for those sins we commit.

It is not your confessing yourselves to be sinners, it is not knowing your condition to be sad and deplorable, so long as you continue in your sins; your care and endeavours should be, to get the heart thoroughly affected therewith, that you may feel yourselves to be lost and undone creatures, for CHRIST came to save such as are lost; and if you are enabled to groan under the weight and burden of your sins, then CHRIST will ease you and give you rest.

And till you are thus sensible of your misery and lost condition, you are a servant to sin and to your lusts, under the bondage and command of Satan, doing his drudgery: thou art under the curse of GOD, and liable to his judgment. Consider how dreadful thy state will be at death, and after the day of judgment, when thou wilt be exposed to such miseries which the ear hath not heard, neither can the heart conceive, and that to all eternity, if you die impenitent.

But I hope better things of you, my brethren, though I thus speak, and things which accompany salvation; go to GOD in prayer, and be earnest with him, that by his Spirit he would convince you of your miserable condition by nature, and make you truly sensible thereof. O be humbled, be humbled, I beseech you, for your sins. Having spent so many years in sinning, what canst thou do less, than be concerned to spend some hours in mourning and sorrowing for the same, and be humbled before GOD.

Look back into your lives, call to mind thy sins, as many as possible thou canst, the sins of thy youth, as well as of thy riper years; see how you have departed from a gracious Father, and wandered in the way of wickedness, in which you have lost yourselves, the favour of GOD, the comforts of his Spirit, and the peace of your own consciences; then go and beg pardon of the LORD, through the blood of the Lamb, for the evil thou hast committed, and for the good thou hast omitted. Consider, likewise, the heinousness of thy sins; see what very aggravating circumstances thy sins are attended with, how you have abused the patience of GOD, which should have led you to repentance; and when thou findest thy heart hard, beg of

GOD

GOD to soften it, cry mightily unto him, and he will take away thy stony heart, and give thee a heart of flesh.

Resolve to leave all thy sinful lusts and pleasures; renounce, forsake, and abhor thy old sinful course of life, and serve GOD in holiness and righteousness all the remaining part of life. If you lament and bewail past sins, and do not forsake them, your repentance is in vain, you are mocking of GOD, and deceiving your own soul; you must put off the old man with his deeds, before you can put on the new man, CHRIST JESUS.

You, therefore, who have been swearers and cursers, you, who have been harlots and drunkards, you, who have been thieves and robbers, you, who have hitherto followed the sinful pleasures and diversions of life, let me beseech you, by the mercies of GOD in CHRIST JESUS, that you would no longer continue therein, but that you would forsake your evil ways, and turn unto the LORD, for he waiteth to be gracious unto you, he is ready, he is willing to pardon you of all your sins; but do not expect CHRIST to pardon you of sin, when you run into it; and will not abstain from complying with the temptations; but if you will be persuaded to abstain from evil and chuse the good, to return unto the LORD, and repent of your wickedness, he hath promised he will abundantly pardon you, he will heal your back-slidings, and will love you freely. Resolve now this day to have done with your sins for ever; let your old ways and you be separated; you must resolve against it, for there can be no true repentance without a resolution to forsake it. Resolve for CHRIST, resolve against the devil and his works, and go on fighting the LORD's battles against the devil and his emissaries; attack him in the strongest holds he has, fight him as men, as christians, and you will soon find him to be a coward; resist him and he will fly from you. Resolve, through grace, to do this, and your repentance is half done; but then take care that you do not ground your resolutions on your own strength, but in the strength of the LORD JESUS CHRIST; he is the way, he is the truth, and he is the life; without his assistance you can do nothing, but through his grace strengthening thee, thou wilt be enabled to do all things; and the more thou art sensible of thy own weakness and inability, the more ready CHRIST will be to help thee; and what can all the men of the world do to thee when

CHRIST is for thee? thou wilt not regard what they say against thee, for you will have the testimony of a good conscience.

Resolve to cast thyself at the feet of CHRIST in subjection to him, and throw thyself into the arms of CHRIST for salvation by him. Consider, my dear brethren, the many invitations he has given you to come unto him, to be saved by him; "GOD has laid on him the iniquity of us all." O let me prevail with you, above all things, to make choice of the LORD JESUS CHRIST; resign yourselves unto him, take him, O take him, upon his own terms, and whosoever thou art, how great a sinner soever you have been, this evening, in the name of the great GOD, do I offer JESUS CHRIST unto thee; as thou valuest thy life and soul refuse him not, but stir up thyself to accept of the LORD JESUS, take him wholly as he is, for he will be applied wholly unto you, or else not at all. JESUS CHRIST must be your whole wisdom, JESUS CHRIST must be your whole righteousness, JESUS CHRIST must be your whole sanctification, or he will never be your eternal redemption.

What though you have been ever so wicked and profligate, yet, if you will now abandon your sins, and turn unto the LORD JESUS CHRIST, thou shalt have him given to thee, and all thy sins shall be freely forgiven. O why will you neglect the great work of your repentance? do not defer the doing of it one day longer, but to-day, even now, take that CHRIST who is freely offered to you.

Now as to the *causes* hereof, the first cause is GOD; he is the author, "we are born of GOD," GOD hath begotten us, even GOD, the Father of our LORD JESUS CHRIST; it is he that stirs us up to will and to do of his own good pleasure: and another cause is, GOD's free grace; it is owing to the "riches of his free grace," my brethren, that we have been prevented from going down to hell long ago; it is because the compassions of the LORD fail not, they are new every morning, and fresh every evening.

Sometimes the instruments are very unlikely: a poor despised minister, or member of JESUS CHRIST, may, by the power of GOD, be made an instrument in the hands of GOD, of bringing you to true evangelical repentance; and this may be done to shew, that the power is not in men, but that it is entirely owing to the good pleasure of GOD; and if there

has

has been any good done among many of you, by preaching the word, as I trust there has, though it was preached in a field, if GOD has met and owned us, and blessed his word, though preached by an enthusiastic babbler, a boy, a madman; I do rejoice, yea, and will rejoice, let foes say what they will. I shall now

Thirdly, Shew the reasons why repentance is necessary to salvation.

And this, my brethren, is plainly revealed to us in the word of GOD, " The soul that does not repent and turn unto the LORD, shall die in its sins, and their blood shall be required at their own heads." It is necessary, as we have sinned, we should repent; for a holy GOD could not, nor ever can, or will, admit any thing that is unholy into his presence: this is the beginning of grace in the soul; there must be a change in heart and life, before there can be a dwelling with a holy GOD. You cannot love sin and GOD too, you cannot love GOD and mammon; no unclean person can stand in the presence of GOD, it is contrary to the holiness of his nature; there is a contrariety between the holy nature of GOD, and the unholy nature of carnal and unregenerate men.

What communication can there be between a sinless GOD, and creatures full of sin, between a pure GOD and impure creatures? If you were to be admitted into heaven with your present tempers, in your impenitent condition, heaven itself would be a hell to you; the songs of angels would be as enthusiasm, and would be intolerable to you; therefore you must have these tempers changed, you must be holy, as GOD is: he must be your GOD here, and you must be his people, or you will never dwell together to all eternity. If you hate the ways of GOD, and cannot spend an hour in his service, how will you think to be easy, to all eternity, in singing praises to him that sits upon the throne, and to the Lamb for ever.

And this is to be the employment, my brethren, of all those who are admitted into this glorious place, where neither sin nor sinner is admitted, where no scoffer ever can come, without repentance from his evil ways, a turning unto GOD, and a cleaving unto him: this must be done, before any can be admitted into the glorious mansions of GOD, which are

prepared

prepared for all that love the LORD JESUS CHRIST in sincerity and truth: repent ye then of all your sins. O my dear brethren, it makes my blood run cold, in thinking that any of you should not be admitted into the glorious mansions above. O that it was in my power, I would place all of you, yea, you my scoffing brethren, and the greatest enemy I have on earth, at the right-hand of JESUS; but this I cannot do: however, I advise and exhort you, with all love and tenderness, to make JESUS your refuge; fly to him for relief; JESUS died to save such as you; he is full of compassion; and if you go to him, as poor, lost, undone sinners, JESUS will give you his spirit; you shall live and reign, and reign and live, you shall love and live, and live and love with this JESUS to all eternity.

I am, *Fourthly*, to exhort all of you, high and low, rich and poor, one with another, to repent of all your sins, and turn unto the LORD.

And I shall speak to each of you; for you have either repented, or you have not, you are believers in CHRIST JESUS, or unbelievers.

And first, you who never have truly repented of your sins, and never have truly forsaken your lusts, be not offended if I speak plain to you; for it is love, love to your souls, that constrains me to speak: I shall lay before you your danger, and the misery to which you are exposed, while you remain impenitent in sin. And O that this may be a means of making you fly to CHRIST for pardon and forgiveness.

While thy sins are not repented of, thou art in danger of death, and if you should die, you would perish for ever. There is no hope of any who live and die in their sins, but that they will dwell with devils and damned spirits to all eternity. And how do we know we shall live much longer: we are not sure of seeing our own habitations this night in safety. What mean ye then being at ease and pleasure while your sins are not pardoned. As sure as ever the word of GOD is true, if you die in that condition, you are shut out of all hope and mercy for ever, and shall pass into easeless and endless misery.

What is all thy pleasures and diversions worth? They last but for a moment, they are of no worth, and but of short continuance. And sure it must be gross folly, eagerly to pursue

those

those sinful lusts and pleasures, which war against the soul, which tend to harden the heart, and keep us from closing with the LORD JESUS; indeed, these are destructive of our peace here, and without repentance, will be of our peace hereafter.

O the folly and madness of this sensual world; sure if there were nothing in sin but present slavery, it would keep an ingenuous spirit from it. But to do the devils drudgery! and if we do that, we shall have his wages, which is eternal death and condemnation; O consider this, my guilty brethren, you that think it no crime to swear, whore, drink, or scoff and jeer at the people of GOD; consider how your voices will then be changed, and you that counted their lives madness, and their end without honour, shall howl and lament at your own madness and folly, that should bring you to so much woe and distress. Then you will lament and bemoan your own dreadful condition; but it will be of no signification: for he that is now your merciful Saviour, will then become your inexorable Judge. Now he is easy to be entreated; but then, all your tears and prayers will be in vain: for GOD hath allotted to every man a day of grace, a time of repentance, which if he doth not improve, but neglects and despises the means which are offered to him, he cannot be saved.

Consider, therefore, while you are going on in a course of sin and unrighteousness, I beseech you, my brethren, to think of the consequence that will attend your thus mispending your precious time; your souls are worth being concerned about: for if you can enjoy all the pleasures and diversions of life, at death you must leave them; that will put an end to all your worldly concerns. And will it not be very deplorable, to have your good things here, all your earthly, sensual, devilish pleasures, which you have been so much taken up with, all over: and the thought for how trifling a concern thou hast lost eternal welfare, will gnaw thy very soul.

Thy wealth and grandeur will stand in no stead; thou canst carry nothing of it into the other world: then the consideration of thy uncharitableness to the poor, and the ways thou didst take to obtain thy wealth, will be a very hell unto thee.

Now you enjoy the means of grace, as the preaching of his word, prayer, and sacraments; and God has sent his ministers out into the fields and highways, to invite, to woo you to come in; but they are tiresome to thee, thou hadst rather be at thy pleasures: ere long, my brethren, they will be over, and you will be no more troubled with them; but then thou wouldst give ten thousand worlds for one moment of that merciful time of grace which thou hast abused; then you will cry for a drop of that precious blood which now you trample under your feet; then you will wish for one more offer of mercy, for Christ and his free grace to be offered to you again; but your crying will be in vain: for as you would not repent here, God will not give you an opportunity to repent hereafter: if you would not in Christ's time, you shall not in your own. In what a dreadful condition will you then be? What horror and astonishment will possess your souls? Then all thy lies and oaths, thy scoffs and jeers at the people of God, all thy filthy and unclean thoughts and actions, thy mispent time in balls, plays, and assemblies, thy spending whole evenings at cards, dice, and masquerades, thy frequenting of taverns and alehouses, thy worldliness, covetousness, and thy uncharitableness, will be brought at once to thy remembrance, and at once charged upon thy guilty soul. And how can you bear the thoughts of these things? Indeed I am full of compassion towards you, to think that this should be the portion of any who now hear me. These are truths, though awful ones; my brethren, these are the truths of the gospel; and if there was not a necessity for thus speaking, I would willingly forbear: for it is no pleasing subject to me, any more than it is to you; but it is my duty to shew you the dreadful consequences of continuing in sin. I am only now acting the part of a skilful surgeon, that searches a wound before he heals it: I would shew you your danger first, that deliverance may be the more readily accepted by you.

Consider, that however you may be for putting the evil day away from you, and are now striving to hide your sins, at the day of judgment there shall be a full discovery of all; hidden things on that day shall be brought to light; and after all thy sins have been revealed to the whole world, then you must

depart

depart into everlasting fire in hell, which will not be quenched night and day; it will be without intermission, without end. O then, what stupidity and senselesness hath possessed your hearts, that you are not frighted from your sins. The fear of *Nebuchadnezzar's* fiery furnace, made men do any thing to avoid it; and shall not an everlasting fire make men, make you, do any thing to avoid it?

O that this would awaken and cause you to humble yourselves for your sins, and to beg pardon for them, that you might find mercy in the LORD.

Do not go away, let not the devil hurry you away before the sermon is over; but stay, and you shall have a JESUS offered to you, who has made full satisfaction for all your sins.

Let me beseech you to cast away your transgressions, to strive against sin, to watch against it, and to beg power and strength from CHRIST, to keep down the power of those lusts that hurry you on in your sinful ways.

But if you will not do any of these things, if you are resolved to sin on, you must expect eternal death to be the consequence; you must expect to be seized with horror and trembling, with horror and amazement, to hear the dreadful sentence of condemnation pronounced against you: and then you will run and call upon the mountains to fall on you, to hide you from the LORD, and from the fierce anger of his wrath.

Had you now a heart to turn from your sins unto the living GOD, by true and unfeigned repentance, and to pray unto him for mercy, in and through the merits of JESUS CHRIST, there were hope; but at the day of judgment, thy prayers and tears will be of no signification; they will be of no service to thee, the Judge will not be entreated by thee: as you would not hearken to him when he called unto thee, but despised both him and his ministers, and would not leave your iniquities; therefore, on that day he will not be entreated, notwithstanding all thy cries and tears; for GOD himself hath said, "Because I have called, and you refused; I have stretched out my hand, and no man regarded, but ye have set at nought all my counsel, and would have none of my reproof; I will also laugh at your calamity, and mock when your fear cometh as desolation, and your destruction cometh as a whirlwind; when diſtreſs and anguiſh cometh upon you, then ſhall they call upon me, but I will not anſwer, they ſhall ſeek me early, but they ſhall not find me."

Now you may call this enthuſiaſm and madneſs; but at that great day, if you repent not of your ſins here, you will find, by woeful experience, that your own ways were madneſs indeed; but God forbid it ſhould be left undone till then: ſeek after the LORD while he is to be found; call upon him while he is near, and you ſhall find mercy: repent this hour, and CHRIST will joyfully receive you.

What ſay you? Muſt I go to my Maſter, and tell him you will not come unto him, and will have none of his counſels? No; do not ſend me on ſo unhappy an errand: I cannot, I will not tell him any ſuch thing. Shall not I rather tell him, you are willing to repent and to be converted, to become new men, and take up a new courſe of life: this is the only wiſe reſolution you can make. Let me tell my Maſter, that you will come unto, and will wait upon him: for if you do not, it will be your ruin in time, and to eternity.

You will at death wiſh you had lived the life of the righteous, that you might have died his death. Be adviſed then; conſider what is before you, CHRIST and the world, holineſs and ſin, life and death: chooſe now for yourſelves; let your choice be made immediately, and let that choice be your dying choice.

If you would not chuſe to die in your ſins, to die drunkards, to die adulterers, to die ſwearers and ſcoffers, &c. live not out this night in the dreadful condition you are in. Some of you, it may be, may ſay, You have not power, you have no ſtrength: but have not you been wanting to yourſelves in ſuch things that were within your power? Have you not as much power to go to hear a ſermon, as to go into a playhouſe, or to a ball, or to a maſquerade? You have as much power to read the Bible, as to read plays, novels, and romances; and you can aſſociate as well with the godly, as with the wicked and prophane: this is but an idle excuſe, my brethren, to go on in your ſins: and if you will be found in the means of grace, CHRIST hath promiſed he will give you ſtrength. While *Peter* was preaching, the Holy Ghoſt fell on all that heard the word: how then ſhould you be found in the way of your duty?

Jesus Christ will then give thee strength; he will put his Spirit within thee; thou shalt find he will be thy wisdom, thy righteousness, thy sanctification, and thy redemption. Do but try what a gracious, a kind, and loving Master he is; he will be a help to thee in all thy burdens: and if the burden of sin is on thy soul, go to him as weary and heavy laden, and thou shalt find rest.

Do not say, that your sins are too many and too great to expect to find mercy: No; be they ever so many, or ever so great, the blood of the Lord Jesus Christ will cleanse you from all sins. God's grace, my brethren, is free, rich, and sovereign. *Manassah* was a great sinner, and yet he was pardoned; *Zaccheus* was gone far from God, and went out to see Christ, with no other view but to satisfy his curiosity; and yet Jesus met him, and brought salvation to his house. *Manassah* was an idolater and murderer, yet he received mercy; the other was an oppressor and extortioner, who had gotten riches by fraud and deceit, and by grinding the faces of the poor: so did *Matthew* too, and yet they found mercy.

Have you been blasphemers and persecutors of the saints and servants of God? So was St. *Paul*, yet he received mercy: Have you been common harlots, filthy and unclean persons? so was *Mary Magdalene*, and yet she received mercy: Hast thou been a thief? the thief upon the cross found mercy. I despair of none of you, however vile and profligate you have been; I say, I despair of none of you, especially when God has had mercy on such a wretch as I am.

Remember the poor Publican, how he found favour with God, when the proud, self-conceited Pharisee, who, puffed up with his own righteousness, was rejected. And if you will go to Jesus, as the poor Publican did, under a sense of your own unworthiness, you shall find favour as he did: there is virtue enough in the blood of Jesus, to pardon greater sinners than he has yet pardoned. Then be not discouraged, but come unto Jesus, and you will find him ready to help in all thy distresses, 'to lead thee into all truth, to bring thee from darkness to light, and from the power of Satan unto God.

Do not let the devil deceive you, by telling you, that then all your delights and pleasures will be over: No; this is so far from depriving you of all pleasure, that it is an inlet unto
unspeakable

unspeakable delights, peculiar to all who are truly regenerated. The new birth is the very beginning of a life of peace and comfort; and the greatest pleasantness is to be found in the ways of holiness.

Solomon, who had experience of all other pleasures, yet saith of the ways of godliness, " That all her ways are ways of pleasantness, and all her paths are paths of peace." Then sure you will not let the devil deceive you; it is all he wants, it is that he aims at, to make religion appear to be melancholy, miserable, and enthusiastic : but let him say what he will, give no ear to him, regard him not, for he always was and will be a liar.

What words, what entreaties shall I use, to make you come unto the LORD JESUS CHRIST ? The little love I have experienced since I have been brought from sin to GOD, is so great, that I would not be in a natural state for ten thousand worlds; and what I have felt is but little to what I hope to feel; but that little love which I have experienced, is a sufficient buoy against all the storms and tempests of this boisterous world : and let men and devils do their worst, I rejoice in the LORD JESUS, yea, and I will rejoice.

And O if you repent and come to JESUS, I would rejoice on your accounts too; and we should rejoice together to all eternity, when once passed on the other side of the grave. O come to JESUS. The arms of JESUS CHRIST will embrace you; he will wash away all your sins in his blood, and will love you freely.

Come, I beseech you to come unto JESUS CHRIST. O that my words would pierce to the very soul ! O that JESUS CHRIST was formed in you ! O that you would turn to the LORD JESUS CHRIST, that he might have mercy upon you !

I would speak till midnight, yea, I would speak till I could speak no more, so it might be a means to bring you to JESUS: let the LORD JESUS but enter your souls, and you shall find peace which the world can neither give nor take away. There is mercy for the greatest sinner amongst you; go unto the LORD as sinners, helpless and undone without it, and then you shall find comfort in your souls, and be admitted at last amongst those who sing praises unto the LORD to all eternity.

Now,

Now, my brethren, let me speak a word of exhortation to those of you, who are already brought to the LORD JESUS, who are born again, who do belong to GOD, to whom it has been given to repent of your sins, and are cleansed from their guilt; and that is, be thankful to GOD for his mercies towards you. O admire the grace of GOD, and bless his name for ever! Are you made alive in CHRIST JESUS? Is the life of GOD begun in your souls, and have you the evidence thereof? Be thankful for this unspeakable mercy to you: never forget to speak of his mercy. And as your life was formerly devoted to sin, and to the pleasures of the world, let it now be spent wholly in the ways of GOD; and O embrace every opportunity of doing and of receiving good. Whatsoever opportunity you have, do it vigorously, do it speedily, do not defer it. If thou seest one hurrying on to destruction, use the utmost of thy endeavour to stop him in his course; shew him the need he has of repentance, and that without it he is lost for ever; do not regard his despising of you; still go on to shew him his danger: and if thy friends mock and despise, do not let that discourage you; hold on, hold out to the end, so you shall have a crown which is immutable, and that fadeth not away.

Let the love of JESUS to you, keep you also humble; do not be high-minded, keep close unto the LORD, observe the rules which the LORD JESUS CHRIST has given in his word, and let not the instructions be lost which you are capable of giving. O consider what reason you have to be thankful to the LORD JESUS CHRIST for giving you that repentance you yourselves had need of: a repentance which worketh by love. Now you find more pleasure in walking with GOD one hour, than in all your former carnal delights, and all the pleasures of sin. O! the joy you feel in your own souls, which all the men of this world, and all the devils in hell, though they were to combine together, could not destroy. Then fear not their wrath or malice, for through many tribulations we must enter into glory.

A few days, or weeks, or years more, and then you will be beyond their reach, you will be in the heavenly *Jerusalem*; there is all harmony and love; there is all joy and delight; there the weary soul is at rest.

Now we have many enemies, but at death they are all loft; they cannot follow us beyond the grave: and this is a great encouragement to us not to regard the scoffs and jeers of the men of this world.

O let the love of Jesus be in your thoughts continually. It was his dying that brought you life; it was his crucifixion that paid the satisfaction for your sins; his death, burial, and resurrection that compleated the work; and he is now in heaven, interceding for you at the right-hand of his Father. And can you do too much for the Lord Jesus Christ, who has done so much for you? His love to you is unfathomable. O the height, the depth, the length and breadth of this love, that brought the King of glory from his throne, to die for such rebels as we are, when we had acted so unkindly against him, and deserved nothing but eternal damnation. He came down and took our nature upon him; he was made of flesh and dwelt among us; he was put to death on our account; he paid our ransom: surely this should make us love the Lord Jesus Christ; should make us rejoice in him, and not do as too many do, and as we ourselves have too often, crucify this Jesus afresh. Let us do all we can, my dear brethren, to honour him.

Come, all of you, come, and behold him stretched out for you; see his hands and feet nailed to the cross. O come, come, my brethren, and nail your sins thereto; come, come and see his side pierced; there is a fountain open for sin, and for uncleanness: O wash, wash and be clean: come and see his head crowned with thorns, and all for you. Can you think of a panting, bleeding, dying Jesus, and not be filled with pity towards him? He underwent all this for you. Come unto him by faith; lay hold on him: there is mercy for every soul of you that will come unto him. Then do not delay; fly unto the arms of this Jesus, and you shall be made clean in his blood.

O what shall I say unto you to make you come to Jesus: I have shewed you the dreadful consequence of not repenting of your sins: and if after all I have said, you are resolved to persist, your blood will be required at your own heads; but I hope better things of you, and things that accompany salvation. Let me beg of you to pray in good earnest for the

grace

grace of repentance. I may never see your faces again; but at the day of judgment I will meet you: there you will either bless GOD that ever you were moved to repentance; or else this sermon, though in a field, will be as a swift witness against you. Repent, repent therefore, my dear brethren, as *John the Baptist*, and as our blessed Redeemer himself earnestly exhorted, and turn from your evil ways, and the LORD will have mercy on you.

Shew them, O Father, wherein they have offended thee; make them to see their own vileness, and that they are lost and undone without true repentance; and O give them that repentance, we beseech of thee, that they may turn from sin unto thee the living and true GOD. These things, and whatever else thou seest needful for us, we entreat that thou wouldst bestow upon us, on account of what the dear JESUS CHRIST has done and suffered; to whom, with Thyself, and holy Spirit, three persons, and one GOD, be ascribed, as is most due, all power, glory, might, majesty, and dominion, now, henceforth, and for evermore. *Amen.*

SERMON XXXIII.

The Gospel Supper.

LUKE xiv. 22, 23, 24.

And the servant said, Lord, it is done as thou hast commanded, and yet there is room. And the lord said unto the servant, Go out into the high-ways, and hedges, and compel them to come in, that my house may be filled. For I say unto you, that none of those men which were bidden, shall taste of my supper.

THOUGH here is a large and solemn assembly, yet I suppose you are all convinced, that you are not to live in this world always. May I not take it for granted, that even the most prophane amongst you, do in your hearts believe, what the sacred oracles have most clearly revealed, " That as it is appointed for all men once to die, so after death comes the judgment?" Yes, I know you believe, that nothing is more certain, than that we are to " appear before the judgment-seat of CHRIST, to be rewarded according to the deeds done in the body, whether they have been good, or whether they have been evil." And, however hard the saying may seem to you at the first hearing, yet I cannot help informing you, that I am thoroughly persuaded, as many will be driven from that judgment-seat, with a " Depart ye cursed into everlasting fire," for pursuing things in themselves lawful, out of a wrong principle, and in too intense a degree; as for drunkenness, adultery, fornication, or any other gross enormity whatsoever. Bad as the world is, blessed be GOD, there are great numbers yet left amongst us, who either through the restraints of a religious education, or self-love,

and

and outward reputation, abstain from gross sin themselves, and look with detestation and abhorrence upon others, who indulge themselves in it. But then, through an over-eager pursuit after the things of sense and time, their souls are insensibly lulled into a spiritual slumber, and by degrees become as dead to God, and as deaf to all the gracious invitations of the gospel, as the most abandoned prodigals. It is remarkable, therefore, that our Saviour, knowing how desperately wicked and treacherous the heart of man was, in this, as well as other respects, after he had cautioned his disciples, and us in them, to "take heed that their hearts were not at any time overcharged with surfeiting and drunkenness," immediately adds, " and the cares (the immoderate anxious cares) of this life." For they are of a distracting, intoxicating nature, and soon overcharge and weigh down the hearts of the children of men. To prevent or remedy this evil, our Lord, during the time of his tabernacling here below, spake many parables, but not one more pertinent, not one, in which the freeness of the gospel-call, and the frivolous pretences men frame to excuse themselves from embracing it, and the dreadful doom they incur by so doing, are more displayed, or set off in livelier colours, than that to which the words of the text refer. "And the lord said unto the servant, Go out into the highways and hedges, and compel them to come in, that my house may be filled: For I say unto you, that none of those that were bidden shall taste of my supper."

In order to have a clear view of the occasion, scope, and contents of the parable, to which these words belong, it is necessary for us to look back to the very beginning of this chapter. "And it came to pass, as he went into the house of one of the chief pharisees to eat bread, on the sabbath day, that they watched him." The person here spoken of, as going into this Pharisee's house, is our blessed Saviour. For as he came eating and drinking, agreeable to his character, he was free, courteous and affable to all; and therefore though it was on the sabbath-day, he accepted an invitation, and went into the house of one of the chief Pharisees to eat bread, notwithstanding he knew the Pharisees were his professed enemies, and that they watched him, hoping to find some occasion to upbraid him, either for his discourse or behaviour. If the

Pharisee into whose house our Lord went, was one of this stamp, his invitation bespeaks him to be a very ill man, and may serve to teach us, that much rancour and heart-enmity against Jesus Christ, may be concealed and cloaked under a great and blazing profession of religion. However, our Saviour was more than a match for all his enemies, and by accepting this invitation, hath warranted his ministers and disciples, to comply with the like invitations, and converse freely about the things of God, though those who invite them, may not have real religion at heart. For how knowest thou, O man, but thou mayest drop something, that may benefit their souls, and make them religious indeed? And supposing they should watch thee, watch thou unto prayer, whilst thou art in their company, and that same Jesus, who went into this Pharisee's house, and was so faithful and edifying in his conversation when there, will enable thee to go and do likewise.

That our Lord's conversation was not trifling, but such as tended to the use of edifying, and that he behaved among the guests as a faithful physician, rather than as a careless, indifferent companion, is evident from the 7th verse of this chapter, where we are told, that " he marked how they chose the chief rooms ;" or, to speak in our common way, were desirous of sitting at the upper end of the table. And whether we think of it or not, the Lord Jesus takes notice of our behaviour, even when we are going to sit down only at our common meals. Would to God, all that make a profession of real christianity, considered this well ! Religion then would not be so much confined to church, or meeting, but be brought home to our private houses, and many needless unchristian compliments be prevented. For (with grief I speak it) is it not too true, that abundance of professors love, and are too fond of the uppermost places in houses, as well as synagogues? This was what our Lord blamed in the guests where he now was. He marked, he took notice, he looked before he spake (as we should always do, if we would speak to the purpose) how they chose out the chief rooms. Therefore, though they were rich in this world's goods, and were none of his guests, yet unwilling to suffer the least sin upon them, or lose any opportunity of giving instruction, he gave them a lecture upon humility, saying unto them, or directing his difcourfe to all in general, though probably he fpake to one in particular, who fat near him, and whom, it may be, he took notice of, as more than ordinarily folicitous in choofing a chief room, or couch, on which they lay at meals, after the cuftom of the *Romans*; " When thou art bidden of any man to a wedding (which feems to intimate that this was a wedding-feaft) fit not down in the higheft room, left a more honourable man than thou be bidden of him; and he that bade thee and him come and fay to thee, Give this man place; and thou begin with fhame to take the loweft room. But when thou art bidden, go and fit down in the loweft room; that when he that bade thee cometh, he may fay unto thee, Friend, go up higher: then fhalt thou have worfhip (or refpect) in the prefence of them who fit at meat with thee." O glorious example of faithfulnefs and love to fouls! How ought minifters efpcially, to copy after their bleffed Mafter, and, with fimplicity and godly fincerity, mildly and opportunely rebuke the faults of the company they are in, though fuperior to them in outward circumftances? What rightly informed perfon, after reading this paffage, can think they teach right and agreeable to the word of GOD in this refpect, who fay, we muft not, at leaft need not, reprove natural men? Surely fuch doctrine cometh not from above! For are we not commanded, in any wife, to reprove our neighbour (whether he be a child of GOD or no) and not to fuffer fin upon him? Is it not more than probable, that all thefe guefts were natural men? And yet our LORD reproved them. Help us then, O Saviour, in this and every other inftance of thy moral conduct, to walk as thou haft fet us an example!

Neither did our LORD ftop here; but obferving that none but the rich, the mighty, and the noble, were called to the feaft, he took occafion alfo from thence, to give even his hoft (for the beft return we make our friends for their kindnefs, is to be faithful to their fouls) one of the chief Pharifees, a wholefome piece of advice. " Then faid he alfo to him that bade him, when thou makeft a dinner or a fupper, call not thy friends, nor thy brethren, neither thy kinfmen nor thy rich neighbours, left they alfo bid thee again, and a recompence be made thee. But when thou makeft a feaft, call the poor, the maimed, the lame, the blind, and thou shalt be blessed; for they cannot recompence thee; For thou shalt be recompenced at the resurrection of the just!" Thus did our LORD entertain the company. Words spoken in such due season, how good are they! Would CHRIST's followers thus exert themselves, and, when in company, begin some useful discourse for their great master, they know not what good they might do, and how many might be influenced, by their good example, to second them in it.

An instance of this we have in the 14th verse: " And when one of them that sat at meat with him heard these things, he said unto him, Blessed is he that shall eat bread in the kingdom of GOD." Happy they who shall be recompenced at that resurrection of the just, which thou hast been speaking of. A very pertinent saying this! every way suitable to persons sitting down to eat bread on earth, which we should never do, without talking of, and longing for that time, when we shall sit down and eat bread in the kingdom of heaven. This opened to our LORD a fresh topic of conversation, and occasioned the parable, which is to be the more immediate subject of your present meditation. As though he had said to the person that spoke last, Thou sayest right: blessed are they indeed, who shall sit down to eat bread in the kingdom of GOD: But alas! most men, especially you Pharisees, act as if you did not believe this; and therefore he said unto him, " A certain man made a great supper, and bade many;" by the certain man making a great supper, we are to understand GOD the Father, who has made provision for perishing souls, by the obedience and death of his beloved Son CHRIST JESUS. This provision is here represented under the character of a supper, because the *Cæna* or supper, among the ancients, was their grand meal: Men could never have made such provision for themselves, or angels for them. No, our salvation is all from GOD, from the beginning to the end. He made it, and not we ourselves; and it is wholly owing to the divine wisdom, and not our own, that we are become GOD's people, and the sheep of his pasture. This provision for perishing souls, may be justly called *great*, because there is rich and ample provision made in the gospel for a great many souls. For however CHRIST's flock may be but a little flock, when

asunder,

asunder, yet when they come all together, they will be a multitude which no man can number. And it is especially called *great*, because it was purchased at so great a price, the price of CHRIST's most precious blood. And therefore, when the apostle would exhort the christians to glorify GOD in their souls and bodies, he makes use of this glorious motive, " That they were bought with a price." He does not say what price, but barely a *price*, emphatically so called; as though all the prices in the world were nothing (as indeed they are not) when compared to this price of CHRIST's most precious blood.

For these reasons, JESUS said in the parable, " A certain man made a great supper, and bade many, and sent his servant at supper-time, to say to them that were bidden, Come, for all things are now ready." He bade many; the eternal GOD took the *Jews* for his peculiar people, under the *Mosaic* dispensation; and by types, shadows, and prophesies of the Old Testament, invited them to partake of the glorious privileges of the gospel. " But at supper-time," in the fulness of time, which GOD the Father had decreed from eternity, in the evening of the world (for which reason the gospel times are called the last times) " he sent his servant," CHRIST his Son, here called his servant, because acting as Mediator he was inferior to the Father; therefore says the prophet *Isaiah*, " Behold my servant whom I have chosen:" " to say to them that were bidden," to the professing *Jews*, called by St. *John*, " his own," that is, his peculiar professing people — with this message, " Come;" repent and believe the gospel. Nothing is required on man's part, but to come, or accept of the gospel offer. It is not according to the old covenant, " Do and live;" but only " come, believe, and thou shalt be saved." All things are ready. Nothing is wanting on GOD's part. " All things are now ready." There seems to be a particular emphasis to be put upon NOW, implying, this was an especial season of grace, and GOD was now exerting his last efforts, to save lost man. Well then, if the great GOD be at so great an expence, to make so great a supper, for perishing creatures, and sends so great a person as his own Son, in the form of a servant, to invite them to come to it; one would imagine, that all who heard these glad tidings, should readily say, LORD, lo we come. But instead of this, we are told, "They all, (the greatest part of the *Jews*) with one consent began to make excuse." Conscience told them they ought to come, and in all probability they had some faint desire to come; and they had nothing, as we hear of, to object either against the person who prepared the supper, or the person that invited them, or the entertainment itself; neither do we hear that they treated either with contempt, as is the custom of too many in the days wherein we live. In all probability, they acknowledged all was very good, and that it was kind in that certain man, to send them such an invitation. But being very busy, and as they thought very lawfully engaged, they begun to make excuse.

But the excuses they made, rendered their refusal inexcusable. "The first said unto him, I have bought a piece of ground, and I must needs go and see it:" Thou fool, buy a piece of ground, and then go see it! A prudent man would have gone and seen the ground first, and bought it afterwards. Why must he *needs* go? At least, why must he needs go *now*? The land was his own, could he not therefore have accepted the invitation to-day, and gone and seen his estate, or plantation, on the morrow? As he had bought it, he need not fear losing his bargain, by anothers buying it from him. But notwithstanding all this, there is a needs must for his going, and therefore says he, "I pray thee, have me excused," and improve thy interest with thy master in my behalf. This was a bad excuse.

The second was rather worse. For what says the evangelist, verse 19? "And another said, I have bought five yoke of oxen, and I go to prove them:" One, it seems, had been buying an estate; another, cattle, to stock an estate already bought; and both equally foolish in making their bargains. For this second had bought five yoke of oxen, which must needs cost them a considerable sum, perhaps all he had in the world, and now he must go and prove them. A wise dealer would have proved the oxen first, and bought them afterwards: But our Saviour speaks this, to shew us, that we will trust one another, nay I may add, the devil himself, more than we will trust God.

The excuse which the third makes, is worst of all. "I have married a wife, and therefore I cannot come." Had he

said,

said, I will not come, he had spoken the real sentiments of his heart: for it is not so much mens impotency, as their want of a will, and inclination, that keeps them from the gospel-feast. But why cannot he come? He has "married a wife." Has he so? Why then, by all means he should come. For the supper to which he was invited, as it should seem, was a wedding-supper, and would have saved him the trouble of a nuptial entertainment. It was a great supper, and consequently there was provision enough for him, and his bride too. And it was made by a great man, who sent out his servant to bid many, so that he need not have doubted of meeting with a hearty welcome, though he should bring his wife with him. Or supposing his wife was unwilling to come, yet as the husband is the head of the wife, he ought to have laid his commands on her, to accompany him. For we cannot do better for our yoke-fellows, than to bring them to the gospel-feast. Or, supposing after all, she would not be prevailed upon, he ought to have gone without her: for "those that have wives, must be as though they had none;" and we must not let carnal affection get such an ascendancy over us, as to be kept thereby from spiritual entertainments. *Adam* paid dear for hearkening to the voice of his wife: and sometimes, unless we forsake wives, as well as houses and lands, we cannot be the LORD's disciples.

This then was the reception the servant met with, and such were the excuses, and answers, that were sent back. And what was the consequence? "So that servant came (no doubt with a sorrowful heart) and shewed his LORD these things." However little it be thought of, yet ministers must shew the LORD, what success their ministry meets with. We must shew it to our LORD here. We must spread the case before him in prayer. We must shew it to our LORD hereafter, before the general assembly of the whole world. But how dreadful is it, when ministers are obliged to go upon their knees, crying, "O! my leanness, my leanness!" and *Elias*-like, to intercede as it were against those, to whom they would not only have imparted the gospel, but even their own lives. It is a heart-breaking consideration. But thus it must be; "The servant came and shewed the LORD these things;" so must we. Well, and what says the LORD?

We are told, verse 21ſt, that "the maſter of the houſe was angry?" Not with the ſervant: for though *Iſrael* be not gathered, yet ſhall CHRIST be glorious; and faithful miniſters ſhall be rewarded, whether people obey the goſpel or not. "We are a ſweet favour unto GOD, whether the word be a favour of life unto life, or a favour of death unto death." The maſter of the houſe therefore was angry, not with the ſervant, but with theſe-worldly-minded, pleaſure-taking refuſers of his gracious invitation; who, in all probability, went to ſee and ſtock their eſtates, and attend upon their brides, not doubting, but their excuſes would be taken, becauſe they were lawfully employed. And, indeed, in one ſenſe, their excuſes were accepted. For I do not hear that they were ever invited any more. GOD took them at their word, though they would not take him at his. They begged to be excuſed, and they were excuſed, as we ſhall ſee in the ſequel of this parable. Let us not therefore harden our hearts, as in the day of provocation; "Now is the accepted time, now is the day of ſalvation." But muſt the feaſt want gueſts? No, if they cannot, or will not come, others ſhall, and will. The maſter of the houſe therefore being angry, ſent the ſervant upon a ſecond errand. "Go out quickly into the ſtreets, and lanes of the city, and bring in hither the poor, and the maimed, and the halt, and the blind." Every word beſpeaks a ſpirit of reſentment and importunity. Go out quickly, make no delay, dread no attempt or danger, into the ſtreets and lanes of the city, and bring in hither, not only call them, but bring them in (for the maſter here, to encourage the ſervant, aſſures him of ſucceſs) the poor, and the maimed, and the halt, and the blind. This was fulfilled, when JESUS CHRIST, after the goſpel was rejected by the *Jews*, went and invited the *Gentiles*, and when the publicans and harlots took the kingdom of GOD by a holy violence, whilſt the ſelf-righteous ſcribes and Phariſees rejected the kingdom of GOD againſt themſelves. This was alſo a home reproof to the rich Phariſee, at whoſe houſe the LORD JESUS was, as well as a cutting leſſon to the other gueſts. For our Saviour would hereby ſhew them, that GOD took a quite different method from his hoſt, and was not above receiving the poor, and halt, and blind, and maimed, to the goſpel ſupper, though he had called none

ſuch

such to sit down at his table. Whether the guests resented it or not, we are not told. But if they were not quite blind, both host and guests might easily see that the parable was spoken against them. But to proceed,

The servant again returns, but with a more pleasing answer than before, " Lord, it is done as thou hast commanded, and yet there is room." The words bespeak the servant to be full of joy at the thoughts of the success he had met with. None can tell, but those who experience it, what comfort ministers have in seeing their labours blest. " Now I live, (says the apostle) if you stand fast in the LORD. Ye are our joy and crown of rejoicing in the day of the LORD JESUS." " Lord, it is done as thou hast commanded. The poor, and maimed, and halt, and blind, have been called, and have obeyed the summons, and I have brought them with me; yet, LORD, thy house, and thy supper is so great, there is room for more. Hereby he insinuated that he wanted to be employed again, in calling more souls; and the more we do, the more may we do for GOD: " To him that hath, shall be given;" and present success is a great encouragement to future diligence. Such hints are pleasing to our Saviour. He delights to see his ministers ready for new work, and waiting for fresh orders. " The Lord, therefore, we are told, ver. 23, said unto his servant, (the same servant,) Go out into the highways and hedges, and compel them to come in, that my house may be filled; 24. For I say unto you, that none of those who are bidden, shall taste of my supper." O cutting words to those that sat at meat, if they had hearts to make the application! But glad tidings of great joy to the publicans, harlots, and Gentiles, who were rejected by the proud Pharisees, as aliens to the commonwealth of *Israel*, and strangers to the covenant of promise! This was fulfilled, when our LORD sent the apostles, not only into the streets and lanes of the city, and places bordering upon *Jerusalem* and *Judea*; but when he gave them a commission to go out into all the world, and preach the gospel to every creature, *Gentile* as well as *Jew*; and not only gave them a command, but blessed their labours with such success, that three thousand were converted in one day. And I am not without hopes that it will be still further fulfilled, by the calling of some of

you

you home this day: For however this parable was spoken originally to the *Jews*, and upon a particular occasion, as at a feast, yet it is applicable to us, and to our children, and to as many as are afar off; yea, to as many as the LORD our GOD shall call. It gives a sanction, methinks, to preaching in the fields, and other places besides the synagogues; and points out the reception the gospel meets with in these days, in such a lively manner, that one would think it had a particular reference to the present age. For is it not too, too plain, that the gospel-offers, and gospel-grace, have been slighted, and made light of, by many professors of this generation? We have been in the churches, telling them, again and again, that GOD has made a great supper (and has invited many, even them) and sent us by his providence and his spirit, " to say unto them that were bidden, Come, for all things are now ready. Believe on the LORD JESUS, and you shall be saved." But the generality of the laity have made light of it, they have given us the hearing, but are too busy in their farms and their merchandizes, their marrying and giving in marriage, to come and be blessed in the LORD of life. We have told them, again and again, that we do not want them to hide themselves from the world, but to teach them how they may live in, and yet not be of it. But all will not do. Many of the clergy also (like the letter-learned Scribes and Pharisees in our Saviour's time) reject the kingdom of GOD against themselves, and deny us the use of the pulpits, for no other reason but because we preach the doctrine of justification in the sight of GOD by faith alone, and invite sinners to come and taste of the gospel feast freely, without money and without price.

Whatever they may think, we are persuaded, the great master of the house is angry with them, for being angry with us without a cause. He therefore now, by his providence, bids us " Go out quickly into the streets and lanes of the city, and bring in the poor, and the maimed, and the halt, and the blind," or call in the publicans and harlots, the common cursers and swearers, and sabbath-breakers, and adulterers, who, perhaps, never entered a church door, or heard that JESUS CHRIST died for such sinners as they are. We, through grace, have obeyed the command, we have gone out, though
exposed

exposed to much contempt for so doing, and, blessed be GOD, our labour has not been in vain in the LORD. For many have been made willing in the day of GOD's power; and, we would speak it with humility, we can go chearfully to our Saviour, and say, " It is done, LORD, as thou hast commanded, and yet there is room." He is therefore pleased, in spite of all opposition from men or devils, to continue, and renew, and enlarge our commission; he hath sent us literally into the highways and hedges; and, I trust, has given us a commission to compel sinners to come: For, could we speak with the tongues of men and angels, yet if the LORD did not attend the word with his power, and sweetly inclined men's wills to comply with the gospel-call, we should be as a sounding brass, or a tinkling cymbal. But this we believe our Saviour will do, for his house must be filled: every soul for whom he has shed his blood, shall finally be saved, " and all that the Father hath given him, shall come unto him, and whosoever cometh unto him he will in no wise cast out." This comforted our LORD, when his gospel was rejected by the *Jews*. As though he had said, Well, tho' you despise the offers of my grace, yet I shall not shed my blood in vain; for all that the Father hath given me shall come unto me.

Supported by this consideration, I am not ashamed to come out this day into the highways and hedges, and to confess that my business is to call the poor, and the maimed, and the halt, and the blind, self-condemned, helpless sinners, to the marriage-feast of the supper of the Lamb. My cry is, Come, believe on the LORD JESUS; throw yourselves at the footstool of his mercy, and you shall be saved; for all things are now ready. GOD the Father is ready, GOD the Son is ready, GOD the Holy Ghost is ready; the blessed angels above are ready, and the blessed saints below are ready, to welcome you to the gospel-feast. A perfect and everlasting righteousness is now wrought out by JESUS CHRIST. GOD, now, upon honourable terms, can acquit the guilty. GOD can now be just, and yet justify the ungodly. " For he hath made CHRIST to be sin for us, who knew no sin, that we might be made the righteousness of GOD in him." The fatted calf is now killed, and " CHRIST, our passover, is

I   sacrificed

sacrificed for us." Come, sinners, and feed upon him in your hearts by faith, with thanksgiving. For JESUS CHRIST's sake, do not with one consent begin to make excuse. Do not let a piece of ground, five yoke of oxen, or even a wife, keep you from this great supper. These you may enjoy, as the gifts of GOD, and make use of them for the Mediator's glory, and yet be present at the gospel-feast. True and undefiled religion does not take away, but rather greatly enhances the comforts of life; and our LORD did not pray that we should be taken out of the world, but "that we should be delivered from the evil of it." O then that you would all, with one consent, say, Lo! we come. Assure yourselves there is provision enough. For it is a great supper. In our Father's house there is bread enough and to spare. And though a great GOD makes the supper, yet he is as good and condescending as he is great. Though he be the high and lofty one that inhabiteth eternity, yet he will dwell with the humble and contrite heart, even with the man that trembleth at his word. Neither can you complain for want of room; "for yet there is room. In our Father's house are many mansions." If it was not so, our Saviour would have told us. The grace of CHRIST is as rich, as free, and as powerful as ever. He is "the same yesterday, to-day, and for ever:" He is full of grace and truth, and out of his fulness, all that come to him may receive grace for grace. He giveth liberally, and upbraideth not. He willeth not the death of a sinner, but rather that he should believe and live. Come then, all ye halt, poor, maimed, and blind sinners; take comfort, the LORD JESUS has sent his servant to call you. It is now supper-time, and a day of uncommon grace. The day may be far spent. Haste, therefore, and away to the supper of the Lamb. If you do not come, I know the master will be angry. And who can stand before him when he is angry? "Harden not therefore your hearts, as in the day of provocation, as in the day of temptation in the wilderness." Do not provoke the LORD to say, "None of those that were bidden shall taste of my supper." O dreadful words! Much more is implied in them than is expressed. It is the same with that in the psalms, "I sware in my wrath, that they should not enter into my rest." And if you do not enter into GOD's rest, nor taste of CHRIST's supper, you must lift up your

your eyes in torments, where you will have no reſt, and muſt ſup with the damned devils for ever more.

Knowing therefore the terrors of the LORD, we perſuade you to haſte away, and make no more frivolous excuſes. For there is no excuſe againſt believing. Perhaps you ſay, You call to the halt, and maimed, and blind, and poor. But if we are halt, and maimed, how can we come? If we are blind, how can we ſee our way? If we are poor, how can we expect admiſſion to ſo great a table? Ah! Happy are ye, if you are ſenſible, that you are halt and maimed. For if you feel yourſelves ſo, and are lamenting it, who knows but whilſt I am ſpeaking, GOD may ſend his Spirit with the word, and fetch you home? Though you are blind, JESUS has eye-ſalve to anoint you. Though you are poor, yet you are welcome to this rich feaſt. It coſt JESUS CHRIST a great price, but you ſhall have it gratis. For ſuch as you was it deſigned. " Bleſſed are the poor in ſpirit, for theirs is the kingdom of heaven." Rich, ſelf-righteous, ſelf-ſufficient ſinners, I know, will ſcorn both the feaſt and its great provider. They have done ſo already, therefore the LORD has ſent us into the highways and hedges, to bring ſuch poor ſouls as you are in. Venture then, my dear friends, and honour GOD, by taking him at his word. Come to the marriage-feaſt. Believe me, you will there partake of moſt delicious fare.

Tell me, ye that have been made to taſte that the LORD is gracious, will you not recommend this feaſt to all? Are you not, whilſt I am ſpeaking, ready to cry out, Come all ye that are without, come ye, obey the call, for we have ſat under the Redeemer's ſhadow with great delight, and his fruit has been pleaſant to our taſte. Whilſt I am ſpeaking, does not the fire kindle, do not your hearts burn with a deſire that others may come and be bleſſed too? If you are chriſtians indeed, I know you will be thus minded, and the language of your hearts will be, LORD, whilſt he is calling, let thy Spirit compel them to come in. O that the LORD may ſay, *Amen!* And why ſhould we doubt? Surely our Saviour will not let me complain this day that I have laboured in vain, and ſpent my ſtrength for nought. Methinks I ſee many deſiring to come. O how ſhall I compel you to come forwards. I will not uſe fire or ſword, as the *Papists* do, by terribly perverting this text of scripture. But I will tell you of the love of GOD, the love of GOD in CHRIST, and surely that must compel you, that must constrain you, whether you will or not. Sinners, my heart is enlarged towards you. I could fill my mouth with arguments. Consider the greatness of the GOD who makes the supper. Consider the greatness of the price, wherewith it was purchased. Consider the greatness of the provision made for you. What would you have more? Consider GOD's infinite condescension, in calling you now, when you might have been in hell, "where the worm dieth not, and the fire is not quenched." And that you might be without excuse, he has sent his servant into the highways and hedges to invite you there. O that you tasted what I do now! I am sure you would not want arguments to induce you to come in: No, you would fly to the gospel-feast, as doves to the windows.

But, poor souls! many of you, perhaps, are not hungry. You do not feel yourselves halt, or maimed, or blind, and therefore you have no relish for this spiritual entertainment. Well, be not angry with me for calling you; be not offended if I weep over you, because you know not the day of your visitation: If I must appear in judgment as a swift witness against you, I must. But that thought chills my blood! I cannot bear it; I feel that I could lay down my life for you. But I am not willing to go without you. What say you, my dear friends? I would put the question to you once more, Will you taste of CHRIST's supper, or will you not? You shall all be welcome. There is milk at this feast for babes, as well as meat for strong men, and for persons of riper years. There is room and provision for high and low, rich and poor, one with another; and our Saviour will thank you for coming. Amazing condescension! Astonishing love! The thought of it quite overcomes me. Help me, help me, O believers, to bless and praise him.

And O! that his love may excite us to come afresh to him, as though we had never come before! For, though we have been often feasted, yet our souls will starve, unless we renew our acts of faith, and throw ourselves, as lost, undone sinners, continually at the feet of CHRIST. Feeding upon past experiences will not satisfy our souls, any more than what we did eat yesterday will sustain our bodies to day. No, believers must look for fresh influences of divine grace, and beg of the LORD to water them every moment. The parable therefore speaks to saints as well as sinners. Come ye to the marriage-feast; you are as welcome now as ever. And may GOD set your souls a longing for that time when we shall sit down and eat bread in the kingdom of heaven! There we shall have full draughts of divine love, and enjoy the glorious Emmanuel for ever more. Even so, LORD JESUS, *Amen*.

SERMON XXXIV.

The Pharisee and Publican.

LUKE xviii. 14.

I tell you, this man went down to his house justified rather than the other: For every one that exalteth himself, shall be abased; and he that humbleth himself, shall be exalted.

THOUGH there be some who dare to deny the LORD JESUS, and disbelieve the revelation he has been pleased to give us, and thereby bring upon themselves swift destruction; yet I would charitably hope there are but few if any such among you, to whom I am now to preach the kingdom of GOD. Was I to ask you, how you expect to be justified in the sight of an offended GOD? I suppose you would answer, only for the sake of our LORD JESUS CHRIST. But, was I to come more home to your consciences, I fear that most would make the LORD JESUS but in part their Saviour, and go about, as it were, to establish a righteousness of their own. And this is not thinking contrary to the rules of christian charity: for we are all self-righteous by nature; it is as natural for us to turn to a covenant of works, as for the sparks to fly upwards. We have had so many legal and so few free-grace preachers, for these many years, that most professors now seem to be settled upon their lees, and rather deserve the title of *Pharisees* than christians.

Thus it was with the generality of the people during the time of our LORD's public ministration: and therefore, in almost all his discourses, he preached the gospel to poor sinners, and denounced terrible woes against proud self-justiciaries. The parable, to which the words of the text belong, looks both thefe ways: For the evangelift informs us (ver. 9.) that our LORD "fpake it unto certain who trufted in themfelves that they were righteous, and defpifed others." And a notable parable it is; a parable worthy of your moft ferious attention. "He that hath ears to hear, let him hear," what JESUS CHRIST fpeaks to all vifible profeffors in it.

Ver. 10. "Two men went up to the temple to pray (and never two men of more oppofite characters) the one a Pharifee and the other a Publican." The Pharifees were the ftricteft fect among the *Jews*. "I was of the ftricteft fect, of the Pharifees," fays *Paul*. They prayed often; not only fo, but they made long prayers; and, that they might appear extraordinary devout, they would pray at the corners of the ftreet, where two ways met, that people going or coming, both ways, might fee them. "They made broad (as our LORD informs us) the borders of their phylacteries," they had pieces of parchment fown to their long robes, on which fome parts of the Scripture were written, that people might from thence infer, that they were lovers of the law of GOD. They were fo very punctual and exact in outward purifications, that they wafhed at their going out and coming in. They held the wafhing of pots, brazen veffels and tables, and many other fuch-like things they did. They were very zealous for the traditions of the fathers, and for the obfervation of the rites and ceremonies of the church, notwithftanding they frequently made void the law of GOD by their traditions. And they were fo exceedingly exact in the outward obfervation of the fabbath, that they condemned our LORD for making a little clay with his fpittle; and called him a finner, and faid, he was not of GOD, becaufe he had given fight to a man born blind, on the fabbath-day. For thefe reafons they were had in high veneration among the people, who were fadly mifled by thefe blind guides: they had the uppermoft places in the fynagogues, and greetings in the market-places (which they loved dearly) and were called of men, *Rabbi*; in fhort, they had fuch a reputation for piety, that it became a proverb among the *Jews*, that, if there were but two men faved, the one of them muft be a Pharifee.

As for the Publicans, it was not fo with them. It feems they were fometimes *Jews*, or at leaft profelytes of the gate;

for we find one here coming up to the temple; but for the generality, I am apt to think they were *Gentiles*; for they were gatherers of the *Roman* taxes, and used to amass much wealth (as appears by the confession of *Zaccheus*, one of the chief of them) by wronging men with false accusations. They were so universally infamous, that our LORD himself tells his disciples, " the excommunicated man should be to them as a heathen man, or a Publican." And the Pharisees thought it a sufficient impeachment of our LORD's character, that he was a friend to Publicans and sinners, and went to sit down with them at meat.

But, however they disagreed in other things, they agreed in this, that public worship is a duty incumbent upon all: for they both came up to the temple. The very heathens were observers of temple-worship. We have very early notice of mens sacrificing to, and calling upon the name of the LORD, in the Old Testament; and I find it no where contradicted in the New. Our LORD, and his apostles, went up to the temple; and we are commanded by the apostle, " not to forsake the assembling ourselves together," as the manner of too many is in our days; and such too, as would have us think well of them, though they seldom or never tread the courts of the LORD's house. But, though our devotions begin in our closets, they must not end there. And, if people never shew their devotions abroad, I must suspect they have little or none at home. " Two men went up to the temple." And what went they thither for? Not (as multitudes amongst us do) to make the house of GOD a house of merchandize, or turn it into a den of thieves; much less to ridicule the preacher, or disturb the congregation; no, they came to the temple, says our LORD, " to pray." Thither should the tribes of GOD's spiritual *Israel* go up, to talk with, and pour out their hearts before the mighty GOD of *Jacob*.

" Two men went up to the temple to pray." I fear one of them forgot his errand. I have often been at a loss what to call the *Pharisee*'s address; it certainly does not deserve the name of a prayer: he may rather be said to come to the temple to *boast*, than to pray; for I do not find one word of confession of his original guilt; not one single petition for pardon of his past actual sins, or for grace to help and assist him for the

time

time to come: he only brings to GOD, as it were, a reckoning of his performances; and does that, which no flesh can justly do, I mean, glory in his presence.

Ver. 11. " The Pharisee stood, and prayed thus with himself; GOD, I thank thee that I am not as other men are, extortioners, unjust, adulterers, or even as this Publican."

Our LORD first takes notice of his posture; " the Pharisee *stood*," he is not to be condemned for that; for standing, as well as kneeling, is a proper posture for prayer. " When you stand praying," says our LORD; though sometimes our LORD kneeled, nay, lay flat on his face upon the ground; his apostles also kneeled, as we read in the *Acts*, which has made me wonder at some, who are so bigotted to standing in family, as well as public prayer, that they will not kneel, notwithstanding all kneel that are around them. I fear there is something of the Pharisee in this conduct. Kneeling and standing are indifferent, if the knee of the soul be bent, and the heart upright towards GOD. We should study not to be particular in indifferent things, lest we offend weak minds. What the Pharisee is remarked for, is his " standing by himself:" for the words may be rendered, he stood by himself, upon some eminent place, at the upper part of the temple, near the Holy of holies, that the congregation might see what a devout man he was: or it may be understood as we read it, he prayed by himself, or of himself, out of his own heart; he did not pray by form; it was an extempore prayer: for there are many Pharisees that pray and preach too, extempore. I do not see why these may not be acquired, as well as other arts and sciences. A man, with a good elocution, ready turn of thought, and good memory, may repeat his own or other mens sermons, and, by the help of a *Wilkins* or *Henry*, may pray seemingly excellently well, and yet not have the least grain of true grace in his heart; I speak this, not to cry down extempore prayer, or to discourage those dear souls who really pray by the spirit; I only would hereby give a word of reproof to those who are so bigotted to extempore prayer, that they condemn, at least judge, all that use forms, as though not so holy and heavenly, as others who pray without them. Alas! this is wrong. Not every one that prays extempore is a spiritual, nor every one that prays with a form, a formal man. Let us not judge one another; let not him that uses a form, judge him that prays extempore, on that account; and let not him that prays extempore, defpife him who ufes a form.

"The Pharifee ſtood, and prayed thus by himſelf." Which may fignify alſo praying inwardly in his heart; for there is a way (and that an excellent one too) of praying when we cannot ſpeak; thus *Anna* prayed, when ſhe ſpoke not aloud, only her lips moved. Thus GOD ſays to *Moſes*, "Why crieſt thou?" when, it is plain, he did not ſpeak a word. This is what the apoſtle means by the "ſpirit making interceſſion (for believers) with groanings which cannot be uttered." For there are times when the ſoul is too big to ſpeak; when GOD fills it as it were, and overſhadows it with his preſence, ſo that it can only fall down, worſhip, adore, and lye in the duſt before the LORD. Again, there is a time when the ſoul is benumbed, barren and dry, and the believer has not a word to ſay to his heavenly Father; and then the heart only can ſpeak. And I mention this for the encouragement of weak chriſtians, who think they never are accepted but when they have a flow of words, and fancy they do not pleaſe GOD at the bottom, for no other reaſon but becauſe they do not pleaſe themſelves. Such would do well to conſider, that GOD knows the language of the heart, and the mind of the ſpirit; and that we make uſe of words, not to inform GOD, but to affect ourſelves. Whenever therefore any of you find yourſelves in ſuch a frame, be not diſcouraged: offer yourſelves up in ſilence before GOD, as clay in the hands of the potter, for him to write and ſtamp his own divine image upon your ſouls. But I believe the Phariſee knew nothing of this way of prayer: he was ſelf-righteous, a ſtranger to the divine life; and therefore either of the former explanations may be beſt put upon theſe words.

"He ſtood, and prayed thus with himſelf; GOD, I thank thee that I am not as other men are, extortioner, unjuſt, adulterer, or even as this Publican." Here is ſome appearance of devotion, but it is only in appearance. To thank GOD that we are not extortioners, unjuſt, adulterers, and as wicked in our practices as other men are, is certainly meet, right, and our bounden duty: for whatever degrees of goodneſs there may be in us, more than in others, it is owing to GOD's reſtraining, preventing, and aſſiſting grace. We are all equally conceived and born in ſin; all are fallen ſhort of the glory of GOD, and

liable

liable to all the curses and maledictions of the law; so that
" he who glorieth, must glory only in the LORD." For none
of us have any thing which we did not receive; and whatever
we have received, we did not in the least merit it, nor could
we lay the least claim to it on any account whatever: we are
wholly indebted to free grace for all. Had the Pharisee thought
thus, when he said, " GOD, I thank thee that I am not as
other men are," it would have been an excellent introduction
to his prayer: but he was a free-willer, as well as self-righteous
(for he that is one must be the other) and thought by his own
power and strength, he had kept himself from these vices. And
yet I do not see what reason he had to trust in himself that he
was righteous, merely because he was not an extortioner, unjust, adulterer; for all this while he might be, as he certainly
was (as is also every self-righteous person) as proud as the
devil. But he not only boasts, but lies before GOD (as all
self-justiciaries will be found liars here or hereafter.) He thanks
GOD that he was not unjust: but is it not an act of the highest
injustice to rob GOD of his prerogative? is it not an act of injustice to judge our neighbour? and yet of both these crimes
this self-righteous vaunter is guilty. "Even as this Publican!" He seems to speak with the utmost disdain; this Publican! Perhaps he pointed at the poor man, that others might
treat him with the like contempt. Thou proud, confident
boaster, what hadst thou to do with that poor Publican? supposing other Publicans were unjust, and extortioners, did it
therefore follow that he must be so? or, if he had been such
a sinner, how knowest thou but he has repented of those sins?
His coming up to the temple to pray, is one good sign of a reformation at least. Thou art therefore inexcusable, O Pharisee, who thus judgest the Publican: for thou that judgest
him to be unjust, art, in the very act of judging, unjust thyself: thy sacrifice is only the sacrifice of a fool.

We have seen what the Pharisee's negative goodness comes
to; I think, nothing at all. Let us see how far his positive
goodness extends; for, if we are truly religious, we shall not
only eschew evil, but also do good: " I fast twice in the week,
I give tithes of all that I possess."

The Pharisee is not here condemned for his fasting, for fasting is a christian duty; " when you fast," says our LORD,

thereby

thereby taking it for granted that his difciples would faſt. And " when the bridegroom ſhall be taken away, then ſhall they faſt in thoſe days." " In faſting often," ſays the apoſtle. And all that would not be caſt-aways, will take care, as their privilege, without legal conſtraint, to " keep their bodies under, and bring them into ſubjection." The Phariſee is only condemned for making a righteouſneſs of his faſting, and thinking that GOD would accept him, or that he was any better than his neighbours, merely on account of his faſting: this is what he was blamed for. The Phariſee was not to be diſcommended for faſting twice in a week; I wiſh ſome chriſtians would imitate him more in this: but to depend on faſting in the leaſt, for his juſtification in the ſight of GOD, was really abominable. " I give tithes of all that I poſſeſs." He might as well have ſaid, I pay tithes. But ſelf-righteous people (whatever they may ſay to the contrary) think they give ſomething to GOD. " I give tithes of all that I poſſeſs:" I make conſcience of giving tithes, not only of all that the law requires, but of my mint, anniſe, and cummin, of all things whatſoever I poſſeſs; this was well; but to boaſt of ſuch things, or of faſting, is phariſaical and deviliſh. Now then let us ſum up all the righteouſneſs of this boaſting Phariſee, and ſee what little reaſon he had to truſt in himſelf, that he was righteous, or to deſpiſe others. He is not unjuſt (but we have only his bare word for that, I think I have proved the contrary;) he is no adulterer, no extortioner; he faſts twice in the week, and gives tithes of all that he poſſeſſes; and all this he might do, and a great deal more, and yet be a child of the devil: for here is no mention made of his loving the LORD his GOD with all his heart, which was the " firſt and great commandment of the law;" here is not a ſingle ſyllable of inward religion; and he was not a true *Jew*, who was only one outwardly. It is only an outſide piety at the beſt; inwardly he is full of pride, ſelf-juſtification, free-will and great uncharitableneſs.

Were not the Phariſees, do you think, highly offended at this character? for they might eaſily know it was ſpoken againſt them. And though, perhaps, ſome of you may be offended at me, yet, out of love, I muſt tell you, I fear this parable is ſpoken againſt many of you: for are there not many

of

of you, who go up to the temple to pray, with no better spirit than this Pharisee did? And because you fast, it may be in the *Lent*, or every *Friday*, and because you do no body any harm, receive the sacrament, pay tithes, and give an alms now and then; you think that you are safe, and trust in yourselves that you are righteous, and inwardly despise those, who do not come up to you in these outward duties? this, I am persuaded, is the case of many of you, though, alas! it is a desperate one, as I shall endeavour to shew at the close of this discourse.

Let us now take a view of the Publican, ver. 13. "And the Publican standing afar off, would not lift up so much as his eyes unto heaven, but smote upon his breast, saying, GOD be merciful to me a sinner."

"The Publican standing afar off:" Perhaps in the outward court of the temple, conscious to himself that he was not worthy to approach the Holy of holies; so conscious and so weighed down with a sense of his own unworthiness, that he would not so much as lift up his eyes unto heaven, which he knew was GOD's throne. Poor heart! what did he feel at this time! none but returning Publicans, like himself, can tell. Methinks I see him standing afar off, pensive, oppressed, and even overwhelmed with sorrow; sometimes he attempts to look up; but then, thinks he, the heavens are unclean in GOD's sight, and the very angels are charged with folly; how then shall such a wretch as I dare to lift up my guilty head! And to shew that his heart was full of holy self-resentment, and that he sorrowed after a godly sort, he smote upon his breast; the word in the original implies, that he *struck hard* upon his breast: he will lay the blame upon none but his own wicked heart. He will not, like unhumbled *Adam*, tacitly lay the fault of his vileness upon GOD, and say, The passions which thou gavest me, they deceived me, and I sinned: he is too penitent thus to reproach his Maker; he smites upon his breast, his treacherous, ungrateful, desperately wicked breast; a breast now ready to burst: and at length, out of the abundance of his heart, I doubt not, with many tears, he at last cries out, "GOD be merciful to me a sinner." Not, GOD be merciful to yonder proud Pharisee: he found enough in himself to vent his resentment against, without looking abroad upon others. Not, GOD be merciful to me a saint; for he

knew

knew "all his righteousnesses were but filthy rags." Not, GOD be merciful to such or such a one; but, GOD be merciful to me, even to me a sinner, a sinner by birth, a sinner in thought, word, and deed; a sinner as to my person, a sinner as to all my performances; a sinner in whom is no health, in whom dwelleth no good thing; a sinner, poor, miserable, blind and naked, from the crown of the head to the sole of the feet, full of wounds, and bruises, and putrifying sores; a self-accused, self-condemned sinner. What think you? would this Publican have been offended if any minister had told him that he deserved to be damned? would he have been angry, if any one had told him, that by nature he was half a devil and half a beast? No: he would have confessed a thousand hells to have been his due, and that he was an earthly, devilish sinner. He felt now what a dreadful thing it was to depart from the living GOD: he felt that he was inexcusable every way; that he could in nowise, upon account of any thing in himself, be justified in the sight of GOD; and therefore lays himself at the feet of sovereign mercy, "GOD be merciful to me a sinner." Here is no confidence in the flesh, no plea fetched from fasting, paying tithes, or the performance of any other duty; here is no boasting that he was not an extortioner, unjust, or an adulterer. Perhaps he had been guilty of all these crimes, at least he knew he would have been guilty of all these, had he been left to follow the devices and desires of his own heart; and therefore, with a broken and contrite spirit, he cries out, "GOD be merciful to me a sinner."

This man came up to the temple to pray, and he prayed indeed. And a broken and contrite heart GOD will not despise. "I tell you," says our LORD, I who lay in the bosom of the Father from all eternity; I who am GOD, and therefore know all things; I who can neither deceive, nor be deceived, whose judgment is according to right; I tell you, whatever you may think of it, or think of me for telling you so, "this man," this Publican, this despised, sinful, but broken-hearted man, "went down to his house justified (acquitted, and looked upon as righteous in the sight of GOD) rather than the other."

Let Pharisees take heed that they do not pervert this text: for when it is said, "This man went down to his house justified rather than the other," our Lord does not mean that both were juftified, and that the Publican had rather more juftification than the Pharifee: but it implies, either that the Publican was actually juftified, but the Pharifee was not; or, that the Publican was in a better way to receive juftification, than the Pharifee; according to our Lord's faying, " The Publicans and Harlots enter into the kingdom of heaven before you." That the Pharifee was not juftified is certain; for " God refifteth the proud;" and that the Publican was at this time actually juftified (and perhaps went home with a fenfe of it in his heart) we have great reafon to infer from the latter part of the text, " For every one that exalteth himfelf fhall be abafed, and he that humbleth himfelf fhall be exalted."

The parable therefore now fpeaks to all who hear me this day: for that our Lord intended it for our learning, is evident, from his making fuch a general application; " For every one that exalteth himfelf fhall be abafed, and he that humbleth himfelf fhall be exalted."

The parable of the Publican and Pharifee, is but as it were a glafs, wherein we may fee the different difpofition of all mankind; for all mankind may be divided into two general claffes. Either they truft wholly in themfelves, or in part, that they are righteous, and then they are Pharifees; or they have no confidence in the flefh, are felf-condemned finners, and then they come under the character of the Publican juft now defcribed. And we may add alfo, that the different reception thefe men met with, points out to us in lively colours, the different treatment the felf-jufticiary and felf-condemned criminal will meet with at the terrible day of judgment: " Every one that exalts himfelf fhall be abafed, but he that humbleth himfelf fhall be exalted."

" Every one," without exception, young or old, high or low, rich or poor (for God is no refpecter of perfons) " every one," whofoever he be, that exalteth himfelf, and not freegrace; every one that trufteth in himfelf that he is righteous, that refts in his duties, or thinks to join them with the righteoufnefs of Jesus Christ, for juftification in the fight of God, though he be no adulterer, no extortioner, though he be not outwardly unjuft, nay, though he faft twice in the week,

week, and gives tithes of all that he poſſeſſes; yet ſhall he be abaſed in the ſight of all good men who know him here, and before men and angels, and GOD himſelf, when JESUS CHRIST comes to appear in judgment hereafter. How low, none but the almighty GOD can tell. He ſhall be abaſed to live with devils, and make his abode in the loweſt hell for evermore.

Hear this, all ye ſelf-juſticiaries, tremble, and behold your doom! a dreadful doom, more dreadful than words can expreſs, or thought conceive! If you refuſe to humble yourſelves, after hearing this parable, I call heaven and earth to witneſs againſt you this day, that GOD ſhall viſit you with all his ſtorms, and pour all the vials of his wrath upon your rebellious heads; you exalted yourſelves here, and GOD ſhall abaſe you hereafter; you are as proud as the devil, and with devils ſhall you dwell to all eternity. "Be not deceived, GOD is not mocked;" he ſees your hearts, he knows all things. And, notwithſtanding you may come up to the temple to pray, your prayers are turned into ſin, and you go down to your houſes unjuſtified, if you are ſelf-juſticiaries; and do you know what it is to be unjuſtified? why, if you are unjuſtified, the wrath of GOD abideth upon you; you are in your blood; all the curſes of the law belong to you: curſed are you when you go out, curſed are you when you come in; curſed are your thoughts, curſed are your words, curſed are your deeds; every thing you do, ſay, or think, from morning to night, is only one continued ſeries of ſin. However highly you may be eſteemed in the ſight of men, however you may be honoured with the uppermoſt ſeats in the ſynagogues, in the church militant, you will have no place in the church triumphant. "Humble yourſelves therefore under the mighty hand of GOD:" pull down every ſelf-righteous thought, and every proud imagination, that now exalteth itſelf againſt the perfect, perſonal, imputed righteouſneſs of the dear LORD JESUS: "For he (and he alone) that humbleth himſelf ſhall be exalted."

He that humbleth himſelf, whatever he be: if, inſtead of faſting twice in the week, he has been drunk twice in the week; if, inſtead of giving tithes of all that he poſſeſſes, he has cheated the miniſter of his tithes, and the king of his taxes; notwithſtanding he be unjuſt, an extortioner, an adulterer,

terer, nay, notwithstanding the sins of all mankind center and unite in him; yet, if through grace, like the Publican, he is enabled to humble himself, he shall be exalted; not in a temporal manner; for christians must rather expect to be abased, and to have their names cast out as evil, and to lay down their lives for Christ Jesus in this world: but he shall be exalted in a spiritual sense; he shall be freely justified from all his sins by the blood of Jesus; he shall have peace with God, a peace which passeth all understanding; not only peace, but joy in believing; he shall be translated from the kingdom of Satan, to the kingdom of God's dear Son: he shall dwell in Christ, and Christ in him: he shall be one with Christ, and Christ one with him: he shall drink of divine pleasures, as out of a river: he shall be sanctified throughout in spirit, soul and body; in one word, he shall be filled with all the fulness of God. Thus shall the man that humbleth himself be exalted here; but O, how high shall he be exalted hereafter! as high as the highest heavens, even to the right-hand of God: there he shall sit, happy both in soul and body, and judge angels; high, out of the reach of all sin and trouble, eternally secure from all danger of falling. O sinners, did you but know how highly God intends to exalt those who humble themselves, and believe in Jesus, surely you would humble yourselves, at least beg of God to humble you; for it is he that must strike the rock of your hearts, and cause floods of contrite tears to flow therefrom. O that God would give this sermon such a commission, as he once gave to the rod of *Moses!* I would strike you through and through with the rod of his word, until each of you was brought to cry out with the poor Publican, " God be merciful to me a sinner." What pleasant language would this be in the ears of the Lord of Sabbaoth!

Are there no poor sinners among you? what, are you all Pharisees? Surely, you cannot bear the thoughts of returning home unjustified; can you? what if a fit of the apoplexy should seize you, and your souls be hurried away before the awful Judge of quick and dead? what will you do without Christ's righteousness? if you go out of the world unjustified, you must remain so for ever. O that you would humble yourselves! then would the Lord exalt you; it may be, that, whilst I am

speaking,

speaking, the LORD might justify you freely by his grace. I observed, that perhaps the Publican had a sense of his justification before he went from the temple, and knew that his pardon was sealed in heaven: and who knows but you may be thus exalted before you go home, if you humble yourselves? O what peace, love and joy, would you then feel in your hearts! you would have a heaven upon earth. O that I could hear any of you say (as I once heard a poor sinner, under my preaching, cry out) *He is come, He is come!* How would you then, like him, extol a precious, a free-hearted CHRIST! how would you magnify him for being such a friend to Publicans and sinners? greater love can no man shew, than to lay down his life for a friend; but CHRIST laid down his life for his enemies, even for you, if you are enabled to humble yourselves, as the Publican did. Sinners, I know not how to leave off talking with you; I would fill my mouth with arguments, I would plead with you. " Come, let us reason together;" though your sins be as scarlet, yet, if you humble yourselves, they shall be as white as snow. One act of true faith in CHRIST, justifies you for ever and ever; he has not promised you what he cannot perform; he is able to exalt you: for GOD hath exalted, and given him a name above every name, that at the name of JESUS every knee shall bow; nay, GOD hath exalted him to be not only a Prince, but a Saviour. May he be a Saviour to you! and then I shall have reason to rejoice, in the day of judgment, that I have not preached in vain, nor laboured in vain.

SERMON

SERMON XXXV.

The Conversion of *Zaccheus*.

LUKE xix. 9, 10.

And JESUS *said unto him, This day is salvation come to this house; forasmuch as he also is the Son of Abraham. For the Son of man is come to seek and to save that which was lost.*

SALVATION, every where through the whole scripture, is said to be the free gift of GOD, through JESUS CHRIST our LORD. Not only free, because GOD is a sovereign agent, and therefore may withhold it from, or confer it on, whom he pleaseth; but free, because there is nothing to be found in man, that can any way induce GOD to be merciful unto him. The righteousness of JESUS CHRIST is the sole cause of our finding favour in GOD's sight: this righteousness apprehended by faith (which is also the gift of GOD) makes it our own; and this faith, if true, will work by love.

These are parts of those glad tidings which are published in the gospel; and of the certainty of them, next to the express word of GOD, the experience of all such as have been saved, is the best, and, as I take it, the most undoubted proof. That GOD might teach us every way, he has been pleased to leave upon record many instances of the power of his grace exerted in the salvation of several persons, that we, hearing how he dealt with them, might from thence infer the manner we must expect to be dealt with ourselves, and learn in what way we must look for salvation, if we truly desire to be made partakers of the inheritance with the saints in light.

The conversion of the person referred to in the text, I think, will be of no small service to us in this matter, if rightly

rightly improved. I would hope, most of you know who the person is, to whom the LORD JESUS speaks; it is the publican *Zaccheus*, to whose house the blessed JESUS said, salvation came, and whom he pronounces a Son of *Abraham*.

It is my design (GOD helping) to make some remarks upon his conversion recorded at large in the preceding verses, and then to inforce the latter part of the text, as an encouragement to poor undone sinners to come to JESUS CHRIST. "For the Son of man is come, to seek and to save that which was lost."

The evangelist *Luke* introduces the account of this man's conversion thus, verse 1. " And JESUS entered and passed through *Jericho*." The holy JESUS made it his business to go about doing good. As the sun in the firmament is continually spreading his benign, quickening, and cheering influences over the natural; so the Son of righteousness arose with healing under his wings, and was daily and hourly diffusing his gracious influences over the moral world. The preceding chapter acquaints us of a notable miracle wrought by the holy JESUS, on poor blind *Bartimeus*; and in this, a greater presents itself to our consideration. The evangelist would have us take particular notice of it; for he introduces it with the word " behold :" " and behold, there was a man named *Zaccheus*, who was the chief among the *Publicans*, and he was rich."

Well might the evangelist usher, in the relation of this man's conversion with the word " behold !" For, according to human judgment, how many unsurmountable obstacles lay in the way of it ! Surely no one will say there was any fitness in *Zaccheus* for salvation; for we are told that he was a *Publican*, and therefore in all probability a notorious sinner. The *Publicans* were gatherers of the *Roman* taxes; they were infamous for their abominable extortion; their very name therefore became so odious, that we find the *Pharisees* often reproached our LORD, as very wicked, because he was a friend unto and sat down to meat with them. *Zaccheus* then, being a *Publican*, was no doubt a sinner; and, being chief among the *Publicans*, consequently was chief among sinners. Nay, " he was rich." One inspired apostle has told us, that " not many mighty, not many noble are called." Another

faith,

faith, " GOD has chosen the poor of this world, rich in faith." And he who was the Maker and Redeemer of the apostles, assures us, " that it is easier for a camel, (or cable-rope) to go through the eye of a needle, than for a rich man to enter into the kingdom of GOD." Let not therefore the rich glory in the multitude of their riches.

But rich as he was, we are told, verse 3. that " he sought to see JESUS."· A wonder indeed! The common people heard our LORD gladly, and the poor received the gospel. The multitude; the οχλες, the mob, the people that knew not the law, as the proud high-priests called them, used to follow him on foot into the country, and sometimes staid with him three days together to hear him preach: But did the rich believe or attend on him? No. Our LORD preached up the doctrine of the cross; he preached too searching for them, and therefore they counted him their enemy, persecuted and spoke all manner of evil against him falsly. Let not the ministers of CHRIST marvel, if they meet with the like treatment from the rich men of this wicked and adulterous generation. I should think it no scandal (supposing it true) to hear it affirmed, that none but the poor attended my ministry. Their souls are as precious to our LORD JESUS CHRIST, as the souls of the greatest men. They were the poor that attended him in the days of his flesh: these are they whom he hath chosen to be rich in faith, and to be the greatest in the kingdom of heaven. Were the rich in this world's goods generally to speak well of me, wo be unto me; I should think it a dreadful sign that I was only a wolf in sheep's clothing, that I spoke peace, peace, when there was no peace, and prophesied smoother things than the gospel would allow of. Hear ye this, O ye rich. Let who will dare to do it, GOD forbid that I should despise the poor; in doing so, I should reproach my Maker. The poor are dear to my soul; I rejoice to see them fly to the doctrine of CHRIST, like the doves to their windows. I only pray, that the poor who attend, may be evangelized, and turned into the spirit of the gospel: if so, " Blessed are ye; for yours is the kingdom of heaven."

But we must return to *Zaccheus*: " He sought to see JESUS." That is good news. I heartily wish I could say, it was out of a good principle: but, without speaking contrary to that charity which hopes and believeth all things for the beſt, we may ſay, that the ſame principle drew him after CHRIST, which now draws multitudes (to ſpeak plainly, it may be multitudes of you) to hear a particular preacher, even curioſity: for we are told, that he came not to hear his doctrine, but to view his perſon, or, to uſe the words of the evangeliſt, "to ſee who he was." Our LORD's fame was now ſpread abroad through all *Jeruſalem*, and all the country round about: ſome ſaid he was a good man; others, "Nay, but he deceiveth the people." And therefore curioſity drew out this rich Publican *Zaccheus*, to ſee who this perſon was, of whom he had heard ſuch various accounts. But it ſeems he could not conveniently get a ſight of him for the preſs, and becauſe he was little of ſtature. Alas! how many are kept from ſeeing CHRIST in glory, by reaſon of the preſs! I mean, how many are aſhamed of being ſingularly good, and therefore follow a multitude to do evil, becauſe they have a preſs or throng of polite acquaintance! And, for fear of being ſet at nought by thoſe with whom they uſed to ſit at meat, they deny the LORD of glory, and are aſhamed to confeſs him before men. This baſe, this ſervile fear of man, is the bane of true chriſtianity; it brings a dreadful ſnare upon the ſoul, and is the ruin of ten thouſands: for I am fully perſuaded, numbers are rationally convicted of goſpel-truths; but, not being able to brook contempt, they will not proſecute their convictions, nor reduce them to practice. Happy thoſe, who in this reſpect, like *Zaccheus*, are reſolved to overcome all impediments that lie in their way to a ſight of CHRIST: for, finding he could not ſee CHRIST becauſe of the preſs and the littleneſs of his natural ſtature, he did not ſmite upon his breaſt, and depart, ſaying, "It is in vain to ſeek after a ſight of him any longer, I can never attain unto it." No, finding he could not ſee CHRIST, if he continued in the midſt of, "he ran before the multitude, and climbed up into a ſycamore-tree, to ſee him; for he was to paſs that way."

There is no ſeeing CHRIST in Glory, unleſs we run before the multitude, and are willing to be in the number of thoſe deſpiſed few, who take the kingdom of GOD by violence. The broad way, in which ſo many go, can never be that ſtrait and narrow way which leads to life. Our LORD's flock
was,

was, and always will be, comparatively a little one: and unless we dare to run before the multitude in a holy singularity, and can rejoice in being accounted fools for CHRIST's sake, we shall never see JESUS with comfort, when he appears in glory. From mentioning the sycamore-tree, and considering the difficulty with which *Zaccheus* must climb it, we may farther learn, that those who would see CHRIST, must undergo other difficulties and hardships, besides contempt. *Zaccheus*, without doubt, went through both. Did not many, think you, laugh at him as he ran along, and in the language of *Michal*, *Saul*'s daughter, cry out, " How glorious did the rich *Zaccheus* look to-day, when, forgetting the greatness of his station, he ran before a pitiful, giddy mob, and climbed up a sycamore-tree, to see an enthusiastic preacher!" But *Zaccheus* cares not for all that; his curiosity was strong: if he could but see who JESUS was, he did not value what scoffers said of him. Thus, and much more will it be with all those who have an effectual desire to see JESUS in heaven: they will go on from strength to strength, break through every difficulty lying in their way, and care not what men or devils say of or do unto them. May the LORD make us all thus minded, for his dear Son's sake!

At length, after taking much pains, and going (as we may well suppose) through much contempt, *Zaccheus* has climbed the tree; and there he sits, as he thinks, hid in the leaves of it, and watching when he should see JESUS pass by: " For he was to pass by that way."

But sing, O heavens, and rejoice, O earth! Praise, magnify, and adore sovereign, electing, free, preventing love; JESUS the everlasting GOD, the Prince of peace, who saw *Nathanael* under the fig-tree, and *Zaccheus* from eternity, now sees him in the sycamore-tree, and calls him in time.

Verse 5. " And when JESUS came to the place, he looked up, and saw him, and said unto him, *Zaccheus*, make haste and come down; for this day I must abide at thy house." Amazing love! Well might *Luke* usher in the account with " behold!" It is worthy of our highest admiration. When *Zaccheus* thought of no such thing, nay, thought that CHRIST JESUS did not know him; behold, CHRIST does what we never hear he did before or after, I mean, invite himself to the house of *Zaccheus*, saying, "*Zaccheus*, make haste and come down; for this day I must abide at thy house." Not pray let me abide, but I must abide this day at thy house. He also calls him by name, as though he was well acquainted with him: and indeed well he might; for his name was written in the book of life, he was one of those whom the Father had given him from all eternity: therefore he must abide at his house that day. " For whom he did predestinate, them he also called."

Here then, as through a glass, we may see the doctrine of free grace evidently exemplified before us. Here was no fitness in *Zaccheus*. He was a Publican, chief among the Publicans; not only so, but rich, and came to see CHRIST only out of curiosity: but sovereign grace triumphs over all. And if we do GOD justice, and are effectually wrought upon, we must acknowledge there was no more fitness in us than in *Zaccheus*; and, had not CHRIST prevented us by his call, we had remained dead in trespasses and sins, and alienated from the divine life, even as others. "JESUS looked up, and saw him, and said unto him, *Zacchues*, make haste and come down; for this day I must abide at thy house."

With what different emotions of heart may we suppose *Zaccheus* received this invitation? Think you not that he was surprised to hear JESUS CHRIST call him by name, and not only so, but invite himself to his house? Surely, thinks *Zaccheus*, I dream: it cannot be; how should he know me? I never saw him before: besides, I shall undergo much contempt, if I receive him under my roof. Thus, I say, we may suppose *Zaccheus* thought within himself. But what saith the scripture? " I will make a willing people in the day of my power." With this outward call, there went an efficacious power from GOD, which sweetly over-ruled his natural will: and therefore, verse 6. " He made haste, and came down, and received him joyfully;" not only into his house, but also into his heart.

Thus it is the great GOD brings home his children. He calls them by name, by his word or providence; he speaks to them also by his spirit. Hereby they are enabled to open their hearts, and are made willing to receive the King of glory. For *Zaccheus*'s sake, let us not entirely condemn people that

come

come under the word, out of no better principle than curiofity. Who knows but GOD may call them? It is good to be where the LORD is paſſing by. May all who are now preſent out of this principle, hear the voice of the Son of GOD ſpeaking to their ſouls, and ſo hear that they may live! Not that men ought therefore to take encouragement to come out of curioſity. For perhaps a thouſand more, at other times, came to ſee CHRIST out of curioſity, as well as *Zaccheus*, who were not effectually called by his grace. I only mention this for the encouragement of my own ſoul, and the conſolation of GOD's children, who are too apt to be angry with thoſe who do not attend on the word out of love to GOD: but let them alone. Brethren, pray for them. How do you know but JESUS CHRIST may ſpeak to their hearts? A few words from CHRIST, applied by his ſpirit, will ſave their ſouls. " *Zaccheus*, ſays CHRIST, make haſte and come down. And he made haſte, and came down, and received him joyfully."

I have obſerved, in holy ſcripture, how particularly it is remarked, that perſons rejoiced upon believing in CHRIST. Thus the converted Eunuch went on his way rejoicing; thus the Jaylor rejoiced with his whole houſe; thus *Zaccheus* received CHRIST joyfully. And well may thoſe rejoice who receive JESUS CHRIST; for with him they receive righteouſneſs, ſanctification, and eternal redemption. Many have brought up an ill report upon our good land, and would fain perſuade people that religion will make them melancholy mad. So far from it, that joy is one ingredient of the kingdom of GOD in the heart of a believer; " The kingdom of GOD is righteouſneſs, peace, and joy in the Holy Ghoſt." To rejoice in the LORD, is a goſpel-duty. " Rejoice in the LORD always, and again I ſay, rejoice." And who can be ſo joyful, as thoſe who know that their pardon is ſealed before they go hence and are no more ſeen? The godly may, but I cannot ſee how any ungodly men can, rejoice: they cannot be truly cheerful. What if wicked men may ſometimes have laughter amongſt them? It is only the laughter of fools; in the midſt of it there is heavineſs: At the beſt, it is but like the crackling of thorns under a pot; it makes a blaze, but ſoon goes out. But, as for the godly, it is not ſo with them; their joy is solid and lasting. As it is a joy that a stranger intermeddleth not with, so it is a joy that no man taketh from them: it is a joy in GOD, a " joy unspeakable and full of glory."

It should seem that *Zaccheus* was under soul-distress but a little while; perhaps (says *Guthrie*, in his book intituled, *The Trial concerning a saving Interest in Christ*) not above a quarter of an hour. I add, perhaps not so long: for, as one observes, sometimes the LORD JESUS delights to deliver speedily. GOD is a sovereign agent, and works upon his children in their effectual calling, according to the counsel of his eternal will. It is with the spiritual, as natural birth: all women have not the like pangs; all christians have not the like degree of conviction. But all agree in this, that all have JESUS CHRIST formed in their hearts: and those who have not so many trials at first, may be visited with the greater conflicts hereafter; though they never come into bondage again, after they have once received the spirit of adoption. " We have not, (says *Paul*) received the spirit of bondage again unto fear." We know not what *Zaccheus* underwent before he died: however, this one thing I know, he now believed in CHRIST, and was justified, or acquitted, and looked upon as righteous in GOD's sight, though a Publican, chief among the Publicans, not many moments before. And thus it is with all, that, like *Zaccheus*, receive JESUS CHRIST by faith into their hearts: the very moment they find rest in him, they are freely justified from all things from which they could not be justified by the law of *Moses*; " for by grace are we saved, through faith, and that not of ourselves, it is the gift of GOD."

Say not within yourselves, this is a licentious Antinomian doctrine; for this faith, if true, will work by love, and be productive of the fruits of holiness. See an instance in this convert *Zaccheus*: no sooner had he received JESUS CHRIST by faith into his heart, but he evidences it by his works; for, ver. 8. we are told, " *Zaccheus* stood forth, and said unto the LORD, Behold, LORD, the half of my goods I give unto the poor; and if I have taken any thing from any man by false accusation, I restore him four-fold."

Having believed on JESUS in his heart, he now makes confession of him with his mouth to salvation. " *Zaccheus* stood forth:"

forth :" he was not afhamed, but ftood forth before his brother Publicans; for true faith cafts out all fervile, finful fear of man; " and faid, Behold, LORD." It is remarkable, how readily people in fcripture have owned the divinity of CHRIST immediately upon their converfion. Thus the woman at *Jacob's* well; " Is not this the CHRIST ?" Thus the man born blind; " LORD, I believe; and worfhipped him." Thus *Zaccheus*, " Behold, LORD." An inconteftable proof this to me, that thofe who deny our LORD's divinity, never effectually felt his power: if they had, they would not fpeak fo lightly of him; they would fcorn to deny his eternal power and Godhead. " *Zaccheus* ftood forth, and faid, Behold, LORD, the half of my goods I give to the poor; and if I have taken any thing from any man by falfe accufation, I reftore him four-fold." Noble fruits of a true living faith in the LORD JESUS! Every word calls for our notice. Not fome fmall, not the tenth part, but the *half*. Of what? My goods; things that were valuable. *My* goods, his own, not another's. I give: not, I will give when I die, when I can keep them no longer; but, I give now, even now. *Zaccheus* would be his own executor. For whilft we have time we fhould do good. But to whom would he give half of his goods? Not to the rich, not to thofe who were already clothed in purple and fine linen, of whom he might be recompenfed again; but to the poor, the maimed, the halt, the blind, from which he could expect no recompence till the refurrection of the dead. " I give to the poor." But knowing that he muft be juft before he could be charitable, and confcious to himfelf that in his public adminiftrations he had wronged many perfons, he adds, " And if I have taken any thing from any man by falfe accufation, I reftore him fourfold." Hear ye this, all ye that make no confcience of cheating the king of his taxes, or of buying or felling run goods. If ever GOD gives you true faith, you will never reft, till, like *Zaccheus*, you have made reftitution to the utmoft of your power. I fuppofe, before his converfion, he thought it no harm to cheat thus, no more than you may do now, and pleafed himfelf frequently, to be fure, that he got rich by doing fo: but now he is grieved for it at his heart; he confeffes his injuftice before men, and promifes to make ample reftitution. Go ye cheating Publicans, learn of *Zaccheus*; go away and do likewife. If you do not make reftitution here, the LORD JESUS fhall make you confefs your fins before men and angels, and condemn you for it, when he comes in the glory of his Father to judgment hereafter.

After all this, with good reafon might our LORD fay unto him, " This day is falvation come to this houfe; forafmuch as he alfo is the Son of *Abraham*;" not fo much by a natural as by a fpiritual birth. He was made partaker of like precious faith with *Abraham*: like *Abraham* he believed on the LORD, and it was accounted to him for righteoufnefs: his faith, like *Abraham*'s, worked by love; and I doubt not, but he has been long fince fitting in *Abraham*'s harbour.

And now, are you not afhamed of yourfelves, who fpeak againft the doctrines of grace, efpecially that doctrine of being juftified by faith alone, as though it leaded to licentioufnefs? What can be more unjuft than fuch a charge? Is not the inftance of *Zaccheus*, a fufficient proof to the contrary? Have I ftrained it to ferve my own turn? GOD forbid. To the beft of my knowledge I have fpoken the truth in fincerity, and the truth as it is in JESUS. I do affirm that we are faved by grace, and that we are juftified by faith alone: but I do alfo affirm, that faith muft be evidenced by good works, where there is an opportunity of performing them.

What therefore has been faid of *Zaccheus*, may ferve as a rule, whereby all may judge whether they have faith or not. You fay you have faith; but how do you prove it? Did you ever hear the LORD JESUS call you by name? Were you ever made to obey that call? Did you ever, like *Zaccheus*, receive JESUS CHRIST joyfully into your hearts? Are you influenced by the faith you fay you have, to ftand up and confefs the LORD JESUS before men? Were you ever made willing to own, and humble yourfelves for, your paft offences? Does your faith work by love, fo that you confcientioufly lay up, according as GOD has profpered you, for the fupport of the poor? Do you give alms of all things that you poffefs? And have you made due reftitution to thofe you have wronged? If fo, happy are ye; falvation is come to your fouls, you are fons, you are daughters of, you fhall fhortly be everlaftingly bleffed with, faithful *Abraham*. But, if you are not thus minded, do not

deceive

deceive your own souls. Though you may talk of justification by faith, like angels, it will do you no good; it will only increase your damnation. You hold the truth, but it is in unrighteousness: your faith being without works, is dead: you have the devil, not *Abraham*, for your father. Unless you get a faith of the heart, a faith working by love, with devils and damned spirits shall you dwell for evermore.

But it is time now to enforce the latter part of the text; " For the Son of man is come to seek and to save that which was lost." These words are spoken by our Saviour in answer to some self-righteous Pharisees, who, instead of rejoicing with the angels in heaven, at the conversion of such a sinner, murmured, " That he was gone to be a guest with a man that was a sinner." To vindicate his conduct, he tells them, that this was an act agreeable to the design of his coming: " For the Son of man is come to seek and to save that which was lost." He might have said, the Son of GOD. But O the wonderful condescension of our Redeemer! He delights to stile himself the Son of man. He came not only to save, but *to seek* and to save that which was lost. He came to *Jericho* to seek and save *Zaccheus*; for otherwise *Zaccheus* would never have been saved by him. But from whence came he? Even from heaven, his dwelling-place, to this lower earth, this vale of tears, to seek and save that which was lost; or all that feel themselves lost, and are willing, like *Zaccheus*, to receive him into their hearts to save them; with how great a salvation? Even from the guilt, and also from the power of their sins; to make them heirs of GOD, and joint heirs with himself, and partakers of that glory which he enjoyed with the Father before the world began. Thus will the Son of man save that which is lost. He was made the son of man, on purpose that he might save them. He had no other end but this in leaving his Father's throne, in obeying the moral law, and hanging upon the cross: all that was done and suffered, merely to satisfy, and procure a righteousness for poor, lost, undone sinners, and that too without respect of persons. " That which was lost;" all of every nation and language, that feel, bewail, and are truly desirous of being delivered from their lost state, did the Son of man come down to seek and to save: for he is mighty, not only so, but willing, to save to the uttermost all that come to GOD through him. He will in no wise cast them out: for he is the same to-day, as he was yesterday. He comes now to sinners, as well as formerly; and, I hope, hath sent me out this day to seek, and, under him, to bring home some of you, the lost sheep of the house of *Israel*.

What say you? Shall I go home rejoicing, saying, That many like sheep have went astray, but they have now believed on JESUS CHRIST, and so returned home to the great Shepherd and Bishop of their souls? If the LORD would be pleased thus to prosper my handy-work, I care not how many legalists and self-righteous pharisees murmur against me, for offering salvation to the worst of sinners: for I know the Son of man came to seek and to save them; and the LORD JESUS will now be a guest to the worst Publican, the vilest sinner that is amongst you, if he does but believe on him. Make haste then, O sinners, make haste, and come by faith to CHRIST. Then, this day, even this hour, nay, this moment, if you believe, JESUS CHRIST shall come and make his eternal abode in your hearts. Which of you is made willing to receive the King of glory? Which of you obeys he call, as *Zaccheus* did? Alas! why do you stand still? How know you, whether JESUS CHRIST may ever call you again? Come then, poor, guilty sinners; come away, poor, lost, undone publicans: make haste, I say, and come away to JESUS CHRIST. The LORD condescends to invite himself to come under the filthy roofs of the houses of your souls. Do not be afraid of entertaining him; he will fill you with all peace and joy in believing. Do not be ashamed to run before the multitude, and to have all manner of evil spoke against you falsly for his sake: one sight of CHRIST will make amends for all. *Zaccheus* was laughed at; and all that will live godly in CHRIST JESUS, shall suffer persecution. But what of that? *Zaccheus* is now crowned in glory; as you also shall shortly be, if you believe on, and are reproached for CHRIST's sake. Do not, therefore, put me off with frivolous excuses: there's no excuse can be given for your not coming to CHRIST. You are lost, undone, without him; and if he is not glorified in your salvation, he will be glorified in your destruction; if he does not come and make his abode in your hearts, you must

take

take up an eternal abode with the devil and his angels. O that the LORD would be pleased to pass by some of you at this time! O that he may call you by his Spirit, and make you a willing people in this day of his power! For I know my calling will not do, unless he, by his efficacious grace, compel you to come in. O that you once felt what it is to receive JESUS CHRIST into your hearts! You would soon, like *Zaccheus*, give him every thing. You do not love CHRIST, because you do not know him; you do not come to him, because you do not feel your want of him: you are whole, and not broken hearted; you are not sick, at least not sensible of your sickness; and, therefore, no wonder you do not apply to JESUS CHRIST, that great, that almighty physician: You do not feel yourselves lost, and therefore do not seek to be found in CHRIST. O that GOD would wound you with the sword of his Spirit, and cause his arrows of conviction to stick deep in your hearts! O that he would dart a ray of divine light into your souls! For if you do not feel yourselves lost without CHRIST, you are of all men most miserable: your souls are dead; you are not only an image of hell, but in some degree hell itself: you carry hell about with you, and you know it not. O that I could see some of you sensible of this, and hear you cry out, " LORD, break this hard heart; LORD, deliver me from the body of this death; draw me, LORD, make me willing to come after thee; I am lost; LORD, save me, or I perish!" Was this your case, how soon would the LORD stretch forth his almighty hand, and say, Be of good cheer, it is I; be not afraid? What a wonderful calm would then possess your troubled souls! Your fellowship would then be with the Father and the Son: your life would be hid with CHRIST in GOD.

Some of you, I hope, have experienced this, and can say, I was lost, but I am found; I was dead, but am alive again: the Son of man came and sought me in the day of his power, and saved my sinful soul. And do you repent that you came to CHRIST? Has he not been a good master? Is not his presence sweet to your souls? Has he not been faithful to his promise? And have you not found, that even in doing and suffering for him, there is an exceeding present great reward? I am persuaded you will answer, Yes. O then, ye saints, re-

commend and talk of the love of CHRIST to others, and tell them, O tell them what great things the LORD has done for you! This may encourage others to come unto him. And who knows but the LORD may make you fishers of men? The story of *Zaccheus* was left on record for this purpose. No truly convicted soul, after such an instance of divine grace has been laid before him, need despair of mercy. What if you are Publicans? Was not *Zaccheus* a Publican? What if you are chief among the Publicans? Was not *Zaccheus* likewise? What if you are rich? Was not *Zaccheus* rich also? And yet almighty grace made him more than conqueror over all these hindrances. All things are possible to JESUS CHRIST; nothing is too hard for him: he is the LORD almighty. Our mountains of sins must all fall before this great *Zerubbabel*. On him GOD the Father has laid the iniquities of all that shall believe on him; and in his own body he bare them on the tree. There, there, by faith, O mourners in *Sion*, may you see your Saviour hanging with arms stretched out, and hear him, as it were, thus speaking to your souls; " Behold
" how I have loved you! Behold my hands and my feet!
" Look, look into my wounded side, and see a heart flaming
" with love: love stronger than death. Come into my arms,
" O sinners, come wash your spotted souls in my heart's
" blood. See here is a fountain opened for all sin and all
" uncleanness! See, O guilty souls, how the wrath of GOD
" is now abiding upon you: come, haste away, and hide
" yourselves in the clefts of my wounds; for I am wounded
" for your transgressions; I am dying that you may live for
" evermore. Behold, as *Moses* lifted up the serpent in the
" wilderness, so am I here lifted up upon a tree. See how I
" am become a curse for you: the chastisement of your peace
" is upon me. I am thus scourged, thus wounded, thus cru-
" cified, that you by my stripes may be healed. O look unto
" me, all ye trembling sinners, even to the ends of the earth!
" Look unto me by faith, and you shall be saved: for I came
" thus to be obedient even unto death, that I might save that
" which was lost."

And what say you to this, O sinners? Suppose you saw the King of glory dying, and thus speaking to you; would you believe on him? No, you would not, unless you believe on him now : for though he is dead, he yet speaketh all this in the scripture; nay, in effect, says all this in the words of the text, " The Son of man is come to seek and to save that which is lost." Do not therefore any longer crucify the LORD of glory. Bring those rebels, your sins, which will not have him to reign over them, bring them out to him : though you cannot slay them yourselves, yet he will slay them for you. The power of his death and resurrection is as great now as formerly. Make haste therefore, make haste, O ye publicans and sinners, and give the dear LORD JESUS your hearts, your whole hearts. If you refuse to hearken to this call of the LORD, remember your damnation will be just : I am free from the blood of you all : you must acquit my Master and me at the terrible day of judgment. O that you may know the things that belong to your everlasting peace, before they are eternally hid from your eyes ! Let all that love the LORD JESUS CHRIST in sincerity say, *Amen*.

SERMON

SERMON XXXVI.

The Marriage of *Cana*.

JOHN ii. 11.

This beginning of miracles did Jesus in Cana of Galilee, and manifested forth his glory; and his disciples believed on him.

I Have more than once had occasion to observe, that the chief end St. *John* had in view, when he wrote his gospel, was to prove the divinity of JESUS CHRIST, [that WORD, who not only was from everlasting with GOD, but also was really GOD blessed for evermore] against those arch-heretics *Ebion* and *Cerinthus*, whose pernicious principles too many follow in these last days. For this purpose, you may take notice, that he is more particular than any other Evangelist, in relating our LORD's divine discourses, as also the glorious miracles which he wrought, not by a power derived from another, like *Moses*, and other prophets, but from a power inherent in himself.

The words of the text have a reference to a notable miracle which CHRIST performed, and thereby gave proof of his eternal power and Godhead. " This beginning of miracles did JESUS in *Cana* of *Galilee*, and manifested forth his glory; and his disciples believed on him."

The miracle here spoken of, is that of our LORD's turning water into wine at a marriage feast. I design, at present, by GOD's help, to make some observations on the circumstances and certainty of the miracle, and then conclude with some practical instructions; that you, by hearing how JESUS CHRIST has shewed forth his glory, may, by the operation of GOD's Spirit upon your hearts, with the disciples mentioned in the text, be brought to believe on him.

First,

First, then, I would make some observations on the miracle itself.

Verse 1 and 2. "And the third day there was a marriage in *Cana* of *Galilee*; and the mother of JESUS was there. And both JESUS was called, and his disciples, to the marriage." By our LORD's being at a feast we may learn, that feasting upon solemn occasions is not absolutely unlawful: but then we must be exceeding careful at such seasons, that the occasion be solemn, and that we go not for the sake of eating and drinking, but to edify one another in love. Feasting in any other manner, I think absolutely unlawful for the followers of JESUS CHRIST: because if we eat and drink out of any other view, it cannot be to the glory of GOD. The Son of man, we know, "came eating and drinking." If a pharisee asked him to come to his house, our LORD went, and sat down with him. But then we find his discourse was always such as tended to the use of edifying. We may then, no doubt, go and do likewise.

We may observe farther, that if our LORD was present at a marriage feast, then, to deny marriage to any order of men, is certainly a "doctrine of devils." "Marriage (says the Apostle) is honourable in all." Our LORD graced a marriage feast with his first public miracle. It was an institution of GOD himself, even in paradise: and therefore, no doubt, lawful for all christians, even for those who are made perfect in holiness through the faith of JESUS CHRIST. But then, we may learn the reason why we have so many unhappy marriages in the world; it is because the parties concerned do not call JESUS CHRIST by prayer, nor ask the advice of his true disciples when they are about to marry: No; CHRIST and religion are the last things that are consulted: and no wonder then if matches of the devil's making (as all such are, which are contracted only on account of outward beauty, or for filthy lucre's sake) prove most miserable, and grievous to be borne.

I cannot but dwell a little on this particular, because I am persuaded the devil cannot lay a greater snare for young christians, than to tempt them unequally to yoke themselves with unbelievers: as are all who are not born again of GOD. This was the snare wherein the sons of GOD were entangled before the flood, and one great cause why God brought that flood upon the world. For what says *Moses*, *Gen.* vi. 2, 3. " The sons of God (the posterity of pious *Seth*) saw the daughters of men, (or the posterity of wicked *Cain*) that they were fair, (not that they were pious) and they took them wives of all which they chose:" not which God chose for them. What follows? " And the Lord said, My spirit shall not always strive with man, for that he also is flesh;" that is, even the few righteous souls being now grown carnal by their ungodly marriages, the whole world was altogether become abominable, and had made themselves vessels of wrath fitted for destruction. I might instance farther, the care the ancient patriarchs took to chuse wives for their children out of their own religious families; and it was one great mark of *Esau*'s rebellion against his father, that he took unto himself wives of the daughters of the *Canaanites*, who were strangers to the covenant of promise made unto his fathers. But I forbear. Time will not permit me to enlarge here. Let it suffice to advise all, whenever they enter into a marriage state, to imitate the people of *Cana* in *Galilee*, to call Christ to the marriage: He certainty will hear and chuse for you; and you will always find his choice to be the best. He then will direct you to such yoke-fellows as shall be helps meet for you in the great work of your salvation, and then he will also enable you to serve him without distraction, and cause you to walk, as *Zachary* and *Elizabeth*, in all his commandments and ordinances blameless.

But to proceed. Who these persons were that called our Lord and his disciples to the marriage, is not certain. Some (because it is said, that the mother of Jesus was there) have supposed that they were related to the Virgin, and that therefore our Lord and his disciples were invited on her account. However that be, it should seem they were not very rich, (for what had rich folks to do with a despised Jesus of *Nazareth*, and his mean followers?) because we find they were unfurnished with a sufficient quantity of wine for a large company, and therefore, " when they wanted wine, the mother of Jesus," having, as it should seem by her applying to him so readily on this occasion, even in his private life, seen some instances of his miraculous power, " saith unto him, They have

have no wine." She thought it sufficient only to inform him of the wants of the host, knowing that he was as ready to give as she to ask. In this light the blessed Virgin's request appears to us at the first view; but if we examine our Lord's answer, we shall have reason to think there was something which was not right; for Jesus saith unto her, ver. 4. "Woman, what have I to do with thee?" Observe, he calls her woman, not mother; to shew her, that though she was his mother, as he was man, yet she was his creature, as he was God. "What have I to do with thee?" Think you that I must work miracles at your bidding? Some have thought that she spoke as though she had an authority over him, which was a proud motion, and our Lord therefore checks her for it. And if Jesus Christ would not turn a little water into wine, whilst he was here on earth, at her command, how idolatrous is that church, and how justly do we separate from her, which prescribes forms, wherein the Virgin is desired to command her Son to have compassion on us!

But notwithstanding the holy Virgin was blameable in this respect, yet she hath herein set rich and poor an example which it is your duty to follow. You that are rich, and live in cieled houses, learn of her to go into the cottages of the poor; your Lord was not above it, and why should you? And when you do visit them, like the virgin-mother, examine their wants; and when you see they have no wine, and are ready to perish with hunger, shut not up your bowels of compassion, but bless the Lord for putting it in your power to administer to their necessities. Believe me, such visits would do you good. You would learn then to be thankful that God has given you bread enough, and to spare. And I am persuaded, every mite that you bestow on feeding the hungry and cloathing the naked disciples of Jesus Christ, will afford you more satisfaction at the hour of death, and in the day of judgment, than all the thousands squandered away in balls and assemblies, and such-like entertainments.

You that are poor in this world's goods, and thereby are disabled from helping, yet you may learn from the Virgin, to pray for one another. She could not turn the water into wine, but she could entreat her son to do it: and so may you; and doubt not of the LORD's hearing you; for GOD has chosen the poor in this world, rich in faith: and by your fervent prayers, you may draw down many a blessing on your poor fellow-creatures. O that I may ever be remembered by you before the throne of our dear LORD JESUS! But what shall we say? Will our LORD entirely disregard this motion of his mother? No; though he check her with, "Woman, what have I to do with thee?" yet he intimates that he would do as she desired by-and-by: "Mine hour is not yet come." As though he had said, The wine is almost, but not quite out; when they are come to an extremity, and sensible of the want of my assistance, then will I shew forth my glory, that they may behold it, and believe on me.

Thus, Sirs, hath our LORD been frequently pleased to deal with me, and, I doubt not, with many of you also. Often, often when I have found his presence as it were hidden from my soul, and his comforts well nigh gone, I have went unto him complaining that I had no visit and token of his love, as usual. Sometimes he has seemed to turn a deaf ear to my request, and as it were said, "What have I to do with thee?" which has made me go sorrowing all the day long; so foolish was I, and faithless before him: for I have always found he loved me notwithstanding, as he did *Lazarus*, though he stayed two days after he heard he was sick. But when my hour of extremity has been come, and my will broken, then hath he lifted up the light of his blessed countenance afresh; he has shewed forth his glory, and made me ashamed for disbelieving him, who often hath turned my water into wine. Be not then discouraged, if the LORD does not immediately seem to regard the voice of your prayer, when you cry unto him. The holy Virgin we find was not; no, she was convinced his time was the best time, and therefore, verse 5. "saith unto the servants, (O that we could follow her advice!) whatsoever he saith unto you, do it."

And now, behold the hour is come, when the eternal Son of GOD will shew forth his glory. The circumstance of the miracle is very remarkable; ver. 6. "And there were set six water-pots of water, after the manner of the purifying of the *Jews*, containing two or three firkins a-piece." The manner of this purifying we have an account of in the other Evangelists,

Evangelists, especially St. *Mark*, who informs us, that the pharisees, and all the *Jews*, except they wash their hands oft, eat not; and when they come from the market, except they wash they eat not. This was a superstitious custom; but, however, we may learn from it, whenever we come in from conversing with those that are without, to purify our hearts by self-examination and prayer; for it is hard to go through the world, and to be kept unspotted from it.

Observe further, verse 7. " JESUS saith unto them," not to his own disciples, but unto the servants of the house, who were strangers to the holy JESUS, and whom the virgin had before charged to do whatsoever he said unto them; " Fill the water-pots with water. And they filled them to the brim. And he saith unto them, draw out now, and bear to the governor of the feast. And they bear it." How our LORD turned the water into wine we are not told. What have we to do with that? Why should we desire to be wise above what is written? It is sufficient for the manifestation of his glorious godhead, that we are assured he did do it. For we are told, verse 9, 10. " When the ruler of the feast had tasted the water that was made wine, and knew not whence it was (but the servants that drew the water knew) the governor of the feast called the bridegroom, and saith unto him, every man at the beginning doth set forth good wine, and when they have well drunk, that which is worse; but thou hast kept the good wine until now."

To explain this passage, you must observe, it was the custom of the *Jews*, nay even of the heathens themselves, (to the shame of our christian baptized heathens be it spoken) at their public feasts to chuse a governor, who was to oversee and regulate the behaviour of the guests, and to take care that all things were carried on with decency and order. To this person then did the servants bear the wine; and we may judge how rich it was by his commendation of it, " Every man at the beginning, &c." Judge ye then, whether JESUS did not shew forth his glory, and whether you have not good reason, like the disciples here mentioned, to believe on him?

Thus, my brethren, I have endeavoured to make some observations on the miracle itself. But alas! this is only the outward court thereof, the veil is yet before our eyes; turn that aside, and we shall see such mysteries under it, as will make our hearts to dance for joy, and fill our mouths with praise for evermore!

But here I cannot help remarking what a sad inference one of our masters of *Israel*, in a printed sermon, has lately drawn from this commendation of the bridegroom. His words are these. "Our blessed Saviour came eating and drinking, was present at weddings, and other entertainments, (though I hear of his being only at one;) nay, at one of them (which I suppose is that of which I am now discoursing) worked a miracle to make wine, when it is plain there had been more drank than was absolutely necessary for the support of nature, and consequently something had been indulged to pleasure and chearfulness."*

I am sorry such words should come from the mouth and pen of a dignified clergyman of the Church of *England*. Alas! how is she fallen! or at least, in what danger must her tottering ark be, when such unhallowed hands are stretched out to support it! Well may I bear patiently to be stiled a blasphemer, and a setter forth of strange doctrines, when my dear Lord Jesus is thus traduced; and when those who pretend to preach in his name, urge this example to patronize licentiousness and excess. It is true (as I observed at the beginning of this discourse) our blessed Saviour did come eating and drinking; he was present at a wedding, and other entertainments; nay, at one of them worked a miracle to make wine, (you see I have been making some observations on it) but then it is not plain there had been more wine drank than was absolutely necessary for the support of nature; much less does it appear, that something had been indulged to pleasure and chearfulness.

The governor does indeed say, "When men have well drunken," but it no where appears that they were the men. Is it to be supposed, that the most holy and unspotted Lamb of God, who was manifested to destroy the works of the devil, and who, when at a Pharisee's house, took notice of even the gestures of those with whom he sat at meat; is it to be supposed, that our dear Redeemer, whose constant practice it was to tell people they must deny themselves, and take up

---

* See Dr. *Trap*'s sermon against being righteous over-much, p. 17.

their crosses daily; who bid his disciples to take heed, lest at any time their hearts might be over-charged with surfeiting and drunkenness; can it be supposed, that such a self-denying JESUS should now turn six large water-pots of water into the richest wine, to encourage excess and drunkenness in persons, who, according to this writer, had indulged to pleasure and chearfulness already? Had our LORD sat by, and seen them indulge, without telling them of it, would it not be a sin? But to insinuate he not only did this, but also turned water into wine, to increase that indulgence; this is making CHRIST a minister of sin indeed. What is this, but using him like the Pharisees of old, who called him a glutton, and a wine-bibber? Alas! how may we expect our dear LORD's enemies will treat him, when he is thus wounded in the house of his seeming friends? Sirs, if you follow such doctrine as this, you will not be righteous, but I am persuaded you will be *wicked over-much*.

But GOD forbid you should think our LORD behaved so much unlike himself in this matter. No, he had nobler ends in view, when he wrought this miracle. One, the evangelist mentions in the words of the text, " to shew forth his glory," or to give a proof of his eternal power and godhead.

Here seems to be an allusion to the appearance of GOD in the tabernacle, which this same evangelist takes notice of in his first chapter, where he says, " The Word (JESUS CHRIST) was made flesh, and dwelt (or, as it is rendered in the margin, tabernacled) amongst us." Our dear LORD, though very GOD of very GOD, and also most perfect and glorious in himself as man, was pleased to throw a veil of flesh over this his great glory, when he came to make his soul an offering for sin. And that the world might know and believe in him as the Saviour of all men, he performed many miracles, and this in particular; for thus speaks the evangelist, " This first," &c.

This then was the chief design of our LORD's turning the water into wine. But there are more which our LORD may be supposed to have had in view, some of which I shall proceed to mention.

Secondly, he might do this to reward the host for calling him and his disciples to the marriage. JESUS CHRIST will not be behind-hand with those who receive him or his followers, for his name's sake. Those who thus honour him, he will honour. A cup of cold water given in the name of a disciple, shall in no wise lose its reward. He will turn water into wine. Though those who abound in alms-deeds, out of a true faith in, and love for JESUS, may seem as it were to throw their bread upon the waters, yet they shall find it again after many days. For they who give to the poor out of this principle, lend unto the LORD; and look, whatsoever they lay out, it shall be repaid them again. Even in this life, GOD often orders good measure pressed down and running over, to be returned into his servants bosoms. It is the same in spirituals. To him that hath, and improves what he hath, for the sake of CHRIST and his disciples, shall be given, and he shall have abundance. Brethren, I would not boast; but, to my master's honour and free grace be it spoken, I can prove this to be true by happy experience. When I have considered that I am a child, and cannot speak, and have seen so many of you come out into the wilderness to be fed, I have often said within myself, what can I do with my little stock of grace and knowledge among so great a multitude? But, at my LORD's command, I have given you to eat of such spiritual food as I had, and before I have done speaking, have had my soul richly fed with the bread which cometh down from heaven. Thus shall it be done to all such who are willing to spend and be spent for CHRIST or his disciples; for there is no respect of persons with GOD.

Thirdly, Our LORD's turning the water, which was poured out so plentifully, into wine, is a sign of the plentiful pouring out of his Spirit into the hearts of believers. The holy Spirit is in scripture compared unto wine; and therefore the prophet calls us to buy wine as well as milk, that is, the spirit of love, which fills and gladdens the soul as it were with new wine. The apostle alludes to this, when he bids the *Ephesians* " not to be drunk with wine, wherein is excess, but be filled with the Spirit." And our LORD shews us thus much by chusing wine; to shew forth the strength and refreshment of his blood, in the blessed sacrament. I know these terms are unintelligible to natural men, they can no more understand me, than if I spake to them in an unknown tongue, for they are only to be spiritually discerned. To

you

you then that are spiritual do I speak, to you who are justified by faith, and feel the blessed Spirit of JESUS CHRIST working upon your hearts, you can judge of what I say; you have already (I am persuaded) been as it were filled with new wine by the inspiration of his Holy Spirit. But alas! you have not yet had half your portion; these are only earnests, and in comparison but shadows of good things to come; our LORD keeps his best wine for you till the last; and though you have drank deep of it already, yet he intends to give you more: He will not leave you, 'till he has filled you to the brim, 'till you are ready to cry out, LORD, stay thine hand, thy poor creatures can hold no more! Be not straitened in your own bowels, since JESUS CHRIST is not straitened in his. Open your hearts as wide as ever you will, the Spirit of the LORD shall fill them. CHRIST deals with true believers, as *Elijah* did with the poor woman, whose oil increased, to pay her husband's debts; as long as she brought pitchers, the oil continued. It did not cease till she ceased bringing vessels to contain it. My brethren, our hearts are like those pitchers; open them freely by faith, and the oil of GOD's free gift, the oil of gladness, the love of GOD through CHRIST, shall be continually pouring in; for believers are to be filled with all the fulness of GOD.

Fourthly, Our LORD's turning water into wine, and keeping the best until last, may shew forth the glory of the latter days of his marriage feast with his church. Great things GOD has done already, whereat millions of saints have rejoiced, and do yet rejoice. Great things GOD is doing now, but yet, my brethren, we shall see greater things than these. It is meet, right, and our bounden duty, to give thanks unto GOD, even the Father; for many righteous men have desired to see the things which we see, and have not seen them; and to hear the things which we hear, and have not heard them. But still there are more excellent things behind. Glorious things are spoken of these times, " when the earth shall be filled with the knowledge of the LORD, as the waters cover the sea." There is a general expectation among the people of GOD, when the partition-wall between *Jew* and *Gentile* shall be broken down, and all *Israel* be saved. Happy those who live when GOD does this. They shall see *Satan*, like lightning, fall from heaven. They shall not weep, as the *Jews* did at the building of the second temple. No, they shall rejoice

joice with exceeding great joy. For all the former glory of the christian church shall be nothing in comparison of that glory which shall excel. Then shall they cry out with the governor of the feast, " thou hast kept thy good wine until now!"

Fifthly, and lastly, This shews us the happiness of that blessed state, when we shall all sit together at the marriage supper of the Lamb, and drink of the new wine in his eternal and glorious kingdom!

The rewards which JESUS CHRIST confers on his faithful servants, and the comforts of his love wherewith he comforts them, whilst pilgrims here on earth, are often so exceeding great, that was it not promised, it were almost presumption for them to hope for any reward hereafter. But, my brethren, all the manifestations of GOD that we can possibly be favoured with here, when compared with the glory that is to be revealed in us, are no more than a drop of water when compared with an unbounded ocean. Though CHRIST frequently fills his saints even to the brim, yet their corruptible bodies weigh down their souls, and cause them to cry, " Who shall deliver us from these bodies of death?" These earthly tabernacles can hold no more: But, blessed be GOD, these earthly tabernacles are to be dissolved; this corruptible is to put on incorruption; this mortal is to put on immortality: and when GOD shall cause all his glory to pass before us, then shall we cry out, LORD, thou hast kept thy good wine until now. We have drank deeply of thy spirit; we have heard glorious things spoken of this thy city, O GOD! but we now find, that not the half, not the thousandth part hath been told us. O the invisible realities of the world of faith! Eye hath not seen, ear hath not heard, neither hath it entered into the heart of the greatest saint to conceive how CHRIST will shew forth his glory there! St. *Paul*, who was carried up into the third heavens, could give us little or no account of it. And well he might not—for he heard and saw such things as is not possible for a man cloathed with flesh and blood to utter. Whilst I am thinking, and only speaking of those things unto you, I am almost carried beyond myself. Methinks, I now receive some little foretastes of that new wine which I hope to drink with you in the heavenly kingdom for ever and ever.

And

And wherefore do you think I have been saying these things? Many, perhaps, may be ready to say, To manifest thy own vain-glory. But it is a small matter with me to be judged of man's judgment. He that judgeth me is the LORD. He knows that I have spoken of his miracle, only for the same end for which he at first performed it, and which I at first proposed, that is, " to shew forth his glory," that you also may be brought to believe on him.

Did I come to preach myself, and not CHRIST JESUS my Lord, I would come to you, not in this plainness of speech, but with the enticing words of man's wisdom. Did I desire to please natural men, I need not preach here in the wilderness. I hope my heart aims at nothing else, than what our LORD's great fore-runner aimed at, and which ought to be the business of every gospel minister, that is, to point out to you the God-man CHRIST JESUS. " Behold then (by faith behold) the Lamb of GOD, who taketh away the sins of the world." Look unto him, and be saved. You have heard how he manifested, and will yet manifest his glory to true believers; and why then, O sinners, will you not believe in him? I say, O sinners, for now I have spoken to the saints, I have many things to say to you. And may GOD give you all an hearing ear, and an obedient heart!

The LORD JESUS who shewed forth his glory above 1700 years ago, has made a marriage feast, and offers to espouse all sinners to himself, and to make them flesh of his flesh, and bone of his bone. He is willing to be united to you by one spirit. In every age, at sundry times, and after divers manners, he hath sent forth his servants, and they had bidden many, but yet, my brethren, there is room. The LORD therefore now has given a commission in these last days to others of his servants, even to compel poor sinners by the cords of love to come in. For our master's house must and shall be filled. He will not shed his precious blood in vain. Come then, come to the marriage. Let this be the day of your espousals with JESUS CHRIST, he is willing to receive you, though other lords have had dominion over you. Come then to the marriage. Behold the oxen and fatlings are killed, and all things are ready; let me hear you say, as *Rebecca* did, when they asked her, whether she would go and be a wife to *Isaac*; O let me hear you say, we will come, Indeed you will not repent it. The LORD shall turn your water into wine. He shall fill your souls with marrow and fatness, and cause you to praise him with joyful lips.

Do not say, you are miserable, and poor, and blind, and naked, and therefore ashamed to come, for it is to such that this invitation is now sent. The polite, the rich, the busy, self-righteous Pharisees of this generation have been bidden already, but they have rejected the counsel of GOD against themselves. They are too deeply engaged in going, one to his country house, another to his merchandize. They are so deeply wedded to the pomps and vanities of this wicked world, that they, as it were with one consent, have made excuse. And though they have been often called in their own synagogues, yet all the return they make, is to thrust us out, and thereby in effect say, they will not come. But GOD forbid, my brethren, that you should learn of them; no, since our LORD condescends to call first, (because if left to yourselves you would never call after him) let me beseech you to answer him, as he answered for you, when called upon by infinite offended justice to die for your sins, " Lo! I come to do thy will, O GOD!" What if you are miserable, and poor, and blind, and naked, that is no excuse; faith is the only wedding garment which CHRIST requires; he does not call you because you already are, but because he intends to make you saints. It pities him to see you naked. He wants to cover you with his righteousness. In short, he desires to shew forth his glory, that is, his free love through your faith in him. Not but that he will be glorified, whether you believe in him or not; for the infinitely free love of JESUS CHRIST will be ever the same, whether you believe it, and so receive it, or the contrary. But our LORD will not always send out his servants in vain, to call you; the time will come when he will say, None of those which were bidden, and would not come, shall taste of my supper. Our LORD is a GOD of justice, as well as of love; and if sinners will not take hold of his golden sceptre, verily he will bruise them with his iron rod. It is for your sakes, O sinners, and not his own, that he thus condescends to invite you: suffer him then to shew forth his glory, even the glory of the exceeding riches of his free grace, by believ-

ing

ing on him, "For we are saved by grace through faith." It was grace, free grace, that moved the Father so to love the world, as to "give his only begotten Son, that whosoever believeth in him should not perish, but have everlasting life!" It was grace, that made the Son to come down and die. It was grace, free grace, that moved the Holy Ghost to undertake to sanctify the elect people of GOD: and it was grace, free grace, that moved our LORD JESUS CHRIST to send forth his ministers to call poor sinners this day. Let me not then, my brethren, go without my errand. Why will you not believe in him? Will the devil do such great and good things for you as CHRIST will? No indeed, he will not. Perhaps, he may give you to drink at first of a little brutish pleasure; but what will he give you to drink at last? a cup of fury and of trembling; a never-dying worm, a self-condemning conscience, and the bitter pains of eternal death. But as for the servants of JESUS CHRIST, it is not so with them. No, he keeps his best wine till the last. And though he may cause you to drink of the brook in the way to heaven, and of the cup of affliction, yet he sweetens it with a sense of his goodness, and makes it pleasant drink, such as their souls do love. I appeal to the experience of any saint here present, (as I doubt not but there are many such in this field) whether CHRIST has not proved faithful, ever since you have been espoused to him? Has he not shewed forth his glory, ever since you have believed on him?

And now, sinners, what have you to object? I see you are all silent, and well you may. For if you will not be drawn by the cords of infinite and everlasting love, what will draw you? I could urge many terrors of the LORD to persuade you; but if the love of JESUS CHRIST will not constrain you, your case is desperate. Remember then this day I have invited all, even the worst of sinners, to be married to the LORD JESUS. If you perish, remember you do not perish for lack of invitation. You yourselves shall stand forth at the last day, and I here give you a summons to meet me at the judgment seat of CHRIST, and to clear both my master and me. Would weeping, would tears prevail on you, I could wish my head were waters, and my eyes fountains of tears, that I might weep out every argument, and melt you into

love.

love. Would any thing I could do or suffer, influence your hearts, I think I could bear to pluck out my eyes, or even to lay down my life for your sakes. Or was I sure to prevail on you by importunity, I could continue my discourse till midnight, I would wrestle with you even till the morning watch, as *Jacob* did with the angel, and would not go away till I had overcome. But such power belongeth only unto the LORD, I can only invite; it is He only can work in you both to will and to do after his good pleasure; it is his property to take away the heart of stone, and give you a heart of flesh; it is his spirit that must convince you of unbelief, and of the everlasting righteousness of his dear Son; it is He alone must give faith to apply his righteousness to your hearts; it is He alone can give you a wedding garment, and bring you to sit down and drink new wine in his kingdom. As to spirituals we are quite dead, and have no more power to turn to GOD of ourselves, than *Lazarus* had to raise himself, after he had lain stinking in the grave four days. If thou canst go, O man, and breathe upon all the dry bones that lye in the graves, and bid them live; if thou canst take thy mantle and divide yonder river, as *Elijah* did the river *Jordan*; then will we believe thou hast a power to turn to GOD of thyself: But as thou must despair of the one, so thou must despair of the other, without CHRIST's quickening grace; in him is thy only help; fly to him then by faith; say unto him, as the poor leper did, " LORD, if thou wilt," thou canst make me willing; and he will stretch forth the right-hand of his power to assist and relieve you: He will sweetly guide you by his wisdom on earth, and afterwards take you up to partake of his glory in heaven.

To his mercy therefore, and Almighty protection, do I earnestly, humbly, and most affectionately commit you: the LORD bless you and keep you; the LORD lift up the light of his blessed countenance upon you, and give you all peace and joy in believing, now and for evermore!

SERMON XXXVII.

The Duty of searching the Scriptures.

JOHN v. 39.

Search the Scriptures.

WHEN the Sadducees came to our blessed LORD, and put to him the question, "whose wife that woman should be in the next life, who had seven husbands in this," he told them " they erred, not knowing the scriptures." And if we would know whence all the errors, that have over-spread the church of CHRIST, first arose, we should find that, in a great measure, they flowed from the same fountain, ignorance of the word of GOD.

Our blessed LORD, though he was the eternal GOD, yet as man, he made the scriptures his constant rule and guide. And therefore, when he was asked by the lawyer, which was the great commandment of the law, he referred him to his Bible for an answer, "What readest thou?" And thus, when led by the Spirit to be tempted by the devil, he repelled all his assaults, with "it is written."

A sufficient confutation this, of their opinion, who say, " the Spirit only, and not the Spirit by the Word, is to be our rule of action." If so, our Saviour, who had the Spirit without measure, needed not always have referred to the written word.

But how few copy after the example of CHRIST? How many are there who do not regard the word of GOD at all, but throw the sacred oracles aside, as an antiquated book, fit only for illiterate men?

Such do greatly err, not knowing what the scriptures are, or for what they are designed.

I shall,

I shall, therefore,

First, Shew, that it is every one's duty to search them.

And, *Secondly*, Lay down some directions for you, to search them with advantage.

I. I am to shew, that it is every person's duty to search the Scriptures.

By the Scriptures, I understand the law and the prophets, and those books which have in all ages been accounted canonical, and which make up that volume commmonly called the Bible.

These are emphatically stiled the *Scriptures*, and, in one place, the " Scriptures of Truth," as though no other books deserved the name of true writings or scripture in comparison of them.

They are not of any private interpretation, authority, or invention, but holy men of old wrote them, as they were moved by the Holy Ghost.

The foundation of GOD's revealing himself thus to mankind, was our fall in *Adam*, and the necessity of our new birth in CHRIST JESUS. And if we search the scriptures as we ought, we shall find the sum and substance, the *Alpha* and *Omega*, the beginning and end of them, is to lead us to a knowledge of these two great truths.

All the threats, promises and precepts, all the exhortations and doctrines contained therein, all the rites, ceremonies and sacrifices appointed under the *Jewish* law; nay, almost all the historical parts of holy scripture, suppose our being fallen in *Adam*, and either point out to us a Mediator to come, or speak of him as already come in the flesh.

Had man continued in a state of innocence, he would not have needed an outward revelation, because the law of GOD was so deeply written in the tables of his heart. But having eaten the forbidden fruit, he incurred the displeasure of GOD, and lost the divine Image, and, therefore, without an external revelation, could never tell how GOD would be reconciled unto him, or how he should be saved from the misery and darkness of his fallen nature.

That

That these truths are so, I need not refer you to any other book, than your own hearts.

For unless we are fallen creatures, whence those abominable corruptions which daily arise in our hearts? We could not come thus corrupt out of the hands of our Maker, because he being goodness itself could make nothing but what is like himself, holy, just, and good. And that we want to be delivered from these disorders of our nature, is evident, because we find an unwillingness within ourselves to own we are thus depraved, and are always striving to appear to others of a quite different frame and temper of mind than what we are.

I appeal to the experience of the most learned disputer against divine revelation, whether he does not find in himself, that he is naturally proud, angry, revengeful, and full of other passions contrary to the purity, holiness, and long-suffering of GOD. And is not this a demonstration that some way or other he is fallen from GOD? And I appeal also, whether at the same time that he finds these hurtful lusts in his heart, he does not strive to seem amiable, courteous, kind and affable; and is not this a manifest proof, that he is sensible he is miserable, and wants, he knows not how, to be redeemed or delivered from it?

Here then, GOD by his word steps in, and opens to his view such a scene of divine love, and infinite goodness in the holy scriptures, that none but men, of such corrupt and reprobate minds as our modern deists, would shut their eyes against it.

What does GOD in his written word do more or less, than shew thee, O man, how thou art fallen into that blindness, darkness, and misery, of which thou feelest and complainest? And, at the same time, he points out the way to what thou desirest, even how thou mayest be redeemed out of it by believing in, and copying after the Son of his love.

As I told you before, so I tell you again, upon these two truths rest all divine revelation. It being given us for no other end, but to shew us our misery, and our happiness; our fall and recovery; or, in one word, after what manner we died in *Adam*, and how in CHRIST we may again be made alive.

Hence then arises the necessity of searching the scriptures: for since they are nothing else but the grand charter of our salvation, the revelation of a covenant made by God with men in Christ, and a light to guide us into the way of peace; it follows, that all are obliged to read and search them, because all are equally fallen from God, all equally stand in need of being informed how they must be restored to, and again united with him.

How foolishly then do the disputing infidels of this generation act, who are continually either calling for signs from heaven, or seeking for outward evidence to prove the truth of divine revelation? Whereas, what they so earnestly seek for is nigh unto, nay, within them. For let them but consult their own hearts, they cannot but feel what they want. Let them but consult the lively oracles of God, and they cannot but see a remedy revealed for all their wants, and that the written word does as exactly answer the wants and desires of their hearts, as face answers to face in the water. Where then is the scribe, where is the wise, where is the solidity of the reasoning of the disputers of this world? Has not God revealed himself unto them, as plain as their own hearts could wish? And yet they require a sign: but there shall no other sign be given them. For if they believe not a revelation which is every way so suited to their wants, neither will they be persuaded though one should rise from the dead.

But this discourse is not designed so much for them that believe not, as for them, who both know and believe that the scriptures contain a revelation which came from God, and that it is their duty, as being chief parties concerned, not only to read but search them also.

I pass on, therefore, in the

Second place, to lay down some directions, how you may search them with advantage.

First, Have always in view, the end for which the scriptures were written, even to shew us the way of salvation, by Jesus Christ.

"Search the scriptures," says our blessed Lord, "for they are they that testify of me." Look, therefore, always for Christ in the scripture. He is the treasure hid in the field, both

both of the Old and New Testament. In the Old, you will find him under prophesies, types, sacrifices, and shadows; in the New, manifested in the flesh, to become a propitiation for our sins as a Priest, and as a Prophet to reveal the whole will of his heavenly Father.

Have CHRIST, then, always in view when you are reading the word of GOD, and this, like the star in the east, will guide you to the Messiah, will serve as a key to every thing that is obscure, and unlock to you the wisdom and riches of all the mysteries of the kingdom of GOD.

Secondly, Search the scriptures with an humble child-like disposition.

For whosoever does not read them with this temper, shall in no wise enter into the knowledge of the things contained in them. For GOD hides the sense of them, from those that are wise and prudent in their own eyes, and reveals them only to babes in CHRIST: who think they know nothing yet as they ought to know; who hunger and thirst after righteousness, and humbly desire to be fed with the sincere milk of the word, that they may grow thereby.

Fancy yourselves, therefore, when you are searching the scriptures, especially when you are reading the New Testament, to be with *Mary* sitting at the feet of the holy JESUS; and be as willing to learn what GOD shall teach you, as *Samuel* was, when he said, "Speak, LORD, for thy servant heareth."

Oh that the unbelievers would pull down every high thought and imagination that exalts itself against the revealed will of GOD! O that they would, like new-born babes, desire to be fed with the pure milk of the word! then we should have them no longer scoffing at Divine Revelation, nor would they read the Bible any more with the same intent the *Philistines* brought out *Sampson*, to make sport at it; but they would see the divine image and superscription written upon every line. They would hear GOD speaking unto their souls by it, and, consequently, be built up in the knowledge and fear of him, who is the Author thereof.

Thirdly, Search the scriptures, with a sincere intention to put in practice what you read.

F 2   A de-

A desire to do the will of GOD is the only way to know it; if any man will do my will, says JESUS CHRIST, "He shall know of my doctrine, whether it be of GOD, or whether I speak of myself." As he also speaks in another place to his disciples, "To you, (who are willing to practise your duty) it is given to know the mysteries of the kingdom of GOD, but to those that are without, (who only want to raise cavils against my doctrine) all these things are spoken in parables, that seeing they may see and not understand, and hearing they may hear and not perceive."

For it is but just in GOD to send those strong delusions, that they may believe a lie, and to conceal the knowledge of himself from all such as do not seek him with a single intention.

JESUS CHRIST is the same now, as formerly, to those who desire to know from his word, who he is that they may believe on, and live by; and to him he will reveal himself as clearly as he did to the woman of *Samaria*, when he said, "I that speak to thee am he," or as he did to the man that was born blind, whom the *Jews* had cast out for his name's sake, "He that talketh with thee, is he." But to those who consult his word with a desire neither to know him, nor keep his commandments, but either merely for their entertainment, or to scoff at the simplicity of the manner in which he is revealed, to those, I say, he never will reveal himself, though they should search the scriptures to all eternity. As he never would tell those whether he was the *Messiah* or not, who put that question to him either out of curiosity, or that they might have whereof to accuse him.

Fourthly, In order to search the scriptures still more effectually, make an application of every thing you read to your own hearts.

For whatever was written in the book of GOD, was written for our learning. And what CHRIST said unto those aforetime, we must look upon as spoken to us also: for since the holy scriptures are nothing but a revelation from GOD, how fallen man is to be restored by JESUS CHRIST: all the precepts, threats, and promises, belong to us and to our children, as well as to those, to whom they were immediately made known.

Thus

Thus the Apostle, when he tells us that he lived by the faith of the Son of God, adds, "who died and gave himself for me." It is this application of Jesus Christ to our hearts, that makes his redemption effectual to each of us.

And it is this application of all the doctrinal and historical parts of scripture, when we are reading them over, that must render them profitable to us, as they were designed for reproof, for correction, for instruction in righteousness, and to make every child of God perfect, thoroughly furnished to every good work.

I dare appeal to the experience of every spiritual reader of holy writ, whether or not, if he consulted the word of God in this manner, he was not at all times and at all seasons, as plainly directed how to act, as though he had consulted the Urim and Thummim, which was upon the high-priest's breast. For this is the way God now reveals himself to man: not by making new revelations, but by applying general things that are revealed already to every sincere reader's heart.

And this, by the way, answers an objection made by those who say, "The word of God is not a perfect rule of action, "because it cannot direct us how to act or how to determine "in particular cases, or what place to go to, when we are in "doubt, and therefore, the Spirit, and not the word, is to "be our rule of action."

But this I deny, and affirm on the contrary, that God at all times, circumstances, and places, though never so minute, never so particular, will, if we diligently seek the assistance of his Holy Spirit, apply general things to our hearts, and thereby, to use the words of the holy Jesus, will lead us into all truth, and give us the particular assistance we want: But this leads me to a

Fifth direction how to search the scriptures with profit: Labour to attain that Spirit by which they were written.

For the natural man discerneth not the words of the Spirit of God, because they are spiritually discerned; the words that Christ hath spoken, they are spirit, and they are life, and can be no more understood as to the true sense and meaning of them, by the mere natural man, than a person who never had learned a language can understand another speaking in it. The scriptures, therefore, have not unfitly been compared, by some, to the cloud which went before the *Israelites*, they are dark and hard to be understood by the natural man, as the cloud appeared dark to the *Egyptians*; but they are light, they are life to christians indeed, as that same cloud which seemed dark to *Pharaoh* and his house, appeared bright and altogether glorious to the *Israel* of GOD.

It was the want of the assistance of this Spirit, that made *Nicodemus*, a teacher of *Israel*, and a ruler of the *Jews*, so utterly ignorant in the doctrine of regeneration: for being only a natural man, he could not tell how that thing could be; it was the want of this Spirit that made our Saviour's disciples, though he so frequently conversed with them, daily mistake the nature of the doctrines he delivered; and it is because the natural veil is not taken off from their hearts, that so many who now pretend to search the scriptures, yet see no farther than into the bare letter of them, and continue entire strangers to the spiritual meaning couched under every parable, and contained in almost all the precepts of the book of GOD.

Indeed, how should it be otherwise, for GOD being a spirit, he cannot communicate himself any otherwise than in a spiritual manner to the hearts of men; and consequently if we are strangers to his Spirit, we must continue strangers to his word, because it is altogether like himself, spiritual. Labour, therefore, earnestly for to attain this blessed Spirit; otherwise, your understandings will never be opened to understand the scriptures aright: and remember, prayer is one of the most immediate means to get this Holy Spirit. Therefore,

Sixthly, Let me advise you, before you read the scriptures, to pray, that CHRIST, according to his promise, would send his Spirit to guide you into all truth; intersperse short ejaculations whilst you are engaged in reading; pray over every word and verse, if possible; and when you close up the book, most earnestly beseech GOD, that the words which you have read, may be inwardly engrafted into your hearts, and bring forth in you the fruits of a good life.

Do this, and you will, with a holy violence, draw down GOD's Holy Spirit into your hearts; you will experience his gracious influence, and feel him enlightening, quickening, and inflaming your souls by the word of GOD; you will then not only read, but mark, learn, and inwardly digest what you

read:

read: and the word of God will be meat indeed, and drink indeed unto your souls; you then will be as *Apollos* was, powerful in the scriptures; be scribes ready instructed to the kingdom of God, and bring out of the good treasures of your heart, things both from the Old and New Testament, to entertain all you converse with. One

Direction more, which shall be the last, *Seventhly*, Read the scripture constantly, or, to use our Saviour's expression in the text, " search the scriptures;" dig in them as for hid treasure; for here is a manifest allusion to those who dig in mines; and our Saviour would thereby teach us, that we must take as much pains in constantly reading his word, if we would grow wise thereby, as those who dig for gold and silver. The scriptures contain the deep things of God, and therefore, can never be sufficiently searched into by a careless, superficial, cursory way of reading them, but by an industrious, close, and humble application.

The Psalmist makes it the characteristic of a good man, that he " meditates on God's law day and night." And " this book of the law, (says God to *Joshua*) shall not go out of thy mouth, but thou shalt meditate therein day and night;" for then thou shalt make thy way prosperous, and thou shalt have good success. Search, therefore, the scriptures, not only devoutly but daily, for in them are the words of eternal life; wait constantly at wisdom's gate, and she will then, and not till then, display and lay open to you her heavenly treasures. You that are rich, are without excuse if you do not; and you that are poor, ought to take heed and improve that little time you have: for by the scriptures you are to be acquitted, and by the scriptures you are to be condemned at the last day.

But perhaps you have no taste for this despised book; perhaps plays, romances, and books of polite entertainment, suit your taste better: if this be your case, give me leave to tell you, your taste is vitiated, and unless corrected by the Spirit and word of God, you shall never enter into his heavenly kingdom: for unless you delight in God here, how will you be made meet to dwell with him hereafter. Is it a sin then, you will say, to read useless impertinent books; I answer, Yes: And that for the same reason, as it is a sin to indulge useless conversation, because both immediately tend to grieve and quench that Spirit, by which alone we can be sealed to the day of redemption. You may reply, How shall we know this? Why, put in practice the precept in the text; search the scripture in the manner that has been recommended, and then you will be convinced of the danger, sinfulness, and unsatisfactoriness of reading any others than the book of GOD, or such as are wrote in the same spirit. You will then say, when I was a child, and ignorant of the excellency of the word of GOD, I read what the world calls harmless books, as other children in knowledge, though old in years, have done, and still do; but now I have tasted the good word of life, and am come to a more perfect knowledge of CHRIST JESUS my LORD, I put away these childish, trifling things, and am determined to read no other books but what lead me to a knowledge of myself and of CHRIST JESUS.

Search, therefore, the scriptures, my dear brethren; taste and see how good the word of GOD is, and then you will never leave that heavenly manna, that angel's food, to feed on dry husks, that light bread, those trifling, sinful compositions, in which men of false taste delight themselves: no, you will then disdain such poor entertainment, and blush that yourselves once were fond of it. The word of GOD will then be sweeter to you than honey, and the honey-comb, and dearer than gold and silver; your souls by reading it, will be filled as it were, with marrow and fatness, and your hearts insensibly moulded into the spirit of its blessed Author. In short, you will be guided by GOD's wisdom here, and conducted by the light of his divine word into glory hereafter.

SERMON

SERMON XXXVIII.

The Indwelling of the Spirit, the common Privilege of all Believers.

JOHN vii. 37, 38, 39.

In the laſt day, that great day of the feaſt, JESUS *ſtood and cried, ſaying, If any man thirſt, let him come unto me and drink. He that believeth on me, as the ſcripture hath ſaid, out of his belly ſhall flow rivers of living water. But this ſpake he of the Spirit, which they that believe on him ſhould receive.*

NOTHING has rendered the croſs of CHRIST of leſs effect; nothing has been a greater ſtumbling-block and rock of offence to weak minds, than a ſuppoſition, now current among us, that moſt of what is contained in the goſpel of JESUS CHRIST, was deſigned only for our LORD's firſt and immediate followers, and conſequently calculated but for one or two hundred years. Accordingly, many now read the life, ſufferings, death, and reſurrection of JESUS CHRIST, in the ſame manner as *Cæſar's Commentaries,* or the *Conqueſts of Alexander* are read: as things rather intended to afford matter for ſpeculation, than to be acted over again in and by us.

As this is true of the doctrines of the goſpel in general, ſo it is of the operation of GOD's Spirit upon the hearts of believers in particular; for we no ſooner mention the neceſſity of our receiving the Holy Ghoſt in theſe laſt days, as well as formerly, but we are looked upon by ſome, as enthuſiaſts and madmen; and by others, repreſented as wilfully deceiving the people, and undermining the eſtabliſhed conſtitution of the church.

Judge

Judge ye then, whether it is not high time for the true ministers of JESUS CHRIST, who have been made partakers of this heavenly gift, to lift up their voices like a trumpet; and if they would not have those souls perish, for which the LORD JESUS has shed his precious blood, to declare, with all boldness, that the Holy Spirit is the common privilege and portion of all believers in all ages; and that we as well as the first christians, must receive the Holy Ghost, before we can be truly called the children of GOD.

For this reason, (and also that I might answer the design of our church in appointing the present festival *) I have chosen the words of the text.

They were spoken by JESUS CHRIST, when he was at the feast of tabernacles. Our LORD attended on the temple-service in general, and the festivals of the *Jewish* church in particular. The festival at which he was now present, was that of the feast of tabernacles, which the *Jews* observed according to GOD's appointment in commemoration of their living in tents. At the last day of this feast, it was customary for many pious people to fetch water from a certain place, and bring it on their heads, singing this anthem out of *Isaiah*, "And with joy shall they draw water out of the wells of salvation." Our LORD observing this, and it being his constant practice to spiritualize every thing he met with, cries out, "If any man thirst, let him come unto me, (rather than unto that well) and drink. He that believeth on me, as the scripture hath spoken, (where it is said, GOD will make water to spring out of a dry rock, and such-like) out of his belly shall flow rivers of living water." And that we might know what our Saviour meant by this living water, the Evangelist immediately adds, "But this spake he of the Spirit, which they that believe on him should receive."

The last words I shall chiefly insist on in the ensuing discourse: And

> *First*, I shall briefly shew, what is meant by the word *Spirit*.
>
> *Secondly*, That this Spirit is the common privilege of all believers.

* Whitsuntide.

Thirdly,

Thirdly, I shall shew the reason on which this doctrine is founded. And

Lastly, Conclude with a general exhortation to believe on Jesus Christ, whereby alone we can receive this Spirit.

First, I am to shew, what is meant by the word *Spirit*.

By the Spirit, is evidently to be understood the Holy Ghost, the third person in the ever-blessed Trinity, consubstantial and co-eternal with the Father and the Son, proceeding from, yet equal to them both. For, to use the words of our Church in this day's office, that which we believe of the glory of the Father, the same we believe of the Son, and of the Holy Ghost, without any difference or inequality.

Thus, says St. *John*, in his first epistle, chap. v. ver. 7. " There are three that bare record in heaven, the Father, the Word, and the Holy Ghost, and these three are one." And our Lord, when he gave his Apostles commission to go and teach all nations, commanded them to baptize in the name of the Holy Ghost, as well as of the Father and the Son. And St. *Peter*, *Acts* v. 3. said to *Ananias*, " Why hath Satan filled thine heart to lie to the Holy Ghost?" And ver. 4. he says, " Thou hast not lied unto men, but unto God." From all which passages, it is plain, that the Holy Ghost, is truly and properly God, as well as the Father and the Son. This is an unspeakable mystery, but a mystery of God's revealing, and, therefore, to be assented to with our whole hearts: seeing God is not a man that he should lie, nor the son of man that he should deceive. I proceed,

Secondly, To prove that the Holy Ghost is the common privilege of all believers.

But, here I would not be understood of so receiving the Holy Ghost, as to enable us to work miracles, or shew outward signs and wonders. I allow our adversaries, that to pretend to be inspired, in this sense, is being wise above what is written. Perhaps it cannot be proved, that God ever interposed in this extraordinary manner, but when some new revelation was to be established, as at the first settling of the

Mosaic and gospel dispensation: and as for my own part, I cannot but suspect the spirit of those who insist upon a repetition of such miracles at this time. For the world being now become nominally christian, (though, GOD knows, little of the power is left among us) there need not outward miracles, but only an inward co-operation of the Holy Spirit with the word, to prove that JESUS is the Messiah which was to come into the world.

Besides, if it was possible for thee, O man, to have faith, so as to be able to remove mountains, or cast out devils; nay, couldst thou speak with the tongue of men and angels, yea, and bid the sun stand still in the midst of heaven; what would all these gifts of the Spirit avail thee, without being made partaker of his sanctifying graces? *Saul* had the spirit of government for a while, so as to become another man, and yet probably was a cast-away. And many, who cast out devils in CHRIST's name, at the last will be disowned by him. If, therefore, thou hadst only the gifts, and was destitute of the graces of the Holy Ghost, they would only serve to lead thee with so much the more solemnity to hell.

Here then we join issue with our adversaries, and will readily grant, that we are not in this sense to be inspired, as were our LORD's first Apostles. But unless men have eyes which see not, and ears that hear not, how can they read the latter part of the text, and not confess that the Holy Spirit, in another sense, is the common privilege of all believers, even to the end of the world? " This spake he of the Spirit, which they that believe on him should receive." Observe, he does not say, they that believe on him for one or two ages, but they that believe on him in general, or, at all times, and in all places. So that, unless we can prove, that St. *John* was under a delusion when he wrote these words, we must believe that even we also, shall receive the Holy Ghost, if we believe on the LORD JESUS with our whole hearts.

Again, our LORD, just before his bitter passion, when he was about to offer up his soul an offering for the sins of the elect world; when his heart was most enlarged, and he would undoubtedly demand the most excellent gift for his disciples, prays, " That they all may be one, as thou, Father, art in me, and I in thee; that they also may be one in us, I in
them,

them, and thou in me, that they may be made perfect in one;" that is, that all his true followers might be united to him by his holy Spirit, by as real, vital, and myſtical an union, as there was between JESUS CHRIST and the Father. I ſay all his *true followers*; for it is evident, from our LORD's own words, that he had us, and all believers, in view, when he put up this prayer; " Neither pray I for theſe alone, but for them alſo which ſhall believe on me through their word;" ſo that, unleſs we treat our LORD as the high prieſts did, and count him a blaſphemer, we muſt confeſs, that all who believe in JESUS CHRIST, through the word, or miniſtration of his ſervants, are to be joined to JESUS CHRIST, by being made partakers of the Holy Spirit.

A great noiſe hath been made of late, about the word *enthuſiaſt*, and it has been caſt upon the preachers of the goſpel, as a term of reproach; but every chriſtian, in the proper ſenſe of the word, muſt be an enthuſiaſt; that is, muſt be inſpired of GOD, or have GOD, by his Spirit, in him. St. *Peter* tells us, " we have many great and precious promiſes, that we may be made partakers of the divine nature;" our LORD prays, " that we may be one, as the Father and he are one;" and our own church, in conformity to theſe texts of Scripture, in her excellent communion-office, tells us, that thoſe who receive the ſacrament worthily, " dwell in CHRIST, and CHRIST in them; that they are one with CHRIST, and CHRIST with them." And yet, chriſtians muſt have their names caſt out as evil, and miniſters in particular, muſt be looked upon as deceivers of the people, for affirming, that we muſt be really united to GOD, by receiving the Holy Ghoſt. Be aſtoniſhed, O heavens, at this!

Indeed, I will not ſay, all our letter-learned preachers deny this doctrine in expreſs words; but however, they do in effect; for they talk profeſſedly againſt inward feelings, and ſay, we may have GOD's Spirit without feeling it, which is in reality to deny the thing itſelf. And had I a mind to hinder the progreſs of the goſpel, and to eſtabliſh the kingdom of darkneſs, I would go about, telling people, they might have the Spirit of GOD, and yet not feel it.

But to return: When our LORD was about to aſcend to his Father and our Father, to his GOD and our GOD, he gave
his

his apostles this commission, "Go and teach all nations, baptizing them in the name of the Father, and of the Son, and of the Holy Ghost." And accordingly, by authority of this commission, we do teach and baptize in this, and every age of the church. And though we translate the words, " baptizing them in the *name*;" yet, as the name of GOD, in the LORD's prayer, and several other places, signifies his nature, they might as well be translated thus, " baptizing them into the *nature* of the Father, into the *nature* of the Son, and into the *nature* of the Holy Ghost." Consequently, if we are all to be baptized into the nature of the Holy Ghost, before our baptism be effectual to salvation, it is evident, that we all must actually receive the Holy Ghost, and ere we can say, we truly believe in JESUS CHRIST. For no one can say, that JESUS is my LORD, but he that has thus received the Holy Ghost.

Numbers of other texts might be quoted to make this doctrine, if possible, still more plain; but I am astonished, that any who call themselves members; much more, that many, who are preachers in the church of *England*, should dare so much as to open their lips against it. And yet, with grief I speak it, GOD is my Judge, persons of the established church seem more generally to be ignorant of it, than any dissenters whatsoever.

But, my dear brethren, what have you been doing? how often have your hearts given your lips the lye? how often have you offered to GOD the sacrifice of fools, and had your prayers turned into sin, if you approve of, and use our church-liturgy, and yet deny the Holy Spirit to be the portion of all believers? In the daily absolution, the minister exhorts the people to pray, that " GOD would grant them repentance, and his Holy Spirit;" in the Collect for *Christmas-day*, we beseech GOD, " that he would daily renew us by his Holy Spirit;" in the last week's Collect, we prayed that " we may evermore rejoice in the comforts of the Holy Ghost;" and in the concluding prayer, which we put up every day, we pray, not only that the grace of our LORD JESUS CHRIST, and the love of GOD, but that " the fellowship of the Holy Ghost" may be with us all evermore.

But farther, a solemn season, to some, is now approaching; I mean the *Ember-days*, at the end of which, all that are to be be ordained to the office of a deacon, are in the sight of God, and in the presence of the congregation, to declare, that " they trust they are inwardly moved by the Holy Ghost, to take upon them that administration;" and to those, who are to be ordained priests, the bishop is to repeat these solemn words, " Receive thou the Holy Ghost, now committed unto thee, by the imposition of our hands." And yet, O that I had no reason to speak it, many that use our forms, and many who have witnessed this good confession, yet dare to both talk and preach against the necessity of receiving the Holy Ghost now; and not only so, but cry out against those, who do insist upon it, as madmen, enthusiasts, schismatics, and underminers of the established constitution.

But you are the schismatics, you are the bane of the church of *England*, who are always crying out, " the temple of the Lord, the temple of the Lord;" and yet starve the people out of our communion, by feeding them only with the dry husks of dead morality, and not bringing out to them the fatted calf; I mean, the doctrines of the operations of the blessed Spirit of God. But here is the misfortune; many of us are not led by, and therefore no wonder that we cannot talk feelingly of, the Holy Ghost; we subscribe to our articles, and make them serve for a key to get into church-preferment, and then preach contrary to those very articles to which we have subscribed. Far be it from me, to charge all the clergy with this hateful hypocrisy; no, blessed be God, there are some left among us, who dare maintain the doctrines of the Reformation, and preach the truth as it is in Jesus: But I speak the truth in Christ, I lye not; the generality of the clergy are fallen from our articles, and do not speak agreeable to them, or to the form of sound words delivered in the Scriptures; wo be unto such blind leaders of the blind! how can you escape the damnation of hell? It is not all your learning (falsely so called) it is not all your preferments can keep you from the just judgment of God. Yet a little while, and we shall all appear before the tribunal of Christ; there, there will I meet you; there Jesus Christ, the great Shepherd and Bishop of souls, shall determine who are the false prophets, who are the wolves in sheep's cloathing. Those who

say,

say, that we must now receive and feel the Holy Ghost, or those who exclaim against it, as the doctrine of devils.

But I can no more; it is an unpleasing task to censure any order of men, especially those who are in the ministry; nor would any thing excuse it but necessity: that necessity which extorted from our LORD himself so many woes against the Scribes and Pharisees, the letter-learned rulers and teachers of the *Jewish* church; and surely, if I could bear to see people perish for lack of knowledge, and yet be silent towards those who keep from them the key of true knowledge, the very stones would cry out.

Would we restore the church to its primitive dignity, the only way is to live and preach the doctrine of CHRIST, and the articles to which we have subscribed; then we shall find the number of dissenters will daily decrease, and the church of *England* become the joy of the whole earth.

I am, in the *Third* place, to shew the reasonableness of this doctrine.

I say, the reasonableness of this doctrine; for however it may seem foolishness to the natural man, yet to those, who have tasted of the good word of life, and have felt the power of the world to come, it will appear to be founded on the highest reason; and is capable, to those who have eyes to see, even of a demonstration; I say of demonstration: for it stands on this self-evident truth, that we are fallen creatures, or, to use the scripture-expression, "have all died in *Adam*."

I know indeed, it is now no uncommon thing amongst us, to deny the doctrine of original sin, as well as the divinity of JESUS CHRIST; but it is incumbent on those who deny it, first to disprove the authority of the holy Scriptures; if thou canst prove, thou unbeliever, that the book, which we call *The Bible*, does not contain the lively oracles of GOD; if thou canst shew, that holy men of old, did not write this book, as they were inwardly moved by the Holy Ghost, then will we give up the doctrine of original sin; but unless thou canst do this, we must insist upon it, that we are all conceived and born in sin; if for no other, yet for this one reason, because that GOD, who cannot lye, has told us so.

But what has light to do with darkness, or polite infidels with the Bible? Alas! as they are strangers to the power, so they

they are generally as great strangers to the word of GOD. And therefore, if we will preach to them, we must preach to and from the heart: for talking in the language of scripture, to them, is but like talking in an unknown tongue. Tell me then, O man, whosoever thou art, that denieſt the doctrine of original sin, if thy conſcience be not ſeared as with a hot iron! tell me, if thou doſt not find thyſelf, by nature, to be a motly mixture of brute and devil? I know theſe terms will ſtir up the whole Phariſee in thy heart; but let not Satan hurry thee hence; ſtop a little, and let us reaſon together; doſt thou not find, that by nature thou art prone to pride? otherwiſe, wherefore art thou now offended? Again, doſt not thou find in thyſelf the ſeeds of malice, revenge, and all un-charitableneſs? and what are theſe but the very tempers of the devil? Again, do we not all by nature follow, and ſuffer ourſelves to be led by our natural appetites, always looking downwards, never looking upwards to that GOD, in whom we live, move, and have our being? and what is this but the very nature of the beaſts that periſh? Out of thy own heart, therefore, will I oblige thee to confeſs, what an inſpired apoſtle has long ſince told us, that " the whole world (by nature) lies in the wicked one;" we are no better than thoſe whom St. *Jude* calls " brute beaſts;" for we have tempers in us all by nature, that prove to a demonſtration, that we are earthly, ſenſual, devilish.

And this will ſerve as another argument, to prove the reality of the operations of the bleſſed Spirit on the hearts of believers, againſt thoſe falſe profeſſors, who deny there is any ſuch thing as influences of the Holy Spirit, that may be felt. For if they will grant that the devil worketh, and ſo as to be felt in the hearts of the children of diſobedience (which they muſt grant, unleſs they will give an apoſtle the lye) where is the wonder that the good Spirit ſhould have the ſame power over thoſe who are truly obedient to the faith of JESUS CHRIST?

If it be true then, that we are all by nature, ſince the fall, a mixture of brute and devil, it is evident, that we all muſt receive the Holy Ghoſt, ere we can dwell with and enjoy GOD.

When you read, how the prodigal, in the goſpel, was reduced to ſo low a condition, as to eat huſks with ſwine, and how *Nebuchadnezzar* was turned out, to graze with oxen; I am confident, you pity their unhappy state. And when you hear, how JESUS CHRIST will say, at the last day, to all that are not born again of GOD, "Depart from me, ye cursed, into everlasting fire, prepared for the devil and his angels," do not your hearts shrink within you, with a secret horror? And if creatures, with only our degree of goodness, cannot bear even the thoughts of dwelling with beasts or devils, to whose nature we are so nearly allied, how do we imagine GOD, who is infinite goodness, and purity itself, can dwell with us, while we are partakers of both their natures? we might as well think to reconcile heaven and hell.

When *Adam* had eaten the forbidden fruit, he fled and hid himself from GOD; why? because he was naked; he was alienated from the life of GOD, the due punishment of his disobedience. Now, we are all by nature naked and void of GOD, as he was at that time, and consequently, until we are changed, renewed, and cloathed with a divine nature again, we must fly from GOD also.

Hence then appears the reasonableness of our being obliged to receive the Spirit of GOD. It is founded on the doctrine of original sin: and, therefore, you will always find, that those who talk against feeling the operations of the Holy Ghost, very rarely, or slightly at least, mention our fall in *Adam*; no, they refer St. *Paul*'s account of the depravity of unbelievers, only to those of old time. Whereas it is obvious, on the contrary, that we are all equally included under the guilt and consequences of our first parent's sin, even as others; and to use the language of our own church-article, "bring into the world with us, a corruption, which renders us liable to GOD's wrath, and eternal damnation."

Should I preach to you any other doctrine, I should wrong my own soul; I should be found a false witness towards GOD and you; and he that preaches any other doctrine, howsoever dignified and distinguished, shall bear his punishment, whosoever he be.

From this plain reason then appears the necessity why we, as well as the first apostles, in this sense, must receive the Spirit of GOD.

For

For the great work of sanctification, or making us holy, is particularly referred to the Holy Ghost; therefore, our LORD says, "Unless a man be born of the Spirit, he cannot enter into the kingdom of GOD."

JESUS CHRIST came down to save us, not only from the guilt, but also from the power of sin: and however often we have repeated our creed, and told GOD we believe in the Holy Ghost, yet, if we have not believed in him, so as to be really united to JESUS CHRIST by him, we have no more concord with JESUS CHRIST than *Belial* himself.

And now, my brethren, what shall I say more? tell me, are not many of you offended at what has been said already? do not some of you think, though I mean well, yet I have carried the point a little too far? are not others ready to cry out, if this be true, who then can be saved? is not this driving people into despair?

Yes, I ingenuously confess it is; but into what despair? a despair of mercy through CHRIST? no, GOD forbid; but a despair of living with GOD without receiving the Holy Ghost. And I would to GOD, that not only all you that hear me this day, but that the whole world was filled with this despair. Believe me, I have been doing no more than you allow your bodily physicians to do every day: if you have a wound, and are in earnest about a cure, you bid the surgeon probe it to the very bottom; and shall not the physician of your souls be allowed the same freedom? What have I been doing but searching your natural wounds, that I might convince you of your danger, and put you upon applying to JESUS CHRIST for a remedy? Indeed I have dealt with you as gently as I could; and now I have wounded, I will attempt to heal you. For I was in the

Last place, to exhort you all to come to JESUS CHRIST by faith, whereby you, even you also, shall receive the Holy Ghost. "For this spake he of the Spirit, which they that *believe* on him should receive."

This, this is what I long to come to. Hitherto I have been preaching only the law; but behold I bring you glad tidings of great joy. If I have wounded you, be not afraid; behold, I now bring a remedy for all your wounds. Notwithstanding you are sunk into the nature of the beast and devil, yet, if you truly

truly believe on JESUS CHRIST, you shall receive the quickening Spirit promised in the text, and be restored to the glorious liberties of the sons of GOD; I say, if you believe on JESUS CHRIST. "For by faith we are saved; it is not of works, lest any one should boast." And, however some men may say, there is a fitness required in the creature, and that we must have a righteousness of our own, before we can lay hold on the righteousness of CHRIST; yet, if we believe the scripture, salvation is the free gift of GOD, in CHRIST JESUS our LORD; and whosoever believeth on him with his whole heart, though his soul be as black as hell itself, shall receive the gift of the Holy Ghost. Behold then, I stand up, and cry out in this great day of the feast, let every one that thirsteth come unto JESUS CHRIST and drink. "He that believeth on him, out of his belly shall flow (not only streams or rivulets, but whole) rivers of living water." This I speak of the Spirit, which they that believe on JESUS shall certainly receive. For JESUS CHRIST is the same yesterday, to-day, and for ever; he is the way, the truth, the resurrection, and the life; "whosoever believeth on him, though he were dead, yet shall he live." There is no respect of persons with JESUS CHRIST; high and low, rich and poor, one with another, may come to him with an humble confidence, if they draw near by faith; from him we may all receive grace upon grace; for JESUS CHRIST is full of grace and truth, and ready to save to the uttermost, all that by a true faith turn unto him. Indeed, the poor generally receive the gospel, and "GOD has chosen the poor in this world, rich in faith." But though not many mighty, not many noble are called; and though it be easier for a camel to go through the eye of a needle, than for a rich man to enter into the kingdom of GOD, yet, even to you that are rich, do I now freely offer salvation, by JESUS CHRIST, if you will renounce yourselves, and come to JESUS CHRIST as poor sinners; I say, as poor sinners; for the "poor in spirit" are only so blessed, as to have a right to the kingdom of GOD. And JESUS CHRIST calls none to him, but those who thirst after his righteousness, and feel themselves weary, and heavy laden with the burden of their sins. JESUS CHRIST justifies the ungodly; he came not to call the righteous, but sinners to repentance.

Do not then say you are unworthy; for this is a faithful and true saying, and worthy of all men to be received, "that JESUS CHRIST came into the world to save sinners;" and if you are the chief of sinners, if you feel yourselves such, verily JESUS CHRIST came into the world chiefly to save you. When *Joseph* was called out of the prison-house to *Pharoah*'s court, we are told, that he staid some time to prepare himself; but do you come with all your prison cloaths about you; come poor, and miserable, and blind, and naked, as you are, and GOD the Father shall receive you with open arms, as was the returning prodigal. He shall cover your nakedness with the best robe of his dear Son's righteousness, shall seal you with the signet of his Spirit, and feed you with the fatted calf, even with the comforts of the Holy Ghost. O, let there then be joy in heaven over some of you, as believing; let me not go back to my Master, and say, LORD, they will not believe my report. Harden no longer your hearts, but open them wide, and let the King of glory enter in; believe me, I am willing to go to prison or death for you; but I am not willing to go to heaven without you. The love of JESUS CHRIST constrains me to lift up my voice like a trumpet. My heart is now full; out of the abundance of the love which I have for your precious and immortal souls, my mouth now speaketh; and I could now not only continue my discourse until midnight, but I could speak until I could speak no more. And why should I despair of any? no, I can despair of no one, when I consider JESUS CHRIST has had mercy on such a wretch as I am; but the free grace of CHRIST prevented me; he saw me in my blood, he passed by me, and said unto me, Live; and the same grace which was sufficient for me, is sufficient for you also; behold, the same blessed Spirit is ready to breathe on all your dry bones, if you will believe on JESUS CHRIST, whom GOD has sent; indeed, you can never believe on, or serve a better master, one that is more mighty, or more willing to save; I can say, the LORD CHRIST is gracious, his yoke is easy, his burden exceeding light; after you have served him many years, like the servants under the law, was he willing to discharge you, you would say, we love our Master, and will not go from him. Come then, my guilty brethren, come and believe on the LORD that bought you with his precious blood; look up by faith, and see him whom you have pierced; behold him bleeding, panting, dying! behold him with arms stretched out ready to receive you all; cry unto him as the penitent thief did, LORD, remember us now thou art in thy kingdom, and he shall say to your souls, shortly shall you be with me in paradise. For those whom CHRIST justifies, them he also glorifies, even with that glory which he enjoyed with the Father, before the world began. Do not say, I have bought a piece of ground, and must needs go see it; or I have bought a yoke of oxen, and must needs go prove them; or I have married a wife, I am engaged in an eager pursuit after the lust of the eye, and the pride of life, and therefore cannot come. Do not fear having your name cast out as evil, or being accounted a fool for CHRIST's sake; yet a little while, and you shall shine like the stars in the firmament for ever. Only believe, and JESUS CHRIST shall be to you wisdom, righteousness, sanctification, and eternal redemption; your bodies shall be fashioned like unto his glorious body, and your souls be partakers of all the fulness of GOD.

Which GOD of his infinite mercy, &c.

SERMON

SERMON XXXIX.

The Resurrection of *Lazarus*.

JOHN xi. 43, 44.

And when he had thus spoken, he cried with a loud voice, Lazarus come forth. And he that was dead, came forth, bound hand and foot with grave-cloaths: and his face was bound about with a napkin. JESUS *saith unto them, Loose him, and let him go.*

WHEN JESUS CHRIST, the eternal Word, was pleased to make all things by the word of his power, his last works were the best. When he looked back upon, and beheld the first products of his almighty power, he pronounced them "good;" but when that last, that lovely creature man, was formed, he pronounced them "very good." So, the same JESUS, when he came to tabernacle among us, and to begin and carry on a new and second creation, though all his works were miracles of wonder, and manifested forth the glory of his eternal Godhead, yet the nearer he came to the end of his public ministrations, the greater and more noble did the miracles which he wrought appear. The resurrection of *Lazarus*, that is to be the subject of the following discourse, I think, is a sufficient proof of this. To an eye of sense, it seems to be one of the greatest, if not the very greatest miracle of all which our blessed LORD performed. When our Saviour bid *John*'s disciples go and tell their Master what things they had seen and heard, he commands them to inform him, that by his divine power "the dead were raised;" alluding no doubt to the Ruler's daughter, who was raised immediately after her decease; and the Widow's son, who at the command of JESUS, rose out of his coffin, as they were carrying his corpse to the burial. These were pregnant proofs,

proofs, that JESUS was indeed the Meſſiah that was to come into the world. But his raiſing of *Lazarus* from the dead, after he had lain four days dead, and ſaw corruption, is ſtill, if poſſible, a greater miracle; and conſequently a ſtronger proof of his being the Anointed, the CHRIST of GOD. The evangeliſt *John* is very particular in giving us an account of this miracle; even ſo particular, as to ſpend a whole chapter in relating the circumſtances which preceded, attended, and followed after it. And as he was undoubtedly directed herein by the all-wiſe, unerring Spirit of GOD, does it not point out unto us, that this miracle, with all its reſpective circumſtances, calls for our particular and moſt ſerious meditation? It appears to me in this light; and therefore, as the LORD ſhall be pleaſed to aſſiſt, I ſhall go back to the beginning of this chapter, follow the evangeliſt ſtep by ſtep, and conſider the particulars of this wonderous miracle, make ſome practical obſervations as I go along, and conclude with ſome ſuitable inſtructions and exhortations, which will naturally ariſe from the body of the diſcourſe.

The evangeliſt in the firſt verſe, makes mention of the ſickneſs of *Lazarus*. "Now, a certain man was ſick, named *Lazarus* of *Bethany*, the town of *Mary*, and her ſiſter *Martha*." Some think theſe ſiſters were very wealthy, ſo as to own good part of the town, or, as the original word ſeems to imply, the village.. But then it is probable the evangeliſt would have ſaid the town of *Lazarus*, eſtates uſually deſcending, as with us, in the male line: it means therefore no more, than that *Martha* and *Mary* lived in *Bethany*. The Holy Ghoſt pointing out to us hereby, that nothing makes a town ſo worthy of a gracious ſoul's remark or eſteem, as its having many of GOD's dear children for its inhabitants. *Bethany*, though a little place, is more famous becauſe it was the town of *Martha* and *Mary*, than if *Alexander* had fought in it one of his greateſt battles. Both theſe women loved JESUS in ſincerity, and were as good as they were great. But *Mary*, though the younger ſiſter, ſeems to be the moſt eminent: for the evangeliſt in the ſecond verſe, ſpeaks of her in a very diſtinguiſhing manner. "It was that *Mary*, (that never-to-be-forgotten *Mary*) which anointed the LORD with ointment (expenſive as it was) and wiped his feet, (after ſhe had

had washed them with tears of love) with her hair," even the hair of her head. What notice is taken of this action! With what an eulogy, and in what a high strain of commendation is it here spoken of? And such are the honours of all GOD's saints. Though all our good works are not recorded as *Mary*'s are, yet GOD is not unmindful, that he should forget our works of faith, and labours which have proceeded of love. Every tear we shed, every sigh we fetch, every alms we give, though it be only a cup of cold water, are all recorded in the Lamb's book of remembrance, and shall be produced to our eternal honour, and rewarded with a reward of grace, though not of debt, at the great and terrible day of the LORD. "I was an hungered, and ye gave me meat, I was thirsty, and ye gave me drink, naked, and ye cloathed me, sick and in prison, and ye came unto me." What reason have we then to be "stedfast and unmoveable, always abounding in the work of the LORD, forasmuch as we are assured, that our labours will not be in vain or forgotten by the LORD?" It was that *Mary* that anointed the LORD with ointment, and wiped his feet with her hair. And what follows? "Whose brother *Lazarus* was sick." So that being related to CHRIST, or his disciples, will not exempt persons from sickness. In this life, time and chance happen to all, only with this material difference, those afflictions which harden the obstinately impenitent, soften and purify the heart of a true believer. "My son, therefore despise not the chastening of the LORD (on one hand), nor faint when thou art rebuked of him (on the other): for whom the LORD loveth he chasteneth, and scourgeth every son whom he receiveth."

JESUS loved *Lazarus*, and yet *Lazarus* was sick. And what do his sisters do for him now he is sick? No doubt they applied to a physician, for it is tempting GOD to neglect making use of means for the recovery of our health, when it is impaired. But then they were not guilty of *Asa*'s crime, "who sought to the physicians, but not to the LORD." No; they knew the most skilful prescriptions would be of no effect, unless attended with a blessing from JESUS the Great and Almighty Physician; and therefore his sisters sent unto him, probably at the beginning of their brother's illness. How unlike is their conduct, to that of the generality of people,

especially

especially the rich and great! How unfashionable is it now-a-days for persons to send to JESUS in behalf of their sick relations! It is so very uncustomary, that in some places, if a minister be sent for to a sick person, it is a sad symptom that the patient is almost past hopes of recovery. Thus did not *Martha* and her sister *Mary*; they sent unto JESUS, though he was now beyond *Jordan*, (chap. x. 40.) where he abode, or chiefly resided, for some time. Hence it was that they knew where to send to him. But what kind of message did they send? A very humble and suitable one. " LORD, Behold, he whom thou lovest is sick." They might have said, LORD, he who loveth thee is sick. But they knew, that our love was not worth mentioning, and that we love JESUS only because he first loved us. Besides, here is no prescribing to our LORD what he should do, or what means he should make use of. They do not so much as say, We pray thee to come, or only speak the word, and our sick brother shall be restored. They simply tell JESUS the case, knowing it was sufficient barely to lay it before an infinitely compassionate Redeemer, and leave it to him to act according to his own sovereign good-will and pleasure. " LORD, Behold he whom thou lovest is sick." Oh how sweet is it when the soul is brought to this! And with what a holy confidence may we pray to, and intercede with the holy JESUS, when we have reason to hope, that those we pray and intercede for, are lovers of, and are beloved of him! For his eyes are in a peculiar manner over the righteous, and his ears always open to their prayers. This was their message, and it soon reached JESUS CHRIST. And how does he receive it? We are told, verse 4. " When JESUS heard that, (that he whom he loved was sick) He said, this sickness is not unto death, but unto the glory of GOD, that the Son of GOD may be glorified thereby." To whom these words were spoken is not certain. In all probability, JESUS spake them to the persons that delivered *Martha*'s and *Mary*'s message. And if so, it was no doubt a comfortable answer for the present, though it must afterwards puzzle them as well as the disciples how to explain it, when they found that *Lazarus* was actually dead. " This sickness is not unto death," not unto an abiding death, because he intended to raise him again, soon after his decease. It is like that expression of our
LORD

Lord in St. *Mark*, " The damsel is not dead, but sleepeth;" which must not be understood in a literal, but metaphorical sense. And this and such-like instances, ought to teach us to weigh carefully our blessed Lord's words, and to wait for an explication of them, by subsequent providences; otherwise we shall be in danger of misapplying them, and thereby bring our souls into unspeakable bondage. " This sickness is not unto death, but unto the glory of God, that the Son of God may be glorified thereby." This is the end both of the afflictions and the deaths of God's people. By all that happens to them he will be glorified one way or another, and cause every thing to work together for their good. And who then but would be content to be sick, or willing to submit to death itself, if so be the Son of God may be glorified thereby? This answer, no doubt, proceeded from love. For we are told,

Verse 5. that " Jesus loved *Martha* and her sister, and *Lazarus.*" Oh happy family! Three in it beloved of Jesus, with a peculiar, everlasting love. " Very often it so happens, (to use the words of the pious Bishop *Beveridge*) that there " is but one in a city, and two in a country of this stamp." But here are two sisters and a brother, all lovers of, and beloved by the glorious Jesus. What shall we say to these things? Why, that our Saviour's grace is free and sovereign, and he may do what he will with his own. They who are thus so highly favoured as to have so many converted in one house, ought to be doubly thankful! Such a blessing have not all his saints. No; many, very many, go mourning over their perverse and graceless relations all their lives long; and find, even to their dying day, that their greatest foes are those of their own houshold. Surely these three relations lived a heaven upon earth. For what can they want, what could make them miserable, who are assured of Jesu's love? But surely if Jesus loves this dear little family, the next news one might think we should hear, would be, that he went immediately and healed *Lazarus*; or at least cured him at a distance. But instead of that, we are told, verse 6. " When he had heard that he was sick, he abode two days still in the same place where he was." A strange way this, in the eye of natural reason, of expressing love; but not so strange in the eye of faith: for the LORD JESUS very often sheweth his love, by deferring to give immediate answers to our prayers. Hereby he tries our faith and patience, and exercises all our passive graces. We have a proof of this in the *Syrophenician* woman, upon whom the blessed JESUS frowned, and spake roughly to at first, only that he might afterwards turn unto her and say, "O woman, great is thy faith." Let not those then who believe, make too much haste; or immediately in their hearts repine against the LORD, because he may not answer their requests, in their own time and way. GOD's time and way is best. And we shall find it to be so in the end. *Martha* and *Mary* experienced the truth of this, though undoubtedly our LORD's seeming delay, to come and heal their brother, cost them great searchings of heart. But will the LORD JESUS forget his dear *Lazarus*, whom his soul loveth? "Can a woman forget her sucking child?" Indeed she may; but the LORD never faileth those that fear him. Neither is he slack concerning his promise, as some men count slackness: for his very delays are answers. The vision is for an appointed time; in the end it will speak and not lie.

Though our LORD abode two days where he was, to try the faith of these sisters, yet after this, he said unto his disciples, verse 7. "Let us go into *Judea* again." With what a holy familiarity does JESUS converse with his dear children! Our Saviour seems to speak to his disciples, as though he was only their brother, and as it were upon a level with them; "Let us go into *Judea* again." How gently, according to what was predicted of him, does he lead those that are with young! JESUS very well knew the weakness of his disciples, and also what a dangerous place *Judea* was: how gradually therefore does he make known unto them, his design of going thither! And how does he admit his disciples to expostulate with him on this account! "Master, say they, the *Jews* of late sought to stone thee, and goest thou thither again?" They were amazed at our LORD's boldness, and were ready to call it presumption; as we generally are prone to censure and condemn other zealous and enterprizing persons, as carrying matters too far; it may be for no other reason, if we examine the bottom of our hearts, but because they go before, and

excel

excel ourselves. The disciples, no doubt, thought that they spoke out of love to their LORD, and assuredly they did; but what a deal of self-love was there mixed and blended with it? They seem much concerned for their Master, but they were more concerned for themselves. However JESUS overlooks their weakness, and mildly replies, verse 9, and 10. " Are there not twelve hours in the day? If any man walk in the day, he stumbleth not, because he seeth the light of the world; but if any man walk in the night, he stumbleth, because there is no light in him." As though our LORD had said, My dear disciples, I thank you for your care and concern for me. *Judea* is a dangerous place, and what you say of the treatment I met with from its inhabitants, is just and true: but be not afraid of going there upon my account. For as a man walketh safely twelve hours of the day, because he walketh in the light: so as long as the time appointed by my Father for my public administration lasts, I shall be as secure from the hands of my enemies, as a man that walks in broad-day is secure from falling. But as a man stumbleth if he walketh in the night, so when the night of my passion cometh, then, but not till then, shall I be given up into the hands of my spiteful foes. Oh what comfort have these words, by the blessing of GOD, frequently brought to my soul! How may all CHRIST's ministers strengthen themselves with this consideration, that so long as GOD hath work for them to do, they are immortal! And if after our work is over, our LORD should call us to lay down our lives for the brethren, and to seal the truth of our doctrine with our blood, it would certainly be the highest honour that can be put upon us. " To you it is given not only to believe, but also to suffer," says the apostle to the *Philippians*.

" These things (the evangelist tells us, ver. 11.) said JESUS, and after that, (to satisfy them that he was not going into *Judea* without a proper call) he saith unto them, Our friend *Lazarus* sleepeth." Our friend. Amazing! For what is a friend? As one's own soul. How dear then, and near are true believers to the most adorable JESUS! " Our friend *La-zarus*." Still more amazing! Here is condescension, here is unparalleled familiarity indeed. And what of him? " He sleepeth." A figurative way of expression. For what is death to the lovers of JESUS CHRIST, but a sleep, and a refreshing one too? Thus it is said of *Stephen* when he died, that "he fell asleep." CHRIST indeed died, but believers only sleep. And "those that sleep in JESUS, (says the scripture) will GOD bring with him." "Our friend *Lazarus* sleepeth." For though he be dead, I shall raise him from the grave so soon, that his dying will be only like a person's taking a short sleep. "Our friend *Lazarus* sleepeth, but I go that I may awake him out of sleep." By this time, one would imagine, our LORD's disciples should have understood him: But how unwilling are we to believe any thing that we do not like. "Then said his disciples, LORD, if he sleep he shall do well." Oh fearful, and slow of heart to believe! How fain would they excuse themselves from going into *Judea*, for fear of a few stones! By this way of talking, how do they in effect impeach their blessed Master's conduct, and under a pretence of preserving his person, sister, and as it were plead for their own (though perhaps undiscerned) cowardice and unbelief? That charity, which hopeth and believeth all things for the best, teacheth us to judge thus favourably of them. For, "Howbeit JESUS spake of his death: they thought that he had spoken of taking rest in sleep." The great and compassionate High-priest knowing and remembering they were but dust, throws a veil of love over their infirmity; and at length, verse 14. "Saith unto them plainly (for if we wait on JESUS, we shall know his will plainly, one way or another) *Lazarus* is dead." And even then, lest they should be swallowed up with overmuch sorrow, he immediately adds, verse 15. "And I am glad for your sakes that I was not there, to the intent ye may believe," or have more faith, or have that faith which you already possess increased and confirmed. A plain proof this, that all JESU's delays to answer prayer, are only to strengthen our faith.

"Nevertheless, says our LORD, let us go unto him." This was a sufficient hint, if they knew how to improve it, that he intended to do something extraordinary, though he would not tell them directly what he intended. For the LORD JESUS will keep those whom he loves, at his foot, and dependant on him. "Let us go unto him." He still speaks as though they were his equals. Oh that Christians in general, Oh that ministers in particular, would learn of him their great exemplar, to condescend to men of low degree! Well, the secret is now out. JESUS has said unto them plainly, *Lazarus* is dead. And what reception does this melancholy news meet with? With great condolance, especially from *Thomas*; for verse 16. "Then said *Thomas*, who is called *Didymus*, unto his fellow disciples, let us also go and die with him;" i. e. according to some, with *Lazarus*, with whom, it may be, *Thomas* had contracted an intimate acquaintance. But granting it was so; shall I commend him for this passionate expression? I commend him not. Surely he spake unadvisedly with his lips; "Let us also go and die with him." As though there was no comfort henceforward to be expected in the world, now his friend *Lazarus* was gone. This was a great fault, and yet a fault that many of GOD's children run into daily, by mourning for their deceased relations overmuch, like persons that have no hope. But this infirmity ought not to be indulged. For if our friends and dear relatives are dead, JESUS, that friend of sinners, is not dead. He will be better to us than seven sons, and will abundantly supply the place of all creature-comforts. But I am more inclined to think that the word *him*, refers to JESUS his dear Master; and if so, he is so far from being blamed, that he spake like a good soldier of JESUS CHRIST. Let us also go, that we may die with him. If our dear master will go into *Judea*, and hazard his precious life, let us not any longer make such frivolous excuses, but let us manfully accompany him; and if the *Jews* should not only be permitted to stone, but also to kill him, let us also go and die with him, we cannot die in a better cause. This was a speech worthy of a christian hero, and *Thomas* herein hath set us an example, that we should follow his steps, by exciting and provoking one another closely to adhere to the blessed JESUS, especially when his cause and interest is in any immediate danger. This exhortation, it seems, had a proper effect. They all went, and as far as we know, chearfully accompanied their glorious Master.

How their thoughts were exercised on the road, we are not told. But I am apt to believe they were a little discouraged when they came to *Bethany*. For " When JESUS came, he

found

found that *Lazarus* had lien in the grave for four days already." And what would it avail them, to come so many miles only to see a dead man's tomb? But how wisely were all things ordered by the blessed JESUS, to manifest his glory in the most extraordinary manner, that not only his disciples might have their faith confirmed, but many also of the *Jews* might believe on him. This *Bethany*, it seems, verse 18. " was nigh unto *Jerusalem*, about fifteen furlongs off;" or about two miles ; and *Martha* and *Mary*, being what we may call people of fashion, and devout likewise; many of the devout, and we may suppose many of the wealthy *Jews* came from the metropolis, as well as other adjacent places, verse 19. to *Martha* and *Mary*; not to pay an idle, trifling, but a serious, profitable visit, " to comfort them concerning their brother." This was kind and neighbourly. To weep with those that weep, and to visit the afflicted in their distresses, is one essential branch of true and undefiled religion. And O how sweet is it when we visit surviving friends, that we have reason to think that their departed relations died in the LORD! And we can therefore give them comfort concerning them: For " blessed are the dead, that die in the LORD, even so saith the Spirit, for they rest from their labours." This and suchlike arguments, no doubt, these visitors made use of, to comfort *Martha* and *Mary*. And indeed they stood in much need of consolation. For we have reason to suppose, from our LORD's answer, " This sickness is not unto death, but the glory of GOD;" that they had entertained thoughts of the recovery of their brother. But who can tell what these two holy souls must feel, when they found their brother did not recover, but was dead, laid out, and now stinking in the silent grave ! What hard thoughts, without judging them, may we suppose they entertained concerning JESUS ! Think ye not that they were ready to cry out in the language of the prophet, " Thou hast deceived us, and we are deceived ?" But man's extremity is JESU's opportunity. In the multitude of the sorrows that they had in their hearts, the news of CHRIST's coming refreshes their souls. Somebody or another, commendably officious, privately informs *Martha* of it. " Who, as soon as she heard that JESUS was come (without making any apology to the company for her rudeness) went

and-

and met him: But *Mary* sat still in the house." But why so, *Mary?* I thought thou hadst been most forward to attend on JESUS, and thy sister *Martha* more prone to be cumbered about the many things of this life. Why sittest thou still? It may be the news was brought only privately to *Martha* (for it is plain from verse 31st, that the *Jews* who were in the house knew not of it;) and *Martha* knowing how our LORD had chid her once, was resolved he should have no reason on the same account to chide her any more; therefore when the news was brought, she would not so much as stay to inform her sister, but went out to see whether it were true or not, and if so, as the eldest sister, she would invite the blessed JESUS in. How happy is it, when CHRIST's reproofs for past neglects, excite our future zeal to come out and meet him! Such reproofs are an excellent oil. Or, it may be, the news reached *Mary*'s ears, as well as *Martha*'s, but being overcome with sorrow, she thought it too good news to be true, and therefore sat still in the house. O how careful ought believers to be, to cherish and maintain, even in the midst of tribulation, a holy confidence and joy in GOD! For the joy of the LORD is a believer's strength. Whereas giving way to melancholy and unbelief, raises gloom and vapours in the mind, clouds the understanding, clogs us in the way of duty, and gives the enemy, who loves to fish in troubled waters, a very great advantage over us.

Mary, perhaps, through the prevalence of this, and being also naturally of a sedentary disposition, "sat still in the house," while her sister *Martha* got the start of her, and went out to meet JESUS. And how does she accost him? Why, in a language bespeaking the distress of a burdened and disordered mind. For she said unto JESUS, verse 21, "LORD, if thou hadst been here, my brother had not died." Here is a mixture of faith and unbelief. Faith made her say, "LORD, if thou hadst been here, my brother had not died." But unbelief made her confine CHRIST's power to his bodily presence. Besides, here was a tacit accusation of the blessed JESUS of unkindness, for not coming when they sent unto him the message, "LORD, he whom thou lovest is sick." Once she charged JESUS with want of care; "LORD, carest thou not, that my sister hath left me to serve alone?" Now she taxes him

him with want of kindness. "If thou hadst been here;" as much as to say, if thou hadst been so kind as to have come when we sent for thee, " my brother had not died;" and by saying thus, she does as it were lay her brother's death to JESUS CHRIST. O how apt are even those whom JESUS loves in a peculiar manner, to charge him foolishly! How often does the enmity of our desperately wicked hearts rise against CHRIST, when we are under the afflicting hand of his providence! Are not the very best of us frequently tempted, in such circumstances, to say within ourselves at least, Why does GOD thus cruelly deal with us? Why did not he keep off this stroke, seeing it was in his power to have prevented it? How should we be ashamed and confounded before him upon this account? How should we pray and labour to be delivered from this remaining enmity of the heart, and long for that time, when mortality shall be swallowed up of life, and we shall never feel one single rising of heart, against a good and gracious, and all-wise and glorious Redeemer, any more? However, to do *Martha* justice, she pretty well recovers herself, verse 22. "But I know, that even now, whatsoever thou wilt ask of GOD, GOD will give it to thee." Whether these words imply an actual belief of our LORD's divinity, is not certain. To me they do; because we shall presently find, that she did believe our LORD was the Son of GOD, and the Messiah which was to come into the world. Therefore when she said, she knew that whatsoever he asked of GOD, GOD would give it to him, she may be understood as referring to GOD the Father, under whom the LORD JESUS acted as Mediator, though equal to him in respect to his eternal glory and godhead. This mystery we may well suppose her acquainted with, because JESUS had been frequently preaching at her house, and consequently, had opened that mystery unto her. O what a blessed thing must it be to have such a Mediator! such an high-priest and intercessor at the Father's right-hand, that whatever he asks the Father in our behalf, he will give unto us! JESUS takes this kindly at *Martha's* hand, and passes over her infirmity. For if the LORD was exact to mark every thing that we say or do amiss, alas! who could abide? He only calmly says unto her, verse 23. "Thy brother shall rise again."

Glad

Glad tidings these of great joy. This should comfort us concerning our deceased, pious relations, that ere long they shall rise again, and soul and body be for ever with the LORD. Howbeit JESUS spake here of an immediate resurrection, though he did not speak plainly: For CHRIST loves to exercise the faith and patience of his disciples, and frequently leaves them to find out his meaning by degrees. It is best for us in our present state, that it should be so. In heaven it will be otherwise. " Thy brother, (says CHRIST to *Martha*) shall rise again." She might immediately have replied, When, LORD? But she fetches a circuit as it were, and labours to find out the mind of JESUS by degrees. " I know, says she, that he shall rise again at the resurrection of the last day." These words seem to imply, that she had some distant thought of our LORD's design to raise her brother now, and that she spoke thus only to draw our Saviour to speak, and tell her plainly whether he meant to do so or not. Those who are acquainted with JESUS, are taught an holy art by the blessed Spirit, in dealing with their blessed master. " I know, says she, he shall rise again at the resurrection of the last day," (a notable proof this, by the way, that the pious *Jews* believed the resurrection of the body). It is just the same as though she had said, LORD, dost thou mean that my brother shall rise again before that time? Our Saviour wisely keeps off from giving her a direct answer, but chuses rather to preach to her heart. " JESUS said unto her, I am the resurrection and the life: He that believeth in me, though he were dead, yet shall he live." On this *Martha*'s faith, if in exercise, might take hold. O glorious words! How encouraging to you poor sinners lying in your blood! Though you are dead in trespasses and sins, and might justly be condemned to die the second death, yet if you believe on the LORD JESUS you shall live. He adds, " And whosoever believeth in me shall never die;" never die as to their souls, never die eternally, and consequently never finally fall away from GOD. This is an encouraging soul-comforting declaration for you, O believers, who are thus kept, as it were, in a garrison, by the mighty power of GOD, through faith, unto salvation! " Believest thou this?" says CHRIST to *Martha*, verse 26. What avail all the many great and precious promises of the gospel, unless they are applied and brought home in particular to each of our souls? The word does not profit unless it is mixed with faith. We therefore do well, when we are reading CHRIST's words, to put this question to ourselves; O my soul, believest thou this? And well would it be for us, if upon putting this question to ourselves, we could with the same holy confidence, and in the same delightful frame, say with *Martha*, verse 27. "Yea, LORD: I believe that thou art the CHRIST, the Son of GOD, which should come into the world." This I think is a direct confession of our LORD's divinity. How full was her heart when she spoke these words! I am persuaded it burnt within her. What a divine warmth had she contracted by talking with JESUS! How does she long that her sister might share in her holy joy! For when she had so said, verse 28. "she went away;" full of love, no doubt, and called *Mary* her sister, as all will labour to call their near relations, who have felt the LORD JESUS to be the resurrection and the life themselves. But *Martha* took care, in the midst of her zeal (as we should always do) to behave with prudence; and therefore " she called her sister secretly, saying, The master is come, and calleth for thee." The master is come. She need say no more; *Mary* knew very well whom she meant. For holy souls easily understand one another when talking of their master JESUS. The divine *Herbert* used to delight (when speaking of JESUS) to say, " My Master;" perhaps he learned it of *Martha*, who said here, " The Master is come, and calleth for thee." But what is this thou sayest, *Martha?* The Master is come, and calleth for thee? Surely a woman of thy exalted piety will not tell a deliberate lie, and in order to induce thy sister to come to JESUS, acquaint her that JESUS called her, when indeed he did not. Thou needest not put thyself to such an expence, or do so much evil, that good may come of it. Only mention JESUS to *Mary*, and let her know for a certainty that the Master is indeed come, and I am persuaded she will sit no longer. *Martha* no doubt knew, and therefore I cannot judge her as some do, as though in her haste she said what was not true. For JESUS might bid her to call her sister, though it be not directly mentioned in this chapter. And it is very probable, that our LORD did enquire after *Mary*, because she used to take such great delight in sitting at his feet, and hearing the gracious words that proceeded out of his mouth. " The Master is come (saith *Martha*

Martha to her sister) and calleth for thee." And so say I to all poor sinners. JESUS, your LORD and Master, your Prince and Saviour, is come, come unto this lower world, and is come this day in his word, and by me, who am less than the least of all his servants, and calleth for you. O that he may also come in the demonstration of the Spirit, and by his mighty power bow your stubborn hearts and wills to obey the call, as holy *Mary* did.

For we are told, verse 29. "When she heard that, she rose quickly, and came to JESUS." Sinners, when will you do so? Or why do you not do so? How know you whether JESUS will call for you any more, before he calls you by death to judgment? Linger, O linger no longer. Fly, fly for your lives. Arise quickly, and with *Mary* come to JESUS. She obeyed the call so very speedily, that her haste was taken notice of by her visitors. "The *Jews* then, who were with her in the house, and comforted her, when they saw *Mary* that she rose up hastily (without any ceremony at all) and went out, followed her, saying, she goeth to the grave, to weep there." How wisely does our LORD permit and order all this, to bring the *Jews* out to behold the wonderful miracle that he was about to perform! Little did *Mary* and the *Jews* think for what end they were thus providentially led out. But when JESUS hath work to be done, he will bring souls to the place where he intends to call them, in spite of men or devils. But how does *Mary* behave when she comes to JESUS? We may be assured, not without great humility. No wonder then we are told, verse 32. that "when she saw him, she immediately fell down at his feet (a place *Mary* had been used to, and in an agony of grief, says, as her sister had done before her) LORD, if thou hadst been here, my brother had not died." Poor *Mary!* Her concern was great indeed. Though she was a holy woman, she could not well bear the loss of her brother. She knew very well, that the world would miss him, and no doubt he had been a kind and tender brother to her. But I am afraid she was sinfully overcome with overmuch sorrow. However, had we been there, the sight must have affected us. It seems to have affected the visitors, especially the blessed JESUS. He, instead of blaming her, for her tacitly accusing him of unkindness, and for not coming to her brother's relief, pities and sympathizes both with *Mary* and her weeping friends! "When Jesus saw her weep, and the *Jews* also weeping, he groaned in his Spirit, and was troubled." Troubled: Not with any sinful perturbation we may be assured: nothing of that nature could possibly be in his sinless soul. And, therefore, some have judiciously enough compared the trouble our Lord now felt, to some chrystal water shaken in a glass or bottle; you may shake it, but there will be no sediment: it will be chrystal water still. "He groaned in his spirit." I do not see why this may not be understood of his praying in the spirit, which maketh intercession for the saints, with αλαλητοις στεναγμοις, "groanings that cannot be uttered." Methinks I see the immaculate Lamb of God, secretly, but powerfully agonizing with his Father; his heart is big with sympathy! At length, out of the fulness of it, he said, ver. 34. "Where have ye laid him? They (I suppose *Mary* and *Martha*) say unto him, Lord, come and see." He came, he saw, "He wept," ver. 35. It is put in a verse by itself, that we might pause a while, and ask, why Jesus wept?

He wept, to shew us, that it was no sin to shed a tear of love and resignation at the grave of a deceased friend; he wept, to see what havock sin had made in the world, and how it had reduced man, who was originally little lower than the angels, (by making him subject to death) to a level with the beasts that perish: but above all, he wept at the foresight of the people's unbelief; he wept, to think how many then present, would not only not believe on, but would be hardened, and have their prejudices increased more and more against him, though he should raise *Lazarus* from the dead before their eyes. Well then may ministers be excused, who, whilst they are preaching, now and then drop a few tears, at the consideration of their sermons being, through the perverseness and unbelief of many of their audience, a favour of death unto death, instead of a favour of life unto life. Upon a like occasion Jesus wept. What an affecting sight was here! Let us for a while suppose ourselves placed amidst these holy mourners; let us imagine that we see the sepulchre just before us, and the *Jews*, and *Mary*, and the blessed Jesus weeping round it. Surely, the most obdurate of us all must drop a tear, or at least be affected with the sight; we find that it affected those who were really by-standers: for then said the

Jews, ver. 36. " Behold, how he loved him." And did they say, Behold, how he loved him, when JESUS only shed a few tears over the grave of his departed *Lazarus?* Come then, O sinners, and view CHRIST dying and pouring out his precious heart's blood for you upon an accursed tree, and then surely you must needs cry out, Behold, how he loved us!

But alas, though all were affected, yet, it seems, all were not well affected at seeing JESUS weep! For we are told, ver. 37. that some of them said, " Could not this man, who opened the eyes of the blind, have caused that even this man should not have died?" One would imagine, that Satan himself could scarce have uttered a more perverse speech: every word is full of spite and rancour. Could not this man, this fellow, this deceiver, who pretends to say, that he opened the eyes of the blind, have caused that this man, whom he seems to love so, should not have died? Is not this a sufficient proof that he is a cheat? Have we catched him at last? Is it likely that he really helped others, when he could not help his own friend?——O how patient ought the servants of our LORD to be! And how may they expect to be censured, and have their good deeds questioned, and lessened, when their blessed Master has been thus treated before them! However, JESUS will do good, notwithstanding all these slights put upon him; and therefore, again groaning in himself, " he cometh to the grave; it was a cave, (or vault, as is customary in great families) and a stone lay upon it; JESUS said, ver. 39. Take ye away the stone." How gradually does our LORD proceed, in order to engage the people's attention the more! Methinks I see them all eye, all ear, and eagerly waiting to see the issue of this affair. But *Martha* now returning with the rest of the company, seems to have lost that good frame which she was in when she went to call her sister; " She saith unto him, (ver. 39.) LORD, by this time he stinketh: for he hath been *either* dead *or* buried four days." O the dismal effects of carnal reasoning! How naturally do we fall into doubts and fears, when we have not our eye simply directed to the blessed JESUS! *Martha*, instead of looking up to him, looks down into the grave, and poring upon her brother's stinking corpse, falls into a fit of unbelief: " By this time he stinketh;" and, therefore, a sight of him will only be offensive. Perhaps she might think our LORD only wanted to take a view of her brother *Lazarus*; JESUS, therefore, to give her yet a further hint, that he intended to do something extraordinary, faith unto her, ver. 40. "Said I not unto thee, that if thou wouldst believe, thou shouldst see the glory of GOD?" Our LORD speaks here with some degree of warmth: for nothing displeases him more than the unbelief of his own disciples. "Said I not unto thee, if thou wouldst believe, thou shouldst see the glory of GOD?" When CHRIST first spoke these words unto her, we are not told; it might be, this was part of their conversation upon another occasion some time before: however, he checks her openly for her unbelief now: for those whom JESUS loves, must expect to be rebuked sharply by him, whenever they dishonour him by unbelief. The reproof is taken.

Without making any more objections, "They took away the stone from the place where the dead was laid." And now behold with what solemnity the holy JESUS prepares himself to execute his gracious design! "And JESUS lift up his eyes, and said, Father, I thank thee that thou hast heard me; and I knew that thou hearest me always: but because of the people which stand by, I said it, that they may believe that thou hast sent me." Who can express with what fervor and intenseness of spirit, our glorious High-priest uttered these words! They are a thanksgiving arising from an assurance that his Father had heard him: for CHRIST, as Mediator, was inferior to the Father. "I knew that thou hearest me always (and so may every believer in his degree say too); but because of the people which stand by, I said it."—Said what? We do not hear that JESUS said any thing by way of prayer before; and that is true, if we mean vocally, but mentally he did say something, even when he groaned in the spirit once and again, and was troubled. There is a way of praying, even when we do not, and cannot speak. "Why cryest thou," said GOD to *Moses*; though we do not hear that he spoke one single word: but he cried in his heart. And I observe this for the comfort of some weak, but real christians, who think they never pray, unless they can have a great flow of words; but this is a great mistake: for we often pray best, when we can speak least. There are times when the heart is too big to speak: and the spirit itself maketh intercession for the saints, and that too according to the will of GOD, with

groanings

groanings that cannot be uttered. Such was *Hannah*'s prayer for a son, " She spake not, only her lips moved:" and such was our LORD's way of praying at this time. And perhaps the soul is never in a better frame, than when in a holy stillness, and unspeakable serenity, it can put itself as a blank in JESUS's hand, for him to stamp on it just what he pleases.

And now the hour of our Saviour's performing this long-expected miracle, is come. Ver. 43. " When he thus had spoken, he cried with a loud voice, *Lazarus*, come forth." With the word there went an irresistible power: he spake, and it was done: he cried, and behold, " He that was dead came forth bound hand and foot with grave cloaths; and his face was bound about with a napkin." What a sight was here! Methinks I see surprize sit upon each spectator's face: as the body rises, their wonder rises too. See how they gaze! See how their looks bespeak the language of astonished hearts; and all with a kind of silent, but expressive oratory, ready to say, What manner of man is this? Surely this is the Messiah that was to come into the world. How did the hearts of *Martha* and *Mary*, as we may very well suppose, leap for joy! How were they ashamed of themselves, for charging JESUS foolishly, and taxing him with unkindness, for not coming to prevent their brother's dying! It is true, CHRIST suffered him to die, but behold he is now alive again! JESUS never denies us one thing, but he intends to give us something better in the stead of it. Think you not that *Martha* and *Mary* were now the most officious to obey our blessed LORD's command, " Loose him, and let him go?" That same power that raised *Lazarus* from the dead, might have also taken the grave-cloaths from him: but JESUS CHRIST never did, and never will work a needless miracle. Others could unloose his grave-cloaths, but JESUS alone could unloose the bands of death.

And now, perhaps, some may be ready to ask, What news hath *Lazarus* brought from the other world! But stop, O man, thy vain curiosity! It is forbidden, and therefore useless knowledge. The scriptures are silent concerning it. Why should we desire to be wise above what is written? It becomes us rather to be wholly employed in adoring the gracious hand of that mighty Redeemer who raised him from the dead,

dead, and to see (now we have heard the history) what improvement we can make of such a remarkable and instructive transaction.

Would to GOD that my preaching upon the resurrection of *Lazarus* to-day, may have the same blessed effects upon you, as the sight of it had upon some of the standers-by: For we are told, ver. 45. " Then many of the *Jews* who came to *Mary*, and had seen the things which JESUS did, believed on him." A profitable visit this! The best, no doubt, that they ever paid in their lives. And this was in answer to our Saviour's prayer, " But because of the people who stand by, I said it, that they may believe, that thou hast sent me." One would imagine, that all who saw this miracle, were induced thereby, really to believe on him: But alas! I could almost say, that I can tell you of a greater miracle than raising *Lazarus* from the dead. And what is that? Why, that some of these very persons who were on the spot, instead of believing on him, " went their way to the Pharisees, and told them what JESUS had done." ver. 46. It was so far from convincing them, that it only excited their envy, stirred up the whole hell of their self-righteous hearts, and made them, from that day forward, " take counsel together," to execute what they had long before designed, to put the innocent JESUS to death. See how busy they are, ver. 47. " Then gathered the chief priests and the Pharisees a council, and said, What do we? For this man doeth many miracles." Envy itself, it seems, could not deny that. And need they say then, " What do we," or what should we do? Believe in, to be sure, and submit to him; take up the cross, and follow him. No; on the contrary, say they, ver. 48. " If we let him thus alone, (which they would not have done so long, had not GOD put a hook in the Leviathan's jaws) all men will believe on him." And suppose they did? Then all men would be blessed indeed, and have a title to true happiness. No, say they, " then the *Romans* shall come and take away both our place and nation." But were not the *Romans* come already? Were they not at this time tributaries to *Cæsar*? But they were afraid of the church as well as the state: " They will come and take away our place," our place of worship: and consequently, they look upon JESUS CHRIST and his proceedings, and adherents, as dangerous both to church and state.

This

This hath been always the method of Pharisees and high-priests, when they have been taking counsel against the Lord Jesus, and his dear anointed ones. But they need not have been afraid on this account: for our Saviour's kingdom neither was, nor is of this world; and the only way to have preserved their place and nation, was to have countenanced, and as much as in them lay, caused all to believe on Jesus. How miserably were they out in their politics! The death of Jesus, which they thought would save, was the grand cause of the utter destruction both of their place and nation: And so will all politics formed against Christ and his gospel end at last in the destruction of those who contrived them.

O the desperate wickedness and treachery of man's deceitful heart! Where are the scribes, where are the infidels, where are the letter-learned disputers of this world, who are daily calling for a repetition of miracles, in order to confirm and evidence the truth of the christian religion? Surely if they believe not *Moses* and the prophets, neither would they believe, though one rose from the dead. Here was one raised from the dead before many witnesses, and yet all those witnesses did by no means believe on Jesus. For divine faith is not wrought in the heart by moral persuasion (though moral suasion is very often made use of as a means to convey it); faith is the peculiar gift of God: no one can come to Jesus unless the Father draw him: and, therefore, that I may draw near the close of this discourse, let me shut up all with a word of exhortation.

Come, ye dead, Christless, unconverted sinners, come and see the place where they laid the body of the deceased *Lazarus*; behold him laid out, bound hand and foot with grave-cloaths, locked up and stinking in a dark cave, with a great stone placed on the top of it! View him again and again; go nearer to him; be not afraid; smell him, ah! how he stinketh. Stop there now, pause a while; and whilst thou art gazing upon the corpse of *Lazarus*, give me leave to tell thee with great plainness, but greater love, that this dead, bound, entombed, stinking carcase, is but a faint representation of thy poor soul in its natural state: for, whether thou believest it or not, thy spirit which thou bearest about with thee, sepulchred in flesh and blood, is as literally dead to God, and as truly

dead

dead in trespasses and sins, as the body of *Lazarus* was in the cave. Was he bound hand and foot with grave-cloaths? So art thou bound hand and foot with thy corruptions: and as a stone was laid on the sepulchre, so is there a stone of unbelief upon thy stupid heart. Perhaps thou hast lain in this state, not only four days, but many years, stinking in GOD's nostrils. And, what is still more affecting, thou art as unable to raise thyself out of this loathsome, dead state, to a life of righteousness and true holiness, as ever *Lazarus* was to raise himself from the cave in which he lay so long. Thou mayest try the power of thy own boasted free-will, and the force and energy of moral persuasion and rational arguments (which, without all doubt, have their proper place in religion); but all thy efforts, exerted with never so much vigour, will prove quite fruitless and abortive, till that same JESUS, who said, "Take away the stone," and cried, "*Lazarus*, come forth," comes by his mighty power, removes the stone of unbelief, speaks life to thy dead soul, looses thee from the fetters of thy sins and corruptions, and by the influences of his blessed Spirit, enables thee to arise, and to walk in the way of his holy commandments. And O that he would now rend the heavens, and come down amongst you! O that there may be a stirring among the dry bones this day! O that whilst I am speaking, and saying, "Dead sinners, come forth," a power, an almighty power might accompany the word, and cause you to emerge into new life!

If the LORD should vouchsafe me such a mercy, and but one single soul in this great congregation, should arise and shake himself from the dust of his natural state; according to the present frame of my heart, I should not care if preaching this sermon here in the fields, was an occasion of hastening my death, as raising *Lazarus* hastened the death of my blessed Master. For methinks death, in some respects, is more tolerable, than to see poor sinners day by day lying sepulchred, dead and stinking in sin. O that you saw how loathsome you are in the sight of GOD, whilst you continue in your natural state! I believe you would not so contentedly hug your chains, and refuse to be set at liberty.

Methinks I see some of you affected at this part of my discourse. What say you? Are there not some ready to complain, alas! we have some relations present, who are so notoriously wicked, that they not only hug their chains, but make a mock of sin, and stink not only in the sight of GOD, but man. Dear souls! you are ready to urge this, as a reason why JESUS will not raise them; and think it hard, perhaps, that JESUS does not come, in answer to your repeated groans and prayers, to convert and save them. But what JESUS said unto *Martha*, I say unto you, "Believe, and you shall see the glory of GOD." Think it not a thing incredible, that GOD should raise their dead souls. Think not hard of JESUS for delaying an answer to your prayers: assure yourselves he heareth you always. And who knows, but this day JESUS may visit some of your dear relations hearts, upon whose account you have travelled in birth till CHRIST be formed in them? You have already sympathized with *Martha* and *Mary*, in their doubts and fears; who knows but you may also be partakers of that joy which their souls experienced, when they received their risen brother into their longing arms.

O Christless souls, you do not know what grief your continuance in sin occasions to your godly relations! You do not know how you grieve the heart of JESUS. I beseech you give him no fresh cause to weep over you upon account of your unbelief: let him not again groan in his spirit and be troubled. Behold how he has loved you, even so as to lay down his life for you. What could he do more? I pray you, therefore, dead sinners, come forth; arise and sup with JESUS. This was an honour conferred on *Lazarus*, and the same honour awaits you: Not that you shall sit down with him personally in this life, as *Lazarus* did; but you shall sit down with him at the table of his ordinances, especially at the table of the Lord's-supper, and ere long sit down with him in the kingdom of heaven.

Happy, thrice happy ye, who are already raised from spiritual death, and have an earnest of an infinitely better and more glorious resurrection in your hearts. You know a little, how delightful it must have been to *Martha* and *Mary* and *Lazarus*, to sit down with the blessed JESUS here below; but how infinitely more delightful will it be, to sit down, not only with *Mary* and *Martha*, but with *Abraham*, *Isaac*, and *Jacob*, and all your other dear brethren and sisters, in the kingdom of heaven. Do you not long for that time, when JESUS shall say unto you, " Come up hither?" Well! blessed be GOD, yet a little while, and that same JESUS, who cried with a loud voice, " *Lazarus*, come forth ;" shall with the same voice, and with the same power, speak unto all that are in their graves, and they shall come forth. That all who hear me this day may be then enabled to lift up their heads and rejoice, that the day of their compleat redemption is indeed fully come, may JESUS CHRIST grant, for his infinite mercy's sake. *Amen*, and *Amen*.

SERMON

SERMON XL.

The Holy Spirit convincing the World of Sin, Righteousness, and Judgment.

JOHN xvi. 8.

And when he is come, he will reprove the world of sin, and of righteousness, and of judgment.

THESE words contain part of a gracious promise, which the blessed JESUS was pleased to make to his weeping and sorrowful disciples. The time was now drawing near, in which the Son of man was first to be lifted up on the cross, and afterwards to heaven. Kind, wondrous kind! had this merciful High-priest been to his disciples, during the time of his tabernacling amongst them. He had compassion on their infirmities, answered for them when assaulted by their enemies, and set them right when out of the way, either in principle or practice. He neither called nor used them as servants, but as friends; and he revealed his secrets to them from time to time. He opened their understandings, that they might understand the scriptures; explained to them the hidden mysteries of the kingdom of GOD, when he spoke to others in parables: nay, he became the servant of them all, and even condescended to wash their feet. The thoughts of parting with so dear and loving a Master as this, especially for a long season, must needs affect them much. When on a certain occasion he intended to be absent from them only for a night, we are told, he was obliged to constrain them to leave him; no wonder then, that when he now informed them he must entirely go away, and that the Pharisees in his absence should put them out of their synagogues, and excommunicate them; yea, that the time should come, that whosoever killed them, would think they did God service (a prophecy, one would imagine, in an especial manner designed for the suffering ministers of this generation); no wonder, I say, considering all this, that we are told, ver. 6. Sorrow had filled their hearts: "Because I have said these things unto you, sorrow hath filled your hearts." The expression is very emphatical; their hearts were so full of concern, that they were ready to burst. In order, therefore, to reconcile them to this mournful dispensation, our dear and compassionate Redeemer shews them the necessity he lay under to leave them; "Nevertheless I tell you the truth; it is expedient for you that I go away:" As though he had said, Think not, my dear disciples, that I leave you out of anger: no, it is for your sakes, for your profit, that I go away: for if I go not away, if I die not upon the cross for your sins, and rise again for your justification, and ascend into heaven to make intercession, and plead my merits before my Father's throne; the Comforter, the Holy Ghost, will not, cannot come unto you; but if I depart, I will send him unto you. And that they might know what he was to do, "When he is come, he will reprove the world of sin, and of righteousness, and of judgment."

The person referred to in the words of the text, is plainly the Comforter, the Holy Ghost; and the promise was first made to our Lord's apostles. But though it was primarily made to them, and was literally and remarkably fulfilled at the day of Pentecost, when the Holy Ghost came down as a mighty rushing wind, and also when three thousand were pricked to the heart by *Peter*'s preaching; yet, as the Apostles were the representatives of the whole body of believers, we must infer, that this promise must be looked upon as spoken to us, and to our children, and to as many as the Lord our God shall call.

My design from these words, is to shew the manner in which the Holy Ghost generally works upon the hearts of those, who, through grace, are made vessels of mercy, and translated from the kingdom of darkness into the kingdom of God's dear Son.

I say, *generally*: For, as God is a sovereign agent, his sacred Spirit bloweth not only on whom, but when and how it listeth. Therefore, far be it from me to confine the Almighty to one way of acting, or say, that all undergo an equal degree of conviction: no, there is a holy variety in GOD's methods of calling home his elect. But this we may affirm assuredly, that, wherever there is a work of true conviction and conversion wrought upon a sinner's heart, the Holy Ghost, whether by a greater or less degree of inward soul-trouble, does that which our LORD JESUS told the disciples, in the words of the text, that he should do when he came.

If any of you ridicule inward religion, or think there is no such thing as our feeling or receiving the Holy Ghost, I fear my preaching will be quite foolishness to you; and that you will understand me no more than if I spoke to you in an unknown tongue. But as the promise in the text, is made to the world, and as I know it will be fulfilling till time shall be no more, I shall proceed to explain the general way whereby the Holy Ghost works upon every converted sinner's heart; and I hope that the LORD, even whilst I am speaking, will be pleased to fulfil it in many of your hearts. " And when he is come, he will reprove the world of sin, of righteousness, and of judgment."

The word, which we translate *reprove*, ought to be rendred *convince*; and in the original it implies a conviction by way of argumentation, and coming with a power upon the mind equal to a demonstration. A great many scoffers of these last days, will ask such as they term pretenders to the Spirit, how they feel the Spirit, and how they know the Spirit? They might as well ask, how they know, and how they feel the sun when it shines upon the body? For with equal power and demonstration does the Spirit of GOD work upon and convince the soul. And,

First, It convinces of sin; and generally of some enormous sin, the worst perhaps the convicted person ever was guilty of. Thus, when our LORD was conversing with the woman of *Samaria*, he convinced her first of her adultery: " Woman, go call thy husband. The woman answered, and said, I have no husband. JESUS said unto her, Thou hast well said, I have no husband: for thou hast had five husbands, and he whom thou now hast, is not thy husband: in this saidst thou truly." With this there went such a powerful conviction of all her other actual sins, that soon after, "she left her waterpot, and went her way into the city, and faith to the men, Come, and see a man that told me all things that ever I did: is not this the CHRIST?" Thus our LORD also dealt with the persecutor *Saul:* he convinced him first of the horrid sin of persecution; "*Saul, Saul,* why persecutest thou me?" Such a sense of all his other sins, probably at the same time revived in his mind, that immediately he died; that is, died to all his false confidences, and was thrown into such an agony of soul, that he continued three days, and neither did eat nor drink. This is the method the Spirit of GOD generally takes in dealing with sinners; he first convinces them of some heinous actual sin, and at the same time brings all their other sins into remembrance, and as it were sets them in battle-array before them: "When he is come, he will reprove the world of sin."

And was it ever thus with you, my dear hearers? (For I must question you as I go along, because I intend, by the Divine help, to preach not only to your heads, but your hearts). Did the Spirit of GOD ever bring all your sins thus to remembrance, and make you cry out to GOD, "Thou writest bitter things against me?" Did your actual sins ever appear before you, as though drawn in a map? If not, you have great reason (unless you were sanctified from the womb) to suspect that you are not convicted, much more not converted, and that the promise of the text was never yet fulfilled in your hearts.

Farther: When the Comforter comes into a sinner's heart, though it generally convinces the sinner of his actual sin first, yet it leads him to see and bewail his original sin, the fountain from which all these polluted streams do flow.

Though every thing in the earth, air, and water; every thing both without and within, concur to prove the truth of that assertion in the scripture, "in *Adam* we all have died;" yet most are so hardened through the deceitfulness of sin, that notwithstanding they may give an assent to the truth of the proposition in their heads, yet they never felt it really in their hearts. Nay, some in words professedly deny it, though their works too, too plainly prove them to be degenerate sons of a degenerate father. But when the Comforter, the Spirit of GOD,

God, arrests a sinner, and convinces him of sin, all carnal reasoning against original corruption, every proud and high imagination, which exalteth itself against that doctrine, is immediately thrown down; and he is made to cry out, "Who shall deliver me from the body of this death?" He now finds that concupiscence is sin; and does not so much bewail his actual sins, as the inward perverseness of his heart, which he now finds not only to be an enemy to, but also direct enmity against God.

And did the Comforter, my dear friends, ever come with such a convincing power as this into your hearts? Were you ever made to see and feel, that in your flesh dwelleth no good thing; that you are conceived and born in sin; that you are by nature children of wrath; that God would be just if he damned you, though you never committed an actual sin in your lives? So often as you have been at church and sacrament, did you ever feelingly confess, that there was no health in you; that the remembrance of your original and actual sins was grievous unto you, and the burden of them intolerable? If not, you have been only offering to God vain oblations; you never yet prayed in your lives; the Comforter never yet came effectually into your souls: consequently you are not in the faith properly so called; no, you are at present in a state of death and damnation.

Again, the Comforter, when he comes effectually to work upon a sinner, not only convinces him of the sin of his nature, and the sin of his life, but also of the sin of his duties.

We all naturally are Legalists, thinking to be justified by the works of the law. When somewhat awakened by the terrors of the Lord, we immediately, like the Pharisees of old, go about to establish our own righteousness, and think we shall find acceptance with God, if we seek it with tears: finding ourselves damned by nature and our actual sins, we then think to recommend ourselves to God by our duties, and hope, by our doings of one kind or another, to inherit eternal life. But, whenever the Comforter comes into the heart, it convinces the soul of these false rests, and makes the sinner to see that all his righteousnesses are but as filthy rags; and that, for the most pompous services, he deserves no better a doom than that of the unprofitable servant, " to be thrown into outer darkness, where is weeping, and wailing, and gnashing of teeth."

And was this degree of conviction ever wrought in any of your souls? Did the Comforter ever come into your hearts, so as to make you sick of your duties, as well as your sins? Were you ever, with the great Apostle of the *Gentiles*, made to abhor your own righteousness which is by the law, and acknowledge that you deserve to be damned, though you should give all your goods to feed the poor? Were you made to feel, that your very repentance needed to be repented of, and that every thing in yourselves is but dung and dross? And that all the arguments you can fetch for mercy, must be out of the heart and pure unmerited love of GOD? Were you ever made to lye at the feet of sovereign Grace, and to say, LORD, if thou wilt, thou mayest save me; if not, thou mayest justly damn me; I have nothing to plead, I can in no wise justify myself in thy sight; my best performances, I see, will condemn me; and all I have to depend upon is thy free grace? What say you? Was this ever, or is this now, the habitual language of your hearts? You have been frequently at the temple; but did you ever approach it in the temper of the poor Publican, and, after you have done all, acknowledge that you have done nothing; and, upon a feeling experimental sense of your own unworthiness and sinfulness every way, smite upon your breasts, and say, " GOD be merciful to us sinners?" If you never were thus minded, the Comforter never yet effectually came into your souls, you are out of CHRIST; and if GOD should require your souls in that condition, he would be no better to you than a consuming fire.

But there is a fourth sin, of which the Comforter, when he comes, convinces the soul, and which alone (it is very remarkable) our LORD mentions, as though it was the only sin worth mentioning; for indeed it is the root of all other sins whatsoever: it is the reigning as well as the damning sin of the world. And what now do you imagine that sin may be? It is that cursed sin, that root of all other evils, I mean the sin of *unbelief*. Says our LORD, verse 9. " Of sin, because, they believe not on me."

But does the christian world, or any of you that hear me this day, want the Holy Ghost to convince you of unbelief?

Are

Are there any infidels here? Yes, (O that I had not too great reason to think so!) I fear most are such: not indeed such infidels as professedly deny the LORD that bought us (though I fear too many even of such monsters are in every country); but I mean such unbelievers, that have no more faith in CHRIST than the devils themselves. Perhaps you may think you believe, because you repeat the Creed, or subscribe to a Confession of Faith; because you go to church or meeting, receive the sacrament, and are taken into full communion. These are blessed privileges; but all this may be done, without our being true believers. And I know not how to detect your false hypocritical faith better, than by putting to you this question: How long have you believed? Would not most of you say, as long as we can remember; we never did disbelieve? Then this is a certain sign that you have no true faith at all; no, not so much as a grain of mustard-seed: for, if you believe now, (unless you were sanctified from your infancy, which is the case of some) you must know that there was a time in which you did not believe on the LORD JESUS CHRIST; and the Holy Ghost, if ever you received it, convinced you of this. Eternal truth has declared, "When he is come, he will convince the world of sin, because they believe not on me."

None of us believe by nature: but after the Holy Ghost has convinced us of the sin of our natures, and the sin of our lives and duties, in order to convince us of our utter inability to save ourselves, and that we must be beholden to GOD, as for every thing else, so for faith (without which it is impossible to please, or be saved by CHRIST) he convinces us also, that we have no faith. "Dost thou believe on the Son of GOD?" is the grand question which the Holy Ghost now puts to the soul: at the same time he works with such power and demonstration, that the soul sees, and is obliged to confess, that it has no faith.

This is a thing little thought of by most who call themselves believers. They dream they are christians, because they live in a christian country: If they were born *Turks*, they would believe on *Mahomet*; for what is that which men commonly call faith, but an outward consent to the established religion? But do not you thus deceive your own selves; true faith is quite another thing. Ask yourselves, therefore, whether or not the Holy Ghost ever powerfully convinced you of the sin of unbelief? You are perhaps so devout (you may imagine) as to get a catalogue of sins; which you look over, and confess in a formal manner, as often as you go to the holy sacrament: but among all your sins, did you ever once confess and bewail that damning sin of unbelief? Were you ever made to cry out, "LORD, give me faith; LORD, give me to believe on thee; O that I had faith! O that I could believe!" If you never were thus distressed, at least, if you never saw and felt that you had no faith, it is a certain sign that the Holy Ghost, the Comforter, never came into and worked savingly upon your souls.

But is it not odd, that the Holy Ghost should be called a Comforter, when it is plain, by the experience of all GOD's children, that this work of conviction is usually attended with sore inward conflicts, and a great deal of soul-trouble? I answer, The Holy Ghost may well be termed a Comforter, even in this work; because it is the only way to, and ends in, true solid comfort. Blessed are they that are thus convicted by him, for they shall be comforted. Nay, not only so, but there is present comfort, even in the midst of these convictions: the soul secretly rejoices in the sight of its own misery, blesses GOD for bringing it out of darkness into light, and looks forward with a comfortable prospect of future deliverances, knowing, that, "though sorrow may endure for a night, joy will come in the morning."

Thus it is that the Holy Ghost convinces the soul of sin. And, if so, how wretchedly are they mistaken, that blend the light of the Spirit with the light of conscience, as all such do, who say, that CHRIST lighteth every man that cometh into the world, and that light, if improved, will bring us to JESUS CHRIST? If such doctrine be true, the promise in the text was needless: our LORD's apostles had already that light; the world hereafter to be convinced, had that light; and, if that was sufficient to bring them to CHRIST, why was it expedient that CHRIST should go away to heaven, to send down the Holy Ghost to do this for them! Alas! all have not this Spirit: it is the special gift of GOD, and, without this special gift, we can never come to CHRIST.

The light of conscience will accuse or convince us of any common sin; but the light of natural conscience never did, never will, and never can, convince of unbelief. If it could, how comes it to pass, that not one of the heathens, who improved the light of nature in such an eminent degree, was ever convinced of unbelief? No, natural conscience cannot effect this; it is the peculiar property of the Holy Ghost the Comforter: " When he is come, he will reprove (or convince) the world of sin, of righteousness, and judgment."

We have heard how he convinces of sin: we come now to shew,

Secondly, What is the righteousness, of which the Comforter convinces the world.

By the word *righteousness*, in some places of scripture, we are to understand that common justice which we ought to practise between man and man; as when *Paul* is said to reason of temperance and righteousness before a trembling *Felix*. But here (as in a multitude of other places in holy writ) we are to understand by the word righteousness, the active and passive obedience of the dear LORD JESUS; even that perfect, personal, all-sufficient righteousness, which he has wrought out for that world which the Spirit is to convince. " Of righteousness, (says our LORD) because I go to the Father, and ye see me no more." This is one argument that the Holy Spirit makes use of to prove CHRIST's righteousness, because he is gone to the Father, and we see him no more. For, had he not wrought out a sufficient righteousness, the Father would have sent him back, as not having done what he undertook; and we should have seen him again.

O the righteousness of CHRIST! It so comforts my soul, that I must be excused if I mention it in almost all my discourses. I would not, if I could help it, have one sermon without it. Whatever infidels may object, or *Arminians* sophistically argue against an *imputed righteousness*; yet whoever know themselves and GOD, must acknowledge, that " JESUS CHRIST is the end of the law for righteousness, (and perfect justification in the sight of GOD) to every one that believeth," and that we are to be made the righteousness of GOD in him. This, and this only, a poor sinner can lay hold of, as a sure anchor of his hope. Whatever other scheme of salvation men may lay, I acknowledge I can see no other foundation whereon to build my hopes of salvation, but on the rock of CHRIST's personal righteousness, imputed to my soul.

Many, I believe, have a rational conviction of, and agree with me in this: but rational convictions, if rested in, avail but little; it must be a spiritual, experimental conviction of the truth, which is saving. And therefore our LORD says, when the Holy Ghost comes in the day of his power, it convinces of this righteousness, of the reality, compleatness, and sufficiency of it, to save a poor sinner.

We have seen how the Holy Ghost convinces the sinner of the sin of his nature, life, duties, and of the sin of unbelief; and what then must the poor creature do? He must, he must inevitably despair, if there be no hope but in himself. When therefore the Spirit has hunted the sinner out of all his false rests and hiding-places, taken off the pitiful fig-leaves of his own works, and driven him out of the trees of the garden (his outward reformations) and placed him naked before the bar of a sovereign, holy, just, and sin-avenging GOD; then, then it is, when the soul, having the sentence of death within itself because of unbelief, has a sweet display of CHRIST's righteousness made to it by the Holy Spirit of GOD. Here it is, that he begins more immediately to act in the quality of a Comforter, and convinces the soul so powerfully of the reality and all-sufficiency of CHRIST's righteousness, that the soul is immediately set a hungering and thirsting after it. Now the sinner begins to see, that though he has destroyed himself, yet in CHRIST is his help; that, though he has no righteousness of his own to recommend him, there is a fulness of grace, a fulness of truth, a fulness of righteousness in the dear LORD JESUS, which, if once imputed to him, will make him happy for ever and ever.

None can tell, but those happy souls who have experienced it, with what demonstration of the Spirit this conviction comes. O how amiable, as well as all-sufficient, does the blessed JESUS now appear! With what new eyes does the soul now see the LORD its righteousness! Brethren, it is unutterable. If you were never thus convinced of CHRIST's righteousness in your own souls, though you may believe it
doctrinally,

doctrinally, it will avail you nothing, if the Comforter never came savingly into your souls, then you are comfortless indeed. But

What will this righteousness avail, if the soul has it not in possession?

Thirdly, The next thing therefore the Comforter, when he comes, convinces the soul of, is judgment.

By the word *judgment*, I understand that well-grounded peace, that settled judgment, which the soul forms of itself, when it is enabled by the Spirit of GOD to lay hold on CHRIST's righteousness, which I believe it always does, when convinced in the matter before-mentioned. " Of judgment (says our LORD) because the Prince of this world is judged;" the soul, being enabled to lay hold on CHRIST's perfect righteousness by a lively faith, has a conviction wrought in it by the Holy Spirit, that the Prince of this world is judged. The soul being now justified by faith, has peace with GOD through our LORD JESUS CHRIST, and can triumphantly say, It is CHRIST that justifies me, who is he that condemns me? The strong man armed is now cast out; my soul is in a true peace; the Prince of this world will come and accuse, but he has now no share in me: the blessed Spirit which I have received, and whereby I am enabled to apply CHRIST's righteousness to my poor soul, powerfully convinces me of this: why should I fear? or of what shall I be afraid, since GOD's Spirit witnesses with my spirit, that I am a child of GOD? The LORD is ascended up on high; he has led captivity captive; he has received the Holy Ghost the Comforter, that best of gifts for men: and that Comforter is come into my heart: he is faithful that hath promised: I, even I, am powerfully, rationally, spiritually convicted of sin, righteousness and judgment. By this I know the Prince of this world is judged.

Thus, I say, may we suppose that soul to triumph, in which the promise of the text is happily fulfilled. And though, at the beginning of this discourse, I said, most had never experienced any thing of this, and that therefore this preaching must be foolishness to such; yet I doubt not but there are some few happy souls, who, through grace, have been enabled to follow me step by step; and notwithstanding the Holy Ghost might not directly work in the same order as I have described, and perhaps they cannot exactly say the time when, yet they have a well-grounded confidence that the work is done, and that they have really been convinced of sin, righteousness and judgment in some way, or at some time or another.

And now, what shall I say to you? O thank God, thank the Lord Jesus, thank the ever-blessed Trinity, for this unspeakable gift: for you would never have been thus highly favoured, had not he who first spoke darkness into light, loved you with an everlasting love, and enlightened you by his Holy Spirit, and that too, not on account of any good thing foreseen in you, but for his own name's sake.

Be humble therefore, O believers, be humble: look to the rock from whence you have been hewn: extol free grace; admire electing love, which alone has made you to differ from the rest of your brethren. Has God brought you into light? Walk as becometh children of light. Provoke not the Holy Spirit to depart from you: for though he hath sealed you to the day of redemption, and you know that the Prince of this world is judged; yet if you backslide, grow luke-warm, or forget your first love, the Lord will visit your offences with the rod of affliction, and your sin with spiritual scourges. Be not therefore high-minded, but fear. Rejoice, but let it be with trembling. As the elect of God, put on, not only humbleness of mind, but bowels of compassion; and pray, O pray for your unconverted brethren! Help me, help me now, O children of God, and hold up my hands, as *Aaron* and *Hur* once held up the hands of *Moses*. Pray, whilst I am preaching, that the Lord may enable me to say, This day is the promise in the text fulfilled in some poor sinners hearts. Cry mightily to God, and, with the cords of holy violence, pull down blessings on your neighbours heads. Christ yet lives and reigns in heaven: the residue of the Spirit is yet in his hand, and a plentiful effusion of it is promised in the latter days of the church. And O that the Holy Ghost, the blessed Comforter, would now come down, and convince those that are Christless amongst you, of sin, of righteousness, and of judgment!

judgment! O that you were once made willing to be convinced!

But perhaps you had rather be filled with wine than with the Spirit, and are daily chasing that Holy Ghost from your souls. What shall I say for you to God? "Father, forgive them, for they know not what they do." What shall I say from God to you? Why? That "God was in Christ reconciling the world unto himself:" Therefore I beseech you, as in Christ's stead, be ye reconciled to God. Do not go away contradicting and blaspheming. I know *Satan* would have you be gone. Many of you may be uneasy, and are ready to cry out, "What a weariness is this!" But I will not let you go: I have wrestled with God for my hearers in private, and I must wrestle with you here in public. Though of myself I can do nothing, and you can no more by your own power come to and believe on Christ, than *Lazarus* could come forth from the grave; yet who knows but God may beget some of you again to a lively hope by this foolishness of preaching, and that you may be some of that world, which the Comforter is to convince of sin, of righteousness, and of judgment? Poor Christless souls! do you know what a condition you are in? Why, you are lying in the wicked one, the devil; he rules in you, he walks and dwells in you, unless you dwell in Christ, and the Comforter is come into your hearts. And will you contentedly lie in that wicked one the devil? What wages will he give you? Eternal death. O that you would come to Christ! The free gift of God through him is eternal life. He will accept of you even now, if you will believe in him. The Comforter may yet come into your hearts, even yours. All that are now his living temples, were once lying in the wicked one, as well as you. This blessed gift, this Holy Ghost, the blessed Jesus received even for the rebellious.

I see many of you affected: but are your passions only a little wrought upon, or are your souls really touched with a lively sense of the heinousness of your sins, your want of faith, and the preciousness of the righteousness of Jesus Christ? If so, I hope the Lord has been gracious, and that the Comforter is coming into your hearts. Do not stifle these convictions!

victions! Do not go away, and straightway forget what manner of doctrine you have heard, and thereby shew that these are only common workings of a few transient convictions, floating upon the surface of your hearts. Beg of GOD that you may be sincere (for he alone can make you so) and that you may indeed desire the promise of the text to be fulfilled in your souls. Who knows but the LORD may be gracious? Remember you have no plea but sovereign mercy; but, for your encouragement also, remember it is the world, such as you are, to whom the Comforter is to come, and whom he is to convince: wait therefore at wisdom's gates. The bare probability of having a door of mercy opened, is enough to keep you striving. CHRIST JESUS came into the world to save sinners, the chief of them: you know not but he came to save you. Do not go and quarrel with GOD's decrees, and say, if I am a reprobate, I shall be damned; if I am elected, I shall be saved; and therefore I will do nothing. What have you to do with GOD's decrees? Secret things belong to to him; it is your business to "give all diligence to make your calling and election sure." If there are but few who find the way that leads to life, do you strive to be some of them: you know not but you may be in the number of those few, and that your striving may be the means which GOD intends to bless, to give you an entrance in. If you do not act thus, you are not sincere; and, if you do, who knows but you may find mercy? For though, after you have done all that you can, GOD may justly cut you off, yet never was a single person damned who did all that he could. Though therefore your hands are withered, stretch them out; though you are impotent, sick, and lame, come, lie at the pool. Who knows but by and by the LORD JESUS may have compassion on you, and send the Comforter to convince you of sin, righteousness, and of judgment? He is a GOD full of compassion and long-suffering, otherwise you and I had been long since lifting up our eyes in torments. But still he is patient with us!

O Christless sinners, you are alive, and who knows but GOD intends to bring you to repentance? Could my prayers or tears effect it, you should have vollies of the one, and floods of the other. My heart is touched with a sense of your condition;

dition: May our merciful High-priest now send down the Comforter, and make you sensible of it also! O the love of CHRIST! It constrains me yet to beseech you to come to him; what do you reject, if you reject CHRIST, the LORD of glory! Sinners, give the dear Redeemer a lodging in your souls. Do not be *Bethshemites*; give CHRIST your hearts, your whole hearts. Indeed he is worthy. He made you, and not you yourselves. You are not your own; give CHRIST then your bodies and souls, which are his! Is it not enough to melt you down, to think that the high and lofty One, who inhabiteth eternity, should condescend to invite you by his ministers? How soon can he frown you to hell? And how know you, but he may, this very instant, if you do not hear his voice? Did any yet harden their hearts against CHRIST, and prosper? Come then, do not send me sorrowful away: do not let me have reason to cry out, O my leanness, my leanness! Do not let me go weeping into my closet, and say, "LORD, they will not believe my report; LORD, I have called them, and they will not answer; I am unto them as a very pleasant song, and as one that plays upon a pleasant instrument; but their hearts are running after the lust of the eye, the lust of the flesh, and the pride of life." Would you be willing that I should give such an account of you, or make such a prayer before GOD? And yet I must not only do so here, but appear in judgment against you hereafter, unless you will come to CHRIST. Once more therefore I intreat you to come. What objections have you to make? Behold, I stand here in the name of GOD, to answer all that you can offer. But I know no one can come, unless the Father draw him: I will therefore address me to my GOD, and intercede with him to send the Comforter into your hearts.

O blessed JESUS, who art a GOD whose compassions fail not, and in whom all the promises are yea and amen; thou that sittest between the cherubims, shew thyself amongst us. Let us now see thy outgoings! O let us now taste that thou art gracious, and reveal thy almighty arm! Get thyself the victory in these poor sinners hearts. Let not the word spoken prove like water spilt upon the ground. Send down,
send

send down, O great High-priest, the Holy Spirit, to convince the world of sin, of righteousness, and of judgment. So will we give thanks and praise to thee, O Father, thee O Son, and thee O blessed Spirit; to whom, as three Persons, but one GOD, be ascribed by angels and archangels, by cherubims and seraphims, and all the heavenly hosts, all possible power, might, majesty, and dominion, now and for evermore. Amen, Amen, Amen.

SERMON

SERMON XLI.

Saul's Conversion.

ACTS ix. 22.

But Saul increased the more in strength, and confounded the Jews which dwelt at Damascus, proving that this is very CHRIST.

IT is an undoubted truth, however paradoxical it may seem to natural men, that "whosoever will live godly in CHRIST JESUS, shall suffer persecution." And therefore it is very remarkable, that our blessed LORD, in his glorious sermon on the mount, after he had been pronouncing those blessed, who were poor in spirit, meek, pure in heart, and such like, immediately adds (and spends no less than three verses in this beatitude " Blessed are they who are persecuted for righteousness sake." No one ever was, or ever will be endowed with the forementioned graces in any degree, but he will be persecuted for it in a measure. There is an irreconcileable enmity between the seed of the woman, and the seed of the serpent. And if we are not of the world, but shew by our fruits that we are of the number of those whom JESUS CHRIST has chosen out of the world, for that very reason the world will hate us. As this is true of every particular christian, so it is true of every christian church in general. For some years past we have heard but little of a public persecution: Why? Because but little of the power of godliness has prevailed amongst all denominations. The strong man armed has had full possession of most professors hearts, and therefore he has let them rest in a false peace. But we may assure ourselves, when JESUS CHRIST begins to gather

in

in his elect in any remarkable manner, and opens an effectual door for preaching the everlasting gospel, persecution will flame out, and *Satan* and his emissaries will do their utmost (though all in vain) to stop the work of GOD. Thus it was in the first ages, thus it is in our days, and thus it will be, till time shall be no more.

Christians and christian churches must then expect enemies. Our chief concern should be, to learn how to behave towards them in a christian manner: For, unless we take good heed to ourselves, we shall imbitter our spirits, and act unbecoming the followers of that LORD, " who, when he was reviled, reviled not again; when he suffered, threatned not; and, as a lamb before his shearers is dumb, so opened he not his mouth." But what motive shall we make use of to bring ourselves to this blessed lamb-like temper? Next to the immediate operation of the Holy Spirit upon our hearts, I know of no consideration more conducive to teach us long-suffering towards our most bitter persecutors, than this, " That, for all we know to the contrary, some of those very persons, who are now persecuting, may be chosen from all eternity by GOD, and hereafter called in time, to edify and build up the church of CHRIST."

The persecutor *Saul*, mentioned in the words of the text, (and whose conversion, GOD willing, I propose to treat on in the following discourse) is a noble instance of this kind.

I say, a persecutor, and that a bloody one: For see how he is introduced in the beginning of this chapter; " And *Saul* yet breathing out threatnings and slaughter against the disciples of our LORD, went unto the high priest, and desired of him letters to *Damascus* to the synagogues, that if he found any of this way, whether they were men or women, he might bring them bound to *Jerusalem*."

" And *Saul* yet breathing out." This implies that he had been a persecutor before. To prove which, we need only look back to the 7th chapter, where we shall find him so very remarkably active at *Stephen*'s death, that " the witnesses laid down their clothes at a young man's feet, whose name was *Saul*." He seems, though young, to be in some authority. Perhaps, for his zeal against the christians, he was preferred in the church, and was allowed to sit in the great council or

Sanhedrim.

Sanhedrim: For we are told, chap. viii. ver. 1. "That *Saul* was consenting unto his death;" and again, at ver. 3. he is brought in as exceeding all in his opposition; for thus speaks the evangelist, "As for *Saul*, he made havock of the church, entring into every house, and haling men and women, committed them to prison." One would have imagined, that this should have satisfied, at least abated the fury of this young zealot. No: being exceedingly mad against them, as he himself informs *Agrippa*, and having made havock of all in *Jerusalem*, he now is resolved to persecute the disciples of the LORD, even to strange cities; and therefore yet breathing out threatnings. "Breathing out." The words are very emphatical, and expressive of his bitter enmity. It was as natural to him now to threaten the christians, as it was for him to breathe: he could scarce speak, but it was some threatnings against them. Nay, he not only breathed out threatnings, but slaughters also (and those who threaten, would also slaughter, if it were in their power) against the disciples of the LORD. Insatiable therefore as hell, finding he could not confute or stop the christians by force of argument, he is resolved to do it by force of arms; and therefore went to the high priest (for there never was a persecution yet without a high priest at the head of it) and desired of him letters, issued out of his spiritual court, to the synagogues or ecclesiastical courts at *Damascus*, giving him authority, "that if he found any of this way, whether they were men or women, he might bring them bound unto *Jerusalem*," I suppose, there to be arraigned and condemned in the high priest's court. Observe how he speaks of the christians. *Luke*, who wrote the *Acts*, calls them "disciples of the LORD," and *Saul* stiles them "Men and women of this way." I doubt not but he represented them as a company of *upstart enthusiasts*, that had lately gotten into a new method or way of living; that would not be content with the temple-service, but they must be righteous over-much, and have their private meetings or conventicles, and break bread, as they called it, from house to house, to the great disturbance of the established clergy, and to the utter subversion of all order and decency. I do not hear that the high priest makes any objection: no, he was as willing to grant letters, as *Saul* was to ask them; and wonderfully

derfully pleased within himself, to find he had such an active zealot to employ against the christians.

Well then, a judicial process is immediately issued out, with the high priest's seal affixed to it. And now methinks I see the young persecutor finely equipped, and pleasing himself with thoughts, how triumphantly he should ride back with the " men and women of this way," dragging them after him to *Jerusalem*.

What a condition may we imagine the poor disciples at *Damascus* were in at this time! No doubt they had heard of *Saul*'s imprisoning and making havock of the saints at *Jerusalem*, and we may well suppose they were apprised of his design against them. I am persuaded this was a growing, because a trying time with these dear people. O how did they wrestle with GOD in prayer, beseeching him either to deliver them from, or give them grace sufficient to enable them to bear up under, the fury of their persecutors? The high priest doubtless with the rest of his reverend brethren, flattered themselves, that they should now put an effectual stop to this growing heresy, and waited with impatience for *Saul*'s return.

But " He that sitteth in heaven laughs them to scorn, the LORD has them in derision." And therefore, ver. 3. " As *Saul* journeyed, and came even near unto *Damascus*," perhaps to the very gates, (our LORD permitting this, to try the faith of his disciples, and more conspicuously to baffle the designs of his enemies) " suddenly (at mid-day, as he acquaints *Agrippa*) there shined round about him a light from heaven," a light brighter than the sun; " and he fell to the earth (why not into hell?) and heard a voice saying unto him, *Saul*, *Saul*, why persecutest thou me?" The word is doubled, " *Saul*, *Saul*:" Like that of our LORD to *Martha*; " *Martha*, *Martha*;" or the prophet, " O earth, earth, earth!" Perhaps these words came like thunder to his soul. That they were spoken audibly, we are assured from verse 7. " His companions heard the voice." Our LORD now arrests the persecuting zealot, calling him by name; for the word never does us good, till we find it spoken to us in particular. " *Saul*, *Saul*, Why persecutest thou Me?" Put the emphasis upon the word *why*, what evil have I done? Put it upon the word *persecutest*,

secutest, why persecutest? I suppose *Saul* thought he was not persecuting; no, he was only putting the laws of the ecclesiastical court into execution; but JESUS, whose eyes are as a flame of fire, saw through the hypocrisy of his heart, that, notwithstanding his specious pretences, all this proceeded from a persecuting spirit, and secret enmity of heart against GOD; and therefore says, " Why persecutest thou me?" Put the emphasis upon the word *me*, why persecutest thou me? alas! *Saul* was not persecuting CHRIST, was he? he was only taking care to prevent innovations in the church, and bringing a company of enthusiasts to justice, who otherwise would overturn the established constitution. But JESUS says, " Why persecutest thou me?" For what is done to CHRIST's disciples, he takes as done to himself, whether it be good, or whether it be evil. He that touches CHRIST's disciples, touches the apple of his eye; and they who persecute the followers of our LORD, would persecute our LORD himself, was he again to come and tabernacle amongst us.

I do not find that *Saul* gives any reason why he did persecute; no, he was struck dumb; as every persecutor will be, when JESUS CHRIST puts this same question to them at the terrible day of judgment. But being pricked at the heart, no doubt with a sense not only of this, but of all his other offences against the great GOD, he said, ver. 5. " Who art thou, LORD?" See how soon GOD can change the heart and voice of his most bitter enemies. Not many days ago, *Saul* was not only blaspheming CHRIST himself, but, as much as in him lay, compelling others to blaspheme also: but now, he, who before was an impostor, is called *Lord*; " Who art thou, LORD?" This admirably points out the way in which GOD's Spirit works upon the heart: it first powerfully convinces of sin, and of our damnable state; and then puts us upon enquiring after JESUS CHRIST. *Saul* being struck to the ground, or pricked to the heart, cries out after JESUS, " Who art thou, LORD?" As many of you that were never so far made sensible of your damnable state, as to be made feelingly to seek after JESUS CHRIST, were never yet truly convicted by, much less converted to, GOD. May the LORD, who struck *Saul*, effectually now strike all my christless hearers, and set them upon enquiring after JESUS, as their all in all! *Saul* said, " Who art thou,

LORD? And the LORD said, I am JESUS, whom thou persecutest." Never did any one enquire truly after JESUS CHRIST, but CHRIST made a saving discovery of himself, to his soul. It should seem, our LORD appeared to him in person; for *Ananias*, afterwards, says, "The LORD who appeared to thee in the way which thou camest;" though this may only imply CHRIST's meeting him in the way; it is not much matter: it is plain CHRIST here speaks to him, and says, "I am JESUS, whom thou persecutest." It is remarkable, how our LORD takes to himself the name of *Jesus*; for it is a name in which he delights: I am JESUS, a Saviour of my people, both from the guilt and power of their sins; "a JESUS, whom thou persecutest." This seems to be spoken to convince *Saul* more and more of his sin; and I doubt not, but every word was sharper than a two-edged sword, and came like so many daggers to his heart; O how did these words affect him! a JESUS! a Saviour! and yet I am persecuting him! this strikes him with horror; but then the word JESUS, though he was a persecutor, might give him some hope. However, our dear LORD, to convince *Saul* that he was to be saved by grace, and that he was not afraid of his power and enmity, tells him, "It is hard for thee to kick against the pricks." As much as to say, though he was persecuting, yet he could not overthrow the church of CHRIST: for he would sit as King upon his holy hill of *Zion*; the malice of men or devils should never be able to prevail against him.

Ver. 6. "And he, trembling and astonished, said, LORD, what wilt thou have me to do?" Those, who think *Saul* had a discovery of JESUS made to his heart before, think that this question is the result of his faith, and that he now desires to know what he shall do, out of gratitude, for what the LORD had done for his soul; in this sense it may be understood; * and I have made use of it as an instance to prove, that faith will work by love; but perhaps it may be more agreeable to the context, if we suppose, that *Saul* had only some distant discovery of CHRIST made to him, and not a full assurance of faith: for we are told, "he trembling and astonished," trembling at the thoughts of his persecuting a JESUS, and astonished at his own vileness, and the infinite condescension of this

* See VOL. V. Sermon 24.

Jesus, cries out, "Lord, what wilt thou have me to do?" Persons under soul-trouble, and sore conviction, would be glad to do any thing, or comply on any terms, to get peace with God. "Arise, (says our Lord) and go into the city, and it shall be told thee what thou shalt do."

And here we will leave *Saul* a while, and see what is become of his companions. But what shall we say? God is a sovereign agent; his sacred Spirit bloweth when and where it listeth; "he will have mercy on whom he will have mercy." *Saul* is taken, but, as far as we know to the contrary, his fellow-travellers are left to perish in their sins: for we are told, ver. 7. "That the men who journeyed with him stood, indeed, speechless, and hearing a confused voice;" I say, a *confused voice*, for so the word signifies, and must be so interpreted, in order to reconcile it with chap. xxii. ver. 9. where *Saul*, giving an account of these men, tells *Agrippa*, "They heard not the voice of him that spake to me." They heard a voice, a confused noise, but not the articulate voice of him that spake to *Saul*, and therefore remained unconverted. For what are all ordinances, all, even the most extraordinary dispensations of providence, without Christ speaks to the soul in them? Thus it is now under the word preached: many, like *Saul's* companions, are sometimes so struck with the outgoings of God appearing in the sanctuary, that they even stand speechless; they hear the preacher's voice, but not the voice of the Son of God, who, perhaps, at the same time is speaking effectually to many other hearts; this I have known often; and what shall we say to these things? O the depth of the sovereignty of God! it is past finding out. Lord, I desire to adore what I cannot comprehend. "Even so, Father, for so it seemeth good in thy sight!"

But to return to *Saul:* the Lord bids him "arise and go into the city;" and we are told, ver. 8. that "*Saul* arose from the earth; and when his eyes were opened, (he was so overpowered with the greatness of the light that shone upon them, that) he saw no man; but they led him by the hand, and brought him into *Damascus*," that very city which was to be the place of his executing or imprisoning the disciples of the Lord. "And he was three days without sight, and neither did eat nor drink." But who can tell what horrors of conscience,

conscience, what convulsions of soul, what deep and pungent convictions of sin he underwent during these three long days? it was this took away his appetite (for who can eat or drink when under a sense of the wrath of GOD for sin?) and, being to be greatly employed hereafter, he must be greatly humbled now; therefore, the LORD leaves him three days groaning under the spirit of bondage, and buffeted, no doubt, with the fiery darts of the devil, that, being tempted like unto his brethren, he might be able hereafter to succour those that were tempted. Had *Saul* applied to any of the blind guides of the *Jewish* church, under these circumstances, they would have said, he was mad, or going besides himself; as many carnal teachers and blind Pharisees now deal with, and so more and more distress, poor souls labouring under awakening convictions of their damnable state. But GOD often at our first awakenings, visits us with sore trials, especially those who are, like *Saul*, to shine in the church, and to be used as instruments in bringing many sons to glory: those who are to be highly exalted, must first be deeply humbled; and this I speak for the comfort of such, who may be now groaning under the spirit of bondage, and perhaps, like *Saul*, can neither eat nor drink; for I have generally observed, that those who have had the deepest convictions, have afterwards been favoured with the most precious communications, and enjoyed most of the divine presence in their souls. This was afterwards remarkably exemplified in *Saul*, who was three days without sight, and neither did eat nor drink.

But will the LORD leave his poor servant in this distress? no; his JESUS (though *Saul* persecuted him) promised (and he will perform) that " it should be told him what he must do. And there was a certain disciple at *Damascus*, named *Ananias*; and unto him, said the LORD, in a vision, *Ananias*; and he said, Behold, I am here, LORD." What a holy familiarity is there between JESUS CHRIST and regenerate souls! *Ananias* had been used to such love-visits, and therefore knew the voice of his beloved. The LORD says, " *Ananias*;" *Ananias* says, " Behold, I am here, LORD." Thus it is that CHRIST now, as well as formerly, often talks with his children at sundry times and after divers manners, as a man talketh with his friend. But what has the LORD to say to *Ananias*?

Ver. 11.

Ver. 11. "And the LORD said unto him, Arise, and go into the street, which is called *Straight*, and enquire in the house of *Judas*, for one called *Saul* of *Tarsus*;" (See here for your comfort, O children of the most high GOD, what notice JESUS CHRIST takes of the street and the house where his own dear servants lodge) "for behold, he prayeth;" but why is this ushered in with the word *behold*? what, was it such a wonder, to hear that *Saul* was praying? why, *Saul* was a Pharisee, and therefore, no doubt, fasted and made long prayers: and, since we are told that he profited above many of his equals, I doubt not but he was taken notice of for his gift in prayer; and yet it seems, that before these three days, *Saul* never prayed in his life; and why? because, before these three days, he never felt himself a condemned creature: he was alive in his own opinion, because without a knowledge of the spiritual meaning of the law; he felt not a want of, and therefore, before now, cried not after a JESUS; and consequently, though he might have said or made a prayer (as many Pharisees do now-a-days) he never prayed a prayer; but now, " behold! he prayed indeed;" and this was urged as one reason why he was converted. None of GOD's children, as one observes, comes into the world still-born; prayer is the very breath of the new creature: and therefore, if we are prayerless, we are christless; if we never had the spirit of supplication, it is a sad sign that we never had the spirit of grace in our souls: and you may be assured you never did pray, unless you have felt yourselves sinners, and seen the want of JESUS to be your Saviour. May the LORD, whom I serve in the gospel of his dear Son, prick you all to the heart, and may it be said of you all, as it was of *Saul*, behold, they pray!

The LORD goes on to encourage *Ananias* to go to *Saul*: says he, ver. 12. " For he hath seen in a vision a man named *Ananias*, coming in, and putting his hand on him, that he might receive his sight." So that though CHRIST converted *Saul* immediately by himself, yet he will carry on the work, thus begun, by a minister. Happy they, who under soul-troubles have such experienced guides, and as well acquainted with JESUS CHRIST as *Ananias* was: you that have such, make much of and be thankful for them; and you who have them not, trust in GOD; he will carry on his own work without them.

Doubtless, *Ananias* was a good man; but shall I commend him for his answer to our LORD? I commend him not: for says he, ver. 13. " LORD, I have heard by many of this man, how much evil he hath done to thy saints at *Jerusalem*: And here, he hath authority from the chief priests to bind all that call upon thy name." I fear this answer proceeded from some relicks of self-righteousness, as well as infidelity, that lay undiscovered in the heart of *Ananias*. " Arise, (said our LORD) and go into the street, which is called *Straight*, and enquire in the house of *Judas*, for one called *Saul* of *Tarsus*; for behold, he prayeth!" One would think this was sufficient to satisfy him; but says *Ananias*, " LORD, I have heard by many of this man (he seems to speak of him with much contempt; for even good men are apt to think too contemptuously of those who are yet in their sins) how much evil he hath done to thy saints in *Jerusalem*: And here, he hath authority from the chief priests, to bind all that call upon thy name." And what then, *Ananias*? Is any thing too hard for the LORD? Who made thee to differ? Could not he who converted thee, convert him also? Surely *Ananias* here forgets himself, or perhaps fears, lest this man, who had authority from the chief priests to bind all that call upon CHRIST's name, should bind him also, if he went unto him; but the LORD silences all objections, with a " Go thy way, for he is a chosen vessel unto me, to bear my name before the *Gentiles*, and kings, and the children of *Israel*. For I will shew him how great things he must suffer for my name's sake." Here GOD stops his mouth immediately, by asserting his sovereignty, and preaching to him the doctrine of election. And the frequent conversion of notorious sinners to GOD, to me is one great proof, amongst a thousand others, of that precious, but too much exploded and sadly misrepresented, doctrine of GOD's electing love; for whence is it that such are taken, whilst thousands, not near so vile, die senseless and stupid? All the answer that can be given, is, *they are chosen vessels*; " Go thy way, (says GOD) for he is a chosen vessel unto me, to bear my name before the *Gentiles*, and kings, and the children of *Israel*: For I will shew him how great things he must suffer for my name's sake."

fake." Observe what a close connection there is between doing and suffering for CHRIST. If any of my brethren in the ministry are present, let them hear what preferment we must expect, if we are called out to work remarkably for GOD: not great prebendaries or bishopricks, but great sufferings for our LORD's name sake; these are the fruits of our labour: and he that will not contentedly suffer great things for preaching CHRIST, is not worthy of him. Suffering will be found to be the best preferment, when we are called to give an account of our ministry at the great day.

I do not hear, that *Ananias* quarrelled with GOD concerning the doctrine of election; no, (O that all good men would, in this, learn of him!) " He went his way, and entered into the house; and put his hands on him, and said, Brother *Saul;*" just now, it was *this man*; now it is *brother Saul:* it is no matter what a man has been, if he be now a christian; the same should be our brother, our sister and mother; GOD blots out every convert's transgressions as with a thick cloud, and so should we; the more vile a man has been, the more should we love him when believing in CHRIST, because CHRIST will be more glorified on his behalf. I doubt not, but *Ananias* was wonderfully delighted to hear that so remarkable a persecutor was brought home to GOD: I am persuaded he felt his soul immediately united to him by love, and therefore addresses him not with, thou persecutor, thou murderer, that camest to butcher me and my friends; but, " brother *Saul.*" It is remarkable that the primitive christians much used the word *brother* and *brethren*; I know it is a term now much in reproach; but those who despise it, I believe, would be glad to be of our brotherhood, when they see us sitting at the right-hand of the Majesty on high. " Brother *Saul,* the LORD (even JESUS that appeared unto thee in the way as thou camest) hath sent me, that thou mightest receive thy sight, and be filled with the Holy Ghost." At this time, we may suppose, he laid his hands upon him. See the consequences.

Ver. 18. " Immediately there fell from his eyes as it had been scales, and he received sight forthwith;" not only bodily, but spiritual sight; he emerged as it were into a new world; he saw, and felt too, things unutterable: he felt a union of soul with GOD; he received the spirit of adoption; he could now,

now, with a full assurance of faith, cry, "Abba, Father." Now was he filled with the Holy Ghost; and had the love of God shed abroad in his heart; now were the days of his mourning ended; now was CHRIST formed in his soul; now he could give men and devils the challenge, knowing that CHRIST had justified him; now he saw the excellencies of CHRIST, and esteemed him the fairest among ten thousand. You only know how to sympathize with the apostle in his joy, who, after a long night of bondage, have been set free by the Spirit, and have received joy in the Holy Ghost. May all that are now mourning, as *Saul* was, be comforted in like manner!

The scales are now removed from the eyes of *Saul's* mind; *Ananias* has done that for him, under GOD: he must now do another office, baptize him, and so receive him into the visible church of CHRIST; a good proof to me of the necessity of baptism where it may be had: for I find here, as well as elsewhere, that baptism is administered even to those who had received the Holy Ghost; *Saul* was convinced of this, and therefore arose and was baptized; and now it is time for him to recruit the outward man, which, by three days abstinence and spiritual conflicts, had been much impaired: we are therefore told, (ver. 19.) " when he had received meat, he was strengthened."

But O, with what comfort did the apostle now eat his food! I am sure it was with singleness, I am persuaded also with gladness of heart; and why? he knew that he was reconciled to GOD; and, for my own part, did I not know how blind and flinty our hearts are by nature, I should wonder how any one could eat even his common food with any satisfaction, who has not some well-grounded hope of his being reconciled to GOD. Our LORD intimates thus much to us: for in his glorious prayer, after he has taught us to pray for our daily bread, immediately adds that petition, " Forgive us our trespasses;" as though our daily bread would do us no service, unless we were sensible of having the forgiveness of our sins.

To proceed: *Saul* hath received meat, and is strengthened; and whither will he go now? to see the brethren; " then was *Saul* certain days with the disciples that were at *Damascus.*" If we know and love CHRIST, we shall also love and desire to

be

be acquainted with the brethren of CHRIST: we may generally know a man by his company. And though all are not saints that associate with saints, (for tares will be always springing up amongst the wheat till the time of harvest) yet, if we never keep company, but are shy and ashamed of the despised children of GOD, it is a certain sign we have not yet experimentally learned JESUS, or received him into our hearts. My dear friends, be not deceived; if we are friends to the Bridegroom, we shall be friends to the children of the Bridegroom. *Saul*, as soon as he was filled with the Holy Ghost, "was certain days with the disciples that were at *Damascus*."

But who can tell what joy these disciples felt when *Saul* came amongst them! I suppose holy *Ananias* introduced him. Methinks I see the once persecuting zealot, when they came to salute him with a holy kiss, throwing himself upon each of their necks, weeping over them with floods of tears, and saying, "O my brother, O my sister, Can you forgive me? "Can you give such a wretch as I the right-hand of fellow-"ship, who intended to drag you behind me bound unto *Je-*"*rusalem!*" Thus, I say, we may suppose *Saul* addressed himself to his fellow-disciples; and I doubt not but they were as ready to forgive and forget as *Ananias* was, and saluted him with the endearing title of "brother *Saul*." Lovely was this meeting; so lovely, that it seemed *Saul* continued certain days with them, to communicate experiences, and to learn the way of GOD more perfectly; to pray for a blessing on his future ministry, and to praise CHRIST JESUS for what he had done for their souls. *Saul*, perhaps, had sat certain years at the feet of *Gamaliel*, but undoubtedly learned more these certain days, than he had learned before in all his life. It pleases me to think how this great scholar is transformed by the renewing of his mind: What a mighty change was here! That so great a man as *Saul* was, both as to his station in life, and internal qualifications, and such a bitter enemy to the christians; for him, I say, to go and be certain days with the people of *this mad way*, and to sit quietly, and be taught of illiterate men, as many of these disciples we may be sure were; what a substantial proof was this of the reality of his conversion!

What a hurry and confusion may we suppose the chief priests were now in! I warrant they were ready to cry out, What! is he also deceived? As for the common people, who knew not the law, and are accursed, for them to be carried away, is no such wonder; but for a man bred up at the feet of *Gamaliel*, for such a scholar, such an enemy to the cause as *Saul*; for him to be led away with a company of silly, deceived men and women, surely it is impossible: we cannot believe it. But *Saul* soon convinces them of the reality of his becoming a fool for CHRIST's sake: for straightway, instead of going to deliver the letters from the high priests, as they expected, in order to bring the disciples that were at *Damascus* bound to *Jerusalem*, " he preached CHRIST in the synagogues, that he is the Son of GOD." This was another proof of his being converted. He not only conversed with christians in private, but he preached CHRIST publicly in the synagogues: especially, he insisted on the divinity of our LORD, proving, notwithstanding his state of humiliation, that he was really the Son of GOD.

But why did *Saul* preach CHRIST thus? Because he had felt the power of CHRIST upon his own soul. And here is the reason why CHRIST is so seldom preached, and his divinity so slightly insisted on in our synagogues: because the generality of those that pretend to preach him, never felt a saving work of conversion upon their own souls. How can they preach, unless they are first taught of, and then sent by GOD? *Saul* did not preach CHRIST before he knew him; no more should any one else. An unconverted minister, though he could speak with the tongues of men and angels, will be but as a sounding brass and tinkling cymbal to those whose senses are exercised to discern spiritual things. Ministers that are unconverted, may talk and declaim of CHRIST, and prove from books that he is the Son of GOD; but they cannot preach with the demonstration of the Spirit and with power, unless they preach from experience, and have had a proof of his divinity, by a work of grace wrought upon their own souls. GOD forgive those, who lay hands on an unconverted man, knowing that he is such: I would not do it for a thousand worlds. LORD JESUS, keep thy own faithful servants pure, and let them not be partakers of other mens sins!

Such

Such an instance as was *Saul*'s conversion, we may be assured, must make a great deal of noise; and, therefore, no wonder we are told, ver. 21. " But all that heard him were amazed, and said, Is not this he that destroyed them who called on this name in *Jerusalem*, and came hither for that intent, that he might bring them bound to the chief priests."

Thus it will be with all that appear publicly for JESUS CHRIST; and it is as impossible for a true christian to be hid, as a city built upon a hill. Brethren, if you are faithful to, you must be reproached and have remarks made on you for CHRIST; especially if you have been remarkably wicked before your conversion. Your friends will say, is not this he, or she, who a little while ago would run to as great an excess of riot and vanity as the worst of us all? What has turned your brain?—Or if you have been close, false, formal hypocrites, as *Saul* was, they will wonder that you should be so deceived, as to think you were not in a safe state before. No doubt, numbers were surprized to hear *Saul*, who was touching the law blameless, affirm that he was in a damnable condition (as in all probability he did) a few days before.

Brethren, you must expect to meet with many such difficulties as these. The scourge of the tongue, is generally the first cross we are called to bear for the sake of CHRIST. Let not, therefore, this move you: It did not intimidate, no, it rather encouraged *Saul:* says the text, " But *Saul* increased the more in strength, and confounded the *Jews* who dwelt at *Damascus*, proving that this is very CHRIST." Opposition never yet did, nor ever will hurt a sincere convert: Nothing like opposition to make the man of GOD perfect. None but a hireling, who careth not for the sheep, will be affrighted at the approach or barking of wolves. CHRIST's ministers are as bold as lions: it is not for such men as they to flee.

And therefore (that I may draw towards a conclusion) let the ministers and disciples of CHRIST learn from *Saul*, not to fear men or their revilings; but, like him, increase in strength, the more wicked men endeavour to weaken their hands. We cannot be christians without being opposed: no; disciples in general must suffer; ministers in particular must suffer great things. But let not this move any of us from our stedfastness in the gospel: He that stood by and strengthened *Saul*, will also stand by and strengthen us: He is a GOD mighty to save all that put their trust in him. If we look up with an eye of faith, we, as well as the first martyr *Stephen*, may see JESUS standing at the right hand of GOD, ready to assist and protect us. Though the LORD's seat is in heaven, yet he has respect to his saints in an especial manner, when suffering here on earth: then the Spirit of CHRIST and of glory rests upon their souls. And, if I may speak my own experience, "I never enjoy more rich communications from GOD, than when despised and rejected of men for the sake of JESUS CHRIST." However little they may design it, my enemies are my greatest friends. What I most fear, is a calm; but the enmity which is in the hearts of natural men against CHRIST, will not suffer them to be quiet long: No; as I hope the work of GOD will increase, so the rage of men and devils will increase also. Let us put on, therefore, the whole armour of GOD: let us not fear the face of men: " Let us fear him only, who can destroy both body and soul in hell:" I say unto you, let us fear him alone. You see how soon GOD can stop the fury of his enemies.

You have just now heard of a proud, powerful zealot stopt in his full career, struck down to the earth with a light from heaven, converted by the almighty power of efficacious grace, and thereupon zealously promoting, nay, resolutely suffering for, the faith, which once with threatenings and slaughters he endeavoured to destroy. Let this teach us to pity and pray for our LORD's most inveterate enemies. Who knows, but in answer thereunto, our LORD may give them repentance unto life? Most think, that CHRIST had respect to *Stephen*'s prayer, when he converted *Saul*. Perhaps for this reason GOD suffers his adversaries to go on, that his goodness and power may shine more bright in their conversion.

But let not the persecutors of CHRIST take encouragement from this to continue in their opposition. Remember, though *Saul* was converted, yet the high-priest, and *Saul*'s companions, were left dead in trespasses and sins: And, if this should be your case, you will of all men be most miserable: for persecutors have the lowest place in hell. And, if *Saul* was struck to the earth by a light from heaven, how will you be able to stand before JESUS CHRIST, when he comes in terrible majesty to take vengeance on all those who have persecuted his gospel? Then the question, " Why persecutest thou me?" will cut you through and through. The secret enmity of your hearts shall be then detected before men and angels, and you shall be doomed to dwell in the blackness of darkness for evermore. Kiss the Son, therefore, lest he be angry: for even you may yet find mercy, if you believe on the Son of GOD: though you persecute him, yet he will be your JESUS. I cannot despair of any of you, when I find a *Saul* among the disciples at *Damascus*. What though your sins are as scarlet, the blood of CHRIST shall wash them as white as snow. Having much to be forgiven, despair not ; only believe, and like *Saul*, of whom I have now been speaking, love much. He counted himself the chiefest sinner of all, and therefore laboured more abundantly than all.

Who is there among you fearing the LORD? Whose hearts hath the LORD now opened to hearken to the voice of his poor unworthy servant? Surely, the LORD will not let me preach in vain. Who is the happy soul that is this day to be washed in the blood of the Lamb? Will no poor sinner take encouragement from *Saul* to come to JESUS CHRIST? You are all thronging round, but which of you will touch the LORD JESUS? What a comfort will it be to *Saul*, and to your own souls, when you meet him in heaven, to tell him, that hearing of his, was a means, under GOD, of your conversion! Doubtless it was written for the encouragement of all poor, returning sinners; he himself tells us so: for " in me GOD shewed all long-suffering, that I might be an example to them that should hereafter believe." Was *Saul* here himself, he would tell you so, indeed he would ; but being dead, by this account of his conversion he yet speaketh. O that GOD may speak by it to your hearts ! O that the arrows of GOD might this day stick fast in your souls, and you made to cry out, " Who art thou, LORD?" Are there any such amongst you? Methinks I feel something of what this *Saul* felt, when he said, " I travail in birth again for you, till CHRIST be formed again in your hearts." O come, come away to JESUS, in

whom

whom *Saul* believed; and then I care not if the high-priests issue out never so many writs, or injuriously drag me to a prison. The thoughts of being instrumental in saving you, will make me sing praises even at midnight: And I know you will be my joy and crown of rejoicing, when I am delivered from this earthly prison, and meet you in the kingdom of GOD hereafter.

Now to GOD, &c.

SERMON XLII.

Marks of having received the Holy Ghost.

ACTS xix. 2.

Have ye received the Holy Ghost since ye believed?

TWO different significations have been given of these words. Some have supposed, that the question here put, is, Whether these disciples, whom St. *Paul* found at *Ephesus*, had received the Holy Ghost by imposition of hands at confirmation? Others think, these disciples had been already baptized into *John*'s baptism; which not being attended with an immediate effusion of the Holy Spirit, the Apostle here asks them, Whether they had received the Holy Ghost by being baptized into JESUS CHRIST? And upon their answering in the negative, he first baptized, and then confirmed them in the name of the LORD JESUS.

Which of these interpretations is the most true, is neither easy nor very necessary to determine. However, as the words contain a most important enquiry, without any reference to the context, I shall from them,

First, Shew who the Holy Ghost here spoken of, is; and that we must all receive him, before we can be stiled true believers.

Secondly, I shall lay down some scripture marks whereby we may know, whether we have thus received the Holy Ghost or not. And

Thirdly, By way of conclusion, address myself to several distinct classes of professors, concerning the doctrine that shall have been delivered.

First, I am to shew who the Holy Ghost spoken of in the the text, is; and that we must all receive him before we can be stiled true believers.

By the Holy Ghost is plainly signified the Holy Spirit, the third Person in the ever-blessed Trinity, consubstantial and co-eternal with the Father and the Son, proceeding from, yet equal to them both. He is emphatically called Holy, because infinitely holy in himself, and the author and finisher of all holiness in us.

This blessed Spirit, who once moved on the face of the great deep; who over-shadowed the blessed Virgin before that holy child was born of her; who descended in a bodily shape, like a dove, on our blessed Lord, when he came up out of the water at his baptism; and afterwards came down in fiery tongues on the heads of all his Apostles at the day of Pentecost: this is the Holy Ghost, who must move on the faces of our souls; this power of the Most High, must come upon us, and we must be baptized with his baptism and refining fire, before we can be stiled true members of Christ's mystical body.

Thus says the Apostle *Paul*, "Know ye not that Jesus Christ is in you, (that is, by his Spirit) unless you are reprobates?" And, "If any man hath not the Spirit of Christ, he is none of his." And again, says St. *John*, "We know that we are his, by the Spirit that he hath given us."

It is not, indeed, necessary that we should have the Spirit now given in that miraculous manner, in which he was at first given to our Lord's Apostles, by signs and wonders; but it is absolutely necessary, that we should receive the Holy Ghost in his sanctifying graces, as really as they did: and so will it continue to be till the end of the world.

For thus stands the case between God and man: God at first made man upright, or as the sacred Penman expresses it, "In the image of God made he man;" that is, his soul was the very copy, the transcript of the divine nature. He, who before, by his almighty fiat, spoke the world into being, breathed into man the breath of spiritual life, and his soul was adorned with a resemblance of the perfections of Deity.

This

This was the finishing stroke of the creation: the perfection both of the moral and material world. And so near did man resemble his divine Original, that God could not but rejoice and take pleasure in his own likeness: And therefore we read, that when God had finished the inanimate and brutish part of the creation, he looked upon it, and beheld it was *good*; but when that lovely, God-like creature man was made, behold it was *very good*.

Happy, unspeakably happy must man needs be, when thus a partaker of the divine nature. And thus might he have still continued, had he continued holy. But God placed him in a state of probation, with a free grant to eat of every tree in the garden of *Eden*, except the tree of knowledge of good and evil: the day he should eat thereof, he was surely to die; that is, not only to be subject to temporal, but spiritual death; and consequently, to lose that divine image, that spiritual life God had not long since breathed into him, and which was as much his happiness as his glory.

These, one would imagine, were easy conditions for a finite creature's happiness to depend on. But man, unhappy man, being seduced by the devil, and desiring, like him, to be equal with his Maker, did eat of the forbidden fruit; and thereby became liable to that curse, which the eternal God, who cannot lie, had denounced against his disobedience.

Accordingly we read, that soon after *Adam* had fallen, he complained that he was naked; naked, not only as to his body, but naked and destitute of those divine graces which before decked and beautified his soul. The unhappy mutiny and disorder which the visible creation fell into, the briars and thorns which now sprung up and overspread the earth, were but poor emblems, lifeless representations of that confusion and rebellion, and those divers lusts and passions which sprung up in, and quite overwhelmed the soul of man immediately after the fall. Alas! he was now no longer the image of the invisible God; but as he had imitated the devil's sin, he became as it were a partaker of the devil's nature, and from an union with, sunk into a state of direct enmity against God.

Now in this dreadful disordered condition, are all of us brought into the world; for as the root is, such must the branches

branches be. Accordingly we are told, " That *Adam* begat a son in his own likeness;" or, with the same corrupt nature which he himself had, after he had eaten the forbidden fruit. And experience as well as scripture proves, that we also are altogether born in sin and corruption; and therefore incapable, whilst in such a state, to hold communion with GOD. For as light cannot have communion with darkness, so GOD can have no communion with such polluted sons of *Belial*.

Here then appears the end and design why CHRIST was manifest in the flesh; to put an end to these disorders, and to restore us to that primitive dignity in which we were at first created. Accordingly he shed his precious blood to satisfy his Father's justice for our sins; and thereby also he procured for us the Holy Ghost, who should once more re-instamp the divine image upon our hearts, and make us capable of living with and enjoying the blessed GOD.

This was the great end of our LORD's coming into the world; nay, this is the only end why the world itself is now kept in being. For as soon as a sufficient number are sanctified out of it, the heavens shall be wrapped up like a scroll, the elements shall melt with fervent heat, the earth, and all that therein is, shall be burnt up.

This sanctification of the Spirit, is that new birth mentioned by our blessed LORD to *Nicodemus*, " without which we cannot see the kingdom of GOD." This is what St. *Paul* calls being " renewed in the spirit of our minds;" and it is the spring of that holiness, without which no man shall see the LORD.

Thus then, it is undeniably certain, we must receive the Holy Ghost ere we can be stiled true members of CHRIST's mystical body. I come in the

Second place to lay down some scriptural marks, whereby we may easily judge, whether we have thus received the Holy Ghost or not. And the

First I shall mention, is, our having received a spirit of prayer and supplication; for that always accompanies the spirit of grace. No sooner was *Paul* converted, but " behold he prayeth." And this was urged as an argument, to convince *Ananias* that he was converted. And GOD's elect are also said to " cry to him day and night."

And

And since one great work of the Holy Spirit is to convince us of sin, and to set us upon seeking pardon and renewing grace, through the all-sufficient merits of a crucified Redeemer, whosoever has felt the power of the world to come, awakening him from his spiritual lethargy, cannot but be always crying out, "LORD, what wouldst thou have me to do?" Or, in the language of the importunate blind *Bartimeus*, "JESUS, thou Son of *David*, have mercy upon me."

The blessed JESUS, as he received the Holy Ghost without measure, so he evidenced it by nothing more, than his frequent addresses at the throne of grace. Accordingly we read, that he was often alone on the mountain praying; that he rose a great while before day to pray: nay, that he spent whole nights in prayer. And whosoever is made partaker of the same Spirit with the holy JESUS, will be of the same mind, and delight in nothing so much, as to "draw nigh unto GOD," and lift up holy hands and hearts in frequent and devout prayer.

It must be confessed, indeed, that this spirit of supplication is often as it were sensibly lost, and decays, for some time, even in those who have actually received the Holy Ghost. Through spiritual dryness and barrenness of soul, they find in themselves a listlessness and backwardness to this duty of prayer; but then they esteem it as their cross, and still persevere in seeking JESUS, though it be sorrowing: and their hearts, notwithstanding, are fixed upon GOD, though they cannot exert their affections so strongly as usual, on account of that spiritual deadness, which GOD, for wise reasons, has suffered to benumb their souls.

But as for the formal believer, it is not so with him: no; he either prays not at all, or if he does enter into his closet, it is with reluctance, out of custom, or to satisfy the checks of his conscience. Whereas the true believer can no more live without prayer, than without food day by day. And he finds his soul as really and perceptibly fed by the one, as his body is nourished and supported by the other. A *Second* scripture mark of our having received the Holy Ghost, is, Not committing sin.

" Whosoever is born of GOD, (says St. *John*) sinneth not, neither can he sin, because his seed remaineth in him."

Neither can he sin. This expression does not imply the impossibility of a christian's sinning: for we are told, that " in many things we offend all:" It only means thus much; that a man who is really born again of GOD, doth not wilfully commit sin, much less live in the habitual practice of it. For how shall he that is dead to sin, as every converted person is, live any longer therein?

It is true, a man that is born again of GOD, may, through surprize, or the violence of a temptation, fall into an act of sin: witness the adultery of *David*, and *Peter*'s denial of his Master. But then, like them, he quickly rises again, goes out from the world, and weeps bitterly; washes the guilt of sin away by the tears of a sincere repentance, joined with faith in the blood of JESUS CHRIST; takes double heed to his ways for the future, and perfects holiness in the fear of GOD.

The meaning of this expression of the Apostle, that " a man who is born of GOD, cannot commit sin," has been * fitly illustrated, by the example of a covetous worldling, to the general bent of whose inclinations, liberality and profuseness are directly opposite: but if, upon some unexpected, sudden occasion, he does play the prodigal, he immediately repents him of his fault, and returns with double care to his niggardliness again. And so is every one that is born again: to commit sin, is as contrary to the habitual frame and tendency of his mind, as generosity is to the inclinations of a miser; but if at any time, he is drawn into sin, he immediately, with double zeal, returns to his duty, and brings forth fruits meet for repentance. Whereas, the unconverted sinner is quite dead in trespasses and sins: or if he does abstain from gross acts of it, through worldly selfish motives, yet, there is some right eye he will not pluck out; some right-hand which he will not cut off; some specious *Agag* that he will not sacrifice for GOD; and thereby he is convinced that he is but a mere *Saul:* and consequently, whatever pretensions he may make to the contrary, he has not yet received the Holy Ghost. A

Third mark whereby we may know, whether or not we have received the Holy Ghost, is, Our conquest over the world.

* Law's *Christian Perfection*.

" For

"For whosoever is born of GOD, (says the Apostle) overcometh the world." By the world, we are to understand, as St. *John* expresses it, " all that is in the world, the lust of the eye, the lust of the flesh, and the pride of life:" And by overcoming of it, is meant, our renouncing these, so as not to follow or be led by them: for whosoever is born from above, has his affections set on things above: he feels a divine attraction in his soul, which forcibly draws his mind heavenwards; and as the hart panteth after the water-brooks, so doth it make his soul to long after the enjoyment of his GOD.

Not that he is so taken up with the affairs of another life, as to neglect the business of this: No; a truly spiritual man dares not stand any day idle; but then he takes care, though he laboureth for the meat which perisheth, first to secure that which endureth to everlasting life. Or, if GOD has exalted him above his brethren, yet, like *Moses*, *Joseph*, and *Daniel*, he, notwithstanding, looks upon himself as a stranger and pilgrim upon earth: having received a principle of new life, he walks by faith and not by sight; and his hopes being full of immortality, he can look on all things here below as vanity and vexation of spirit: In short, though he is in, yet he is not of the world; and as he was made for the enjoyment of GOD, so nothing but GOD can satisfy his soul.

The ever-blessed JESUS was a perfect instance of overcoming the world. For though he went about continually doing good, and always lived as in a press and throng; yet, wherever he was, his conversation tended heavenwards. In like manner, he that is joined to the LORD in one spirit, will so order his thoughts, words, and actions, that he will evidence to all, that his conversation is in heaven.

On the contrary, an unconverted man being of the earth, is earthy; and having no spiritual eye to discern spiritual things, he is always seeking for happiness in this life, where it never was, will, or can be found. Being not born again from above, he is bowed down by a spirit of natural infirmity: the serpent's curse becomes his choice, and he eats of the dust of the earth all the days of his life. A

Fourth scripture mark of our having received the Holy Ghost, is, Our loving one another.

"We know (says St. *John*) we are passed from death unto life, because we love the brethren." "And by this (says CHRIST himself) shall all men know that ye are my disciples, if ye have love one towards another." Love is the fulfilling of the gospel, as well as of the law: for "GOD is love; and whosoever dwelleth in love, dwelleth in GOD.

But by this love we are not to understand a softness and tenderness of mere nature, or a love founded on worldly motives (for this a natural man may have); but a love of our brethren, proceeding from love towards GOD: loving all men in general, because of their relation to GOD; and loving good men in particular, for the grace we see in them, and because they love our LORD JESUS in sincerity.

This is christian charity, and that new commandment which CHRIST gave to his disciples. *New*, not in its object, but in the motive and example whereon it is founded, even JESUS CHRIST. This is that love which the primitive christians were so renowned for, that it became a proverb, *See how these christians love one another*. And without this love, though we should give all our goods to feed the poor, and our bodies to be burnt, it would profit us nothing.

Further, this love is not confined to any particular set of men, but is impartial and catholic: A love that embraces GOD's image wherever it beholds it, and that delights in nothing so much as to see CHRIST's kingdom come.

This is the love wherewith JESUS CHRIST loved mankind: He loved all, even the worst of men, as appears by his weeping over the obstinately perverse; but wherever he saw the least appearance of the divine likeness, that soul he loved in particular. Thus we read, that when he heard the young man say, "All these things have I kept from my youth," that so far he loved him. And when he saw any noble instance of faith, though in a Centurion and a *Syrophenician*, aliens to the commonwealth of *Israel*, how is he said to marvel at, to rejoice in, speak of, and commend it? So every spiritual disciple of JESUS CHRIST will cordially embrace all who worship GOD in spirit and in truth, however they may differ as to the appendages of religion, and in things not essentially necessary to salvation.

I confess, indeed, that the heart of a natural man is not thus enlarged all at once; and a person may really have received the Holy Ghost, (as *Peter*, no doubt, had when he was unwilling to go to *Cornelius*) though he be not arrived to this: but then, where a person is truly in CHRIST, all narrowness of spirit decreases in him daily; the partition wall of bigotry and party zeal is broken down more and more; and the nearer he comes to heaven, the more his heart is enlarged with that love, which there will make no difference between any people, nation, or language, but we shall all, with one heart, and one voice, sing praises to him that sitteth upon the throne for ever. But I hasten to a

Fifth scripture mark, Loving our enemies.

" I say unto you, (says JESUS CHRIST) Love your enemies, bless them that curse you, do good to those that hate you, and pray for them that despitefully use you and persecute you." And this duty of loving your enemies is so necessary, that without it, our righteousness does not exceed the righteousness of the Scribes and Pharisees, or even of Publicans and sinners: " For if you do good to them only, who do good to you, what do you more than others?" What do you extraordinary? " Do not even the Publicans the same?" And these precepts our LORD confirmed by his own example; when he wept over the bloody city; when he suffered himself to be led as a sheep to the slaughter; when he made that mild reply to the traytor *Judas*, " *Judas*, betrayest thou the Son of man with a kiss;" and more especially, when in the agonies and pangs of death, he prayed for his very murderers, " Father, forgive them, for they know not what they do."

This is a difficult duty to the natural man; but whosoever is made partaker of the promise of the Spirit, will find it practicable and easy: for if we are born again of GOD, we must be like him, and consequently delight to be perfect in this duty of doing good to our worst enemies in the same manner, though not in the same degree as he is perfect: He sends his rain on the evil and the good; causeth his sun to shine on the just and unjust; and more especially commended his love towards us, that whilst we were his enemies, he sent forth his Son, born of a woman, made under the law, that he might become a curse for us.

Many

Many other marks are scattered up and down the scriptures, whereby we may know whether or not we have received the Holy Ghost: such as, "to be carnally minded, is death, but to be spiritually minded is life and peace." "Now the fruits of the Spirit are joy, peace, long-suffering, meekness," with a multitude of texts to the same purpose. But as most, if not all of them, are comprehended in the duties already laid down, I dare affirm, whosoever upon an impartial examination, can find the aforesaid marks on his soul, may be as certain, as though an angel was to tell him, that his pardon is sealed in heaven.

As for my own part, I had rather see these divine graces, and this heavenly temper stamped upon my soul, than to hear an angel from heaven saying unto me, Son, be of good cheer, thy sins are forgiven thee.

These are infallible witnesses; these are *Emmanuel*, GOD with and in us; these make up that white stone, which none knoweth, saving he who hath receiveth it; these are the earnests of the heavenly inheritance in our hearts: In short, these are glory begun, and are that good thing, that better part, and which if you continue to stir up this gift of GOD, neither men nor devils shall ever be able to take from us.

I proceed, as was proposed, in the *Third* place, to make an application of the doctrine delivered, to several distinct classes of professors. And

First, I shall address myself to those who are dead in trespasses and sins. And, O how could I weep over you, as our LORD wept over *Jerusalem!* For, alas! how distant must you be from GOD? What a prodigious work have you to finish, who, instead of praying day and night, seldom or never pray at all? And, instead of being born again of GOD, so as not to commit sin, are so deeply sunk into the nature of devils, as to make a mock at it? Or, instead of overcoming the world, so as not to follow or be led by it, are continually making provision for the flesh, to fulfil the lusts thereof. And, instead of being endued with the god-like disposition of loving all men, even your enemies, have your hearts full of hatred, malice, and revenge, and deride those who are the sincere followers of the lowly JESUS. But think you, O sinners,

that

that GOD will admit such polluted wretches into his sight? Or should he admit you, do you imagine you could take any pleasure in him? No; heaven itself would be no heaven to you; the devilish dispositions which are in your hearts, would render all the spiritual enjoyments of those blessed mansions, ineffectual to make you happy. To qualify you to be blissful partakers of that heavenly inheritance with the saints in light, there is a meetness required: to attain which, ought to be the chief business of your lives.

It is true, you, as well as the righteous, in one sense, shall see GOD; (for we must all appear before the judgment-seat of CHRIST) but you must see him once, never to see him more. For as you carry about in you the devil's image, with devils you must dwell: being of the same nature, you must share the same doom. " Repent, therefore, and be converted, that your sins may be blotted out." See that you receive the Holy Ghost, before you go hence: for otherwise, how can you escape the damnation of hell?

Secondly, Let me apply myself to those who deceive themselves with false hopes of salvation. Some, through the influence of a good education, or other providential restraints, have not run into the same excess of riot with other men, and they think they have no need to receive the Holy Ghost, but flatter themselves that they are really born again.

But do you shew it by bringing forth the fruits of the Spirit? Do you pray without ceasing? Do you not commit sin? Have you overcome the world? And do you love your enemies, and all mankind, in the same manner, as JESUS CHRIST loved them?

If these things, brethren, be in you and abound, then may you have confidence towards GOD; but if not, although you may be civilized, yet you are not converted: no, you are yet in your sins. The nature of the old *Adam* still reigneth in your souls; and unless the nature of the second *Adam* be grafted in its room, you can never see GOD.

Think not, therefore, to dress yourselves up in the ornaments of a good nature, and civil education, and say with *Agag*, " surely the bitterness of death is past:" For GOD's justice, notwithstanding that, like *Samuel*, shall hew you to pieces. However you may be highly esteemed in the sight of men, yet, in the sight of God, you are but like the apples of *Sodom*, dunghills covered over with snow, mere whited sepulchres, appearing a little beautiful without, but inwardly full of corruption and of all uncleanness: and consequently will be dismissed at the last day with a "Verily, I know you not."

But the word of God is profitable for comfort as well as correction.

Thirdly, Therefore I address myself to those who are under the drawings of the Father, and are exercised with the Spirit of bondage, and not finding the marks before mentioned, are crying out, Who shall deliver us from the body of this death?

But fear not, little flock; for notwithstanding your present infant state of grace, it shall be your Father's good pleasure to give you the kingdom. The grace of God, through Jesus Christ, shall deliver you, and give you what you thirst after: He hath promised, he will also do it. Ye shall receive the spirit of adoption, that promise of the Father, if you faint not: only persevere in seeking it; and determine not to be at rest in your soul, till you know and feel that you are thus born again from above, and God's Spirit witnesseth with your spirits that you are the children of God.

Fourthly and *Lastly*, I address myself to those who have received the Holy Ghost in all his sanctifying graces, and are almost ripe for glory.

Hail, happy saints! for your heaven is begun on earth: you have already received the first fruits of the Spirit, and are patiently waiting till that blessed change come, when your harvest shall be compleat. I see and admire you, though, alas! at so great a distance from you: your life, I know, is hid with Christ in God. You have comforts, you have meat to eat, which a sinful, carnal, ridiculing world knows nothing of. Christ's yoke is now become easy to you, and his burden light. You have passed through the pangs of the new birth, and now rejoice that Christ Jesus is spiritually formed in your hearts. You know what it is to dwell in Christ, and Christ in you. Like *Jacob*'s ladder, although your bodies are on earth, yet your souls and hearts are in heaven: and by your faith and constant recollection, like the blessed angels, you do always behold the face of your Father which is in heaven.

I need

I need not exhort you to prefs forward, for you know that in walking in the Spirit there is a great reward. Rather will I exhort you, in patience to poffefs your fouls yet a little while, and Jesus Christ will deliver you from the burden of the flefh, and an abundant entrance fhall be adminiftered to you, into the eternal joy and uninterrupted felicity of his heavenly kingdom.

Which God of his infinite mercy grant, through Jesus Christ our Lord: To whom, with the Father, and the Holy Ghoft, three Perfons and one God, be afcribed all honour, power, and glory, for ever and ever.

SERMON XLIII.

The Almost Christian.

Acts xxvi. 28.

Almost thou persuadest me to be a Christian.

THESE words contain the ingenuous confession of king *Agrippa*; which having some reference to, it may not be improper to relate the substance of the preceding verses, with which the words are so closely connected.

The chapter, out of which the text is taken, contains an admirable account which the great St. *Paul* gave of his wonderful conversion from Judaism to Christianity, when he was called to make his defence before *Festus* a *Gentile* governor, and king *Agrippa*. Our blessed LORD had long since foretold, that when the Son of man should be lifted up, " his disciples should be brought before kings and rulers, for his name's sake, for a testimony unto them." And very good was the design of infinite wisdom in thus ordaining it; for Christianity being, from the beginning, a doctrine of the Cross, the princes and rulers of the earth thought themselves too high to be instructed by such mean teachers, or too happy to be disturbed by such unwelcome truths; and therefore would have always continued strangers to JESUS CHRIST, and him crucified, had not the apostles, by being arraigned before them, gained opportunities of preaching to them " JESUS and the resurrection." St. *Paul* knew full well that this was the main reason, why his blessed Master permitted his enemies at this time to arraign him at a public bar; and therefore, in compliance with the divine will, thinks it not sufficient,

sufficient, barely to make his defence, but endeavours at the same time to convert his judges. And this he did with such demonstration of the spirit, and of power, that *Festus*, unwilling to be convinced by the strongest evidence, cries out with a loud voice, " *Paul*, much learning doth make thee mad." To which the brave apostle (like a true follower of the holy JESUS) meekly replies, I am not mad, most noble *Festus*, but speak forth the words of truth and soberness." But in all probability, seeing king *Agrippa* more affected with his discourse, and observing in him an inclination to know the truth, he applies himself more particularly to him. " The king knoweth of these things; before whom also I speak freely; for I am persuaded that none of these things are hidden from him." And then, that if possible he might complete his wished-for conversion, he with an inimitable strain of oratory, addresses himself still more closely, " King *Agrippa*, believest thou the prophets? I know that thou believest them." At which the passions of the king began to work so strongly, that he was obliged in open court, to own himself affected by the prisoner's preaching, and ingenuously to cry out, " *Paul*, almost thou persuadest me to be a Christian."

Which words, taken with the context, afford us a lively representation of the different reception, which the doctrine of CHRIST's ministers, who come in the power and spirit of St. *Paul*, meets with now-a-days in the minds of men. For notwithstanding they, like this great apostle, " speak forth the words of truth and soberness;" and with such energy and power, that all their adversaries cannot justly gainsay or resist; yet, too many, with the noble *Festus* before-mentioned, being like him, either too proud to be taught, or too sensual, too careless, or too worldly-minded to live up to the doctrine, in order to excuse themselves, cry out, that " much learning, much study, or, what is more unaccountable, much piety, hath made them mad." And though, blessed be GOD! all do not thus disbelieve our report; yet amongst those who gladly receive the word, and confess that we speak the words of truth and soberness, there are so few, who arrive at any higher degree of piety than that of *Agrippa*, or are any farther persuaded than to be almost Christians, that I cannot but

think

think it highly neceſſary to warn my dear hearers of the danger of ſuch a ſtate. And therefore, from the words of the text, ſhall endeavour to ſhew theſe three things:

Firſt, What is meant by an almoſt chriſtian.

Secondly, What are the chief reaſons, why ſo many are no more than almoſt chriſtians.

Thirdly, I ſhall conſider the ineffectualneſs, danger, abſurdity, and uneaſineſs which attends thoſe who are but almoſt chriſtians; and then conclude with a general exhortation, to ſet all upon ſtriving not only to be almoſt, but altogether chriſtians.

I. And, *Firſt*, I am to conſider what is meant by an almoſt chriſtian.

An almoſt chriſtian, if we conſider him in reſpect to his duty to GOD, is one that halts between two opinions; that wavers between CHRIST and the world; that would reconcile GOD and *Mammon*, light and darkneſs, CHRIST and *Belial*. It is true, he has an inclination to religion, but then he is very cautious how he goes too far in it: his falſe heart is always crying out, Spare thyſelf, do thyſelf no harm. He prays indeed, that " GOD's will may be done on earth, as it is in heaven." But notwithſtanding, he is very partial in his obedience, and fondly hopes that GOD will not be extreme to mark every thing that he wilfully does amiſs; though an inſpired apoſtle has told him, that " he who offends in one point is guilty of all." But chiefly, he is one that depends much on outward ordinances, and on that account looks upon himſelf as righteous, and deſpiſes others; though at the ſame time he is as great a ſtranger to the divine life as any other perſon whatſoever. In ſhort, he is fond of the form, but never experiences the power of godlineſs in his heart. He goes on year after year, attending on the means of grace, but then, like *Pharaoh*'s lean kine, he is never the better, but rather the worſe for them.

If you consider him in respect to his neighbour, he is one that is strictly just to all; but then this does not proceed from any love to God or regard to man, but only through a principle of self-love: because he knows dishonesty will spoil his reputation, and consequently hinder his thriving in the world.

He is one that depends much upon being negatively good, and contents himself with the consciousness of having done no one any harm; though he reads in the gospel, that " the unprofitable servant was cast into outer darkness," and the barren fig-tree was cursed and dried up from the roots, not for bearing bad, but no fruit.

He is no enemy to charitable contributions in public, if not too frequently recommended: but then he is unacquainted with the kind offices of visiting the sick and imprisoned, cloathing the naked, and relieving the hungary in a private manner. He thinks that these things belong only to the clergy, though his own false heart tells him, that nothing but pride keeps him from exercising these acts of humility; and that JESUS CHRIST, in the 25th chapter of St. *Matthew*, condemns persons to everlasting punishment, not merely for being fornicators, drunkards, or extortioners, but for neglecting these charitable offices, " When the Son of man shall come in his glory, he shall set the sheep on his right-hand, and the goats on his left. And then shall he say unto them on his left-hand, depart from me, ye cursed, into everlasting fire prepared for the devil and his angels: for I was an hungred, and ye gave me no meat; I was thirsty, and ye gave me no drink; I was a stranger, and ye took me not in; naked, and ye cloathed me not; sick and in prison, and ye visited me not. Then shall they also say, LORD, when saw we thee an hungred, or a-thirst, or a stranger, or naked, or sick, or in prison, and did not minister unto thee? Then shall he answer them, Verily I say unto you, inasmuch as ye have not done it unto one of the least of these my brethren, ye did it not unto me: and these shall go away into everlasting punishment." I thought proper to give you this whole passage of scripture at large, because our Saviour lays such a particular stress upon it; and yet it is so little regarded, that were we to judge by the practice of christians, one should be tempted to think there were no such verses in the Bible.

But to proceed in the character of an *almost christian*: If we consider him in respect of himself; as we said he was strictly honest to his neighbour, so he is likewise strictly sober in himself: but then both his honesty and sobriety proceed from the same principle of a false self-love. It is true, he runs not into the same excess of riot with other men; but then it is not out of obedience to the laws of GOD, but either because his constitution will not away with intemperance; or rather because he is cautious of forfeiting his reputation, or unfitting himself for temporal business. But though he is so prudent as to avoid intemperance and excess, for the reasons before-mentioned; yet he always goes to the extremity of what is lawful. It is true, he is no drunkard; but then he has no *christian self-denial*. He cannot think our Saviour to be so austere a Master, as to deny us to indulge ourselves in some particulars: and so by this means he is destitute of a sense of true religion, as much as if he lived in debauchery, or any other crime whatever. As to settling his principles as well as practice, he is guided more by the world, than by the word of GOD: for his part, he cannot think the way to heaven so narrow as some would make it; and therefore considers not so much what scripture requires, as what such and such a good man does, or what will best suit his own corrupt inclinations. Upon this account, he is not only very cautious himself, but likewise very careful of young converts, whose faces are set heavenward; and therefore is always acting the devil's part, and bidding them spare themselves, though they are doing no more than what the scripture strictly requires them to do: The consequence of which is, that " he suffers not himself to enter into the kingdom of GOD, and those that are entering in he hinders."

Thus lives the almost christian: not that I can say, I have fully described him to you; but from these outlines and sketches of his character, if your consciences have done their proper office, and made a particular application of what has been

been said to your own hearts, I cannot but fear that some of you may observe some features in his picture, odious as it is, too near resembling your own; and therefore I cannot but hope, that you will join with the apostle in the words immediately following the text, and wish yourselves " to be not only almost, but altogether christians."

II. I proceed to the second general thing proposed; to consider the reasons why so many are no more than almost christians.

1. And the first reason I shall mention is, because so many set out with false notions of religion; though they live in a christian country, yet they know not what christianity is. This perhaps may be esteemed a hard saying, but experience sadly evinces the truth of it; for some place religion in being of this or that communion; more in morality; most in a round of duties, and a model of performances; and few, very few acknowledge it to be, what it really is, a thorough inward change of nature, a divine life, a vital participation of JESUS CHRIST, an union of the soul with GOD; which the apostle expresses by saying, "He that is joined to the LORD is one spirit." Hence it happens, that so many, even of the most knowing professors, when you come to converse with them concerning the essence, the life, the soul of religion, I mean our new birth in JESUS CHRIST, confess themselves quite ignorant of the matter, and cry out with *Nicodemus*, " How can this thing be?" And no wonder then, that so many are only almost christians, when so many know not what christianity is: no marvel, that so many take up with the form, when they are quite strangers to the power of godliness; or content themselves with the shadow, when they know so little about the substance of it. And this is one cause why so many are almost, and so few are altogether christians.

2. A second reason that may be assigned why so many are no more than almost christians, is a servile fear of man: multitudes there are and have been, who, though awakened to a sense of the divine life, and have tasted and felt the powers of the world to come; yet out of a base sinful fear of being

counted singular, or contemned by men, have suffered all those good impressions to wear off. It is true, they have some esteem for JESUS CHRIST; but then, like *Nicodemus*, they would come to him only by night: they are willing to serve him; but then they would do it secretly, for fear of the *Jews*: they have a mind to see JESUS, but then they cannot come to him because of the press, and for fear of being laughed at, and ridiculed by those with whom they used to sit at meat. But well did our Saviour prophesy of such persons, " How can ye love me, who receive honour one of another?" Alas! have they never read, that " the friendship of this world is enmity with GOD;" and that our LORD himself has threatened, " Whosoever shall be ashamed of me or of my words, in this wicked and adulterous generation, of him shall the Son of man be ashamed, when he cometh in the glory of his Father and of his holy angels?" No wonder that so many are no more than almost christians, since so many " love the praise of men more than the honour which cometh of GOD."

3. A third reason why so many are no more than almost christians, is a reigning love of money. This was the pitiable case of that forward young man in the gospel, who came running to our blessed LORD, and kneeling before him, enquired " what he must do to inherit eternal life;" to whom our blessed Master replied, " Thou knowest the commandments, Do not kill, Do not commit adultery, Do not steal:" To which the young man replied, " All these have I kept from my youth." But when our LORD proceeded to tell him, " Yet lackest thou one thing; Go sell all that thou hast, and give to the poor; He was grieved at that saying, and went away sorrowful, for he had great possessions!" Poor youth! he had a good mind to be a christian, and to inherit eternal life, but thought it too dear, if it could be purchased at no less an expence than of his estate! And thus many, both young and old, now-a-days, come running to worship our blessed LORD in public, and kneel before him in private, and enquire at his gospel, what they must do to inherit eternal life: but when they find they must renounce the self-enjoyment of riches, and forsake all in affection to follow him, they

cry,

cry, "The LORD pardon us in this thing! We pray thee, have us excused."

But is heaven so small a trifle in men's esteem, as not to be worth a little gilded earth? Is eternal life so mean a purchase, as not to deserve the temporary renunciation of a few transitory riches? Surely it is. But however inconsistent such a behaviour may be, this inordinate love of money is too evidently the common and fatal cause, why so many are no more than almost christians.

4. Nor is the love of pleasure a less uncommon, or a less fatal cause why so many are no more than almost christians. Thousands and ten thousands there are, who despise riches, and would willingly be true disciples of JESUS CHRIST, if parting with their money would make them so; but when they are told that our blessed LORD has said, "Whosoever will come after him must deny himself;" like the pitiable young man before-mentioned, "they go away sorrowful:" for they have too great a love for sensual pleasures. They will perhaps send for the ministers of CHRIST, as *Herod* did for *John*, and hear them gladly: but touch them in their *Herodias*, tell them they must part with such or such a darling pleasure; and with wicked *Ahab* they cry out, "Hast thou found us, O our enemy?" Tell them of the necessity of mortification and self-denial, and it is as difficult for them to hear, as if you was to bid them "cut off a right-hand, or pluck out a right-eye." They cannot think our blessed LORD requires so much at their hands, though an inspired apostle has commanded us to "mortify our members which are upon earth." And who himself, even after he had converted thousands, and was very near arrived to the end of his race, yet professed that it was his daily practice to "keep under his body, and bring it into subjection, lest after he had preached to others, he himself should be a cast-away!"

But some men would be wiser than this great apostle, and chalk out to us what they falsely imagine an easier way to happiness. They would flatter us, we may go to heaven without offering violence to our sensual appetites; and enter into the strait gate without striving against our carnal inclinations. And this is another reason why so many are only almost, and not altogether christians.

5. The fifth and last reason I shall assign why so many are only almost christians, is a fickleness and instability of temper.

It has been, no doubt, a misfortune that many a minister and sincere christian has met with, to weep and wail over numbers of promising converts, who seemingly began in the Spirit, but after a while fell away, and basely ended in the flesh; and this not for want of right notions in religion, nor out of a servile fear of man, nor from the love of money, or of sensual pleasure, but through an instability and fickleness of temper. They looked upon religion merely for novelty, as something which pleased them for a while; but after their curiosity was satisfied, they laid it aside again: like the young man that came to see JESUS with a linen cloth about his naked body, they have followed him for a season, but when temptations came to take hold on them, for want of a little more resolution, they have been stripped of all their good intentions, and fled away naked. They at first, like a tree planted by the water-side, grew up and flourished for a while; but having no root in themselves, no inward principle of holiness and piety, like *Jonah*'s gourd, they were soon dried up and withered. Their good intentions are too like the violent motions of the animal spirits of a body newly beheaded, which, though impetuous, are not lasting. In short, they set out well in their journey to heaven, but finding the way either narrower or longer than they expected, through an unsteadiness of temper, they have made an eternal halt, and so " returned like the dog to his vomit, or like the sow that was washed to her wallowing in the mire!"

But I tremble to pronounce the fate of such unstable professors, who having put their hands to the plough, for want of a little more resolution, shamefully look back. How shall I repeat to them that dreadful threatening, " If any man draw back, my soul shall have no pleasure in him:" And again, " It

"It is impossible (that is, exceeding difficult at least) for those that have been once enlightened, and have tasted of the heavenly gift, and the powers of the world to come, if they should fall away, to be renewed again unto repentance." But notwithstanding the gospel is so severe against apostates, yet many that begun well, through a fickleness of temper, (O that none of us here present may ever be such) have been by this means of the number of those that turn back unto perdition. And this is the fifth, and the last reason I shall give, why so many are only almost, and not altogether christians.

III. Proceed we now to the third general thing proposed, namely, to consider the folly of being no more than an almost christian.

1. And the *first* proof I shall give of the folly of such a proceeding is, that it is ineffectual to salvation. It is true, such men are almost good; but almost to hit the mark, is really to miss it. GOD requires us "to love him with all our hearts, with all our souls, and with all our strength." He loves us too well to admit any rival; because, so far as our hearts are empty of GOD, so far must they be unhappy. The devil, indeed, like the false mother that came before *Solomon*, would have our hearts divided, as she would have had the child; but GOD, like the true mother, will have all or none. "My Son, give me thy heart," thy whole heart, is the general call to all: and if this be not done, we never can expect the divine mercy.

Persons may play the hypocrite; but GOD at the great day will strike them dead, (as he did *Ananias* and *Sapphira* by the mouth of his servant *Peter*) for pretending to offer him all their hearts, when they keep back from him the greatest part. They may perhaps impose upon their fellow-creatures for a while; but he that enabled *Elijah* to cry out, "Come in thou wife of *Jeroboam*," when she came disguised to enquire about her sick son, will also discover them through their most artful dissimulations; and if their hearts are not wholly with him, appoint them their portion with hypocrites and unbelievers.

2. But, *secondly,* What renders an half-way-piety more inexcusable is, that it is not only insufficient to our own salvation, but also very prejudicial to that of others.

An almost christian is one of the most hurtful creatures in the world: he is a wolf in sheep's cloathing: he is one of those false prophets, our blessed Lord bids us beware of in his sermon on the mount, who would persuade men, that the way to heaven is broader than it really is; and thereby, as it was observed before, " enter not into the kingdom of God themselves, and those that are entering in they hinder." These, these are the men that turn the world into a lukewarm *Laodicean* spirit; that hang out false lights, and so shipwreck unthinking benighted souls in their voyage to the haven of eternity. These are they who are greater enemies to the cross of Christ, than infidels themselves: for of an unbeliever every one will be aware; but an almost christian, through his subtle hypocrisy, draws away many after him; and therefore must expect to receive the greater damnation.

3. But, *thirdly,* As it is most prejudicial to ourselves and hurtful to others, so it is the greatest instance of ingratitude we can express towards our Lord and Master Jesus Christ. For did he come down from heaven, and shed his precious blood, to purchase these hearts of ours, and shall we only give him half of them? O how can we say we love him, when our hearts are not wholly with him? How can we call him our Saviour, when we will not endeavour sincerely to approve ourselves to him, and so let him see the travail of his soul, and be satisfied!

Had any of us purchased a slave at a most expensive rate, and who was before involved in the utmost miseries and torments, and so must have continued for ever, had we shut up our bowels of compassion from him; and was this slave afterwards to grow rebellious, or deny giving us but half his service; how, how should we exclaim against his base ingratitude! And yet this base ungrateful slave thou art, O man, who acknowledgest thyself to be redeemed from infinite unavoidable misery and punishment by the death of Jesus Christ, and

yet

yet wilt not give thyself wholly to him. But shall we deal with GOD our Maker in a manner we would not be dealt with by a man like ourselves? GOD forbid! No. Suffer me, therefore,

To add a word or two of exhortation to you, to excite you to be not only almost, but altogether christians. O let us scorn all base and treacherous treatment of our King and Saviour, of our GOD and Creator. Let us not take some pains all our lives to go to heaven, and yet plunge ourselves into hell at last. Let us give to GOD our whole hearts, and no longer halt between two opinions: if the world be GOD, let us serve that; if pleasure be a GOD, let us serve that; but if the LORD he be GOD, let us, O let us serve him alone. Alas! why, why should we stand out any longer? Why should we be so in love with slavery, as not wholly to renounce the world, the flesh, and the devil, which, like so many spiritual chains, bind down our souls, and hinder them from flying up to GOD. Alas! what are we afraid of? Is not GOD able to reward our entire obedience? If he is, as the almost christian's lame way of serving him, seems to grant, why then will we not serve him entirely? For the same reason we do so much, why do we not do more? Or do you think that being only half religious will make you happy, but that going farther, will render you miserable and uneasy? Alas! this, my brethren, is delusion all over: for what is it but this *half piety*, this wavering between GOD and the world, that makes so many, that are seemingly well disposed, such utter strangers to the comforts of religion? They chuse just so much of religion as will disturb them in their lusts, and follow their lusts so far as to deprive themselves of the comforts of religion. Whereas on the contrary, would they sincerely leave all in affection, and give their hearts wholly to GOD, they would then (and they cannot till then) experience the unspeakable pleasure of having a mind at unity with itself, and enjoy such a peace of GOD, which even in this life passes all understanding, and which they were entire strangers to before. It is true, if we will devote ourselves entirely to GOD, we must meet with contempt; but then it is because contempt is necessary to heal our pride. We must renounce some sensual pleasures, but then it is because those unfit us for spiritual ones, which are infinitely better. We must renounce the love of the world; but then it is that we may be filled with the love of GOD: and when that has once enlarged our hearts, we shall, like *Jacob* when he served for his beloved *Rachel*, think nothing too difficult to undergo, no hardships too tedious to endure, because of the love we shall then have for our dear Redeemer. Thus easy, thus delightful will be the ways of GOD even in this life: but when once we throw off these bodies, and our souls are filled with all the fulness of GOD, O! what heart can conceive, what tongue can express, with what unspeakable joy and consolation shall we then look back on our past sincere and hearty services. Think you then, my dear hearers, we shall repent we had done too much; or rather think you not, we shall be ashamed that we did no more; and blush we were so backward to give up all to GOD; when he intended hereafter to give us himself?

Let me therefore, to conclude, exhort you, my brethren, to have always before you the unspeakable happiness of enjoying GOD. And think withal, that every degree of holiness you neglect, every act of piety you omit, is a jewel taken out of your crown, a degree of blessedness lost in the vision of GOD. O! do but always think and act thus, and you will no longer be labouring to compound matters between GOD and the world; but, on the contrary, be daily endeavouring to give up yourselves more and more unto him; you will be always watching, always praying, always aspiring after farther degrees of purity and love, and consequently always preparing yourselves for a fuller sight and enjoyment of that GOD, in whose presence there is fulness of joy, and at whose right-hand there are pleasures for ever more. Amen! Amen!

SERMON XLIV.

CHRIST the Believer's Wisdom, Righteousness, Sanctification, and Redemption.

---

1 COR. i. 30.

But of him are ye in CHRIST JESUS, *who of* GOD *is made unto us, wisdom, righteousness, sanctification, and redemption.*

OF all the verses in the book of GOD, this which I have now read to you, is, I believe, one of the most comprehensive: What glad tidings does it bring to believers! what precious privileges are they herein invested with! how are they here led to the fountain of them all, I mean, the love, the everlasting love of GOD the Father! "Of him are ye in CHRIST JESUS, who of GOD is made unto us, wisdom, righteousness, sanctification, and redemption."

Without referring you to the context, I shall from the words,

First, Point out to you the fountain, from which all those blessings flow, that the elect of GOD partake of in JESUS CHRIST, "who of GOD is made unto us." And,

Secondly, I shall consider what these blessings are, "wisdom, righteousness, sanctification, and redemption."

First, I would point out to you the fountain from which all those blessings flow, that the elect of GOD partake of in JESUS, "who of GOD is made unto us," the Father, he it is who is spoken of here. Not as though JESUS CHRIST was not GOD also; but GOD the Father is the fountain of the Deity;

Deity; and, if we consider JESUS CHRIST acting as Mediator, GOD the Father is greater than he; there was an eternal contract between the Father and the Son: "I have made a covenant with my chosen, and I have sworn unto *David* my servant;" now *David* was a type of CHRIST, with whom the Father made a covenant, that if he would obey and suffer, and make himself a sacrifice for sin, he should " see his seed, he should prolong his days, and the pleasure of the LORD should prosper in his hands." This compact our LORD refers to, in that glorious prayer recorded in the 17th chapter of *John*; and therefore he prays for, or rather demands with a full assurance, all that were given to him by the Father: "Father, I will that they also whom thou hast given me, be with me where I am." For this same reason the apostle breaks out into praises of GOD, even the Father of our LORD JESUS CHRIST; for he loved the elect with an everlasting love, or, as our LORD expresses it, "before the foundation of the world;" and therefore, to shew them to whom they were beholden for their salvation, our LORD, in the 25th of *Matthew*, represents himself, saying, "Come, ye blessed children of my Father, receive the kingdom prepared for you from the foundation of the world." And thus, in reply to the mother of *Zebedee*'s children, he says, "It is not mine to give, but it shall be given to them, for whom it is prepared, of the Father." The apostle therefore, when here speaking of the christian's privileges, lest they should sacrifice to their own drag, or think their salvation was owing to their own faithfulness, or improvement of their own free-will, reminds them to look back on the everlasting love of GOD the Father; "who of GOD is made unto us, &c."

Would to GOD, this point of doctrine was considered more, and people were more studious of the covenant of redemption between the Father and the Son! we should not then have so much disputing against the doctrine of election, or hear it condemned (even by good men) as a doctrine of devils. For my own part, I cannot see how true humbleness of mind can be attained without a knowledge of it; and though I will not say, that every one who denies election is a bad man, yet I will say, with that sweet singer, Mr. *Trail*, it is a very bad

sign:

sign: such a one, whoever he be, I think cannot truly know himself: for, if we deny election, we must, partly at least, glory in ourselves; but our redemption is so ordered, that no flesh should glory in the divine presence; and hence it is, that the pride of man opposes this doctrine, because according to this doctrine, and no other, "he that glories, must glory only in the LORD." But what shall I say? Election is a mystery that shines with such resplendent brightness, that, to make use of the words of one who has drank deeply of electing love, it dazzles the weak eyes even of some of GOD's dear children; however, though they know it not, all the blessings they receive, all the privileges they do or will enjoy, through JESUS CHRIST, flow from the everlasting love of GOD the Father: "But of him are you in CHRIST JESUS, who of GOD is made unto us, wisdom, righteousness, sanctification, and redemption."

Secondly, I come to shew what these blessings are, which are here, through CHRIST, made over to the elect. And

1. *First*, CHRIST is made to them *wisdom*; but wherein does true wisdom consist? Was I to ask some of you, perhaps you would say, in indulging the lust of the flesh, and saying to your souls, eat, drink, and be merry; but this is only the wisdom of brutes; they have as good a gust and relish for sensual pleasures, as the greatest epicure on earth. Others would tell me, true wisdom consisted in adding house to house, and field to field, and calling lands after their own names; but this cannot be true wisdom; for riches often take to themselves wings, and fly away, like an eagle towards heaven. Even wisdom itself assures us, "that a man's life doth not consist in the abundance of the things which he possesses;" vanity, vanity, all these things are vanity; for, if riches leave not the owner, the owners must soon leave them; "for rich men must also die, and leave their riches for others;" their riches cannot procure them redemption from the grave, whither we are all hastening apace.

But perhaps you despise riches and pleasure, and therefore place wisdom in the knowledge of books: but it is possible for you

you to tell the numbers of the stars, and call them all by their names, and yet be mere fools; learned men are not always wise; nay, our common learning, so much cried up, makes men only so many accomplished fools; to keep you therefore no longer in suspense, and withal to humble you, I will send you to an heathen to school, to learn what true wisdom is: "Know thyself," was a saying of one of the wise men of *Greece*; this is certainly true wisdom, and this is that wisdom spoken of in the text, and which JESUS CHRIST is made to all elect sinners; they are made to know themselves, so as not to think more highly of themselves than they ought to think. Before they were darkness, now they are light in the LORD; and in that light they see their own darkness; they now bewail themselves as fallen creatures by nature, dead in trespasses and sins, sons and heirs of hell, and children of wrath; they now see that all their righteousnesses are but as filthy rags; that there is no health in their souls; that they are poor and miserable, blind and naked; and that there is no name given under heaven, whereby they can be saved, but that of JESUS CHRIST. They see the necessity of closing with a Saviour; and behold the wisdom of GOD in appointing him to be a Saviour; they are also made willing to accept of salvation upon our LORD's own terms, and to receive him as their all in all: thus CHRIST is made to them wisdom.

2. Secondly, *Righteousness*. "Who of GOD is made unto us, wisdom, righteousness;" CHRIST's whole personal righteousness is made over to, and accounted theirs. Being enabled to lay hold on CHRIST by faith, GOD the Father blots out their transgressions, as with a thick cloud; their sins, and their iniquities he remembers no more; they are made the righteousness of GOD in CHRIST JESUS, "who is the end of the law for righteousness to every one that believeth." In one sense, GOD now sees no sin in them; the whole covenant of works is fulfilled in them; they are actually justified, acquitted, and looked upon as righteous in the sight of GOD; they are perfectly accepted in the beloved; they are compleat in him; the flaming sword of GOD's wrath, which before moved every way, is now removed, and free access given to the tree of life; they are enabled to reach out the arm of faith, and pluck, and

live for evermore. Hence it is that the apostle, under a sense of this blessed privilege, breaks out into this triumphant language; "It is CHRIST that justifies, who is he that condemns?" Does sin condemn? CHRIST's righteousness delivers believers from the guilt of it: CHRIST is their Saviour, and is become a propitiation for their sins: who therefore shall lay any thing to the charge of GOD's elect? Does the law condemn? By having CHRIST's righteousness imputed to them, they are dead to the law, as a covenant of works; CHRIST has fulfilled it for them, and in their stead. Does death threaten them? they need not fear: the sting of death is sin, the strength of sin is the law; but GOD has given them the victory, by imputing to them the righteousness of the LORD JESUS.

And what a privilege is here! Well might the angels at the birth of CHRIST, say to the humble shepherds, "Behold, I bring you glad tidings of great joy;" unto you that believe in CHRIST, "a Saviour is born." And well may angels rejoice at the conversion of poor sinners: for the LORD is their righteousness; they have peace with GOD, through faith in CHRIST's blood, and shall never enter into condemnation. O believers! (for this discourse is intended in a special manner for you) lift up your heads; "Rejoice in the LORD always; again I say, rejoice." CHRIST is made to you of GOD righteousness, what then should you fear? you are made the righteousness of GOD in him; you may be called, "The LORD our righteousness." Of what then should you be afraid? what shall separate you henceforward from the love of CHRIST? "shall tribulation, or distress, or persecution, or famine, or nakedness, or peril, or sword? No, I am persuaded, neither death, nor life, nor angels, nor principalities, nor powers, nor things present, nor things to come, nor height, nor depth, nor any other creature, shall be able to separate you from the love of GOD, which is in CHRIST JESUS our LORD," who of GOD is made unto you righteousness.

This is a glorious privilege, but this is only the beginning of the happiness of believers: For

3. *Thirdly*, CHRIST is not only made to them righteousness, but *sanctification*; by sanctification, I do not mean a bare hypocritical

critical attendance on outward ordinances, though rightly-informed christians will think it their duty and privilege constantly to attend on all outward ordinances. Nor do I mean by sanctification, a bare outward reformation, and a few transient convictions, or a little legal sorrow; for all this an unsanctified man may have; but, by sanctification, I mean a total renovation of the whole man; by the righteousness of CHRIST, believers become legally, by sanctification they are made spiritually, alive; by one they are entitled to, by the other they are made meet for, glory. They are sanctified, therefore, throughout, in spirit, soul and body.

Their understandings, which were before dark, now become light in the LORD; and their wills, before contrary to, now become one with, the will of GOD: their affections are now set on things above; their memory is now filled with divine things; their natural consciences are now enlightened; their members, which were before instruments of uncleanness, and of iniquity unto iniquity, are now instruments of righteousness and true holiness; in short, they are new creatures; "old things are passed away, all things are become new," in their hearts; sin has now no longer dominion over them; they are freed from the power, though not the indwelling and being, of it; they are holy both in heart and life, in all manner of conversation; they are made partakers of a divine nature; and from JESUS CHRIST, they receive grace for grace; and every grace that is in CHRIST, is copied and transcribed into their souls; they are transformed into his likeness; he is formed within them; they dwell in him, and he in them; they are led by the Spirit, and bring forth the fruits thereof; they know that CHRIST is their *Emmanuel*, GOD with and in them; they are living temples of the Holy Ghost. And therefore, being a holy habitation unto the LORD, the whole trinity dwells and walks in them; even here, they sit together with CHRIST in heavenly places, and are vitally united to him, their head, by a living faith; their Redeemer, their Maker, is their husband; they are flesh of his flesh, bone of his bone; they talk, they walk with him, as a man talketh and walketh with his friend; in short, they are one with CHRIST, even as JESUS CHRIST and the Father are one.

Thus

Thus is CHRIST made to believers sanctification. And O what a privilege is this! to be changed from beasts into saints, and from a devilish, to be made partakers of a divine nature; to be translated from the kingdom of Satan, into the kingdom of GOD's dear Son! to put off the old man, which is corrupt, and to put on the new man, which is created after GOD, in righteousness and true holiness. O what an unspeakable blessing is this! I almost stand amazed at the contemplation thereof. Well might the apostle exhort believers to rejoice in the LORD; indeed they have reason always to rejoice, yea, to rejoice on a dying bed; for the kingdom of GOD is in them; they are changed from glory to glory, even by the Spirit of the LORD: well may this be a mystery to the natural, for it is a mystery even to the spiritual man himself, a mystery which he cannot fathom. Does it not often dazzle your eyes, O ye children of GOD, to look at your own brightness, when the candle of the LORD shines out, and your Redeemer lifts up the light of his blessed countenance upon your souls? Are not you astonished, when you feel the love of GOD shed abroad in your hearts, by the Holy Ghost, and GOD holds out the golden sceptre of his mercy, and bids you ask what you will, and it shall be given you? Does not that peace of GOD, which keeps and rules your hearts, surpass the utmost limits of your understandings? and is not the joy you feel unspeakable? is it not full of glory? I am persuaded it is; and in your secret communion, when the LORD's love flows in upon your souls, you are as it were swallowed up in, or, to use the apostle's phrase, "filled with all the fulness of GOD." Are not you ready to cry out with *Solomon,* "And will the LORD, indeed, dwell thus with men!" How is it that we should be thus thy sons and daughters, O LORD GOD Almighty!

If you are children of GOD, and know what it is to have fellowship with the Father and the Son; if you walk by faith, and not by sight; I am assured this is frequently the language of your hearts.

But look forward, and see an unbounded prospect of eternal happiness lying before thee, O believer! what thou hast already received, are only the first-fruits, like the cluster of grapes brought out of the land of *Canaan*; only an earneſt and pledge of yet infinitely better things to come: the harveſt is to follow; thy grace is hereafter to be ſwallowed up in glory. Thy great *Joſhua*, and merciful high Prieſt, ſhall adminiſter an abundant entrance to thee into the land of promiſe, that reſt which awaits the children of GOD: For CHRIST is not only made to believers, wiſdom, righteouſneſs, and ſanctification, but alſo *redemption*.

But, before we enter upon the explanation and contemplation of this privilege,

Firſt, Learn hence the great miſtake of thoſe writers, and clergy, who, notwithſtanding they talk of ſanctification and inward holineſs (as indeed ſometimes they do, though in a very looſe and ſuperficial manner) yet they generally make it the *cauſe*, whereas they ſhould conſider it as the *effect*, of our juſtification. "Of him are ye in CHRIST JESUS, who of GOD is made unto us, wiſdom, righteouſneſs, (and then) ſanctification." For CHRIST's righteouſneſs, or that which CHRIST has done in our ſtead without us, is the ſole cauſe of our acceptance in the ſight of GOD, and of all holineſs wrought in us: to this, and not to the light within, or any thing wrought within, ſhould poor ſinners ſeek for juſtification in the ſight of GOD: for the ſake of CHRIST's righteouſneſs alone, and not any thing wrought in us, does GOD look favourably upon us; our ſanctification at beſt, in this life, is not compleat: though we are delivered from the power, we are not freed from the in-being of ſin; but not only the dominion, but the in-being of ſin, is forbidden by the perfect law of GOD: for it is not ſaid, thou ſhalt not give way to luſt, but, "thou ſhalt not luſt." So that whilſt the principle of luſt remains in the leaſt degree in our hearts, though we are otherwiſe never ſo holy, yet we cannot, on account of that, hope for acceptance with GOD. We muſt firſt, therefore, look for a righteouſneſs without us, even the righteouſneſs of our LORD JESUS CHRIST: for this reaſon the apoſtle mentions it, and puts it before ſanctification in the words of the text. And whoſoever teacheth any other doctrine, doth not preach the truth as it is in JESUS.

Secondly,

Secondly, From hence alfo, the Antinomians and formal hypocrites may be confuted, who talk of CHRIST without, but know nothing, experimentally, of a work of fanctification wrought within them. Whatever they may pretend to, fince CHRIST is not in them, the LORD is not their righteoufnefs, and they have no well-grounded hope of glory: for though fanctification is not the caufe, yet it is the effect of our acceptance with GOD; "Who of GOD is made unto us righteoufnefs and fanctification." He therefore, that is really in CHRIST, is a new creature; it is not going back to a covenant of works, to look into our hearts, and, feeing that they are changed and renewed, from thence form a comfortable and well-grounded affurance of the fafety of our ftates: no, but this is what we are directed to in fcripture; by our bringing forth the fruits, we are to judge whether or no we ever did truly partake of the Spirit of GOD. "We know, (fays *John*) that we are paffed from death unto life, becaufe we love the brethren." And however we may talk of CHRIST's righteoufnefs, and exclaim againft legal preachers; yet, if we are not holy in heart and life, if we are not fanctified and renewed by the Spirit in our minds, we are felf-deceivers, we are only formal hypocrites: for we muft not put afunder what GOD has joined together; we muft keep the medium between the two extremes; not infift fo much on the one hand upon CHRIST without, as to exclude CHRIST within, as an evidence of our being his, and as a preparation for future happinefs; nor, on the other hand, fo depend on inherent righteoufnefs or holinefs wrought in us, as to exclude the righteoufnefs of JESUS CHRIST without us. But

4. *Fourthly*, Let us now go on, and take a view of the other link, or rather the end, of the believer's golden chain of privileges, *redemption*. But we muft look very high; for the top of it, like *Jacob*'s ladder, reaches heaven, where all believers will afcend, and be placed at the right-hand of GOD. "Who of GOD is made unto us, wifdom, righteoufnefs, fanctification, and *redemption*."

This is a golden chain indeed! and, what is beft of all, not one link can ever be broken afunder from another. Was there no other text in the book of GOD, this single one sufficiently proves the final perseverance of true believers: for never did GOD yet justify a man, whom he did not sanctify; nor sanctify one, whom he did not compleatly redeem and glorify; no; as for GOD, his way, his work, is perfect; he always carried on and finished the work he begun; thus it was in the first, so it is in the new creation; when GOD says, "Let there be light," there is light, that shines more and more unto the perfect day, when believers enter into their eternal rest, as GOD entered into his. Those whom GOD has justified, he has in effect glorified: for as a man's worthiness was not the cause of GOD's giving him CHRIST's righteousness, so neither shall his unworthiness be a cause of his taking it away; GOD's gifts and callings are without repentance; and I cannot think, they are clear in the notion of CHRIST's righteousness, who deny the final perseverance of the saints; I fear, they understand justification in that low sense, which I understood it in a few years ago, as implying no more than remission of sins: but it not only signifies remission of sins past, but also a *fœderal right* to all good things to come. If GOD has given us his only Son, how shall he not with him freely give us all things? Therefore, the apostle, after he says, "Who of GOD is made unto us righteousness," does not say, perhaps he may be made to us sanctification and redemption; but, "he is made:" for there is an eternal, indissoluble connection between these blessed privileges. As the obedience of CHRIST is imputed to believers, so his perseverance in that obedience is to be imputed to them also: and it argues great ignorance of the covenant of grace and redemption, to object against it.

By the word *redemption*, we are to understand, not only a compleat deliverance from all evil, but also a full enjoyment of all good both in body and soul: I say, both in body and soul; for the LORD is also for the body; the bodies of the saints in this life are temples of the Holy Ghost; GOD makes a covenant with the dust of believers; after death, though worms destroy them, yet, even in their flesh shall they see GOD. I fear, indeed, there are some *Sadducees* in our days, or at least heretics, who say, either, that there is no resurrection of the body, or that the resurrection is past already, namely, in our regeneration:

regeneration: Hence it is, that our Lord's coming in the flesh, at the day of judgment, is denied; and consequently, we must throw aside the sacrament of the Lord's supper. For why should we remember the Lord's death until he comes to judgment, when he is already come to judge our hearts, and will not come a second time? but all this is only the reasoning of unlearned, unstable men, who certainly know not what they say, nor whereof they affirm. That we must follow our Lord in the regeneration, be partakers of a new birth, and that Christ must come into our hearts, we freely confess; and we hope, when speaking of these things, we speak no more than what we know and feel: but then it is plain, that Jesus Christ will come, hereafter, to judgment, and that he ascended into heaven with the body which he had here on earth; for says he, after his resurrection, "Handle me, and see; a spirit has not flesh and bones, as you see me have." And it is plain, that Christ's resurrection was an earnest of ours: for says the apostle, "Christ is risen from the dead, and become the first-fruits of them that sleep;" and as in *Adam* all die, and are subject to mortality; so all that are in Christ, the second *Adam*, who represented believers as their fœderal head, shall certainly be made alive, or rise again with their bodies at the last day.

Here then, O believers! is one, though the lowest, degree of that redemption which you are to be partakers of hereafter; I mean, the redemption of your bodies: for this corruptible must put on incorruption, this mortal must put on immortality. Your bodies, as well as souls, were given to Jesus Christ by the Father; they have been companions in watching, and fasting, and praying: your bodies therefore, as well as souls, shall Jesus Christ raise up at the last day. Fear not, therefore, O believers, to look into the grave; for to you it is no other than a consecrated dormitory, where your bodies shall sleep quietly until the morning of the resurrection; when the voice of the archangel shall sound, and the trump of God give the general alarm, "Arise ye dead, and come to judgment;" earth, air, fire, water, shall give up your scattered atoms, and both in body and soul shall you be ever with the Lord. I doubt not, but many of you are groaning under crazy bodies, and complain often that the mortal body weighs down the immortal soul; at least this is my case; but let us have a little patience, and we shall be delivered from our earthly prisons; ere long, these tabernacles of clay shall be dissolved, and we shall be clothed with our house which is from heaven; hereafter, our bodies shall be spiritualized, and shall be so far from hindering our souls through weakness, that they shall become strong; so strong, as to bear up under an exceeding and eternal weight of glory; others again may have deformed bodies, emaciated also with sickness, and worn out with labour and age; but wait a little, until your blessed change by death comes; then your bodies shall be renewed and made glorious, like unto CHRIST's glorious body: of which we may form some faint idea, from the account given us of our LORD's transfiguration on the mount, when it is said, " His raiment became bright and glistering, and his face brighter than the sun." Well then may a believer break out in the apostle's triumphant language, " O death, where is thy sting! O grave, where is thy victory!"

But what is the redemption of the body, in comparison of the redemption of the better part, our souls? I must, therefore, say to you believers, as the angel said to *John*, " Come up higher," and let us take as clear a view as we can, at such a distance, of the redemption CHRIST has purchased for, and will shortly put you in actual possession of. Already you are justified, already you are sanctified, and thereby freed from the guilt and dominion of sin: but, as I have observed, the being and indwelling of sin yet remains in you; GOD sees it proper to leave some *Amalekites* in the land, to keep his *Israel* in action. The most perfect christian, I am persuaded, must agree, according to one of our articles, " That the corruption of na-
" ture remains even in the regenerate; that the flesh lusteth
" always against the spirit, and the spirit against the flesh."
So that believers cannot do things for GOD with that perfection they desire; this grieves their righteous souls day by day, and, with the holy apostle, makes them cry out, " Who shall deliver us from the body of this death!" I thank GOD, our LORD JESUS CHRIST will, but not compleatly before the day of our dissolution; then will the very being of sin be destroyed,

and

and an eternal stop put to inbred, indwelling corruption. And is not this a great redemption? I am sure believers esteem it so: for there is nothing grieves the heart of a child of God so much, as the remains of indwelling sin. Again, believers are often in heaviness through manifold temptations; God sees that it is needful and good for them so to be; and though they may be highly favoured, and wrapt up in communion with God, even to the third heavens; yet a messenger of Satan is often sent to buffet them, lest they should be puffed up with the abundance of revelations. But be not weary, be not faint in your minds: the time of your compleat redemption draweth nigh. In heaven the wicked one shall cease from troubling you, and your weary souls shall enjoy an everlasting rest; his fiery darts cannot reach those blissful regions: Satan will never come any more to appear with, disturb, or accuse the sons of God, when once the Lord Jesus Christ shuts the door. Your righteous souls are now grieved, day by day, at the ungodly conversation of the wicked; tares now grow up among the wheat; wolves come in sheeps clothing: but the redemption spoken of in the text, will free your souls from all anxiety on these accounts; hereafter you shall enjoy a perfect communion of saints; nothing that is unholy or unsanctified shall enter into the Holy of holies, which is prepared for you above: this, and all manner of evil whatsoever, you shall be delivered from, when your redemption is hereafter made compleat in heaven; not only so, but you shall enter into the full enjoyment of all good. It is true, all saints will not have the same degree of happiness, but all will be as happy as their hearts can desire. Believers, you shall judge the evil, and familiarly converse with good, angels: you shall sit down with *Abraham*, *Isaac*, *Jacob*, and all the spirits of just men made perfect; and, to sum up all your happiness in one word, you shall see God the Father, Son, and Holy Ghost; and, by seeing God, be more and more like unto him, and pass from glory to glory, even to all eternity.

But I must stop: the glories of the upper world croud in so fast upon my soul, that I am lost in the contemplation of them. Brethren, the redemption spoken of is unutterable; we cannot here find it out; eye hath not seen, nor ear heard, nor has it entered into the hearts of the moſt holy men living, to conceive how great it is. Was I to entertain you whole ages with an account of it, when you come to heaven, you muſt ſay, with the Queen of *Sheba*, " Not half, no, not one thouſandth part was told us." All we can do here, is to go upon mount *Piſgah*, and by the eye of faith, take a diſtant view of the promiſed land: We may ſee it, as *Abraham* did CHRIST, afar off, and rejoice in it; but here we only know in part. Bleſſed be GOD, there is a time coming, when we ſhall know GOD, even as we are known, and GOD be all in all. LORD JESUS, accompliſh the number of thine elect! LORD JESUS, haſten thy kingdom!

And now, where are the ſcoffers of theſe laſt days, who count the lives of chriſtians to be madneſs, and their end to be without honour? Unhappy men! you know not what you do. Were your eyes open, and had you ſenſes to diſcern ſpiritual things, you would not ſpeak all manner of evil againſt the children of GOD, but you would eſteem them as the excellent ones of the earth, and envy their happineſs: your ſouls would hunger and thirſt after it: you alſo would become fools for CHRIST's ſake. You boaſt of wiſdom; ſo did the philoſophers of *Corinth*: but your wiſdom is the fooliſhneſs of folly in the ſight of GOD. What will your wiſdom avail you, if it does not make you wiſe unto ſalvation? Can you, with all your wiſdom, propoſe a more conſiſtent ſcheme to build your hopes of ſalvation on, than what has been now laid before you? Can you, with all the ſtrength of natural reaſon, find out a better way of acceptance with GOD, than by the righteouſneſs of the LORD JESUS CHRIST? Is it right to think your own works can in any meaſure deſerve or procure it? If not, Why will you not believe in him? Why will you not ſubmit to his righteouſneſs? Can you deny that you are fallen creatures? Do not you find that you are full of diſorders, and that theſe diſorders make you unhappy? Do not you find that you cannot change your own hearts? Have you not reſolved many and many a time, and have not your corruptions yet dominion over you? Are you not bond-ſlaves to your luſts, and led captive by the devil at his will? Why then will you not come to CHRIST for ſanctification? Do you not defire to die the death of the righteous, and that your future ftate may be like theirs ? I am perfuaded you cannot bear the thoughts of being annihilated, much lefs of being miferable for ever. Whatever you may pretend, if you fpeak truth, you muft confefs, that confcience breaks in upon you in your more fober intervals whether you will or not, and even conftrains you to believe, that hell is no painted fire. And why then will you not come to CHRIST ? He alone can procure you everlafting redemption. Hafte, hafte away to him, poor beguiled finners. You lack wifdom; afk it of CHRIST. Who knows but he may give it you ? He is able: for he is the wifdom of the Father ; he is that wifdom which was from everlafting. You have no righteoufnefs; away, therefore, to CHRIST : " He is the end of the law for righteoufnefs to every one that believeth." You are unholy ; flee to the LORD JESUS: He is full of grace and truth ; and of his fulnefs all may receive that believe in him. You are afraid to die ; let this drive you to CHRIST: He has the keys of death and hell ; in him is plenteous redemption ; he alone can open the door which leads to everlafting life. Let not, therefore, the deceived reafoner boaft any longer of his pretended reafon. Whatever you may think, it is the moft unreafonable thing in the world, not to believe on JESUS CHRIST, whom GOD hath fent. Why, why will you die ? why will you not come unto him, that you may have life ? " Ho! every one that thirfteth, come unto the waters of life and drink freely : come, buy without money and without price." Were thefe bleffed privileges in the text to be purchafed with money, you might fay, We are poor, and cannot buy : or, were they to be conferred only on finners of fuch a rank or degree, then you might fay, How can fuch finners as we expect to be fo highly favoured ? But they are to be freely given of GOD to the worft of finners. " To us," fays the Apoftle ; to me a perfecutor, to you *Corinthians*, who were " unclean, drunkards, covetous perfons, idolaters." Therefore, each poor finner may fay then, Why not unto me ? Has CHRIST but one bleffing ? What if he has bleffed millions already, by turning them away from their iniquities ; yet, he ftill continues the fame : he lives for ever to make interceffion, and therefore will blefs you, even you alfo. Though, *Efau* like, you have been

been prophane, and hitherto despised your heavenly Father's birth-right; even now, if you believe, "CHRIST will be made to you of GOD, wisdom, righteousness, sanctification, and redemption."

But I must turn again to believers, for whose instruction, as I observed before, this discourse was particularly intended. You see, brethren, partakers of the heavenly calling, what great blessings are treasured up for you in JESUS CHRIST your head, and what you are entitled to by believing on his name. Take heed, therefore, that ye walk worthy of the vocation wherewith ye are called. Think often how highly you are favoured; and remember, you have not chosen CHRIST, but CHRIST hath chosen you. Put on (as the elect of GOD) humbleness of mind, and glory, but let it be only in the LORD: for you have nothing but what you have received of GOD. By nature ye were as foolish, as legal, as unholy, and in as damnable a condition as others. Be pitiful, therefore, be courteous; and, as sanctification is a progressive work, beware of thinking you have already attained. Let him that is holy, be holy still; knowing, that he who is most pure in heart, shall hereafter enjoy the clearest vision of GOD. Let indwelling sin be your daily burden; and not only bewail and lament, but see that you subdue it daily by the power of divine grace; and look up to JESUS continually to be the finisher, as well as author of your faith. Build not on your own faithfulness, but on GOD's unchangeableness. Take heed of thinking you stand by the power of your own free-will. The everlasting love of GOD the Father, must be your only hope and consolation: let this support you under all trials. Remember that GOD's gifts and callings are without repentance; that CHRIST having once loved you, will love you to the end. Let this constrain you to obedience, and make you long and look for that blessed time, when he shall not only be your wisdom, and righteousness, and sanctification, but also compleat and everlasting redemption.

Glory be to GOD in the highest!

SERMON

SERMON XLV.

The Knowledge of Jesus Christ the best Knowledge.

---

1 Cor. ii. 2.

I determined not to know any thing among you, save Jesus Christ, *and him crucified.*

THE persons to whom these words were written, were the members of the church of *Corinth*; who, as appears by the foregoing chapter, were not only divided into different sects, by one saying, " I am of *Paul*, and another, I am of *Apollos*;" but also had many amongst them, who were so full of the wisdom of this world, and so wise in their own eyes, that they set at nought the simplicity of the gospel, and accounted the Apostle's preaching foolishness.

Never had the Apostle more need of the wisdom of the serpent, mingled with the innocency of the dove, than now. What is the sum of all his wisdom? he tells them, in the words of the text, " I determined not to know any thing amongst you, save Jesus Christ, and him crucified."

A resolution this, worthy of the great St. *Paul*; and no less worthy, no less necessary for every minister, and every disciple of Christ, to make always, even unto the end of the world.

In the following discourse, I shall,

First, Explain what is meant by " not knowing any thing, save Jesus Christ, and him crucified."

Secondly, Give some reasons why every christian should determine not to know any thing else. And

Thirdly, Conclude with a general exhortation to put this determination into practice.

First, I am to explain what is meant by " not knowing any thing, save JESUS CHRIST, and him crucified."

By JESUS CHRIST, we are to understand the eternal Son of GOD. He is called JESUS, a Saviour, because he was to save us from the guilt and power of our sins; and, like *Joshua*, by whom he was remarkably typified, to lead GOD's spiritual *Israel* through the wilderness of this world, to the heavenly *Canaan*, the promised inheritance of the children of GOD.

He is called *Christ*, which signifies anointed, because he was anointed by the Holy Ghost at his baptism, to be a prophet to instruct, a priest to make an atonement for, and a king to govern and protect his church. And he was crucified, or hung (O stupendous love!) till he was dead upon the cross, that he might become a curse for us: for it is written, " Cursed is every man that hangeth upon a tree."

The foundation or first cause of his suffering, was our fall in *Adam*; in whom, as the living oracles of GOD declare, " We all died;" his sin was imputed to us all." It pleased GOD, after he had spoken the world into being, to create man after his own divine image, to breathe into him the breath of life, and to place him as our representative in the garden of *Eden*.

But he being left to his own free will, did eat of the forbidden fruit, notwithstanding GOD had told him, " The day in which he eat thereof, he should surely die;" and thereby he, with his whole posterity, in whose name he acted, became liable to the wrath of GOD, and sunk into a spiritual death.

But

But behold the goodness, as well as the severity of GOD! For no sooner had man been convicted as a sinner, but lo! a Saviour is revealed to him, under the character of the *seed of the woman:* the merits of whose sacrifice were then immediately to take place, and who should, in the fulness of time, by suffering death, satisfy for the guilt we had contracted; by obeying the whole moral law, work out for us an everlasting righteousness; and by becoming a principle of new life in us, destroy the power of the devil, and thereby restore us to a better state than that in which we were at first created.

This is the plain scriptural account of that mystery of godliness, GOD manifested in the flesh; and to this our own hearts, unless blinded by the god of this world, cannot but yield an immediate assent.

For, let us but search our own hearts, and ask ourselves, if we could create our own children, whether or not we would not create them with a less mixture of good and evil, than we find in ourselves? Supposing GOD then only to have our goodness, he could not, at first, make us so sinful, so polluted as we are. But supposing him to be as he is, infinitely good, or goodness itself, then it is absolutely impossible that he should create any thing but what is like himself, perfect, entire, lacking nothing. Man then could not come out of the hands of his Maker, so miserably blind and naked, with such a mixture of the beast and devil, as he finds now in himself, but must have fallen from what he was; and as it does not suit with the goodness and justness of GOD, to punish the whole race of mankind with these disorders merely for nothing; and since men bring these disorders into the world with them; it follows, that as they could not sin themselves, being yet unborn, some other man's sin must have been imputed to them; from whence, as from a fountain, all these evils flow.

I know this doctrine of our *original sin*, or fall in *Adam*, is esteemed foolishness by the wise disputer of this world, who will reply, How does it suit the goodness of GOD, to impute

one

one man's sin to an innocent posterity ? But has it not been proved to a demonstration, that it is so ? And therefore, supposing we cannot reconcile it to our shallow comprehensions, that is no argument at all : for if it appears that GOD has done a thing, we may be sure it is right, whether we can see the reasons for it or not.

But this is entirely cleared up by what was said before, that no sooner was the sin imputed, but a CHRIST was revealed; and this CHRIST, this GOD incarnate, who was conceived by the Holy Ghost, that he might be freed from the guilt of our original sin ; who was born of the Virgin *Mary*, that he might be the seed of the woman only ; who suffered under *Pontius Pilate*, a *Gentile* governor, to fulfil these prophecies, which signified what death he should die : This same JESUS, who was crucified in weakness, but raised in power, is that divine person, that *Emmanuel*, that GOD with us, whom we preach, in whom ye believe, and whom alone the Apostle, in the text, was determined to know.

By which word *know*, we are not to understand a bare historical knowledge ; for to know that CHRIST was crucified by his enemies at *Jerusalem*, in this manner only, will do us no more service, than to know that *Cæsar* was butchered by his friends at *Rome*; but the word *know*, means to know, so as to approve of him ; as when CHRIST says, " Verily, I know you not ;" I know you not, so as to approve of you. It signifies to know him, so as to embrace him in all his offices ; to take him to be our prophet, priest, and king ; so as to give up ourselves wholly to be instructed, saved, and governed by him. It implies an experimental knowledge of his crucifixion, so as to feel the power of it, and to be crucified unto the world, as the Apostle explains himself in the epistle to the *Philippians*, where he says, " I count all things but dung and dross, that I might know him, and the power of his resurrection."

This knowledge the Apostle was so swallowed up in, that he was determined not to know any thing else ; he was resolved to make that his only study, the governing principle of his

his life, the point and end in which all his thoughts, words, and actions, should center.

Secondly, I pass on to give some reasons why every christian should, with the Apostle, determine " not to know any thing, save JESUS CHRIST, and him crucified."

First, Without this, our persons will not be accepted in the sight of GOD." " This (and consequently this only) is life eternal, to know thee, the only true GOD, and JESUS CHRIST, whom thou hast sent." As also St. *Peter* says, " There is now no other name given under heaven, whereby we can be saved, but that of JESUS CHRIST."

Some, indeed, may please themselves in knowing the world, others boast themselves in the knowledge of a multitude of languages; but could we speak with the tongue of men and angels, or did we know the number of the stars, and could call them all by their names, yet, without this experimental knowledge of JESUS CHRIST, and him crucified, it would profit us nothing.

The former, indeed, may procure us a little honour, which cometh of man; but the latter only can render us acceptable in the sight of GOD: for, if we are ignorant of CHRIST, GOD will be to us a consuming fire.

CHRIST is the way, the truth, and the life; " No one cometh to the Father, but through him;" " He is the Lamb slain from the foundation of the world;" and none ever were, or ever will be received up into glory, but by an experimental application of his merits to their hearts.

We might as well think to rebuild the tower of *Babel*, or reach heaven with our hands, as to imagine we could enter therein by any other door, than that of the knowledge of JESUS CHRIST. Other knowledge may make you wise in your own eyes, and puff you up; but this alone edifieth, and maketh wise unto salvation.

As the meanest christian, if he knows but this, though he know nothing else, will be accepted; so the greatest master in *Israel*, the most letter-learned teacher, without this, will be rejected. His philosophy is mere nonsense, his wisdom mere foolishness in the sight of GOD.

The author of the words now before us, was a remarkable instance of this; never, perhaps, was a greater scholar, in all what the world calls fine learning, than he: for he was bred up at the feet of *Gamaliel*, and profited in the knowledge of books, as well as in the *Jewish* religion, above many of his equals, as appears by the language, rhetoric, and spirit of his writings; and yet, when he came to know what it was to be a christian, " He accounted all things but loss, so he might win CHRIST." And, though he was now at *Corinth*, that seat of polite learning, yet he was absolutely determined not to know any thing, or to make nothing his study, but what taught him to know JESUS CHRIST, and him crucified.

Hence then, appears the folly of those who spend their whole lives in heaping up other knowledge; and, instead of searching the scriptures, which testify of JESUS CHRIST, and are alone able to make them wise unto salvation, disquiet themselves in a pursuit after the knowledge of such things, as when known, concern them no more, than to know that a bird dropped a feather upon one of the *Pyrenean* mountains.

Hence it is, that so many, who profess themselves wise, because they can dispute of the causes and effects, the moral fitness and unfitness of things, appear mere fools in the things of GOD; so that when you come to converse with them about the great work of redemption wrought out for us by JESUS CHRIST, and of his being a propitiation for our sins, a fulfiller of the covenant of works, and a principle of new life to our souls, they are quite ignorant of the whole matter; and prove, to a demonstration, that, with all their learning, they know nothing yet, as they ought to know.

But, alas! how must it surprize a man, when the Most High is about to take away his soul, to think that he has

passed

passed for a wise man, and a learned disputer in this world, and yet is left destitute of that knowledge which alone can make him appear with boldness before the judgment-seat of JESUS CHRIST? How must it grieve him, in a future state, to see others, whom he despised as illiterate men, because they experimentally knew CHRIST, and him crucified, exalted to the right-hand of GOD; and himself, with all his fine accomplishments, because he knew every thing, perhaps, but CHRIST, thrust down into hell?

Well might the Apostle, in a holy triumph, cry out, "Where is the wise? Where is the scribe? Where is the disputer of this world?" For, GOD will then make foolish the wisdom of this world, and bring to nought the wisdom of those who were so knowing in their own eyes.

I have made this digression from the main point before us, not to condemn or decry human literature; but to shew, that it ought to be used only in subordination to divine; and that a christian, if the Holy Spirit guided the pen of the Apostle, when he wrote this epistle, ought to study no books, but such as lead him to a farther knowledge of JESUS CHRIST, and him crucified.

And there is the more reason for this, because of the great mischief the contrary practice has done to the church of GOD: for, what was it but this learning, or rather this ignorance, that kept so many of the Scribes and Pharisees from the saving knowledge of JESUS CHRIST? And what is it, but this human wisdom, this science, falsely so called, that blinds the understanding, and corrupts the hearts of so many modern unbelievers, and makes them unwilling to submit to the righteousness which is of GOD by faith in CHRIST JESUS? But,

Secondly, Without this knowledge our performances, as well as persons, will not be acceptable in the sight of GOD.

"Through faith," says the Apostle, that is, through a lively faith in a Mediator to come, "*Abel* offered a more acceptable

ceptable facrifice than *Cain*." And it is through a like faith, or an experimental knowledge of the fame divine Mediator, that our facrifices of prayer, praife, and thankfgivings, come up as an incenfe before the throne of grace.

Two perfons may go up to the temple to pray; but he only will return home juftified, who, in the language of our collects, fincerely offers up his prayers through JESUS CHRIST our LORD.

For it is this great atonement, this all-fufficient facrifice, which alone can give us boldnefs to approach with our prayers to the Holy of Holies: and he that prefumes to go without this, acts *Korah*'s crime over again; offers unto GOD ftrange fire, and, confequently, will be rejected by him.

Farther, as our devotions to GOD will not, fo neither, without this knowledge of JESUS CHRIST, will our acts of charity to men be accepted by him. For did we give all our goods to feed the poor, and yet were deftitute of this knowledge, it would profit us nothing.

This our bleffed LORD himfelf intimates in the xxvth of *Matthew*, where he tells thofe who had been rich in good works, "That inafmuch as they did it unto one of the leaft of his brethren, they did it unto him." From whence we may plainly infer, that it is feeing CHRIST in his members, and doing good to them out of an experimental knowledge of his love to us, that alone will render our alms-deeds rewardable at the laft day.

Laftly, As neither our acts of piety nor charity, fo neither will our civil nor moral actions be acceptable to GOD, without this experimental knowledge of JESUS CHRIST.

Our modern pretenders to reafon, indeed, fet up another principle to act from; they talk, I know not what, Of doing moral and civil duties of life, from the moral fitnefs and unfitnefs of things. But fuch men are blind, however they may pretend to fee; and going thus about to eftablifh their own righte-

righteousness, are utterly ignorant of the righteousness which is of God by faith in Christ Jesus.

For though we grant that morality is a substantial part of christianity, and that Christ came not to destroy, or take off the moral law, as a rule of action, but to explain, and so fulfil it; yet we affirm, that our moral and civil actions are now no farther acceptable in the sight of God the Father, than as they proceed from the principle of a new nature, and an experimental knowledge of, or vital faith in his dear Son.

The death of Jesus Christ has turned our whole lives into one continued sacrifice; and whether we eat or drink, whether we pray to God, or do any thing to man, it must all be done out of a love for, and knowledge of him who died and rose again, to render all, even our most ordinary deeds, acceptable in the sight of God.

If we live by this principle, if Christ be the Alpha and Omega of all our actions, then our least are acceptable sacrifices; but if this principle be wanting, our most pompous services avail nothing: we are but spiritual idolaters; we sacrifice to our own net; we make an idol of ourselves, by making ourselves, and not Christ, the end of our actions: and, therefore, such actions are so far from being accepted by God, that, according to the language of one of the Articles of our Church, " We doubt not but they have the nature of " sin, because they spring not from an experimental faith in, " and knowledge of Jesus Christ."

Were we not fallen creatures, we might then act, perhaps, from other principles; but since we are fallen from God in *Adam*, and are restored again only by the obedience and death of Jesus Christ, the face of things is entirely changed, and all we think, speak, or do, is only accepted in and through him.

Justly, therefore, may I, in the

Third and *Last* place, Exhort you to put the Apostle's resolution in practice, and beseech you, with him, to determine,

"Not to know any thing, save JESUS CHRIST, and him crucified."

I say, *determine*; for unless you sit down first, and count the cost, and from a well-grounded conviction of the excellency of this, above all other knowledge whatsoever, resolve to make this your chief study, your only end, your one thing needful, every frivolous temptation will draw you aside from the pursuit after it.

Your friends and carnal acquaintance, and, above all, your grand adversary the devil, will be persuading you to determine not to know any thing, but how to lay up goods for many years, and to get a knowledge and taste of the pomps and vanities of this wicked world; but do you determine not to follow, or be led by them; and the more they persuade you to know other things, the more do you " determine not to know any thing, save JESUS CHRIST, and him crucified." For, this knowledge never faileth; but whether they be riches, they shall fail; whether they be pomps, they shall cease; whether they be vanities, they shall fade away: but the knowledge of JESUS CHRIST, and him crucified, abideth for ever.

Whatever, therefore, you are ignorant of, be not ignorant of this. If you know CHRIST, and him crucified, you know enough to make you happy, supposing you know nothing else; and without this, all your other knowledge cannot keep you from being everlastingly miserable.

Value not then, the contempt of friends, which you must necessarily meet with upon your open profession to act according to this determination. For your Master, whose you are, was despised before you; and all that will know nothing else but JESUS CHRIST, and him crucified, must, in some degree or other, suffer persecution.

It is necessary that offences should come, to try what is in our hearts, and whether we will be faithful soldiers of JESUS CHRIST or not.

Dare ye then to confefs our bleffed Mafter before men, and to fhine as lights in the world, amidft a crooked and perverfe generation? Let us not be content with following him afar off; for then we fhall, as *Peter* did, foon deny him; but let us be altogether chriftians, and let our fpeech, and all our actions declare to the world whofe difciples we are, and that we have indeed " determined not to know any thing, fave JESUS CHRIST, and him crucified." Then, well will it be with us, and happy, unfpeakably happy fhall we be, even here; and what is infinitely better, when others that defpifed us, fhall be calling for the mountains to fall on them, and the hills to cover them, we fhall be exalted to fit down on the right-hand of GOD, and fhine as the fun in the firmament, in the kingdom of our moft adorable Redeemer, for ever and ever.

Which GOD of his infinite mercy grant, &c.

SERMON XLVI,

Of Justification by CHRIST.

---

1 COR. vi. 11.

But ye are justified.

The whole verse is: *And such were some of you; but ye are washed, but ye are sanctified, but ye are justified in the name of our* LORD JESUS CHRIST, *and by the Spirit of our* GOD.

IT has been objected by some, who dissent from, nay, I may add, by others also, who actually are friends to the present ecclesiastical establishment, that the ministers of the Church of *England* preach themselves, and not CHRIST JESUS the LORD; that they entertain their people with lectures of mere morality, without declaring to them the glad tidings of salvation by JESUS CHRIST. How well grounded such an objection may be, is not my business to enquire: All I shall say at present to the point is, that whenever such a grand objection is urged against the whole body of the clergy in general, every honest minister of JESUS CHRIST should do his utmost to cut off all manner of occasion, from those who desire an occasion to take offence at us; that so by hearing us continually sounding forth the word of truth, and declaring with all boldness and assurance of faith, " that there is no other name given under heaven, whereby they can be saved, but that of JESUS CHRIST," they may be ashamed of this their same confident boasting against us.

It was an eye to this objection, joined with the agreeableness and delightfulness of the subject (for who can but delight to talk of that which the blessed angels desire to look into?) that induces me to discourse a little on that great and fundamental article of our faith; namely, our being freely justified by the precious blood of JESUS CHRIST. " But ye are washed, but ye are sanctified, but ye are justified, in the name of our LORD JESUS CHRIST, and by the Spirit of our GOD."

The words beginning with the particle *but*, have plainly a reference to something before; it may not therefore be improper, before I descend to particulars, to consider the words as they stand in relation to the context. The apostle, in the verses immediately foregoing, had been reckoning up many notorious sins, drunkenness, adultery, fornication, and such like, the commission of which, without a true and hearty repentance, he tells the *Corinthians*, would entirely shut them out of the kingdom of GOD. But then, lest they should, on the one hand, grow spiritually proud by seeing themselves differ from their unconverted brethren, and therefore be tempted to set them at nought, and say with the self-conceited hypocrite in the prophet, " Come not nigh me, for I am holier than thou;" or, on the other hand, by looking back on the multitude of their past offences, should be apt to think their sins were too many and grievous to be forgiven: he first, in order to keep them humble, reminds them of their sad state before conversion, telling them in plain terms, " such (or as it might be read, these things) were some of you;" not only one, but all that sad catalogue of vices I have been drawing up, some of you were once guilty of; but then, at the same time, to preserve them from despair, behold he brings them glad tidings of great joy: " But ye are washed; but ye are sanctified, but ye are justified in the name of our LORD JESUS CHRIST, and by the Spirit of our GOD."

The former part of this text, our being *sanctified*, I have in some measure treated of already; I would now enlarge on our being freely justified by the precious obedience and death of JESUS CHRIST: " But ye are justified in the name of our LORD JESUS CHRIST."

From which words I shall consider three things;

First, What is meant by the word *justified*.

Secondly, I shall endeavour to prove that all mankind in general, and every individual person in particular, stands in need of being justified.

Thirdly, That there is no possibility of obtaining this justification, which we so much want, but by the all-perfect obedience, and precious death of JESUS CHRIST.

First, I am to consider what is meant by the word justified.

"But ye are justified," says the apostle; which is, as though he had said, you have your sins forgiven, and are looked upon by GOD as though you never had offended him at all: for that is the meaning of the word justified, in almost all the passages of holy scripture where this word is mentioned. Thus, when this same apostle writes to the *Romans*, he tells them, that "whom GOD called, those he also justified:" And that this word justified, implies a blotting out of all our transgressions, is manifest from what follows, "them he also glorified," which could not be if a justified person was not looked upon by GOD, as though he never had offended him at all. And again, speaking of *Abraham's* faith, he tells them, that "*Abraham* believed on Him that justifies the ungodly," who acquits and clears the ungodly man; for it is a law-term, and alludes to a judge acquitting an accused criminal of the thing laid to his charge. Which expression the apostle himself explains by a quotation out of the *Psalms:* "Blessed is the man to whom the LORD imputeth no sin." From all which proofs, and many others that might be urged, it is evident, that by being justified, we are to understand, being so acquitted in the sight of GOD as to be looked upon as though we never had offended him at all. And in this sense we are to understand that article, which we profess to believe

believe in our creed, when each of us declare in his own perſon, I believe the forgiveneſs of ſins. This leads me to the

Second thing propoſed, to prove that all mankind in general, and every individual perſon in particular, ſtands in need of being juſtified.

And indeed the apoſtle ſuppoſes this in the words of the text: "But ye are juſtified," thereby implying that the *Corinthians* (and conſequently all mankind, there being no difference, as will be ſhewn hereafter) ſtood in need of being juſtified.

But not to reſt in bare ſuppoſitions, in my farther enlargement on this head, I ſhall endeavour to prove, that we all ſtand in need of being juſtified on account of the ſin of our natures, and the ſin of our lives.

1. *Firſt*, I affirm that we all ſtand in need of being juſtified, on account of the ſin of our natures: for we are all chargeable with original ſin, or the ſin of our firſt parents. Which, though a propoſition that may be denied by a ſelf-juſtifying infidel, who "will not come to CHRIST that he may have life;" yet can never be denied by any one who believes that St. *Paul*'s epiſtles were written by divine inſpiration; where we are told, that "in *Adam* all died;" that is, *Adam*'s ſin was imputed to all: and leſt we ſhould forget to make a particular application, it is added in another place, "that there is none that doeth good (that is, by nature) no, not one: That we are all gone out of the way, (of original righteouſneſs) and are by nature the children of wrath." And even *David*, who was a man after GOD's own heart, and, if any one could, might ſurely plead an exemption from this univerſal corruption, yet he confeſſes, that "he was ſhapen in iniquity, and that in ſin did his mother conceive him." And, to mention but one text more, as immediately applicable to the preſent purpoſe, St. *Paul*, in his epiſtle to the *Romans*, ſays, that "Death came upon all men, for the diſobedience of one, namely, of *Adam*, even upon

upon those, (that is, little children) who had not sinned after the similitude of *Adam*'s transgression;" who had not been guilty of actual sin, and therefore could not be punished with temporal death (which came into the world, as this same apostle elsewhere informs us, only by sin) had not the disobedience of our first parents been imputed to them. So that what has been said in this point seems to be excellently summed up in that article of our church, where she declares, that " Original sin standeth not in the following of *Adam*, " but it is the fault and corruption of every man, that na- " turally is engendered of the offspring of *Adam*; whereby " man is very far gone from original righteousness, and is " of his own nature inclined to evil, so that the flesh lusteth " always contrary to the spirit; and therefore in every person " born into this world, it deserveth GOD's wrath and damna- " tion."

I have been more particular in treating of this point, because it is the very foundation of the christian religion: For I am verily persuaded, that it is nothing but a want of being well grounded in the doctrine of original sin, and of the helpless, nay, I may say, damnable condition, each of us comes into the world in, that makes so many infidels oppose, and so many who call themselves christians, so very lukewarm in their love and affections to JESUS CHRIST. It is this, and I could almost say, this only, that makes infidelity abound among us so much as it does. For, alas! we are mistaken if we imagine that men now commence or continue infidels, and set up corrupted reason in opposition to divine revelation merely for want of evidence, (for I believe it might easily be proved, that a modern unbeliever is the most credulous creature living;) no, it is only for want of an humble mind, of a sense of their original depravity, and a willingness to own themselves so depraved, that makes them so obstinately shut their eyes against the light of the glorious gospel of CHRIST. Whereas, on the contrary, were they but once pricked to the heart with a due and lively sense of their natural corruption and liableness to condemnation, we should have them no more scoffing at divine revelation, and looking on it as an idle tale; but they would cry out with

the

the trembling jaylor, " What shall I do to be saved ?" It was an error in this fundamental point, that made so many resist the evidence the Son of GOD himself gave of his divine mission, when he tabernacled amongst us. Every word he spake, every action he did, every miracle he wrought, proved that he came from GOD. And why then did so many harden their hearts, and would not believe his report? Why, he himself informs us, " They will not come unto me that they may have life :" They will obstinately stand out against those means GOD had appointed for their salvation : And St. *Paul* tells us, " that if the gospel be hid, it is hid to them that are lost ; in whom the GOD of this world hath blinded the eyes of them which believe not, lest the light of the glorious gospel of CHRIST, who is the image of GOD, should shine upon them." 2 *Cor.* iv. 3, 4.

If it be asked, how it suits with the divine goodness, to impute the guilt of one man's sin, to an innocent posterity ? I should think it sufficient to make use of the apostle's words : " Nay, but O man, who art thou that repliest against GOD ? Shall the thing formed say to him that formed it, why hast thou made me thus ?" But to come to a more direct reply : Persons would do well to consider that in the first covenant GOD made with man, *Adam* acted as a public person, as the common representative of all mankind, and consequently we must stand or fall with him. Had he continued in his obedience, and not eaten the forbidden fruit, the benefits of that obedience would doubtless have been imputed to us : But since he did not persist in it, but broke the covenant made with him, and us in him ; who dares charge the righteous Judge of all the earth with injustice for imputing that to us also ? I proceed,

Secondly, To prove that we stand in need of being justified, on account of the sin of our lives.

That GOD, as he made man, has a right to demand his obedience, I suppose is a truth no one will deny : that he hath also given us both a natural and a written law, whereby we are to be judged, cannot be questioned by any one who

believes

believes *St. Paul's* epistle to the *Romans* to be of divine authority: For in it we are told of a law written in the heart, and a law given by *Moses*; and that each of us hath broken these laws, is too evident from our sad and frequent experience. Accordingly the holy scriptures inform us that " there is no man which liveth and sinneth not;" that " in many things we offend all;" that " if we say we have no sin we deceive ourselves," and such like. And if we are thus offenders against GOD, it follows, that we stand in need of forgiveness for thus offending Him; unless we suppose GOD to enact laws, and at the same time not care whether they are obeyed or no; which is as absurd as to suppose that a prince should establish laws for the proper government of his country, and yet let every violator of them come off with impunity. But GOD has not dealt so foolishly with his creatures: no, as he gave us a law, he demands our obedience to that law, and has obliged us universally and perseveringly to obey it, under no less a penalty than incurring his curse and eternal death for every breach of it: For thus speaks the scripture; " Cursed is he that continueth not in all things that are written in the law to do them;" as the scripture also speaketh in another place, " The soul that sinneth, it shall die." Now it has already been proved, that we have all of us sinned; and therefore, unless some means can be found to satisfy GOD's justice, we must perish eternally.

Let us then stand a while, and see in what a deplorable condition each of us comes into the world, and still continues, till we are translated into a state of grace. For surely nothing can well be supposed more deplorable, than to be born under the curse of GOD; to be charged with *original guilt*; and not only so, but to be convicted as actual breakers of GOD's law, the least breach of which justly deserves eternal damnation. Surely this can be but a melancholy prospect to view ourselves in, and must put us upon contriving some means whereby we may satisfy and appease our offended judge. But what must those means be? Shall we repent? Alas! there is not one word of repentance mentioned in the first covenant: " The day that thou eatest thereof, thou shalt surely die." So that, if GOD be true, unless there be some

way

way found out to satisfy divine justice, we must perish; and there is no room left for us to expect a change of mind in GOD, though we should seek it with tears. Well then, if repentance will not do, shall we plead the law of works? Alas! " By the law shall no man living be justified: for by the law comes the knowledge of Sin." It is that which convicts and condemns, and therefore can by no means justify us; and " all our righteousnesses (says the prophet) are but as filthy rags." Wherewith then shall we come before the LORD, and bow down before the most high GOD? Shall we come before Him with calves of a year old, with thousands of rams, or ten thousands of rivers of oil? Alas! GOD has shewed thee, O man, that this will not avail: For he hath declared, " I will take no bullock out of thy house, nor he-goat out of thy fold: for all the beasts of the forests are mine, and so are the cattle upon a thousand hills." Will the LORD then be pleased to accept our first-born for our transgression, the fruit of our bodies for the sin of our souls? Even this will not purchase our pardon: for he hath declared that " the children shall not bear the iniquities of their parents." Besides, they are sinners, and therefore, being under the same condemnation, equally stand in need of forgiveness with ourselves. They are impure, and will the LORD accept the blind and lame for sacrifice? Shall some angel then, or archangel, undertake to fulfill the covenant which we have broken, and make atonement for us? Alas! they are only creatures, though creatures of the highest order; and therefore are obliged to obey GOD as well as we; and after they have done all, must say they have done no more than what was their duty to do. And supposing it was possible for them to die, yet how could the death of a finite creature satisfy an infinitely offended justice? O wretched men that we are! Who shall deliver us? I thank GOD, our LORD JESUS CHRIST. Which naturally leads me to the

Third thing proposed, which was to endeavour to prove, that there is no possibility of obtaining this justification, which we so much want, but by the all-perfect obedience and precious

cious death of JESUS CHRIST, " But ye are justified in the name of our LORD JESUS CHRIST."

But this having been in some measure proved by what has been said under the foregoing head, wherein I have shewn that neither our repentance, righteousness, nor sacrifice, no not the obedience and death of angels themselves, could possibly procure justification for us, nothing remains for me to do under this head, but to shew that JESUS CHRIST has procured it for us.

And here I shall still have recourse " to the law and to the testimony." For after all the most subtle disputations on either side, nothing but the lively oracles of GOD can give us any satisfaction in this momentous point : it being such an inconceivable mystery, that the eternal only-begotten Son of GOD should die for sinful man, that we durst not have presumed so much as to have thought of it, had not GOD revealed it in his holy word. It is true, reason may shew us the wound, but revelation only can lead us to the means of our cure. And though the method GOD has been pleased to take to make us happy, may be to the infidel a stumbling-block, and to the wise opiniator and disputer of this world, foolishness ; yet wisdom, that is, the dispensation of our redemption, will be justified, approved of, and submitted to, by all her truly wise and holy children, by every sincere and upright christian.

But to come more directly to the point before us. Two things, as was before observed, we wanted, in order to be at peace with GOD.

1. To be freed from the guilt of the sin of our nature.

2. From the sin of our lives.

And both these (thanks be to GOD for this unspeakable gift) are secured to believers by the obedience and death of JESUS CHRIST. For what says the scripture ?

1. As

1. As to the *first*, it informs us, that " as by the disobedience of one man, (or by one transgression, namely, that of *Adam*) many were made sinners; so by the obedience of one, Jesus Christ (therein including his passive as well as active obedience) many were made righteous." And again, " As by the disobedience of one man, judgment came upon all men unto condemnation;" or all men were condemned on having *Adam*'s sin imputed to them; " so by the obedience of one, that is, Jesus Christ, the free gift of pardon and peace came upon all men, (all sorts of men) unto justification of life." I say all sorts of men; for the apostle in this chapter is only drawing a parallel between the first and second *Adam* in this respect, that they acted both as representatives; and as the posterity of *Adam* had his sin imputed to them, so those for whom Christ died, and whose representative he is, shall have his merits imputed to them also. Whoever run the parallel farther, in order to prove universal redemption (whatever arguments they may draw for the proof of it from other passages of scripture,) if they would draw one from this for that purpose, I think they stretch their line of interpretation beyond the limits of scripture.

2. Pardon for the sin of our lives was another thing, which we wanted to have secured to us, before we could be at peace with God.

And this the holy scriptures inform us, is abundantly done by the death of Jesus Christ. The evangelical prophet foretold that the promised Redeemer should be " wounded for our transgressions, and bruised for our iniquities; that the chastisement of our peace should be upon him; and that by his stripes we should be healed," *Isaiah* liii. 6. The angels at his birth said, that he should " save his people from their sins." And St. *Paul* declares, that " this is a faithful saying, and worthy of all acceptation, that Jesus Christ came into the world to save sinners." And here in the words of the text, " Such (or, as I observed before, these things) were some of you; but ye are washed, &c." and again, " Jesus Christ is the end of the law for righteousness to every one that believeth." And, to shew us that none but Jesus Christ can do all this, the apostle St. *Peter* says, " Neither is their salvation in any other ; for there is no other name under heaven given among men, whereby we must be saved, but the name of Jesus Christ."

How God will be pleased to deal with the *Gentiles*, who yet sit in darkness and under the shadow of death, and upon whom the sun of righteousness never yet arose, is not for us to enquire. " What have we to do to judge those that are without ?" To God's mercy let us recommend them, and wait for a solution of this and every other difficult point, till the great day of accounts, when all God's dispensations, both of providence and grace, will be fully cleared up by methods to us, as yet unknown, because unrevealed. However, this we know, that the judge of all the earth will, most assuredly, do right.

But it is time for me to draw towards a conclusion.

I have now, brethren, by the blessing of God, discoursed on the words of the text in the method I proposed. Many useful inferences might be drawn from what has been delivered ; but as I have detained you, I fear, too long already, permit me only to make a reflection or two on what has been said, and I have done.

If then we are freely justified by the death and obedience of Jesus Christ, let us here pause a while ; and as before we have reflected on the misery of a fallen, let us now turn aside and see the happiness of the believing, soul. But alas ! how am I lost to think that God the Father, when we were in a state of enmity and rebellion against Him, should notwithstanding yearn in his bowels towards us his fallen, his apostate creatures : And because nothing but an infinite ransom could satisfy an infinitely offended justice, that should send his only and dear Son Jesus Christ (who is God, blessed for ever, and who had lain in his bosom from all eternity) to fulfil the covenant of works, and die a cursed, painful, ignominious death, for us and for our salvation ! who can avoid crying out, at the consideration of this mystery of

god-

godliness. "Oh the depth of the riches of GOD's love" to us his wretched, miserable and undone creatures! "How unsearchable is his mercy, and his ways past finding out!" Now know we of a truth, O GOD, that thou hast loved us, "since thou hast not with-held thy Son, thine only Son JESUS CHRIST," from thus doing and dying for us.

But as we admire the Father sending, let us likewise humbly and thankfully adore the Son coming, when sent to die for man. But O! what thoughts can conceive, what words express the infinite greatness of that unparalleled love, which engaged the Son of GOD to come down from the mansions of his Father's glory to obey and die for sinful man! The *Jews*, when he only shed a tear at poor *Lazarus*'s funeral, said, "Behold how he loved him." How much more justly then may we cry out, Behold how he loved us! When he not only fulfilled the whole moral law, but did not spare to shed his own most precious blood for us.

And can any poor truly-convicted sinner, after this, despair of mercy? What, can they see their Saviour hanging on a tree, with arms stretched out ready to embrace them, and yet, on their truly believing on him, doubt of finding acceptance with him? No, away with all such dishonourable, desponding thoughts. Look on his hands, bored with pins of iron; look on his side, pierced with a cruel spear, to let loose the sluices of his blood, and open a fountain for sin, and for all uncleanness; and then despair of mercy if you can! No, only believe in Him, and then, though you have crucified him afresh, yet will he abundantly pardon you; "though your sins be as scarlet, yet shall they be as wool; though deeper than crimson, yet shall they be whiter than snow."

Which GOD of his infinite mercy grant, &c.

SERMON XLVII.

The great Duty of Charity recommended.

---

1 COR. xiii. 8.

Charity never faileth.

NOTHING is more valuable and commendable, and yet, not one duty is lefs practifed, than that of charity. We often pretend concern and pity for the mifery and diftrefs of our fellow-creatures, but yet we feldom commiferate their condition fo much as to relieve them according to our abilities; but unlefs we affift them with what they may ftand in need of, for the body, as well as for the foul, all our wifhes are no more than words of no value or regard, and are not to be efteemed or regarded: for when we hear of any deplorable circumftance, in which our fellow-creatures are involved, be they friends or enemies; it is our duty, as chriftians, to affift them to the utmoft of our power.

Indeed, we are not, my brethren, to hurt ourfelves or our families; this is not that charity which is fo much recommended by St. *Paul*; no, but if we are any ways capable of relieving them without injuring either ourfelves, or families, then it is our duty to do it; and this never faileth, where it proceeds from a right end, and with a right view.

St. *Paul* had been fhewing, in the preceding chapter, that fpiritual gifts were divers; that GOD had difpofed of one bleffing to one, and another to another; and though there was a diverfity of bleffings, GOD did not beftow them to one perfon, but gave to one a bleffing which he denied to another, and gave a blessing, or a gift to the other which might make him as eminent in one way, as the other's gift made him so in another: but though there are these divers spiritual gifts, they are all given for some wise end, even to profit withal, and to that end they are thus diversly bestowed. We are not, on the one hand, to hide those gifts which God has given us: neither are we, on the other, to be so lavish of them, as to spend them upon our lusts and pleasures, to satisfy our sensual appetites, but they are to be used for the glory of God, and the good of immortal souls. After he had particularly illustrated this, he comes to shew, that all gifts, however great they may be in themselves, are of no value unless we have charity, as you may see particularly, by considering from the beginning of this chapter.

But before I go any further, I shall inform you what the apostle means by charity; and that is, LOVE; if there is true love, there will be charity; there will be an endeavour to assist, help, and relieve according to that ability wherewith God has blessed us: and, since this is so much recommended by the apostle, let us see how valuable this charity is, and how commendable in all those who pursue it. I shall,

I. Consider this blessing as relating to the bodies of men.

II. I shall shew how much more valuable it is, when relating to the souls of men.

III. Shall shew you when your charity is of the right kind.

IV. Why this charity, or the grace of love, never faileth.

V. Shall conclude all, with an exhortation to high and low, rich and poor, one with another, to be found in the constant practice of this valuable and commendable duty.

First, I shall consider this duty, as relating to the bodies of men. And,

1. O that the *rich* would confider how praife-worthy this duty is, in helping their fellow-creatures! We were created to be a help to each other; GOD has made no one fo independent as not to need the affiftance of another; the richeft and moft powerful man upon the face of this earth, needs the help and affiftance of thofe who are around him; and though he may be great to-day, a thoufand accidents may make him as low to-morrow; he that is rolling in plenty to-day, may be in as much fcarcity to-morrow. If our rich men would be more charitable to their poor friends and neighbours, it would be a means of recommending them to the favour of others, if Providence fhould frown upon them; but alas, our great men had much rather fpend their money in a playhoufe, at a ball, an affembly, or a mafquerade, than relieve a poor diftreffed fervant of JESUS CHRIST. They had rather fpend their eftates on their hawks and hounds, on their whores, and earthly, fenfual, devilifh pleafures, than comfort, nourifh, or relieve one of their diftreffed fellow-creatures. What difference is there between the king on the throne, and the beggar on the dunghill, when GOD demands their breaths? There is no difference, my brethren, in the grave, nor will there be any at the day of judgment. You will not be excufed becaufe you have had a great eftate, a fine houfe, and lived in all the pleafures that earth could afford you; no, thefe things will be one means of your condemnation; neither will you be judged according to the largenefs of your eftate, but according to the ufe you have made of it.

Now, you may think nothing but of your pleafures and delights, of living in eafe and plenty, and never confider how many thoufands of your fellow-creatures would rejoice at what you are making wafte of, and fetting no account by. Let me befeech you, my rich brethren, to confider the poor of the world, and how commendable and praife-worthy it is to relieve thofe who are diftreffed. Confider, how pleafing this is to GOD, how delightful it is to man, and how many prayers you will have put up for your welfare, by thofe perfons whom you relieve; and let this be a confideration to fpare a little out of the abundance wherewith GOD has blessed you, or the relief of his poor. He could have placed you in their low condition, and they in your high state; it is only his good pleasure that has thus made the difference, and shall not this make you remember your distressed fellow-creatures?

Let me beseech you to consider, which will stand you best at the day of judgment, so much money expended at a horse-race, at a cockpit, at a play or masquerade, or so much given for the relief of your fellow-creatures, and for the distressed members of JESUS CHRIST.

I beseech you, that you would consider how valuable and commendable this duty is: do not be angry at my thus exhorting you to that duty, which is so much recommended by JESUS CHRIST himself, and by all his apostles: I speak particularly to you, my rich brethren, to intreat you to consider those that are poor in this world, and help them from time to time, as their necessity calls for it. Consider, that there is a curse denounced against the riches of those, who do not thus do good with them; namely, "Go to now you rich men, weep and howl for your miseries that shall come upon you; your riches are corrupted, your garments are moth-eaten, your gold and silver is cankered, and the rust of them shall be a witness against you, and shall eat your flesh, as it were fire; ye have heaped your treasure together for the last day." You see the dreadful woe pronounced against all those who hoard up the abundance of the things of this life, without relieving the distresses of those who are in want thereof: and the apostle *James* goes on also to speak against those who have acquired estates by fraud, as too many have in these days. "Behold the hire of the labourers, which have reaped down your fields, which is by you kept back by fraud, crieth; and the cries of them who have reaped, are entered into the ears of the LORD GOD of Sabbaoth. Ye have lived in pleasure on the earth, and been wanton; ye have nourished your hearts, as in a day of slaughter." Thus, if you go on to live after the lust of the flesh, to pamper your bellies, and make them a God, while the poor all round you are starving,

God will make these things a witness against you, which shall be as a worm to your souls, and gnaw your consciences to all eternity; therefore, let me once more recommend charity unto the bodies of men, and beseech you to remember what the blessed Lord Jesus Christ has promised unto those who thus love his members, that " as they have done it to the least of his members, they have done it unto him."

I am not now speaking for myself; I am not recommending my little flock in *Georgia* to you; then you might say, as many wantonly do, that I wanted the money for myself; no, my brethren, I am now recommending the poor of this land to you, your poor neighbours, poor friends, yea, your poor enemies; they are whom I am now speaking for; and when I see so many starving in the streets, and almost naked, my bowels are moved with pity and concern, to consider, that many in whose power it is, to lend their assisting hand, should shut up their bowels of compassion, and will not relieve their fellow-creatures, though in the most deplorable condition for the want thereof.

As I have thus recommended charity particularly to the rich among you; so now I would,

2. *Secondly*, Recommend this to another set of people among us, who, instead of being the most forward in acts of charity, are commonly the most backward; I mean the *clergy* of this land.

Good God! how amazing is the consideration, that those, whom God has called out to labour in spiritual things, should be so backward in this duty, as fatal experience teacheth. Our clergy (that is the generality thereof) are only seeking after preferment, running up and down, to obtain one benefice after another; and to heap up an estate, either to spend on the pleasures of life, or to gratify their sensual appetites, while the poor of their flock are forgotten; nay, worse, they are scorned, hated, and disdained.

I am not now, my brethren, speaking of all the clergy; no, blessed be GOD, there are some among them, who abhor such proceedings, and are willing to relieve the necessitous; but GOD knows, these are but very few, while many take no thought of the poor among them.

They can visit the rich and the great, but the poor they cannot bear in their sight; they are forgetful, wilfully forgetful of the poor members of JESUS CHRIST.

They have gone out of the old paths, and turned into a new polite way, but which is not warranted in the word of GOD: they are sunk into a fine way of acting; but as fine as it is, it was not the practice of the apostles, or of the christians in any age of the church: for they visited and relieved the poor among them; but how rare is this among us, how seldom do we find charity in a clergyman?

It is with grief I speak these things, but woful experience is a witness to the truth thereof: and if all the clergy of this land were here, I would tell them boldly, that they did not keep in the ways of charity, but were remiss in their duty; instead of "selling all and giving to the poor," they will not sell any thing, nor give at all to the poor.

3. *Thirdly*, I would exhort you who are poor, to be charitable to one another.

Though you may not have money, or the things of this life, to bestow upon one another; yet you may assist them, by comforting, and advising them not to be discouraged though they are low in the world; or in sickness you may help them according as you have time or ability: do not be unkind to one another: do not grieve, or vex, or be angry with each other; for this is giving the world an advantage over you.

And if GOD stirs up any to relieve you, do not make an ill use of what his providence, by the hands of some christian,

hath

hath bestowed upon you: be always humble and wait on GOD; do not murmur or repine, if you see any relieved and you are not; still wait on the LORD, and help one another, according to your abilities, from time to time.

Having shewed you how valuable this is to the bodies of men, I now proceed,

Secondly, To shew you how much more valuable this charity is, when it extends to the souls of men.

And is not the soul more valuable than the body? It would be of no advantage, but an infinite disadvantage, to obtain all the world, if we were to lose our souls. The soul is of infinite value, and of infinite concern, and, therefore, we should extend our charity whenever we see it needful, and likewise should reprove, rebuke, and exhort with all godliness and love.

We should, my dear brethren, use all means and opportunities for the salvation of our own souls, and of the souls of others. We may have a great deal of charity and concern for the bodies of our fellow-creatures, when we have no thought, or concern, for their immortal souls: But O how sad is it, to have thought for a mortal, but not for the immortal part; to have charity for the body of our fellow-creatures, while we have no concern for their immortal souls; it may be, we help them to ruin them, but have no concern in the saving of them.

You may love to spend a merry evening, to go to a play, or a horse-race, with them; but on the other hand, you cannot bear the thoughts of going to a sermon, or a religious society, with them; no, you would sing the songs of the drunkard, but you will not sing hymns, with them; this is not polite enough, this is unbecoming a gentleman of taste, unfashionable, and only practised among a parcel of enthusiasts and madmen.

Thus

Thus, you will be so uncharitable as to join hand in hand with those who are hastening to their own damnation, while you will not be so charitable as to assist them in being brought from darkness to light, and from the power of Satan unto God. But this, this, my dear brethren, is the greatest charity, as can be, to save a soul from death: this is of far greater advantage, than relieving the body of a fellow-creature: for the most miserable object as could be, death would deliver it from all. But death, to those who are not born again, would be so far from being a release from all misery, that it would be an inlet to all torment, and that to all eternity. Therefore, we should assist, as much as possible, to keep a soul from falling into the hands of Satan: for he is the grand enemy of souls. How should this excite you to watch over your own and others souls? for unless you are earnest with God, Satan will be too hard for you. Surely, it is the greatest charity to watch over one another's words and actions, that we may forewarn each other when danger is nigh, or when the enemy of souls approaches.

And if you have once known the value of your own souls, and know what it is to be snatched as brands out of the burning fire, you will be solicitous that others may be brought out of the same state. It is not the leading of a moral life, being honest, and paying every man his just due; this is not a proof of your being in a state of grace, or of being born again, and renewed in the spirit of your minds: No, you may die honest, just, charitable, and yet not be in a state of salvation.

It is not the preaching of that morality, which most of our pulpits now bring forth, that is sufficient to bring you from sin unto God. I saw you willing to learn, and yet were ignorant of the necessity of being born again, regenerated, of having all old things done away, and all things becoming new in your souls: I could not bear, my brethren, to see you in the highway to destruction, and none to bring you back. It was love to your souls, it was a desire to see Christ formed

formed in you, which brought me into the fields, the highways, and hedges, to preach unto you JESUS, a crucified JESUS as dying for you. It was charity, indeed it was charity to your souls, which has exposed me to the present ill treatment of my letter-learned brethren.

Therefore, let me advise you to be charitable to the souls of one another; that is, by advising them with all love and tenderness, to follow after CHRIST, and the things which belong to their immortal peace, before they be for ever hid from their eyes.

I now proceed, in the

Third place, to shew when your charity is of the right kind.

And here, my brethren, I shall shew, *First*, When it is not; and, *Secondly*, When it is of the right kind.

1. *First*, Your charity is not of the right kind, when it proceeds from worldly views or ends.

If it is to be seen of men, to receive any advantage from them, to be esteemed, or to gain a reputation in the world; or if you have any pride in it, and expect to reap benefit from GOD merely for it; if all, or each of these is the end of your charity, then it is all in vain; your charity does not proceed from a right end, but you are hereby deceiving your own souls. If you give an alms purely to be observed by man, or as expecting favour from GOD, merely on the account thereof, then you have not the glory of GOD, or the benefit of your fellow-creatures at heart, but merely yourself: this, this is not charity. Nor,

Secondly, Is that true charity, when we give any thing to our fellow-creatures purely to indulge them in vice: this is so far from being charity, that it is a sin, both against GOD, and against our fellow-creatures. And yet, this is as common, as it is sinful, to carry our friends, under a specious pretence of charity, to one or the other entertainment, with no other view, but to make them guilty of excess. Hereby you are guilty of a double sin: we are not to sin ourselves, much less should we endeavour to make another sin likewise. But,

Thirdly, Our charity comes from a right end, when it proceeds from love to GOD, and for the welfare both of the body and soul of our fellow-creatures.

When this is the sole end of relieving our distressed fellow-creatures, then our charity comes from a right end, and we may expect to reap advantage by it: this is the charity which is pleasing to GOD. GOD is well pleased, when all our actions proceed from love, love to himself, and love to immortal souls.

Consider, my dear brethren, that it was love for souls, that brought the blessed JESUS down from the bosom of his Father; that made him, who was equal in power and glory, to come and take upon him our nature; that caused the LORD of life to die the painful, ignominious, and accursed death of the cross. It was love to immortal souls, that brought this blessed JESUS among us. And O that we might hence consider how great the value of souls was and is: it was that which made JESUS to bleed, pant, and die. And surely souls must be of infinite worth, which made the Lamb of GOD to die so shameful a death.

And shall not this make you have a true value for souls? It is of the greatest worth: and this, this is the greatest charity, when it comes from love to GOD, and from love to souls. This will be a charity, the satisfaction of which will last to all eternity. O that this may make you have so much regard for the value of souls, as not to neglect all opportunities for the doing of them good: here is something worth having charity for, because they remain to all eternity. Therefore, let me earnestly beseech you both to consider the worth of immortal souls, and let your charity extend to them, that by your advice and admonition, you may be an instrument, in the hands of GOD, in bringing souls to the LORD JESUS.

I am in the next place to consider,

Fourthly, Why this charity, or grace of love never faileth.

And it never faileth in respect of its proceeding from an unchangeable GOD. We are not to understand, that our charity is always the same: No, there may, and frequently are, ebbs and flowings; but still it never totally faileth: No, the grace of love remaineth for ever. There is, and will be, a charity to all who have erred and run astray from GOD. We cannot be easy to see souls in the highway to destruction, and not use our utmost endeavour to bring them back from sin, and shew them the dreadful consequence of running into evil. Christians cannot bear to see those souls for whom CHRIST died, perish for want of knowledge: and if they see any of the bodies of their fellow-creatures in want, they will do the utmost in their power to relieve them.

Charity will never fail, among those who have a true love to the LORD JESUS, and know the value of souls: they will be charitable to those who are in distress. And thus you see, that true charity, if it proceeds from a right end, never faileth.

I now proceed, my brethren, in the

Last place, to exhort all of you, high and low, rich and poor, one with another, to practice this valuable and commendable duty of charity.

It is not rolling in your coaches, taking your pleasure, and not considering the miseries of your fellow-creatures, that is commendable or praise-worthy; but the relieving your distressed poor fellow-creatures, is valuable and praise-worthy wherever it is found. But alas! how very few of our gay and polite gentlemen consider their poor friends; rather they despise,

despise, and do not regard them. They can indulge themselves in the follies of life, and had much rather spend their estates in lusts and pleasures, while the poor all round them are not thought worthy to be set with the dogs of their flock. If you have an abundance of the things of this world, then you are esteemed as companions for the polite and gay in life; but if you are poor, then you must not expect to find any favour, but be hated, or not thought fit for company or conversation: and if you have an abundance of the things of this life, and do not want any assistance, then you have many ready to help you. My dear brethren, I do not doubt but your own experience is a proof of my assertions; as also, that if any come into distress, then those, who promised to give relief, quite forget what they promise, and will despise, because Providence has frowned. But this is not acting like those who are bound for the heavenly *Jerusalem*; thus our hearts and our actions give our lips the lie: for if we profess the name of CHRIST, and do not depart from all iniquity, we are not those, who are worthy of being esteemed christians indeed.

For, if we have not charity, we are not christians: charity is the great duty of christians: and where is our christianity, if we want charity? Therefore, let me beseech you to exercise charity to your distressed fellow-creatures. Indeed, my dear brethren, this is truly commendable, truly valuable; and therefore, I beseech you, in the bowels of tender mercy to CHRIST, to consider his poor distressed members; exercise, exercise, I beseech you, this charity: if you have no compassion, you are not true disciples of the LORD JESUS CHRIST. I humbly beg you to consider those who want relief, and are really destitute, and relieve them according to your abilities. Consider, that the more favourable Providence has been to you, it should make you the more earnest and solicitous to relieve those whom you may find in distress: it is of the utmost consequence, what is well pleasing to your fellow-creatures, and doing your duty to GOD.

When you are called from hence, then all riches and grandeur will be over; the grave will make no distinction;
great

great eſtates will be of no ſignification in the other world; and if you have made a bad uſe of the talent which God hath put into your hands, it will be only an aggravation of your condemnation at the great day of account, when God ſhall come to demand your ſouls, and to call you to an account, for the uſe to which you have put the abundance of the things of this life.

To conclude, let me once more beſeech each of you to act according to the circumſtances of life, which God, in his rich and free mercy, has given you.

If you were ſenſible of the great conſequences which would attend your acting in this charitable manner, and conſidered it as a proof of your love to God, the loving his members; you could not be uncharitable in your tempers, nor fail to relieve any of your diſtreſſed fellow creatures.

Conſider how eaſy it is for many of you, by putting your mites together, to help one who is in diſtreſs; and how can you tell, but that the little you give, may be the means of bringing one from diſtreſs into flouriſhing circumſtances; and then, if there is a true ſpirit of a chriſtian in them, they can never be ſufficiently thankful to God the author, and to you as the inſtrument, in being ſo great a friend to them in their melancholy circumſtances: conſider alſo, once more, how much better your account will be at the day of judgment, and what peace of conſcience you will enjoy. How ſatisfactory muſt be the thought of having relieved the widow and the fatherleſs? This is recommended by the Lord Jesus Christ, and has been practiſed in all ages of the church: and therefore, my brethren, be ye now found in the practice of this duty.

I have been the larger upon this, becauſe our enemies ſay we deny all moral actions; but, bleſſed be God, they ſpeak againſt us without cauſe: we highly value them; but we ſay, that faith in Christ, the love of God, and being born again, are of infinite more worth; but you cannot be true
chriſtians

christians without having charity to your fellow-creatures, be they friends or enemies, if in distress. And, therefore, exert yourselves in this duty, as is commanded by the blessed JESUS: and if you have true charity, you shall live and reign with him for ever.

Now to GOD the Father, GOD the Son, and GOD the Holy Ghost, be all honour, power, glory, might, majesty, and dominion, both now and for evermore. *Amen.*

SERMON XLVIII.

Satan's Devices.

---

2 Cor. ii. 11.

Lest Satan should get an advantage over us; for we are not ignorant of his devices.

THE occasion of these words was as follows: In the church of *Corinth* there was an unhappy person, who had committed such incest, as was not so much as named among the *Gentiles*, in taking his father's wife; but either on account of his wealth, power, or some such reasons, like many notorious offenders now-adays, he had not been exposed to the censures of the church. St. *Paul*, therefore, in his first epistle, severely chides them for this neglect of discipline, and commands them, " in the name of our Lord Jesus Christ, when they were gathered together, to deliver such a one, whoever he was, to Satan, for the destruction of the flesh, that his Spirit might be saved in the day of the Lord;" that is, they should solemnly excommunicate him; which was then commonly attended with some bodily disease. The *Corinthians*, being obedient to the Apostle, as dear children, no sooner received this reproof, but they submitted to it, and cast the offending party out of the church. But whilst they were endeavouring to amend one fault, they unhappily ran into another; and as they formerly had been too mild and remiss, so now they behaved towards him with too much severity and resentment. The Apostle, therefore, in this chapter, reproves this, and tells them, that " sufficient to the offender's shame, was the punishment which had been inflicted of many:" that he had now suffered enough; and that, therefore, left he should be tempted to say with *Cain*, " My punishment is greater than I can bear;" or to use the Apostle's own words, " Left he should be swallowed up with overmuch sorrow;" they ought, now he had given proof of his repentance, to forgive him, to confirm their love towards him, and so restore him in the spirit of meekness; " Left Satan, (to whose buffetings he was now given, by tempting him to despair) should get an advantage over us:" and so, by representing you as merciless and cruel, cause that holy name to be blasphemed, by which you are called; " for we are not ignorant of his devices:" we know very well how many subtle ways he has to draw aside and beguile unguarded unthinking men.

Thus then, stand the words in relation to the context; but as Satan has many devices, and as his quiver is full of other poisonous darts, besides those which he shoots at us to drive us to despair, I shall, in the following discourse,

First, Briefly observe who we are to understand by Satan. And,

Secondly, Point out to you, what are the chief devices he generally makes use of, to draw off converts from CHRIST, and also prescribe some remedies against them.

First, Who are we to understand by Satan?

The word *Satan*, in its original signification, means an adversary; and in its general acceptation, is made use of, to point out to us the chief of the devils, who, for striving to be as GOD, was cast down from heaven, and is now permitted, " with the rest of his spiritual wickednesses in high places, to walk up and down, seeking whom he may devour." We hear of him immediately after the creation, when in the shape of a serpent, he lay in wait to deceive our first parents. He is called Satan, in the book of *Job*, where we are told, that
" when

"when the sons of GOD came to present themselves before the LORD, Satan also came amongst them." As the scripture also speaketh in the book of *Chronicles*; " and Satan moved *David* to number the people." In the New Testament he goes under different denominations; sometimes he is called the *evil One*, because he is evil in himself, and tempts us to evil. Sometimes, " the Prince of the power of the air;" and, " the Spirit that now ruleth in the children of disobedience;" because he resides chiefly in the air, and through the whole world: and all that are not born of GOD, are said to lie in him.

He is an enemy to GOD and goodness; he is a hater of all truth: Why else did he slander GOD in paradise? Why did he tell *Eve*, " You shall not surely die?" And why did he promise to give all the kingdoms of the world, and the glories of them, to JESUS CHRIST, if he would fall down and worship him?

He is full of malice, envy, and revenge: For what other motives could induce him to molest innocent man in paradise? And why is he still so restless in his attempts to destroy us, who have done him no wrong?

He is a being of great *power*, as appears in his being able to act on the imagination of our blessed LORD, so as to represent to him all the kingdoms of the world, and the glories of them, in a moment of time. As also in carrying his sacred body through the air up to a pinacle of the temple; and his driving a herd of swine so furiously into the deep. Nay, so great is his might, that, I doubt not, was GOD to let him use his full strength, but he could turn the earth upside down, or pull the sun from its orb.

But what he is most remarkable for is, his *subtlety*: for not having power given him from above, to take us by force, he is obliged to wait for opportunities to betray us, and to catch us by guile. He, therefore, made use of the serpent, which was subtle above all the beasts of the field, in order to tempt our first parents; and accordingly he is said, in the New Testament, "To lie in wait to deceive;" and, in the words of the text, the Apostle says, "We are not ignorant of his devices;" thereby implying, that we are more in danger of being seduced by his policy, than over-borne by his power.

From this short description of Satan, we may easily judge whose children they are, who love to make a lie, who speak evil of, and slander their neighbour, and whose hearts are full of pride, subtlety, malice, envy, revenge, and all uncharitableness. Surely they have Satan for their father: for the tempers of Satan they know, and the works of Satan they do. But were they to see either themselves, or Satan as he is, they could not but be terrified at their own likeness, and abhor themselves in dust and ashes.

But, the justice of GOD in suffering us to be tempted, is vindicated from the following considerations: That we are here in a state of disorder; That he has promised not to suffer us to be tempted above what we are able to bear; and not only so, but to him that overcometh he will give a crown of life.

The holy angels themselves, it should seem, were once put to a trial whether they would be faithful or not. The first *Adam* was tempted, even in paradise. And JESUS CHRIST, that second *Adam*, though he was a son, yet was carried, as our representative, by the Holy Spirit, into the wilderness, to be tempted of the devil. And there is not one single saint in paradise, amongst the goodly fellowship of the prophets, the glorious company of the apostles, the noble army of martyrs, and the spirits of just men made perfect, who, when on earth, was not assaulted by the fiery darts of that wicked one, the devil.

What then has been the common lot of all GOD's children, and of the angels, nay, of the eternal Son of GOD himself, we must not think to be exempted from: No, it is sufficient if we are made perfect through temptations, as they were. And, therefore,

therefore, since we cannot but be tempted, unless we could unmake human nature, instead of repining at our condition, we should rather be enquiring, at what time of our lives Satan most violently assaults us? And what those devices are, which he commonly makes use of, in order to " get an advantage over us?"

As to the first question, what time of life? I answer, we must expect to be tempted by him, in some degree or other, all our lives long.—For this life being a continual warfare, we must never expect to have rest from our spiritual adversary the devil, or to say, our combat with him is finished, 'till, with our blessed master, we bow down our heads, and give up the ghost.

But since the time of our conversion, or first entring upon the spiritual life, is the most critical time at which he, for the most part, violently besets us, as well knowing, if he can prevent our setting out, he can lead us captive at his will; and since the wise son of *Sirach* particularly warns us, when we are going to serve the LORD, to prepare our souls for temptation, I shall, in answer to the other question, pass on to the

Second general thing proposed; and point out those devices, which Satan generally makes use of at our first conversion, in order to get an advantage over us.

But let me observe to you, that whatsoever shall be delivered in the following discourse is only designed for such as have actually entered upon the divine life; and not for carnal almost Christians, who have the form of godliness, but never yet felt the power of it in their hearts. This being premised, The

First device I shall mention, which Satan makes use of, is, *to drive us to despair.*

When GOD the Father awakens a sinner by the terrors of the law, and by his Holy Spirit convinceth him of sin, in order to lead him to CHRIST, and shew him the necessity of a Redeemer; then Satan generally strikes in, and aggravates those convictions to such a degree, as to make the sinner doubt of finding mercy thro' the Mediator.

Thus, in all his temptations of the Holy JESUS, he chiefly aimed to make him question, whether he was the Son of GOD? " If thou be the Son of GOD," do so and so. With many such desponding thoughts, no doubt, he filled the heart of the great St. *Paul*, when he continued three days, neither eating bread nor drinking water; and therefore he speaks by experience, when he says, in the words of the text, " We are not ignorant of his devices," that he would endeavour to drive the incestuous person to despair.

But let not any of you be influenced by him, to despair of finding mercy. For it is not the greatness or number of our crimes, but impenitence and unbelief, that will prove our ruin: No, were our sins more in number than the hairs of our head, or of a deeper die than the brightest scarlet; yet the merits of the death of JESUS CHRIST are infinitely greater, and faith in his blood shall make them white as snow.

Answer always, therefore, his despairing suggestions, as your Blessed LORD did, with an " It is written." Tell him, you know that your Redeemer liveth, ever to make intercession for you; that the LORD hath received from him double for all your crimes: And tho' you have sinned much, that is no reason why you should despair, but only why you should love much, having so much forgiven. A

Second device that Satan generally makes use of, to get an advantage over young converts, is, to tempt them to *presume*, or to think more highly of themselves than they ought to think.

When a person has for some little time tasted the good word of life, and felt the powers of the world to come, he is commonly (as indeed well he may) most highly transported with that sudden change he finds in himself. But then, Satan

Satan will not be wanting, at such a time, to puff him up with a high conceit of his own attainments, as if he was some great person; and will tempt him to set at nought his brethren, as though he was holier than they.

Take heed therefore, and let us beware of this device of our spiritual adversary; for as before honour is humility, so a haughty spirit generally goes before a fall; and GOD is obliged, when under such circumstances, to send us some humbling visitation, or permit us to fall, as he did *Peter*, into some grievous sin, that we may learn not to be too high minded.

To check therefore all suggestions to spiritual pride, let us consider, that we did not apprehend CHRIST, but were apprehended of him. That we have nothing but what we have received. That the free grace of GOD has alone made the difference between us and others; and, was GOD to leave us to the deceitfulness of our own hearts but one moment, we should become weak and wicked, like other men. We should farther consider, that being proud of grace, is the most ready way to lose it. "For GOD resisteth the proud, and giveth more grace only to the humble." And were we endowed with the perfections of the seraphim; yet if we were proud of those perfections, they would but render us more accomplished devils. Above all, we should pray earnestly to Almighty GOD, that we may learn of JESUS CHRIST, to be lowly in heart. That his grace, through the subtlety and deceivableness of Satan, may not be our poison. But that we may always think soberly of ourselves, as we ought to think. A

Third device I shall mention, which Satan generally makes use of, " to get an advantage over us," is to tempt us to *uneasiness*, and to have *hard thoughts of* GOD, when we are dead and barren in prayer.

Though this is a term not understood by the natural man, yet, whosoever there are amongst you, who have passed through the

the pangs of the *new birth*, they know full well what I mean, when I talk of deadness and dryness in prayer. And, I doubt not, but many of you, amongst whom I am now preaching the kingdom of GOD, are at this very time labouring under it.

For, when persons are first awakened to the divine life, because grace is weak and nature strong, GOD is often pleased to vouchsafe them some extraordinary illuminations of his Holy Spirit; but when they are grown to be more perfect men in CHRIST, then he frequently seems to leave them to themselves; and not only so, but permits a horrible deadness and dread to overwhelm them; at which times Satan will not be wanting to vex and tempt them to impatience, to the great discomfort of their souls.

But be not afraid; for this is no more than your blessed Redeemer, that spotless Lamb of GOD, has undergone before you: witness his bitter agony in the garden, when his soul was exceeding sorrowful, even unto death. When he sweat great drops of blood, falling on the ground; when the sense of the Divinity was drawn from him; and Satan, in all probability, was permitted to set all his terrors in array before him.

Rejoice, therefore, my brethren, when you fall into the like circumstances; as knowing, that you are therein partakers of the sufferings of JESUS CHRIST. Consider, that it is necessary such inward trials should come, to wean us from the immoderate love of sensible devotion, and teach us to follow CHRIST, not merely for his loaves, but out of a principle of love and obedience. In patience, therefore, possess your souls, and be not terrified by Satan's suggestions. Still persevere in seeking JESUS in the use of means, though it be sorrowing; and though through barrenness of soul, you may go mourning all the day long. Consider that the spouse is with you, though behind the curtain; as he was with *Mary*, at the sepulchre, though she knew it not. That he has withdrawn but for a little while, to make his next visit more welcome. That though he may now seem to frown and look back on you, as he did on the *Syrophenician* woman; yet if you, like her, or blind *Bartimeus*, cry out so much the more earnestly, " Jesus, thou Son of *David*, have mercy on us;" he will be made known unto you again, either in the temple, by breaking of bread, or some other way.

But amongst all the devices that Satan makes use of, " to get an advantage over us," there is none in which he is more successful, or by which he grieves the children of God worse, than a

Fourth device I am going to mention, his troubling you with *blasphemous, profane, unbelieving thoughts*; and sometimes to such a degree, that they are as tormenting as the rack.

Some indeed are apt to impute all such evil thoughts to a disorder of body. But those who know any thing of the spiritual life, can inform you, with greater certainty, that for the generality, they proceed from that wicked one, the devil; who, no doubt, has power given him from above, as well now as formerly, to disorder the body, as he did *Job*'s, that he may, with the more secrecy and success, work upon, ruffle and torment the soul.

You that have felt his fiery darts, can subscribe to the truth of this, and by fatal experience can tell, how often he has bid you, " curse God and die," and darted into your thoughts a thousand blasphemous suggestions, even in your most secret and solemn retirements; the bare looking back on which makes your very hearts to tremble.

I appeal to your own consciencies; Have not some of you, when you have been lifting up holy hands in prayer, been pestered with such a crowd of the most horrid insinuations, that you have been often tempted to rise off from your knees, and been made to believe your prayers were an abomination to the Lord? Nay, when, with the rest of your christian brethren, you have crouded round the holy table, and taken the sacred symbols of Christ's most blessed body and blood

into

into your hands, instead of remembring the death of your Saviour, have you not been employed in driving out evil thoughts, as *Abraham* was in driving away the birds, that came to devour his sacrifice; and thereby have been terrified, lest you have eat and drank your own damnation?

But marvel not, as though some strange thing happened unto you; for this has been the common lot of all GOD's children. We read, even in *Job*'s time, "That when the sons of GOD came to appear before their Maker, (at public worship) Satan also came amongst them," to disturb their devotions.

And think not that GOD is angry with you for these distracting, though ever so blasphemous thoughts: No, he knows it is not you, but Satan working in you; and therefore, notwithstanding he may be displeased with, and certainly will punish him; yet he will both pity and reward you. And though it be difficult to make persons in your circumstances to believe so; yet I doubt not but you are more acceptable to GOD, when performing your holy duties in the midst of such involuntary distractions, than when you are wrapped up by devotion, as it were, into the third heavens; for you are then suffering, as well as doing the will of GOD at the same time; and, like *Nehemiah*'s servants at the building of the temple, are holding a trowel in one hand, and a sword in the other. Be not driven from the use of any ordinance whatever, on account of those abominable suggestions; for then you let Satan get his desired advantage over you; it being his chief design, by these thoughts, to make you fall out with the means of grace; and to tempt you to believe, you do not please GOD, for no other reason, than because you do not please yourselves. Rather persevere in the use of the holy communion especially, and all other means whatever; and when these temptations have wrought that resignation in you, for which they were permitted, GOD will visit you with fresh tokens of his love, as he met *Abraham*, when he returned from the slaughter of the five kings; and will send an angel from heaven, as he did to his Son, on purpose to strengthen you.

Hitherto we have only observed such devices as Satan makes use of immediately by himself; but there is a

Fifth I shall mention, which is not the least, tempting us by our *carnal friends* and *relations*.

This is one of the most common, as well as most artful devices he makes use of, to draw young converts from GOD; for when he cannot prevail over them by himself, he will try what he can do by the influence and mediation of others.

Thus he tempted *Eve*, that she might tempt *Adam*. Thus he stirred up *Job*'s wife, to bid him "Curse GOD and die." And thus he made use of *Peter*'s tongue, to persuade our blessed LORD "to spare himself," and thereby decline those sufferings, by which alone we could be preserved from suffering the vengeance of eternal fire. And thus, in these last days, he often stirs up our most powerful friends and dearest intimates, to dissuade us from going in that narrow way, which alone leadeth unto life eternal.

But our blessed LORD has furnished us with a sufficient answer to all such suggestions. "Get you behind me, my adversaries;" for otherwise they will be an offence unto you; and the only reason why they give such advice is, because they "favour not the things that be of GOD, but the things that be of men."

Whoever, therefore, among you are resolved to serve the LORD, prepare your souls for many such temptations as these; for it is necessary that such offences should come, to try your sincerity, to teach us to cease from man, and to see if we will forsake all to follow CHRIST.

Indeed our modernisers of christianity would persuade us, that the gospel was calculated only for about two hundred years; and that now there is no need of hating father and mother,

mother, or of being persecuted for the sake of CHRIST and his gospel.

But such persons err, not knowing the scriptures, and the power of godliness in their hearts; for whosoever receives the love of GOD in the truth of it, will find, that CHRIST came to send not peace, but a sword upon earth, as much now as ever. That the father-in-law shall be against the daughter-in-law, in these latter, as well as in the primitive times; and that if we will live godly in CHRIST JESUS, we must, as then, so now, from carnal friends and relations, suffer persecution. But the devil hath a

Sixth device, which is as dangerous as any of the former, by *not tempting us at all*, or rather, by *withdrawing himself for a while*, in order to come upon us at an hour when we think not of it.

Thus it is said, that he left JESUS CHRIST only for a season; and our blessed LORD has bid us to watch and pray always, that we enter not into temptation; thereby implying, that Satan, whether we think of it or not, is always seeking how he may devour us.

If we would therefore behave like good soldiers of JESUS CHRIST, we must be always upon our guard, and never pretend to lay down our spiritual weapons of prayer and watching, till our warfare is accomplished by death; for if we do, our spiritual Amalek will quickly prevail against us. What if he has left us? it is only for a season; yet a little while, and, like a roaring lion, with double fury, he will break out upon us again. So great a coward as the devil is, he seldom leaves us at the first onset. As he followed our blessed LORD with one temptation after another, so will he treat his servants. And the reason why he does not renew his attacks, is sometimes, because GOD knows we are yet weak and unable to bear them, sometimes, because our grand adversary thinks to beset us at a more convenient season.

Watch carefully therefore over thy heart, O chriſtian; and whenever thou perceiveſt thyſelf to be falling into a ſpiritual ſlumber, ſay to it, as CHRIST to his diſciples, "Ariſe (my ſoul) why ſleepeſt thou?" Awake, awake; put on ſtrength, watch and pray, or otherwiſe the *Philiſtines* will be upon thee, and lead thee whither thou wouldſt not. Alas! Is this life a time to lie down and ſlumber in? Ariſe, and call upon thy GOD; thy ſpiritual enemy is not dead, but lurketh in ſome ſecret place, ſeeking a convenient opportunity, how he may betray thee. If thou ceaſeſt to ſtrive with him, thou ceaſeſt to be a friend of GOD; thou ceaſeſt to go in that narrow way which leadeth unto life.

Thus have I endeavoured to point out to you ſome of thoſe devices, that Satan generally makes uſe of " to get an advantage over us;" many others there are, no doubt, which he often uſes.

But theſe, on account of my youth and want of experience, I cannot yet appriſe you of; they who have been liſted for many years in their maſter's ſervice, and fought under his banner againſt our ſpiritual Amalek, are able to diſcover more of his artifices; and, being tempted in all things, like unto their brethren, can, in all things, adviſe and ſuccour thoſe that are tempted.

In the mean while, let me exhort my young fellow-ſoldiers, who, like myſelf, are but juſt entring the field, and for whoſe ſake this was written, not to be diſcouraged at the fiery trial wherewith they muſt be tried, if they would be found faithful ſervants of JESUS CHRIST. You ſee, my dearly beloved brethren, by what has been delivered, that our way through the wilderneſs of this world to the heavenly *Canaan*, is beſet with thorns, and that there are ſons of Anak to be grappled with, ere you can poſſeſs the promiſed land. But let not theſe, like ſo many falſe ſpies, diſcourage you from going up to fight the LORD's battles, but ſay with *Caleb* and *Joſhua*, "Nay, but we will go up, for we are able to conquer them." JESUS CHRIST, that great captain of our ſalvation, has in

our

our stead, and as our representative, baffled the grand enemy of mankind, and we have nothing to do, but manfully to fight under his banner, and to go on from conquering to conquer. Our glory does not consist in being exempted from, but in enduring temptations. "Blessed is the man, (says the apostle) that endureth temptation;" and again, "Brethren, count it all joy, when you fall into divers temptations:" And in that perfect form our blessed LORD has prescribed to us, we are taught to pray, not so much to be delivered from all temptation, as " from the evil" of it. Whilst we are on this side eternity, it must needs be that temptations come; and, no doubt, " Satan has desired to have all of us, to sift us as wheat." But wherefore should we fear? For he that is for us, is by far more powerful, than all that are against us. JESUS CHRIST, our great High-priest, is exalted to the right hand of GOD, and there sitteth to make intercession for us, that our faith fail not.

Since then CHRIST is praying, whom should we fear? And since he has promised to make us more than conquerors, of whom should we be afraid? No, though an host of devils are set in array against us, let us not be afraid; though there should rise up the hottest persecution against us, yet let us put our trust in GOD. What though Satan, and the rest of his apostate spirits, are powerful, when compared with us; yet, if put in competition with the Almighty, they are as weak as the meanest worms. GOD has them all reserved in chains of darkness unto the judgment of the great day. So far as he permits them, they shall go, but no farther; and where he pleases, there shall their proud malicious designs be stayed. We read in the gospel, that though a legion of them possessed one man, yet they could not destroy him; nor could they so much as enter into a swine, without first having leave given them from above. It is true, we often find they foil us, when we are assaulted by them; but let us be strong, and very couragious; for, though they bruise our heels, we shall, at length, bruise their heads. Yet a little while, and he that shall come, will come; and then we shall see all our spiritual enemies put under our feet. What if they do come out against us, like so

many

many great Goliahs; yet, if we can go forth, as the ſtripling *David*, in the name and ſtrength of the LORD of hoſts, we may ſay, O Satan, where is thy power? O fallen ſpirits, where is your victory?

Once more therefore, and to conclude; let us be ſtrong, and very couragious, and let us put on the whole armour of GOD, that we may be able to ſtand againſt the fiery darts of the wicked one. Let us renounce ourſelves, and the world, and then we ſhall take away the armour in which he truſteth, and he will find nothing in us for his temptations to work upon. We ſhall then prevent his malicious deſigns; and being willing to ſuffer ourſelves, ſhall need leſs ſufferings to be ſent us from above. Let us have our loins girt about with truth; and for an helmet, the hope of ſalvation; " praying always with all manner of ſupplication." Above all things, " Let us take the ſword of the ſpirit, which is the word of GOD," and " the ſhield of faith," looking always to JESUS, the author and finiſher of our faith, who for the joy that was ſet before him, endured the croſs, deſpiſing the ſhame, and is now ſat down at the right hand of GOD.

> To which happy place, may GOD of his infinite mercy tranſlate us all, through our LORD JESUS CHRIST.

> To whom, with the Father, and the Holy Ghoſt, three perſons and one eternal GOD, be all honour and glory, now and for evermore. Amen.

SERMON XLIX.

On Regeneration.

2 COR. v. 17.

If any man be in CHRIST, *he is a new creature.*

THE doctrine of our regeneration, or new birth in CHRIST JESUS, though one of the moſt fundamental doctrines of our holy religion; though ſo plainly and often preſſed on us in ſacred writ, "that he who runs may read;" nay though it is the very hinge on which the ſalvation of each of us turns, and a point too in which all ſincere chriſtians, of every denomination, agree; yet it is ſo ſeldom conſidered, and ſo little experimentally underſtood by the generality of profeſſors, that were we to judge of the truth of it, by the experience of moſt who call themſelves chriſtians, we ſhould be apt to imagine they had "not ſo much as heard" whether there be any ſuch thing as regeneration or not. It is true, men for the moſt part are orthodox in the common articles of their creed; they believe "there is but one GOD, and one Mediator between GOD and men, even the man CHRIST JESUS;" and that there is no other name given under heaven, whereby they can be ſaved, beſides his: But then tell them, they muſt be regenerated, they muſt be born again, they muſt be renewed in the very ſpirit, in the inmoſt faculties of their minds, ere they can truly call CHRIST, "Lord, Lord," or have an evidence that they have any ſhare in the merits of his precious blood; and they are ready to cry out with *Nicodemus*, "How can theſe things be?" Or with the *Athenians*, on another occaſion, "What will this babler ſay? he ſeemeth to be a ſetter-forth of ſtrange doctrines:"

doctrines;" because we preach unto them Christ, and the new-birth.

That I may therefore contribute my mite towards curing the fatal mistake of such persons, who would thus put asunder what God has inseparably joined together, and vainly think they are justified by Christ, or have their sins forgiven, and his perfect obedience imputed to them, when they are not sanctified, have not their natures changed, and made holy, I shall beg leave to enlarge on the words of the text in the following manner:

First, I shall endeavour to explain what is meant by being in Christ: "If any man be in Christ."

Secondly, What we are to understand by being a new creature: "If any man be in Christ he is a new creature."

Thirdly, I shall produce some arguments to make good the apostle's assertion. And

Fourthly, I shall draw some inferences from what may be delivered, and then conclude with a word or two of exhortation.

First, I am to endeavour to explain what is meant by this expression in the text, "If any man be in Christ."

Now a person may be said to be in Christ two ways.

First, Only by an outward profession. And in this sense, every one that is called a christian, or baptized into Christ's church, may be said to be in Christ. But that this is not the sole meaning of the apostle's phrase before us, is evident, because then, every one that names the name of Christ, or is baptized into his visible church, would be a new creature. Which is notoriously false, it being too plain, beyond all contradiction, that comparatively but few of those that are "born of water," are "born of the Spirit" likewise; to use another spiritual way of speaking, many are baptized with water, which were never baptized with the Holy Ghost.

To be in CHRIST therefore, in the full import of the word, must certainly mean something more than a bare outward profession, or being called after his name. For, as this same apostle tells us, " All are not *Israelites* that are of *Israel*," so when applied to christianity, all are not real christians that are nominally such. Nay, this is so far from being the case, that our blessed LORD himself informs us, that many who have prophesied or preached in his name, and in his name cast out devils, and done many wonderful works, shall notwithstanding be dismissed at the last day, with " depart from me, I know you not, ye workers of iniquity."

It remains therefore, that this expression, " if any man be in CHRIST," must be understood in a

Second and closer signification, to be *in him* so as to partake of the benefits of his sufferings. To be in him not only by an outward profession, but by an inward change and purity of heart, and cohabitation of his holy spirit. To be in him, so as to be mystically united to him by a true and lively faith, and thereby to receive spiritual virtue from him, as the members of the natural body do from the head, or the branches from the vine. To be in him in such a manner as the apostle, speaking of himself, acquaints us he knew a person was, " I knew man in CHRIST," a true christian; or, as he himself desires to be in CHRIST, when he wishes, in his epistle to the *Philippians*, that he might be found in him.

This is undoubtedly the proper meaning of the apostle's expression in the words of the text; so that what he says in his epistle to the *Romans* about circumcision, may very well be applied to the present subject; that he is not a real christian who is only one outwardly; nor is that true baptism, which is only outward in the flesh. But he is a true christian, who is one inwardly, whose baptism is that of the heart, in the spirit, and not merely in the water, whose praise is not of man but of GOD. Or, as he speaketh in another place, "Neither circumcision nor uncircumcision availeth any thing (of itself) but a new creature." Which amounts to what he here declares in the verse now under consideration, that if any man be truly and properly in CHRIST, he is a new creature. Which brings me to shew,

Secondly, What we are to understand by being a *new creature*.

And here it is evident at the first view, that this expression is not to be so explained as though there was a physical change required to be made in us; or as though we were to be reduced to our primitive nothings, and then created and formed again. For, supposing we were, as *Nicodemus* ignorantly imagined, to enter a "second time into our mother's womb, and be born," alas! what would it contribute towards rendering us spiritually new creatures? Since "that which was born of the flesh would be flesh still;" we should be the same carnal persons as ever, being derived from carnal parents, and consequently receiving the seeds of all manner of sin and corruption from them. No, it only means, that we must be so altered as to the qualities and tempers of our minds, that we must entirely forget what manner of persons we once were. As it may be said of a piece of gold, that was once in the ore, after it has been cleansed, purified and polished, that it is a new piece of gold; as it may be said of a bright glass that has been covered over with filth, when it is wiped, and so become transparent and clear, that it is a new glass: Or, as it might be said of *Naaman*, when he recovered of his leprosy, and his flesh returned unto him like the flesh of a young child, that he was a new man; so our souls, though still the same as to essence, yet are so purged, purified and cleansed from their natural dross, filth and leprosy, by the blessed influences of the Holy Spirit, that they may be properly said to be made anew.

How this glorious change is wrought in the soul, cannot easily be explained: For no one knows the ways of the Spirit, save the Spirit of GOD himself. Not that this ought to be any argument against this doctrine; for, as our blessed LORD observed to *Nicodemus*, when he was discoursing on this very subject, " The wind bloweth where it listeth, and thou hearest the sound thereof, but knowest not whence it cometh, and whither it goeth;" and if we are told of natural things, and we understand them not, how much less ought we to wonder, if we cannot immediately account for the invisible workings of the Holy Spirit? The truth of the matter is this: the doctrine of our regeneration, or new birth in CHRIST JESUS, is hard to be understood by the natural man. But that there is really such a thing, and that each of us must be spiritually born again, I shall endeavour to shew under my

Third general head, in which I was to produce some arguments to make good the apostle's assertion.

And here one would think it sufficient to affirm,

First, That GOD himself, in his holy word, hath told us so. Many texts might be produced out of the Old Testament to prove this point, and indeed, one would wonder how *Nicodemus*, who was a teacher in *Israel*, and who was therefore to instruct the people in the spiritual meaning of the law, should be so ignorant of this grand article, as we find he really was, by his asking our blessed LORD, when he was pressing on him this topic, How can these things be? Surely, he could not forget how often the Psalmist had begged of GOD, to make him " a new heart," and " to renew a right spirit within him ;" as likewise, how frequently the prophets had warned the people to make them " new hearts," and new minds, and so turn unto the LORD their GOD. But not to mention these and such like texts out of the Old Testament, this doctrine is so often and plainly repeated in the New, that, as I observed before, he who runs may read. For what says the great Prophet and Instructor of the world himself: " Except a man (every one that is naturally the offspring of *Adam*) be born again of water and the Spirit, he cannot enter into the kingdom of GOD." And lest we should be apt to flight this affertion, and *Nicodemus*-like, reject the doctrine, becaufe we cannot immediately explain "How this thing can be;" our bleffed Mafter therefore affirms it, as it were, by an oath, " Verily, verily, I fay unto you," or, as it may be read, I the Amen; I, who am truth itfelf, fay unto you, that it is the unalterable appointment of my heavenly Father, that " unlefs a man be born again, he cannot enter into the kingdom of GOD."

Agreeable to this, are thofe many paffages we meet with in the epiftles, where we are commanded to be " renewed in the Spirit," or, which was before explained, in the inmoft faculties of our minds; to " put off the Old Man, which is corrupt; and to put on the New Man, which is created after GOD, in righteoufnefs and true holinefs;" that " old things muft pafs away, and that all things muft become new;" that we are to be " faved by the wafhing of regeneration, and the renewing of the Holy Ghoft." Or, methinks, was there no other paffage to be produced befides the words of the text, it would be full enough, fince the apoftle therein pofitively affirms, that " If any man be in CHRIST, he is a *new creature*."

Now, what can be underftood by all thefe different terms of being *born again*, of *putting off the Old Man*, and *putting on the New*, of being *renewed in the fpirit of our minds*, and becoming *new creatures*; but that chriftianity requires a thorough, real inward change of heart? Do we think thefe, and fuch-like forms of fpeaking, are mere metaphors, words of a bare found, without any real folid fignification? Indeed, it is to be feared, fome men would have them interpreted fo; but alas! unhappy men! they are not to be envied in their metaphorical interpretation: it will be well, if they do not interpret themfelves out of their falvation.

Multitudes of other texts might be produced to confirm this fame truth; but thofe already quoted are fo plain and convincing, that one would imagine no one fhould deny it; were we not told, there are fome, " who having eyes, fee

not,

not, and ears, hear not, and that will not understand with their hearts, or hear with their ears, left they should be converted, and CHRIST should heal them."

But I proceed to a

Second argument; and that shall be taken from the purity of GOD, and the present corrupt and polluted state of man.

GOD is described in holy scripture (and I speak to those who profess to know the scripture) as a Spirit; as a being of such infinite sanctity, as to be of " purer eyes than to behold iniquity;" as to be so transcendently holy, that it is said " the very heavens are not clean in his sight; and the angels themselves he chargeth with folly." On the other hand, man is described (and every regenerate person will find it true by his own experience) as a creature altogether " conceived and born in sin;" as having " no good thing dwelling in him;" as being " carnal, sold under sin;" nay, as having " a mind which is at enmity with GOD," and such-like. And since there is such an infinite disparity, can any one conceive how a filthy, corrupted, polluted wretch can dwell with an infinitely pure and holy GOD, before he is changed, and rendered, in some measure, like him? Can he, who is of purer eyes than to behold iniquity, dwell with it? Can he, in whose sight the heavens are not clean, delight to dwell with uncleanness itself? No, we might as well suppose light to have communion with darkness, or CHRIST to have concord with *Belial*. But I pass on to a

Third argument, which shall be founded on the consideration of the nature of that happiness GOD has prepared for those that unfeignedly love him.

To enter indeed on a minute and particular description of heaven, would be vain and presumptuous, since we are told that " eye hath not seen, nor ear heard, neither hath it entered into the heart of man to conceive, the things that are there prepared" for the sincere followers of the holy JESUS, even in this life, much less in that which is to come. However, this we may venture to affirm in general, that as GOD is a Spirit, so the happiness he has laid up for his people is spiritual likewise; and consequently, unless our carnal minds are changed, and spiritualized, we can never be made meet to partake of that inheritance with the saints in light.

It is true, we may flatter ourselves, that, supposing we continue in our natural corrupt estate, and carry all our lusts along with us, we should, notwithstanding, relish heaven, was GOD to admit us therein. And so we might, was it a *Mahometan* paradise, wherein we were to take our full swing in sensual delights. But since its joys are only spiritual, and no unclean thing can possibly enter those blessed mansions, there is an absolute necessity of our being changed, and undergoing a total renovation of our depraved natures, before we can have any taste or relish of those heavenly pleasures.

It is, doubtless, for this reason, that the apostle declares it to be the irrevocable decree of the Almighty, that "without holiness, (without being made pure by regeneration, and having the image of GOD thereby reinstamped upon the soul) no man shall see the LORD." And it is very observable, that our divine Master, in the famous passage before referred to, concerning the absolute necessity of regeneration, does not say, Unless a man be born again, he *shall not*, but " unless a man be born again, he *cannot* enter into the kingdom of GOD." It is founded in the very nature of things, that unless we have dispositions wrought in us suitable to the objects that are to entertain us, we can take no manner of complacency or satisfaction in them. For instance; what delight can the most harmonious music afford to a deaf, or what pleasure can the most excellent picture give to a blind man? Can a tasteless palate relish the richest dainties, or a filthy swine be pleased with the finest garden of flowers? No: and what reason can be assigned for it? An answer is ready; because they have neither of them any tempers of mind correspondent or agreeable to what they are to be diverted with. And thus it is with the soul hereafter: for death makes no more alteration in the foul, than as it inlarges its faculties, and makes it capable of receiving deeper impressions either of pleasure or pain. If it delighted to converse with God here, it will be transported with the sight of his glorious Majesty hereafter. If it was pleased with the communion of saints on earth, it will be infinitely more so with the communion and society of holy angels, and the spirits of just men made perfect in heaven. But if the opposite of all this be true, we may assure ourselves the soul could not be happy, was God himself to admit it (which he never will do) into the regions of the blessed. But it is time for me to hasten to the

Fourth argument, because CHRIST's redemption will not be complete in us, unless we are new creatures.

If we reflect indeed on the first and chief end of our blessed LORD's coming, we shall find it was to be a propitiation for our sins, to give his life a ransom for many. But then, if the benefits of our dear Redeemer's death were to extend no farther than barely to procure forgiveness of our sins, we should have as little reason to rejoice in it, as a poor condemned criminal that is ready to perish by some fatal disease, would have in receiving a pardon from his judge. For christians would do well to consider, that there is not only a legal hinderance to our happiness, as we are breakers of GOD's law, but also a moral impurity in our natures, which renders us incapable of enjoying heaven (as hath been already proved) till some mighty change have been wrought in us. It is necessary therefore, in order to make CHRIST's redemption compleat, that we should have a grant of GOD's holy Spirit to change our natures, and so prepare us for the enjoyment of that happiness our Saviour has purchased by his precious blood.

Accordingly the holy scriptures inform us, that whom CHRIST justifies, or whose sins he forgives, and to whom he imputes his perfect obedience, those he also sanctifies, purifies and cleanses, and totally changeth their corrupted natures. As the scripture also speaketh in another place, " CHRIST is to us juſtification, ſanctification, and then redemption."ᵃ But,

Fourthly, Proceed we now to the next general thing propoſed, to draw ſome inferences from what has been delivered. And,

Firſt, If he that is in CHRIST be a new creature, this may ſerve as a reproof for thoſe who reſt in a bare performance of outward duties, without perceiving any real inward change of heart.

We may obſerve a great many perſons to be very punctual in the regular returns of public and private prayer, as likewiſe of receiving the holy communion, and perhaps now and then too in keeping a faſt. But here is the misfortune, they reſt barely in the uſe of the means, and think all is over, when they have thus complied with thoſe ſacred inſtitutions; whereas, were they rightly informed, they would conſider, that all the inſtituted means of grace, as prayer, faſting, hearing and reading the word of GOD, receiving the bleſſed ſacrament, and ſuch-like, are no farther ſerviceable to us, than as they are found to make us inwardly better, and to carry on the ſpiritual life in the ſoul.

It is true, they are means; but then they are only means; they are part, but not the whole of religion: for if ſo, who more religious than the Phariſee? He faſted twice in the week, and gave tythes of all that he poſſeſſed, and yet was not juſtified, as our Saviour himſelf informs us, in the ſight of GOD.

You perhaps, like the Phariſee, may faſt often, and make long prayers; you may, with *Herod,* hear good ſermons gladly. But yet, if you continue vain and trifling, immoral or worldly-minded, and differ from the reſt of your neighbours barely in going to church, or in complying with ſome outward performances, are you better than they? No, in no wiſe; you are by far much worſe: for if you uſe them, and

at

at the same time abuse them, you thereby encourage others to think there is nothing in them, and therefore must expect to receive the greater damnation. But,

Secondly, If he that is *in* CHRIST be a new creature, then this may check the groundless presumption of another class of professors, who rest in the attainment of some moral virtues, and falsely imagine they are good christians, if they are just in their dealings, temperate in their diet, and do no hurt or violence to any man.

But if this was all that is requisite to make us christians, why might not the heathens of old be good christians, who were remarkable for these virtues? or St. *Paul* before his conversion, who tells us, that he lived in all good conscience? but we find he renounces all dependance on works of this nature, and only desires to be found in CHRIST, and to know the power of his resurrection, or have an experimental proof of receiving the Holy Ghost, purchased for him by the death, and ensured and applied to him by the resurrection of JESUS CHRIST.

The sum of the matter is this: christianity includes morality, as grace does reason; but if we are only mere Moralists, if we are not inwardly wrought upon, and changed by the powerful operations of the Holy Spirit, and our moral actions, proceed from a principle of a new nature, however we may call ourselves christians, we shall be found naked at the great day, and in the number of those, who have neither CHRIST's righteousness imputed to them for their justification in the sight, nor holiness enough in their souls as the consequence of that, in order to make them meet for the enjoyment, of GOD. Nor,

Thirdly, Will this doctrine less condemn those, who rest in a partial amendment of themselves, without experiencing a thorough, real, inward change of heart.

A little acquaintance with the world will furnish us with instances, of no small number of persons, who, perhaps, were before openly profane; but seeing the ill consequences of their vices, and the many worldly inconveniencies it has reduced them to, on a sudden, as it were, grow civilized; and thereupon flatter themselves that they are very religious, because they differ a little from their former selves, and are not so scandalously wicked as once they were: whereas, at the same time, they shall have some secret darling sin or other, some beloved *Dalilah* or *Heredias*, which they will not part with; some hidden lust, which they will not mortify; some vicious habit, which they will not take pains to root out. But wouldst thou know, O vain man! whoever thou art, what the LORD thy GOD requires of thee? thou must be informed, that nothing short of a thorough sound conversion will fit thee for the kingdom of heaven. It is not enough to turn from profaneness to civility; but thou must turn from civility to godliness. Not only some, but " all things must become new" in thy soul. It will profit thee but little to do many things, if yet some one thing thou lackest. In short, thou must not only be an almost, but altogether a new creature, or in vain thou boasteth that thou art a christian.

Fourthly, If he that is in CHRIST be a new creature, then this may be prescribed as an infallible rule for every person of whatever denomination, age, degree or quality, to judge himself by; this being the only solid foundation, whereon we can build a well-grounded assurance of pardon, peace, and happiness.

We may indeed depend on the broken reed of an external profession; we may think we are good enough, if we lead such sober, honest, moral lives, as many heathens did. We may imagine we are in a safe condition, if we attend on the public offices of religion, and are constant in the duties of our closets. But unless all these tend to reform our lives, and change our hearts, and are only used as so many channels of divine grace; as I told you before, so I tell you again, christianity will profit you nothing.

Let each of us therefore seriously put this question to our hearts: Have we received the Holy Ghost since we believed? Are we new creatures in CHRIST, or no? At least, if we are not so yet, is it our daily endeavour to become such? Do we constantly and conscientiously use all the means of grace required thereto? Do we fast, watch and pray? Do we, not lazily seek, but laboriously strive to enter in at the strait gate? In short, do we renounce our own righteousness, take up our crosses and follow CHRIST? If so, we are in that narrow way which leads to life; the good seed is sown in our hearts, and will, if duly watered and nourished by a regular persevering use of all the means of grace, grow up to eternal life. But on the contrary, if we have only heard, and know not experimentally, whether there be any Holy Ghost; if we are strangers to fasting, watching and prayer, and all the other spiritual exercises of devotion; if we are content to go in the broad way, merely because we see most other people do so, without once reflecting whether it be the right one or not; in short, if we are strangers, nay enemies to the cross of CHRIST, by lives of worldly-mindedness, and sensual pleasure, and thereby make others think, that christianity is but an empty name, a bare formal profession; if this be the case, I say, CHRIST is as yet dead in vain, to us; we are under the guilt of our sins; and are unacquainted with a true and thorough conversion.

But beloved, I am persuaded better things of you, and things that accompany salvation, though I thus speak; I would humbly hope that you are sincerely persuaded, that he who hath not the Spirit of CHRIST is none of his; and that, unless the Spirit, which raised JESUS from the dead, dwell in you here, neither will your mortal bodies be quickened by the same Spirit to dwell with him hereafter.

Let me therefore (as was proposed in the *last* place) earnestly exhort you, in the name of our LORD JESUS CHRIST, to act suitable to those convictions, and to live as christians, that are commanded in holy writ, to " put off their former conversation concerning the Old Man, and to put on the

New Man, which is created after God in righteousness and true holiness."

It must be owned indeed, that this is a great and difficult work; but, blessed be God, it is not impossible. Many thousands of happy souls have been assisted by a divine power to bring it about, and why should we despair of success? Is God's hand shortened, that it cannot save? Was he the God of our Fathers, is he not the God of their children also? Yes, doubtless, of their children also. It is a task likewise, that will put us to some pain; it will oblige us to part with some lust, to break with some friend, to mortify some beloved passion, which may be exceeding dear to us, and perhaps as hard to leave, as to cut off a right-hand, or pluck out a right-eye. But what of all this? Will not the being made a real living member of Christ, a child of God, and an inheritor of the kingdom of heaven, abundantly make amends for all this trouble? Undoubtedly it will.

The setting about and carrying on this great and necessary work, perhaps may, nay assuredly will expose us also to the ridicule of the unthinking part of mankind, who will wonder, that we run not into the same excess of riot with themselves; and because we deny our sinful appetites, and are not conformed to this world, being commanded in scripture to do the one, and to have our conversation in heaven, in opposition to the other, they may count our lives folly, and our end to be without honour. But will not the being numbered among the saints, and shining as the stars for ever and ever, be a more than sufficient recompense for all the ridicule, calumny, or reproach, we can possibly meet with here?

Indeed, was there no other reward attended a thorough conversion, but that peace of God, which is the unavoidable consequence of it, and which, even in this life, " passeth all understanding," we should have great reason to rejoice. But when we consider, that this is the least of those mercies God has prepared for those that are in Christ, and become new creatures; that, this is but the beginning of an eternal succession of pleasures; that the day of our deaths, which the unconverted, unrenewed sinner must so much dread, will be, as it were, but the first day of our new births, and open to us an everlasting scene of happiness and comfort; in short, if we remember, that they who are regenerate and born again, have a real title to all the glorious promises of the gospel, and are infallibly certain of being as happy, both here and hereafter, as an all-wise, all-gracious, all-powerful God can make them; methinks, every one that has but the least concern for the salvation of his precious and immortal soul, having such promises, such an hope, such an eternity of happiness set before him, should never cease watching, praying, and striving, till he find a real, inward, saving change wrought in his heart, and thereby doth know of a truth, that he dwells in CHRIST, and CHRIST in him; that he is a new creature, therefore a child of GOD; that he is already an inheritor, and will ere long be an actual possessor of the kingdom of heaven.

Which GOD of his infinite mercy grant, through JESUS CHRIST our LORD.

To whom, &c.

SERMON

SERMON L.

Christians, Temples of the living GOD.

---

2 COR. vi. 16.

Ye are the Temple of the living God.

ISAIAH, speaking of the glory of gospel days, said, "Men have not heard nor perceived by the ear, neither hath the eye seen, O GOD, besides thee, what he hath prepared for him that waiteth for him." Chap. lxiv. 4. Could a world lying in the wicked one, be really convinced of this, they would need no other motive to induce them to renounce themselves, take up their cross, and follow JESUS CHRIST. And had believers this truth always deeply impressed upon their souls, they could not but abstain from every evil, be continually aspiring after every good; and in a word, use all diligence to walk worthy of Him who hath called them to his kingdom and glory. If I mistake not, that is the end purposed by the apostle *Paul*, in the words of the text, "Ye are the temple of the living GOD." Words originally directed to the church of *Corinth*, but which equally belong to us, and to our children, and to as many as the LORD our GOD shall call. To give you the true meaning of, and then practically to improve them, shall be my endeavour in the following discourse.

First, I shall endeavour to give you the true meaning of these words, "Ye are the temple of the living GOD." The expression undoubtedly is metaphorical, or figurative: but under the metaphor, something real, and of infinite importance, is to be understood. And there seems to be a manifest allusion, not only to what we call temples or churches in general, but to the *Jewish temple* in particular. I trust, that but few, if any here, need be informed, that the preparations for this edifice were exceedingly grand, that it was modelled and built by a divine order, and when compleated, was separated from common uses, and dedicated to the service of the incomprehensible Jehovah, with the utmost solemnity.

It is thus that christians are " the temple of the living GOD," of Father, Son, and Holy Ghost; they who once held a consultation to create, are all equally concerned in making preparations for, and effectually bringing about the redemption of man. The Father creates, the Son redeems, and the Holy Ghost sanctifies all the elect people of GOD. Being loved from eternity, they are effectually called in time, they are chosen out of the world, and not only by an external formal dedication at baptism, or at the LORD's supper, but by a free, voluntary, unconstrained oblation, they devote themselves, spirit, soul, and body, to the entire service of Him, who hath loved and given himself for them.

This is true and undefiled religion before GOD our heavenly Father: This is the real christian's *reasonable service*, or, as some think the word imports, this is the service required of us in the word of GOD. It implies no less than a total renunciation of the world; in short, turns the christian's whole life into one continued sacrifice of love to GOD; so that, " whether he eats or drinks, he does all to his glory." Not that I would hereby insinuate, that to be christians, or to keep to the words of our text, in order to be temples of the living GOD, we must become hermits, or shut ourselves up in nunneries or cloysters; this be far from me! No. The religion, which this bible in my hand prescribes, is a social religion, a religion equally practicable by high and low, rich and poor, and which absolutely requires a due discharge of all relative duties, in whatsoever state of life GOD shall be pleased to place and continue us.

That some, in all ages of the church, have literally separated themselves from the world, and from a sincere desire to save their souls, and attain higher degrees of christian perfection, have wholly devoted themselves to solitude and retirement, is what I make no doubt of. But then such a zeal is in no wise according to knowledge; for private christians, as well as ministers, are said to be " the salt of the earth, and the lights of the world," and are commanded to " let their light shine before men." But how can this be done, if we shut ourselves up, and thereby entirely exclude ourselves from all manner of conversation with the world? Or supposing we could take the wings of the morning, and fly into the most distant and desolate parts of the earth, what would this avail us, unless we could agree with a wicked heart and wicked tempter not to pursue and molest us there?

So far should we be from thus getting ease and comfort, that I believe we should on the contrary soon find by our experience the truth of what a hermit himself once told me, that a tree which stands by itself, is most exposed and liable to the strongest blasts. When our Saviour was to be tempted by the devil, he was led by the Spirit into the wilderness. How contrary this to their practice, who go into a wilderness to avoid temptation! Surely such are unmindful of the petition put up for us by our blessed LORD, " Father, I pray not that thou wouldst take them out of the world, but that thou wouldst keep them from the evil." This then is to be a christian indeed; to be in the world, and yet not of it; to have our hands, according to our respective stations in life, employed on earth, and our hearts at the same time fixed on things above. Then, indeed, are we " temples of the living GOD," when with a humble boldness, we can say with a great and good soldier of JESUS CHRIST, we are the same in the parlour, as we are in the closet; and can at night throw off our cares, as we throw off our cloaths; and being at peace with the world, ourselves, and GOD, are indifferent whether we sleep or die.

Farther, the Jewish temple was a house of prayer. " My house (says the Great GOD) shall be called a house of prayer:"

and implies that the hearts of true believers are the seats of prayer. For this end was it built, and adorned with such furniture. *Solomon*, in that admirable prayer which he put up to God at the dedication of the temple, saith, " Hearken therefore unto the supplication of thy servant, and of thy people *Israel*, which they shall make towards this place." And hence I suppose it was that *Daniel*, that man greatly beloved, in the time of captivity, " prayed as aforetime three times a day with his face towards the temple." And what was said of the first, our Lord applies to the second temple, " My house shall be called a house of prayer." On this account also, true believers may be stiled, " the temple of the living God." For being wholly devoted and dedicated to God, even a God in Christ, their heart becomes the seats of prayer, from whence, as so many living altars, a perpetual sacrifice of prayer and praise (like unto, tho' infinitely superior to the perpetual oblation under the Mosaic dispensation) is continually ascending, and offered up, to the Father of Mercies, the God of all Consolations. Such, and such only, who thus worship God in the temple of their hearts, can truly be said to be made priests unto God, or be stiled a royal priesthood; such, and such only, can truly be stiled, " the temple of the living God," because such only pray to him, as one expresses it, in the temple of their hearts, and consequently worship him in spirit and in truth.

Let no one say that such a devotion is impracticable, or at least only practicable by a few, and those such who have nothing to do with the common affairs of life; for this is the common duty and privilege of all true christians. " To pray without ceasing," and " to rejoice in the Lord always," are precepts equally obligatory on all that name the name of Christ. And though it must be owned, that it is hard for persons that are immersed in the world, to serve the Lord without distraction; and though we must confess, that the lamp of devotion, even in the best of saints, sometimes burns too dimly, yet those who are the temple of the living God, find prayer to be their very element: And when those who make this objection, once come to love prayer, as some un-

happy

happy men love swearing, they will find no more difficulty in praying to, and praising GOD always, than these unhappy creatures do in cursing and swearing always. What hath been advanced, is far from being a state peculiar to persons wholly retired from the world.

My brethren, the love of GOD is all in all. When once possessed of this, as we certainly must be, if we are " the temple of the living GOD," meditation, prayer, praise, and other spiritual exercises, become habitual and delightful. When once touched with this divine magnet, for ever after the soul feels a divine attraction, and continually turns to its centre, GOD; and if diverted therefrom, by any sudden or violent temptation, yet when that obstruction is removed, like as a needle touched by a loadstone when your finger is taken away, turns to its rest, its centre, its GOD, its All, again.

The Jewish temple was also a place where the Great Jehovah was pleased in a more immediate manner to reside. Hence, he is said to put and record his name there, and to sit or dwell between the cherubims; and when *Solomon* first dedicated it, we are told, " the house was filled with a cloud, so that the priests could not stand to minister by reason of the cloud, for the glory of the LORD had filled the house." And wherefore all this amazing manifestation of the Divine Glory? Even for this, O man, to shew thee how the High and Lofty One that inhabiteth eternity, would make believers hearts his living temple, and dwell and make his abode in all those that tremble at his word.

To this, the apostle more particularly alludes in the words immediately following our text; for having called the *Corinthians* " the temple of the living GOD," he adds, " as GOD hath said, I will dwell in them, and I will walk in them, and I will be their GOD, and they shall be my people." Strange and strong expressions these! But strange and strong as they are, must be experienced by all who are indeed " the temple of the living GOD." For they are said, to be " chosen to be a holy habitation through the Spirit; to dwell in GOD,

and

and God in them; to have the witness in themselves, and to have God's Spirit witnessing with their spirits that they are the children of God." Which expressions import no more or less, than that prayer of our Lord which he put up for his church and people a little before his bitter passion, "That they may be one, even as we are one, I in them, and thou in me, that they may be made perfect in one:" This glorious passage our church adopts in her excellent communion office, and is so far from thinking that this was only the privilege of the apostles, that she asserts in the strongest terms, that it is the privilege of every worthy communicant. For then (says she) if we receive the sacrament worthily, we are one with Christ, and Christ is one with us; we dwell in Christ, and Christ in us. And what is it, but that inspiration of the Holy Spirit, which we pray for in the beginning of that office, and that fellowship of the Holy Ghost, which the minister, in the conclusion of every day's public prayer, entreats the Lord to be with us all evermore?

Brethren, the time would fail me to mention all the scriptures, and the various branches of our liturgy, articles, and homilies, that speak of this inestimable blessing, the indwelling of the blessed Spirit, whereby we do indeed become, "the temples of the living God." If you have eyes that see, or ears that hear, you may view it almost in every page of the lively oracles, and every part of those offices, which some of you daily use, and hear read to you, in the public worship of Almighty God. In asserting therefore this doctrine, we do not vent the whimsies of a disordered brain, and heated imagination; neither do we broach any new doctrines, or set up the peculiar opinions of any particular sect or denomination of christians whatsoever; but we speak the words of truth and soberness, we shew you the right and good old way, even that, in which the articles of all the reformed churches, and all sincere christians of all parties, however differing in other respects, do universally agree. We are now insisting upon a point, which may properly be termed the christian *shibboleth*, something which is the grand criterion of our most holy religion; and on account of which, the holy *Ignatius*, one of

the

the first fathers of the church, was used to stile himself a *bearer of* GOD, and the people to whom he wrote, *bearers of* GOD : For this, as it is recorded of him, he was arraigned before *Trajan*, who imperiously said, Where is this man, that says, he carries GOD about with him. With an humble boldness he answered, I am he, and then quoted the passage in the text " Ye are the temple of the living GOD ; as GOD hath said, I will dwell in them, and walk in them, and I will be their GOD, and they shall be my people." Upon this, to cure him of his enthusiasm, he was condemned to be devoured by lions.

Blessed be GOD ! we are not in danger of being called before such persecuting *Trajans* now : under our present mild and happy administration, the scourge of the tongue is all that they can legally lash us with. But if permitted to go farther, we need not be ashamed of witnessing this good confession. Suffering grace will be given for suffering times ; and if, like *Ignatius*, we are bearers of GOD, we also shall be enabled to say with him, when led to the devouring lions, Now I begin to be a disciple of CHRIST.

But it is time for me,

Secondly, To make some practical improvement of what has been delivered. You have heard in what sense it is that real christians are " the temple of the living GOD." Shall I ask, Believe ye these things ? I know and am persuaded that some of you do indeed believe them, not because I have told you, but because you yourselves have experienced the same.

I congratulate you from my inmost soul. O that your hearts may be in tune this day to " magnify the LORD," and your spirits prepared to " rejoice in GOD your Saviour." Like the Virgin *Mary*, you are highly favoured, and from henceforth all the generations of GOD's people shall call you blessed. You can call CHRIST, Lord, by the Holy Ghost, and thereby have an internal, as well as external evidence of the divinity, both of his person, and of his holy word. You can now prove that despised book, emphatically called The Scriptures, doth contain the perfect and acceptable will of GOD. You have found the second *Adam* to be a quickening spirit; He hath raised you from death to life. And being thus taught, and born of GOD, however unlearned in other respects, you can say, "Is not this the CHRIST?" O ineffable blessing! inconceivable privilege! GOD's spirit witnesseth with your spirits, that you are the children of GOD. When you think of this, are you not ready to cry out with the beloved disciple, "What manner of love is this, that we should be called the children of GOD!" I believe that holy man was in an extasy when he wrote these words; and tho' he has been in heaven so long, yet his extatic surprize is but now beginning, and will be but as beginning through the ages of eternity. Thus shall it be with all you likewise, whom the high and lofty One, that inhabiteth eternity, hath made his living temples. For He hath sealed you to the day of redemption, and hath given you the earnest of your future inheritance. His eyes and heart shall therefore be upon you continually: and in spite of all opposition from men or devils, the top-stone of this spirituaul building shall be brought forth, and you shall shout Grace, grace unto it: your bodies shall be fashioned like unto the Redeemer's glorious body, and your souls, in which (O infinite condescension!) He now delights to dwell, shall be filled with all the fulness of GOD. You shall then go no more out; you shall then no more need the light of the sun or the light of the moon, for the LORD himself will be your temple, and the Lamb in the midst thereof shall be your glory. Dearly beloved in the LORD, what say you to these things? Do not your hearts burn within you whilst thinking of these deep, but glorious truths of GOD. Whilst I am musing, and speaking of them, methinks a fire kindles even in this cold, icy heart of mine: O! what shall we render unto the LORD for all these mercies! Surely He hath done great things for us: How great is his goodness, and his bounty! O the heighth, the depth, the length, and the breadth of the love of GOD! Surely it passeth knowledge. O for humility! and a soul-abasing, GOD-exalting sense of these things! When the blessed virgin went into the hill country, to pay a visit to her cousin *Elizabeth*, amazed at such a favour, she cried out, "Whence is it that the mother of my LORD vouchsafes to come to me?" And when the great Jehovah filled the temple with his glory, out of the abundance of his heart, king *Solomon* burst forth into this pathetic exclamation, "But will GOD in very deed dwell with men on the earth?" With how much greater astonishment ought we to say, And will the LORD himself in very deed come to us? Will the high and lofty One that inhabiteth eternity, dwell in, and make our earthly hearts his living temples? My brethren, whence is this? From any fitness in us foreseen? No, I know you disclaim such an unbecoming thought. Was it then from the improvement of our own free-will? No, I am persuaded you will not thus debase the riches of GOD's free grace. Are you not all ready to say, Not unto us, not unto us, but unto thy free, thy unmerited, thy sovereign, distinguishing love and mercy, O LORD, be all the glory. It is this, and this alone, hath made the difference between us and others. We have nothing but what is freely given us from above: if we love GOD, it is because GOD first loved us. Let us look then unto the rock from whence we have been hewn, and the hole of the pit from whence we have been digged. And if there be any consolation in CHRIST, if any comfort of love, if any fellowship of the spirit, if any bowels and mercies, let us study and strive to walk as becometh those who are made the temples of the living GOD, or, as the apostle elsewhere expresseth himself, "a holy temple unto the LORD." What manner of persons ought such to be in all holy conversation and godliness? How holily and how purely should we live! As our apostle argues in another place, "For what fellowship hath righteousness with unrighteousness? What communion hath light with darkness? Or what concord hath CHRIST with Belial?" Shall those who are temples of the living GOD, suffer themselves to be dens of thieves and cages of unclean birds? Shall vain unchaste thoughts be suffered to dwell within them? much less shall any thing that is impure be conceived or acted by them? Shall we provoke the LORD to jealousy? GOD forbid! We all know with what distinguished ardor

our

our blessed Redeemer purged an earthly temple; a zeal for his father's house even eat him up: with what a holy vehemence did he overturn the tables of the money-changers, and scourge the buyers and sellers out before him! Why? They made his father's house a house of merchandise: they had turned the house of prayer into a den of thieves.

O my brethren, how often have you and I been guilty of this great evil? How often have the lust of the flesh, the lust of the eye, and the pride of life, insensibly stolen away our hearts from GOD? Once they were indeed houses of prayer; faith, hope, love, peace, joy, and all the other fruits of the blessed Spirit lodged within them; but now, O now, it may be, thieves and robbers. *Hinc illæ lachrymæ.* Hence those hidings of GOD's face, that dryness, and deadness, and barrenness of soul, those wearisome nights and days, which many of us have felt from time to time, and have been made to groan under. Hence those dolorous and heart-breaking complaints, "O that I knew where I might find him! O that it was with me as in days of old, when the candle of the LORD shone bright upon my soul!" Hence those domestic trials, those personal losses and disappointments: and to this perhaps some of us may add, hence all those public rebukes with which we have been visited: they are all only as so many scourges of small cords in the loving Redeemer's hands, to scourge the buyers and sellers out of the temple of our hearts. O that we may know the rod and who hath appointed it! He hath chastised us with whips: may we be wise, and by a more close and circumspect walk prevent his chastising us in time to come with scorpions! But who is sufficient for this thing? None but thou, O LORD, to whom alone all hearts are open, all desires known, and from whom no secrets are hidden! Cleanse thou therefore the thoughts of our hearts by the inspiration of thy blessed Spirit, that henceforward we may more perfectly love thee, and more worthily magnify thy holy name!

But are not some of you ready to object, and to fear, that the LORD hath forgotten to be gracious, that he hath shut up his loving kindnefs in difpleafure, and that he will be no more entreated? Thus the pfalmift once thought, when vifited for his backflidings with GOD's heavy hand. But he acknowledged this to be his infirmity; and whether you think of it or no, I tell you, this is your infirmity. O ye dejected, defponding, diftruftful fouls, hear ye the word of the LORD, and call to mind his wonderful declarations of old to his people. "I, even I am He that blotteth out thy tranfgreffions: for a fmall moment have I forfaken thee, but with everlafting mercies will I gather thee. Can a woman forget her fucking child? Yes fhe may, but the LORD will not forget you, O ye of little faith, For as a father pitieth his own children, fo doth the LORD pity them that fear him. How fhall I give thee up, O *Ephraim?* How fhall I make thee as *Admah?* How fhall I fet thee as *Zeboim?*" And what is the refult of all thefe interrogations? "My repentings are kindled together: I will not return to execute the fiercenefs of my anger againft *Ephraim:* For I am GOD, and not man." And is not the language of all thefe endearing paffages, like that of *Jofeph* to his felf-convicted, troubled brethren? "Come near to me." O that it may be faid of you, as it is faid of them, "And they came near unto him." Then fhould you find by happy experience, that the LORD, the LORD GOD, merciful and gracious, is indeed flow to anger and of great kindnefs, and repenteth him of the evil. Who knows but he may come down this day, this hour, nay this moment, and fuddenly revifit the temple of your hearts? Who knows but he may revive his work in your precious fouls, caufe you to return to your firft love, help you to do your firft works, and even exceed your hopes, and caufe the glory of this fecond vifitation even to furpafs that glory which filled your hearts, in that happy, never to be forgotten day, in which he firft vouchfafed to make you his living temples? Even fo, Father, let it feem good in thy fight!

But the improvement of our fubject muft not end here. Hitherto I have been giving bread to the children; and it is my meat and drink fo to do: but muft nothing be faid to thofe of you who are without? I mean to fuch who cannot yet

yet say, that they are "the temple of the living God." And O how great, put you all together, may the number of you be: by far, in all probability, the greatest part of this auditory. Say not I am uncharitable; the God of truth, hath said it, "Strait is the gate, and narrow is the way, which leadeth unto life, and few there be that find it." Suffer me to speak plainly to you, my brethren; you have heard what has been said upon the words of our text, and what must be wrought in us, ere we can truly say that we are "the temple of the living God." Is it so with you? Are ye separated from the world and worldly tempers? Are your hearts become houses of prayer? Doth the Spirit of God dwell in your souls? and whether you eat or drink, or whatsoever you do, as to the habitual bent of your minds, do you do all to the glory of God? These are short, but plain, and let me tell you very important questions. What answer can you make to them? Say not, "Go thy way, and at a more convenient season I will call for thee." I will not, I must not suffer you to put me off so; I demand an answer in the name of the Lord of Hosts. What say ye? Methinks, I hear you say, We have been dedicated to God in baptism, we go to church or meeting, we say our prayers, repeat our creeds, or have subscribed the articles, and the confession of faith; we are quite orthodox, and great friends to the doctrines of grace; we do no body any harm, we are honest moral people, we are churc-hmembers, we keep up family-prayer, and constantly go to the table of the Lord." All these things are good in their places.. But thus far, nay much farther may you go, and yet be far from the kingdom of God. The unprofitable servant did no one any harm; and the foolish virgins had a lamp of an outward profession, and went up even to heaven's gate, calling Christ, "Lord, Lord." These things may make you whited sepulchres, but not "the temples of the living God." Alas! Alas! one thing you yet lack, the one chief thing, and without which all is nothing; I mean the indwelling of God's blessed Spirit, without which you can never become "the temples of the living God."

Awake

Awake therefore, ye deceived formalists, awake; who, vainly puffed up with your model of performances, boastingly cry out, "The temple of the Lord, the temple of the Lord, the temple of the Lord are we." Awake, ye outward-court worshippers: ye are building on a sandy foundation: take heed lest you also go to hell by the very door of heaven. Behold, and remember, I have told you before.

And as for you who have done none of these things, who instead of making an outward profession of religion, have as it were renounced your baptism, proclaim your sin like *Sodom*, and wilfully and daringly live as without God in the world; I ask you, how can you think to escape, if you persist in neglecting such a great salvation. Verily, I should utterly despair of your ever attaining the blessed privilege of being temples of the living God, did I not hear of thousands, who through the grace of God have been translated from a like state of darkness into his marvellous light. Such, says the apostle *Paul*, writing to these very *Corinthians* who were now God's living temples, (drunkards, whoremongers, adulterers, and such like) "such were some of you. But ye are washed, but ye are sanctified, but ye are justified in the name of the Lord Jesus, and by the Spirit of our God." O that the same blessed Spirit may this day vouchsafe to come and pluck you also as brands out of the burning! Behold, I warn you to flee from the wrath to come. Go home, and meditate on these things; and think whether it is not infinitely better, even here, to be temples of the living God, than to be bond-slaves to every brutish lust, and to be led captive by the devil at his will. The Lord Jesus can, and if you fly to him for refuge, he will set your souls at liberty. He hath led captivity captive, he hath ascended up on high, on purpose to receive this gift of the blessed Spirit of God for men, "even for the rebellious," that he might dwell in your hearts by faith here, and thereby prepare you to dwell with Him and all the heavenly host in his kingdom hereafter.

That this may be the happy lot of you all, may God of his infinite mercy grant, for the sake of his dear Son Christ Jesus

JESUS our LORD; to whom with the Father, and the blessed Spirit, three persons, but one GOD, be ascribed all power, might, majesty, and dominion, now and for evermore. Amen! and Amen!

SERMON LI.

CHRIST the only Preservative against a Reprobate Spirit.

---

2 COR. xiii. 5.

Know ye not your ownselves, how that JESUS CHRIST *is in you, except ye be Reprobates.*

THE doctrines of the gospel are doctrines of peace, and they bring comfort to all who believe in them; they are not like the law given by *Moses*, which consisted of troublesome and painful ceremonies; neither do they carry with them that terror which the law did; as, "cursed is every one who continueth not to do all things which are written in the book of the law:" If you were to keep the whole law, and break but in one point, you are guilty of the breach of all. The law denounces threatnings against all who do not conform to her strict commands; but the gospel is a declaration of grace, peace and mercy; here you have an account of the blood of CHRIST, blood which speaketh better things than that of *Abel*; for *Abel*'s blood cried aloud for vengeance, vengeance: But JESUS CHRIST's crieth mercy, mercy, mercy upon the guilty sinner. If he comes to CHRIST, confesses and forsakes his sin, then JESUS will have mercy upon him: And if, my brethren, you are but sensible of your sins, convinced of your iniquities, and feel yourselves lost, undone sinners, and come and tell CHRIST of your lost condition, you will soon find how ready he is to help you;

he

he will give you his spirit; and if you have his spirit you cannot be reprobates: you will find his spirit to be quickening and refreshing; not like the spirit of the world, a spirit of reproach, envy, and all uncharitableness.

Most of your own experiences will confirm the truth hereof; for are not you reproached and slandered, and does not the world say all manner of evil against you, merely because you follow Jesus Christ; because you will not go to the same excess of riot with them? While they are singing the songs of the drunkard, you are singing psalms and hymns: while they are at a playhouse, you are hearing a sermon: while they are drinking, revelling and mispending their precious time, and hastening on their own destruction, you are reading, praying, meditating, and working out your salvation with fear and trembling. This is matter enough for a world to reproach you; you are not polite and fashionable enough for them. If you will live godly, you must suffer persecution; you must not expect to go through this world without being persecuted and reviled. If you were of the world, the world would love you; for it always loves its own; but if you are not of the world, it will hate you; it has done so in all ages, it never loved any but those who were pleased with its vanities and allurements. It has been the death of many a lover of Jesus, merely because they have loved him: And, therefore, my brethren, do not be surprized if you meet with a fiery trial, for all those things will be a means of sending you to your master the sooner.

The spirit of the world is hatred; that of Christ is love: the spirit of the world is vexation; that of Christ is pleasure: the spirit of the world is sorrow; that of Christ is joy: the spirit of the world is evil, and that of Christ is good: the spirit of the world will never satisfy us, but Christ's spirit is all satisfaction: the spirit of the world is misery; that of Christ is ease. In one word, the spirit of the world has nothing lasting; but the spirit of Christ is durable, and will last through an eternity of ages: the spirit of Christ will remove every difficulty, satisfy every doubt,

and

and be a means of bringing you to himself, to live with him for ever and ever.

From the words of my text, I shall shew you,

I. The necessity of receiving the spirit of CHRIST.

II. Who CHRIST is, whose spirit you are to receive. And then

Shall conclude with an exhortation to all of you, high and low, rich and poor, to come unto the LORD JESUS CHRIST, and to beg that you may receive his spirit, so that you may not be reprobates.

First, I am to shew you the necessity there is of receiving the spirit of CHRIST.

And here, my brethren, it will be necessary to consider you as in your first state; that is, when GOD first created *Adam*, and placed him in the garden of *Eden*, and gave him a privilege of eating of all the trees in the garden, except the tree of knowledge of good and evil, which stood in the midst thereof. Our first parents had not been long in this state of innocence, before they fell from it, they broke the divine commands, and involved all their posterity in guilt; for as *Adam* was our representative, so we were to stand or fall in him; and as he was our foederal head, his falling involved all our race under the power of death, for death came into the world by sin; and we all became liable to the eternal punishment due from GOD, for man's disobedience to the divine command.

Now as man had sinned, and a satisfaction was demanded, it was impossible for a finite creature to satisfy him, who was a GOD of so strict purity as not to behold iniquity: And man by the justice of GOD would have been sent down into the pit, which was prepared of old for the devil and his angels; but when justice was going to pass the irrevocable sentence, then the LORD JESUS CHRIST came and offered himself a ransom a ranfom for poor finners. Here was admirable condefcenfion of the Lord Jesus Christ! that he who was in the bofom of his father, fhould come down from all that glory, to die for fuch rebels as you and I are, who if it lay in our power, would pull the Almighty from his throne: Now can you think that if there was no need of Christ's death, can you think that if there could have been any other ranfom found, whereby poor finners might have been faved, God would not have fpared his only begotten Son, and not have delivered him up for all that believe in him?

This, my brethren, I think proves to a demonftration, that it was neceffary for Christ to die: But confider, it will be of no fervice to know that Christ died for finners, if you do not accept of his fpirit, that you may be fanctified, and fitted for the reception of that Jesus, who died for all thofe who believe in him. The fin of your nature, your original fin, is fufficient to fink you into torments, of which there will be no end; therefore unlefs you receive the fpirit of Christ you are reprobates, and you cannot be faved: Nothing fhort of the blood of Jesus applied to your fouls, will make you happy to all eternity: Then, feeing this is fo abfolutely neceffary, that you cannot be faved without having received the fpirit of Christ, but that ye are reprobates, do not reft contented 'till you have good hopes, through grace, that the good work is begun in your fouls; that you have received a pardon for your fins; that Christ came down from heaven, died, and made fatisfaction for your fins. Don't flatter yourfelves that a little morality will be fufficient to fave you; that going to church, or prayers, and facrament, and doing all the duties of religion in an external manner, will ever carry you to heaven; no, you muft have grace in your hearts; there muft be a change of the whole man.

You muft be born again, and become new creatures, and have the fpirit of Christ within you: And until you have that fpirit of Christ, however you may think to the contrary, and pleafe yourfelves in your own imagination, I fay, you are no better than reprobates. You may content yourselves with leading civil, outward decent lives, but what will that avail you, unless you have the spirit of the LORD JESUS CHRIST in your hearts: His kingdom must be set up in your souls; there must be the life of GOD in the soul of man, else you belong not to the LORD JESUS CHRIST; and until you belong to him, you are reprobates.

This may seem as enthusiasm to some of you, but if it is so, it is what the apostle *Paul* taught; and therefore, my brethren, they are the words of truth. I beseech you, in the mercies of GOD in CHRIST JESUS, not to despise these words, as if they do not concern you, but were only calculated for the first ages of christianity, and, therefore, of no signification: If you think thus, you are wronging your own souls; for whatever is written, was written for you in these times, as well as for the christians in the first ages of the church.

For the case stands thus between GOD and man: GOD, at first, made man upright, or, as the sacred penman expresses it, "In the image of GOD made he man;" his soul was the very copy, the transcript of the divine nature. He who had, by his almighty power, spoken the world into being, breathed into man the breath of spiritual life; and his soul became adorned with purity and perfection. This was the finishing stroke of the creation; the perfection both of the moral and material world; and it so resembled the divine Original, that GOD could not but rejoice and take pleasure in his own likeness: Therefore, we read, that when GOD had finished the inanimate and brutish part of the creation, "he looked, and behold it was good." But when that lovely, god-like creature man was made, "behold it was very good."

Happy, unspeakably happy, to be thus partaker of a divine Nature; and thus man might have continued still, had he continued holy; but GOD placed him in a state of probation, with a free grant to eat of every tree in the garden, except the tree of knowledge of good and evil. The day he did eat thereof he was not only to become subject to temporal, but spiritual death; and so lose that divine image, that spiritual life which God had breathed into him, and which was as much his happiness as his glory.

But man, unhappy man, being seduced by the devil, did eat of the forbidden fruit, and thereby became liable to that curse which the eternal God had pronounced on him for his disobedience. And we read, that soon after *Adam* was fallen, he complained that he was naked; naked, not only as to his body, but naked and destitute of those divine graces which before beautified his soul.

An unhappy mutiny and disorder then fell upon this world; those briars and thorns which now spring up and overspread the earth, were but poor emblems, lifeless representations of that confusion and rebellion which sprung up in, and overwhelmed, the soul of man, immediately after the fall. He now sunk into the temper of a beast and devil.

In this dreadful and disordered condition are all of us brought into the world: We are told, my brethren, that " *Adam* had a son in his own likeness," or with the same corrupt nature which he himself had sunk into, after eating the forbidden fruit: And experience, as well as scripture, proves, that we are altogether born in sin, and, therefore, uncapable, whilst in such a state, to have communion with God.

For as light cannot have communion with darkness, so God can have no communion with such polluted sons of *Belial*. Here, here, appears the great and glorious end, why Christ was manifest in the flesh, to put an end to these disorders, and to restore us unto the favour of God. He came down from heaven and shed his precious blood upon the cross, to satisfy the divine justice of his Father, for our sins; and so, he purchased this Holy Ghost, who must once more re-stamp the divine image on our hearts, and make us capable of living with, and enjoying of God. We must be renewed by the spirit of God; he must dwell in us before we can be new creatures, and be freed from a reprobate spirit: the spirit of CHRIST muſt bring us home unto that fold where all his ſheep are, and implant his grace in our hearts, and take from us that ſpirit of ſin which reigns in us: And till this is rooted out of our hearts, however we may flatter ourſelves with being good chriſtians, becauſe we are good moraliſts, and lead civil, moral, decent lives, yet if we live and die, my brethren, in this way, we are only flattering ourſelves into hell.

I think I have proved, to a demonſtration, the neceſſity there is of receiving the ſpirit of CHRIST. I now come to ſhew you,

Secondly, Who CHRIST is, whoſe ſpirit you are to receive.

My brethren, JESUS CHRIST is coequal, coeſſential, coeternal, and conſubſtantial with the Father, very GOD of very GOD; and as there was not a moment of time in which GOD the Father was not, ſo there was not a moment of time in which GOD the Son was not.

Arians and *Socinians* deny this godhead of CHRIST, and eſteem him only as a creature: The *Arians* look on him as a titular Deity, as a created and ſubordinate God; but, if they would humbly ſearch the ſcriptures they would find divine homage paid to CHRIST. He is called GOD in ſcripture, particularly when the great evangelical Prophet ſays, " He ſhall be called the mighty GOD, the everlaſting Father, and the government ſhall be upon his ſhoulders:" And JESUS CHRIST himſelf ſays, that he is the Alpha and Omega;" and that " the world was made by him:" But though this be ever ſo plain, our gay airy ſparks of this age will not believe the LORD JESUS CHRIST to be equal with his Father, and that for no other reaſon, but becauſe it is a faſhionable and polite doctrine to deny his divinity, and eſteem him only as a created God.

Our *Socinians* do not go ſo far; they look upon CHRIST only to be a good man ſent from GOD, to ſhew the people the way they should go, on their forsaking of Judaism; that he was to be also an example to the world, and that his death was only to prove the truth of his doctrines.

Many of those who call themselves members, yea, teachers of the church of *England*, have got into this polite scheme. Good God! my very soul shudders at the thoughts of the consequence that will attend such a belief. O my brethren, do not think so dishonourably of the LORD who bought you; of the JESUS who died for you: he must be all in all unto your souls, if ever you are saved by him: CHRIST must be your active, as well as passive obedience; his righteousness must be imputed to you. The doctrine of CHRIST's righteousness being imputed, is a comfortable, a desirable doctrine to all real christians: And to you, sinners, who are enquiring what you must do to be saved? how uncomfortable would it be to tell you, by your own good works, when, perhaps, you have never done one good work in all your lives: This would be driving you to despair indeed; no, " believe in the LORD JESUS CHRIST and you shall be saved;" come to the LORD JESUS by faith, and he shall receive you. He is able and willing to save you.

This second person in the Trinity, who is God-man, the mediator of the new covenant; he, my brethren, hath virtue enough, in his blood, to atone for the sins of millions of worlds: As man he died, he was crucified, nailed to, and pierced on the accursed tree: This was the love of the LORD JESUS CHRIST for you; and will you then have low and dishonourable thoughts of JESUS CHRIST, after his having done so much for you? O my dear brethren, don't be so polite as to deny the Deity of CHRIST; though you may be counted fools in the eye of the world, yet in GOD's account, you shall be esteemed wise, wise for salvation.

You may now be looked upon as fools and madmen, as a parcel of rabble, and, in a short time, fit for Bedlam. They may say you are going to undermine the established church; but GOD, who knows the secrets of all hearts, knows our innocency;

innocency; and I speak the truth in CHRIST, I lie not, I should rejoice to see all the world adhere to her articles; I should rejoice to see the teachers, the ministers of the church of *England*, preach up those very articles they have subscribed to; but those ministers who do preach them up, they esteem as madmen, and look on them, as the off-scouring of the earth, unfit for company and conversation.

The evil things they say of me, blessed be GOD, are without foundation; I am a friend to the church homilies; I am a friend to her liturgy, and if they did not thrust me out of their churches, I would read it every day.

My brethren, I am not for limiting the spirit of GOD, but am for uniting all in the bonds of love; I love all that love the LORD JESUS CHRIST: This will make more christians, than will the spirit of persecution.

The Pharisees may think it madness to mention persecution in a christian country, but the spirit of persecution resides in many: their will is as great, but blessed be GOD, they want the power; if they had that, my brethren, fire and faggot is what we must expect, for the devil's temple is shaken. Many are coming unto JESUS, I hope many of you are already come, and many more coming; this must make Satan rage, to see his kingdom weakened; he will stir up all his malice against the people of GOD. We must expect, that a suffering time will certainly come; it is now hastening on, it is ripening a-pace; then it will be proved, to a demonstration, whether you are hypocrites or not; for suffering times are always trying times. O my brethren, do not be afraid of a little reproach, but look on it as a fore-runner of what will be the attendant upon it: Therefore let me, by way of application,

Exhort all of you, high and low, rich and poor, one with another, to come unto the LORD JESUS CHRIST, that he may give you strength to undergo whatsoever he, in his wisdom, calls you to. Come, come, my brethren, to JESUS

Christ, and he will give you grace, which will make you willing and ready to suffer all things for Jesus Christ.

It is not being pointed at; it is not being despised and looked on as mad, and a deluded people: Alas! what does this signify to a soul who has Jesus Christ? Do not be afraid to confess the blessed Jesus; dare to be singularly good: Don't be afraid of singing of hymns, or of meeting together to build each other up in the ways of the Lord: Shine ye as lights in the world amidst a crooked and perverse generation.

It is necessary that offences should come, to try what is in our hearts, and whether we will be faithful soldiers of Jesus Christ or not: Be not content with following Christ afar off, for then we shall, as *Peter* did, soon deny him; but let us be altogether christians. Let our speech and all our actions declare to the whole world, whose disciples we are, and that we have determined to know nothing but Jesus Christ, and him crucified. O then, then, will it be well with us, happy, unspeakably happy, shall we be, even here; and what is infinitely better, when others that despised us shall be calling for the mountains to fall on them, and the hills to cover them, we shall be exalted to sit down on the right hand of God, and shine as the sun in the firmament, and live for ever with our Redeemer. And will not this be a sufficient recompence for all the sufferings you have undergone here? Therefore, do not strive to have the greatness, the riches, the honour, and pleasures of this world, but strive to have Jesus Christ.

Your friends and carnal acquaintance, and, above all, your grand adversary the devil, will be persuading you not to have Christ until you are grown old; he would have you lay up goods for many years; to see plays, play at cards; go to balls, and masquerades; and to make you the more willing, to draw you in, he calls sinful pleasures, innocent diversions.

A late learned Rabbi of our church, told the people, in a sermon, which I myself heard, that if people went to church of a Sunday, and said the prayers while there, that it was no harm, neither would GOD count it a sin, to take their recreation, after the service of the church was over: But I say, my brethren, and the command of GOD says so too, that the whole sabbath must be kept holy; and that as GOD has allowed you six days for yourselves, to do the duties in those several stations wherein Providence has placed you, he expects you should give him one day to himself; and will you waste that sabbath which should be spent in gathering provisions for your souls? GOD forbid!

You had ten thousand times better be ignorant of all the polite diversions of the age, than to be ignorant of the spirit of CHRIST's being within you, and that it must be, before you are *new creatures*, and are in CHRIST; and if you have not an interest in CHRIST, you are lost, your damnation is hastening on. " He that believeth shall be saved, and he that believeth not shall be damned."

If you stand out against CHRIST, you are fighting against yourselves. O come unto him, do not stay to bring good works with you, for they will be of no service; all your works will never carry you to heaven, they will never pardon one sin, nor give you the least comfort in a dying hour; if you have nothing more than your own works to recommend you to GOD, they will not prevent your sinking into that eternal abyss, where there is no bottom.

But come unto CHRIST, and he will give you that righteousness which will stand you in good account at the great day of the LORD, when he shall come to take notice of them that love him, and of those who have the wedding garment on.

Let all your actions spring from the love of JESUS; let him be the Alpha and Omega of all your actions; then, my brethren, our indifferent ones are acceptable sacrifices; but if this principle be wanting, our most pompous services avail nothing; we are only spiritual idolaters; we sacrifice to our own net, and make an idol of ourselves, by making ourselves,

and

and not CHRIST, the spring of our actions; and therefore, my brethren, such actions are so far from being accepted by GOD, that according to the language of one of the articles of our church, "We doubt not but that they have the nature of sin, because they spring not from an experimental faith in, and knowledge of JESUS CHRIST."

Were we not fallen creatures, we might then act upon other principles; but since we are fallen in *Adam*, and are restored again only by the death of JESUS CHRIST, the face of things is intirely changed, and all we think, speak, or do, is only accepted in and through him.

Therefore, my brethren, I beseech you, in the bowels of love and compassion, that you would come unto JESUS: Do not go away scoffing, offended, or blaspheming. Indeed, all I say is in love to your souls; and if I could be but an instrument of bringing you to JESUS CHRIST, if you were to be never so much exalted, I should not envy, but rejoice in your happiness: If I was to make up the last of the train of the companions of the blessed JESUS, it would rejoice me to see you above me in glory. I do not speak out of a false humility, a pretended sanctity; no, GOD is my judge, I speak the truth in CHRIST, I lie not, I would willingly go to prison, or to death for you, so I could but bring one soul from the devil's strong holds, into the salvation which is by CHRIST JESUS.

Come then unto CHRIST every one that hears me this night; I offer JESUS CHRIST, pardon, and salvation to all you, who will accept thereof. Come, O ye drunkards, lay aside your cups, drink no more to excess; come and drink of the water which CHRIST will give you, and then you will thirst no more : come, O ye thieves; let him that has stolen, steal no more, but fly unto CHRIST and he will receive you. Come unto him, O ye harlots; lay aside your lusts and turn unto the LORD, and he will have mercy upon you, he will cleanse you of all your sins, and wash you in his blood.

Come,

Come, all ye liars; come, all ye Pharisees; come, all ye fornicators, adulterers, swearers, and blasphemers, come to Christ, and he will take away all your filth, he will cleanse you from your pollution, and your sins shall be done away. Come, come, my guilty brethren; I beseech you for Christ's sake, and for your immortal soul's sake, to come unto Christ: Do not let me knock at the door of your hearts in vain, but open and let the King of Glory in, and he will dwell with you, he will come and sup with you this night; this hour, this moment he is ready to receive you, therefore come unto him.

Do not consult with flesh and blood, let not the world hinder you from coming to the Lord of life: What are a few transitory pleasures of this life worth? They are not worth your having, but Jesus Christ is a pearl of great price, he is worth the laying out all you have, to buy.

And if you are under afflictions, fly not to company to divert you, neither read what the world calls harmless books; they only tend to harden the heart, and to keep you from closing with the Lord Jesus Christ.

When I was a child, yea, when I came to riper years, God knows, it is with grief I speak it, when ignorant of the excellency of the word of God, I read as many of these harmless books as any one; but now I have tasted the good word of life, and am come to a more perfect knowledge of Christ Jesus my Lord; I put away these childish, trifling things, and am determined to read no other books but what lead me to a knowledge of myself, and Jesus Christ.

Methinks I could speak till midnight unto you, my brethren; I am full of love towards you; let me beseech you to fly to Christ for succour: "Now is the accepted time, now is the day of salvation;" therefore delay not, but strive to enter in at the strait gate; do not go the broad way of the polite world, but choose to suffer affliction with the

people

people of GOD, rather than to enjoy the pleasures of sin for a season: You will have a reward afterwards, that will make amends for all the taunts, jeers, and calamities you may undergo here.

And will not the presence of CHRIST be a sufficient reward for all you have suffered for his name's sake? Why will you not accept of the LORD of glory? Do not say you have not heard of CHRIST, for he is now offered to you, and you will not accept of him; do not blame my master, he is willing to save you, if you will but lay hold on him by faith; and if you do not, your blood will be required of your own heads.

But I hope that you will not let the blood of JESUS be shed in vain, and that you will not let my preaching be of no signification. Would you have me go and tell my master, you will not come, and that I have spent my strength in vain; I cannot bear to carry so unpleasing a message unto him, I would not, indeed, I would not be a swift witness against any of you at the great day of accounts; but if you will refuse these gracious invitations, and not accept of them, I must do it: and will it not move your tender hearts to see your friends taken up into heaven, and you yourselves thrust down into hell? But I hope better things of most of you, even that you will turn unto the LORD of love, the JESUS who died for you, that in the day when he shall come to take his people to the mansions of everlasting rest, you may hear his voice, "Come, ye blessed of my Father, enter into the kingdom prepared for you before the foundation of the world." And that we may all enter into that glory, do thou, O JESUS, prepare us, by thy grace; give us thy spirit; and may our hearts be united to thee: May the word that has now been spoken, take deep root in thy people's hearts, that it may spring up and bring forth fruit, in some thirty, in some forty, and in some an hundred fold; do thou preserve them while in this life from all evil, and keep them from falling, and at last present them faultless before thy Father, when thou comest to judge the world, that where thou art, they may

be

be alſo. Grant this, O Lord Jesus Christ, with whatever elſe thou ſeeſt needful for us, both at this time and for evermore.

Now to God the Father, God the Son, and God the Holy Ghoſt, be aſcribed all honour, power, glory, might, majeſty and dominion, both now and for evermore, Amen.

SERMON LII.

The heinous Sin of Drunkenness.

EPHESIANS v. 18.

Be not drunk with Wine, wherein is Excess; but be filled with the Spirit.

THE persons to whom these words were written, were the inhabitants of *Ephesus*, as we are told in the *Acts*, had been worshipppers of the great goddess *Diana*, and, in all probability, worshipped the God *Bacchus* also; at the celebration of whose festivals, it was always customary, nay, part of their religion, to get drunk; as though there was no other way to please their God, but by turning themselves into brutes.

The apostle therefore in this chapter, amongst many other precepts more especially applicable to them, lays down this in the text; and exhorts them, as they had now, by the free grace of GOD, been turned from heathenish darkness to the light of the gospel, to walk as children of light, and no longer make it part of their religion or practice to be " drunk with wine, wherein is excess;" but, on the contrary, strive to " be filled with the Spirit" of that Saviour, after whose name they were called, and whose religion taught them to abstain from a filthy sin, and to live soberly as they ought to live.

The world being now christian, and the doctrines of the gospel every where received, one would imagine, there should be no reason for repeating the precept now before us. But alas,

alas, christians! I mean christians falsely so called, are led captive by all sin in general, and by this of drunkenness in particular; that was St. *Paul* to rise again from the dead, he might be tempted to think most of us were turned back to the worship of dumb idols; had set up temples in honour of *Bacchus*; and made it part of our religion, as the *Ephesians* did of theirs, " to be drunk with wine, wherein is excess."

Some of our civil magistrates have not been wanting to use the power given them from above, for the punishment and restraint of such evil doings; and I wish it could be said this plague of drinking, by what they have done, had been stayed amongst us. But alas! though their labour, we trust, has not been altogether in vain in the LORD, yet thousands, and I could almost say ten thousands, fall daily at our right-hand, by this sin of drunkenness, in our streets; nay, men seem to have made a covenant with hell, and though the power of the civil magistrate is exerted against them, nay, though they cannot but daily see the companions of their riot hourly, by this sin, brought to the grave, yet " they will rise up early to follow strong drink, and cry, To-morrow shall be as to-day, and so much the more abundantly; when we awake, we will seek it yet again."

It is high time therefore, for thy ministers, O GOD, to lift up their voices like a trumpet; and since human threats cannot prevail, to set before them the terrors of the LORD, and try if these will not persuade them to cease from the evil of their doings.

But alas! how shall I address myself to them? I fear excess of drinking has made them such mere *Nabals*, that there is no speaking to them. And many of GOD's servants have toiled all their life-time in dissuading them from this sin of drunkenness, yet they will not forbear. However, at thy command, I will speak also, though they be a rebellious house. Magnify thy strength, O LORD, in my weakness, and grant that I may speak with such demonstration of the Spirit, and power,

that

that from henceforward they may cease to act so unwisely, and this sin of drunkenness may not be their ruin.

Believe me, ye unhappy men of *Belial*, (for such, alas! this sin has made you) it is not without the strongest reasons, as well as utmost concern for your precious and immortal souls, that I now conjure you, in the Apostle's words, " Not to be drunk with wine, or any other liquor, wherein is excess." For,

First, Drunkenness is a sin which must be highly displeasing to GOD; because it is an abuse of his good creatures.

When GOD first made man, and had breathed into him the breath of life, he gave him dominion over the works of his hands; and every herb bearing seed, and every tree, in which was the fruit of a tree yielding seed, to him was given for meat: but when *Adam* had tasted the forbidden fruit, which was the only restraint laid upon him, he forfeited this privilege, and had no right, after he had disobeyed his Creator, to the use of any one of the creatures.

But, blessed be GOD, this charter, as well as all other privileges, is restored to us by the death of the second *Adam*, our LORD and Master JESUS CHRIST. Of every beast of the field, every fish of the sea, and whatsoever flieth in the air, or moveth on the face of the earth, that is fit for food, " we may freely eat," without scruple take and eat; but then, with this limitation, that we use them moderately. For GOD, by the death of JESUS, has given no man licence to be intemperate; but, on the contrary, has laid us under the strongest obligations to live soberly, as well as godly, in this present world.

But the drunkard, despising the goodness and bounty of GOD, in restoring to us what we had so justly forfeited, turns his grace into wantonness; and as though the creature was not of itself enough subject to vanity, by being cursed for our sake, he abuses it still more, by making it administer to his lusts;

lusts; and turns that wine which was intended to make glad his heart, into a deadly poison.

But thinkest thou, O drunkard, whosoever thou art, thou shalt escape the righteous judgment of GOD? No, the time will shortly come that thou must be no longer steward, and then the Sovereign LORD of all the earth will reckon with thee for thus wasting his goods. Alas! wilt thou then wrest scripture any longer to thy own damnation? And because JESUS CHRIST turned water into wine at the marriage-feast, to supply the wants of his indigent host, say, that it is therefore meet to make merry, and be drunken. No, thou shalt be silent before him; and know, that though thou hast encouraged thyself in drunkenness by such-like arguments, yet for all these things GOD will bring thee into judgment. But,

Secondly, What makes drunkenness more exceedingly sinful, is, that a man, by falling into it, sinneth against his own body.

When the apostle would dissuade the *Corinthians* from fornication, he urges this as an argument, " Flee fornication, brethren; for he that committeth fornication, sinneth against his own body." And may not I as justly cry out, Flee drunkenness, my brethren, since he that committeth that crime, sinneth against his own body? For, from whence come so many diseases and distempers in your bodies? Come they not from hence, even from your intemperance in drinking? Who hath pains in the head? Who hath rottenness in the bones? Who hath redness of eyes? He that tarries long at the wine, he that rises early to seek new wine. How many walking skeletons have you seen, whose bodies were once exceeding fair to look upon, fat and well-favoured; but, by this sin of drinking, how has their beauty departed from them, and how have they been permitted to walk to and fro upon the earth, as though GOD intended to set them up, as he did *Lot*'s wife, for monuments of his justice, that others might learn not to get drunk? Nay, I appeal to yourselves: are not many, for

this

this cause, even now sickly among you? And have not many of your companions, whom you once saw so flourishing, like green bay trees, been brought by it with sorrow to their graves?

We might, perhaps, think ourselves hardly dealt with by God, was he to send us, as he did the royal Psalmist, to choose one plague out of three, whereby we should be destroyed. But had the Almighty decreed to cut off man from the face of the earth, and to shorten his days, he could not well send a more effectual plague, than to permit men, as they pleased, to over-charge themselves with drunkenness; for though it be a slow, yet it is a certain poison. And if the sword has slain its thousands, drunkenness has slain its ten thousands.

And will not this alarm you, O ye transgressors? Will not this persuade you to spare yourselves, and to do your bodies no harm? What, have you lost the first principles of human nature, the fundamental law of self-preservation? You seem to have a great fondness for your bodies; why, otherwise, to gratify the inordinate appetites, do you drink to excess? But surely, if you truly loved them, you would not thus destroy them; and was there no other argument to be urged against drunkenness, the consideration that it will destroy those lives you are so fond of, one would imagine, should be sufficient.

I know, indeed, that it is a common answer, which drunkards make to those, who, out of love, would pull them as firebrands out of the fire, we are no body's enemy but our own. But this, instead of being an excuse for, is an aggravation of their guilt: for (not to mention that the drunkenness of one man has cloathed many a family with rags, and that it is scarce possible for a person to be drunk, without tempting his neighbour also) not to mention these, and many other ill consequences, which would prove such an excuse to be entirely false: yet what is dearer to a man than himself? And if he himself be lost, what would all the whole world avail him? But how wilt thou stand, O man, before the judgment-seat of CHRIST, and make such an excuse, when thou shalt be arraigned before him as a self-murderer? Will it then be sufficient, thinkest thou, to say, I was no man's enemy but my own? No; GOD will then tell thee, that thou oughtest to have glorified him with thy spirit, and with thy body, which were his; and since thou hast, by intemperance, destroyed thy body, he will destroy both thy body and soul in hell. But,

Thirdly, What renders drunkenness more inexcusable, is, that it robs a man of his reason.

Reason is the glory of a man; the chief thing whereby GOD has made us to differ from the brute creation. And our modern unbelievers have exalted it to such a high degree, as even to set it in opposition to revelation, and so deny the LORD that bought them. But though, in doing this, they greatly err, and whilst they profess themselves wise, become real fools; yet we must acknowledge, that reason is the candle of the LORD, and whosoever puts it out, shall bear his punishment, whosoever he be.

But yet, this the drunkard does. *Nebuchadnezzar*'s curse he makes his choice, his reason departeth from him; and then what is he better than a brute?

The very heathen kings were so sensible of this, that, in order to deter their young princes from drinking, they used to make their slaves get drunk, and be exposed before them. And didst thou but see thine own picture, O drunkard, when, after having drowned thy reason, thou staggerest to and fro, like one of the fools in *Israel*, and seest thy very companions making songs upon thee, surely thou wouldst not return to thy vomit again, but abhor thyself in dust and ashes!

When *David*, in a holy ecstacy, was dancing before the ark, *Michal*, *Saul*'s daughter, despised him in her heart; and when he came home, she said, " How glorious was the king of *Israel* to-day, who uncovered himself to-day in the eyes of the hand-maids of his servants, as one of the vain fellows shamelessly uncovereth himself." But may not every one that meets a drunkard, more justly say, How glorious does he, that was made a little lower than the angels, look to-day, when, unmindful of his dignity, he has by drinking robbed himself of his reason, and reduced himself to a level with the beasts that perish.

But what if GOD, in the midst of one of these drunken fits, should arrest thee by death, and say unto thee, " Thou fool, this moment shall thy soul be required of thee." O! how wouldst thou appear in those filthy garments before that GOD, in whose sight the heavens are not clean. And how knowest thou, O man, but this may be thy lot? Hast thou not known many summoned at such an unguarded hour? and what assurance hast thou, that thou shalt not be the next? Because GOD has forborn thee so long, thinkest thou he will forbear always? No, this is rather a sign that he will come at an hour thou lookest not for him; and since his goodness and long-suffering has not led thee to repentance, he will cut thee down, and not permit thee to cumber the ground any longer. Consider this then, all ye that count it a pleasure to turn yourselves into brutes, lest GOD pluck you away by a sudden death, and there be none to deliver you.

Fourthly, There is a farther aggravation of this crime, that it is an inlet to, and forerunner of many other sins; for it seldom comes alone.

We may say of drunkenness, as *Solomon* does of strife, that it is like the letting out of water; for we know not what will be the end thereof. Its name is *Legion*; behold a troop of sins cometh after it. And, for my own part, when I see a drunkard, with the holy Prophet, when he looked in *Hazael's* face, I can hardly forbear weeping, to consider how many vices he may fall into, ere he comes to himself again.

What horrid incest did righteous *Lot* commit with his own daughters, when they had made him drunk? And, I doubt not,

not, but there are many amongst you, who have committed such crimes when you have deprived yourselves of your reason by drinking, that were you to hear of them, your heart, like *Nabal*'s, after he was told how he had abused *David* when he was drunk, would die within you. And, had any one told you, when you were sober, that you would have been guilty of such crimes, you would have cried out, with *Hazael* before-mentioned, "Are thy servants so many dogs, that they should do thus?"

But no marvel that drunkards commit such crimes; for drunkenness drives the Holy Spirit from them; they become mere machines for the devil to work up to what he pleases; he enters into them, as he entered into the herd of swine; and no wonder if they then commit all uncleanness, and any other crime, with greediness. But this leads me to a

Fifth consideration, which highly aggravates the sin of drunkenness, it separates the Holy Spirit from us.

It is to be hoped, that no one here present need be informed, that before we can be assured we are christians indeed, we must receive the Holy Ghost, must be born again from above, and have the Spirit of GOD witnessing with our spirits, that we are the sons of GOD. This, this alone is true christianity; and without the cohabitation of this blessed Spirit in our hearts, our righteousness does not exceed the righteousness of the Scribes and Pharisees, and we shall in no wise enter into the kingdom of GOD.

But now, drunkards do in effect bid this blessed Spirit to depart from them: for what has he to do with such filthy swine? They have no lot or share in the Spirit of the Son of *David*. They have chased him out of their hearts, by defiling his temple; I mean their bodies. And he can no more hold communion with them, than light can have communion with darkness, or CHRIST have concord with *Belial*.

The apostle, therefore, in the words of the text, exhorts the *Ephesians*, " not to be drunk with wine, wherein is excess, but to be filled with the Spirit;" thereby implying, that drunkenness and the Spirit of GOD could never dwell in the same heart. And in another epistle, he bids them to avoid unprofitable conversation, as a thing which grieved the Holy Spirit: whereby alone they could be sealed to the day of redemption. And if unprofitable conversation grieves the Holy Spirit, at what an infinite distance must drunkenness drive him from the hearts of men?

O that you were wise! that you would consider what a dreadful thing it is to have the Spirit of the living GOD depart from you! for, assure yourselves, if you live without him, you will live without GOD in the world. You are in the same miserable forlorn condition as *Saul* was, when an evil spirit of the LORD came upon him; and you are only so many vessels of wrath fitted for destruction. But this brings me to a

Sixth reason against the sin of drunkenness; it absolutely unfits a man for the enjoyment of GOD in heaven, and exposes him to his eternal wrath.

To see and enjoy GOD, and to be like the blessed angels; always beholding the face of our heavenly Father, in the glories of his kingdom; is such an unspeakable happiness, that even wicked men, though they will not live the life of the righteous, cannot but wish their future state to be like his.

But think you, O ye drunkards, that you shall ever be partakers of this inheritance with the saints in light? Do you flatter yourselves, that you, who have made them often the subject of your drunken songs, shall now be exalted to sing with them the heavenly songs of *Sion?* No, as by drunkenness you have made your hearts cages of unclean birds, with impure and unclean spirits must you dwell.

A burning *Tophet*, kindled by God's wrath, is prepared for your reception, where you must suffer the vengeance of eternal fire, and in vain cry out for a drop of water to cool your tongues. Indeed you shall drink, but it shall be a cup of God's fury: for in the hand of the Lord there will be a cup of fury, it will be full mixed; and as for the dregs thereof, all the drunkards of the land shall suck them out.

But perhaps you may not believe this report. These words may be looked upon by you as idle tales, and I may seem to you as *Lot* did to his sons-in-law, when he came to warn them to get up out of *Sodom*, "as one that mocketh." But if you believe not me, believe eternal truth itself, which has positively declared, that no drunkard shall ever enter into his kingdom.

And I call heaven and earth to witness against you this day, that as surely as the Lord rained fire and brimstone, as soon as *Lot* went out of *Sodom*, so surely will God cast you into a lake of fire and brimstone, when he shall come to take vengeance on them that know not God, and have not obeyed the gospel of our Lord Jesus Christ.

Behold then I have told you before; remember, that you this day were informed what the end of drunkenness would be. And I summon you, in the name of that God whom I serve, to meet me at the judgment-seat of Christ, that you may acquit both my Master and me; and confess, with your own mouths, that your damnation was of yourselves, and that we are free from the blood of you all.

But, Lord, has no one believed our report? Wilt thou suffer so many words to be spoken in vain, if it be yet in vain? No, methinks I see some pricked to the heart, and ready to cry out, in the language of *David* to *Abigail*, "Blessed be the Lord God of *Israel*, which sent thee this day to speak unto us." For surely, unless he had sent thee, this sin of drunkenness had been our ruin: but now, since we find whither it will lead us, we are refolved to drink no liquor to excefs while the world ftands, left we fhould be tormented in the flames of hell.

But alas! how fhall we be delivered from the power of this fin? Can the *Ethiopian* change his fkin, or the leopard his fpots? So hard, almoft, will it be for you who have been accuftomed to be intemperate, to learn to live fober.

But do not defpair; for what is impoffible with man, is poffible with GOD. Of whom then fhould you feek for fuccour, but of him your LORD? Who, though for this fin of drunkennefs, he might juftly turn away his face from you; yet obferve,

Firft, If you pour out your hearts before him in *daily prayer*, and afk affiftance from above, it may be GOD will endue you with power from on high, and make you more than conquerors through JESUS CHRIST. Had you kept up communion with him in prayer, you would not fo long, by drunkennefs, have had communion with devils. But, like the Prodigal, you have defired to be your own mafters; you have lived without prayer, depended on your own ftrength; and now fee, alas! on what a broken reed you have leaned. How foon have you made yourfelves like the beafts that have no underftanding? But turn ye, turn ye from your evil ways. Come to him with the repenting Prodigal, faying, " Father we have finned;" we befeech thee, let not this fin of drunkennefs have any longer dominion over us. Lay hold on CHRIST by faith, and lo! it fhall happen to you even as you will. A

Second means I would recommend to you, in order to get the better of drunkennefs, is to *avoid evil company:* For it is the evil communication of wicked men, that has drawn many thoufands into this fin, and fo corrupted their good manners.

But you may fay, If I leave my companions, I muft expect contempt: for they will certainly defpife me for being fingu-
lar.

ly. And thinkest thou, O man, ever to enter in at the strait gate by a true conversion, without being had in derision of them that are round about thee? No; though thou mayst be despised, and not go to heaven, yet thou canst not go to heaven without being despised: "For the friendship of the world is enmity with GOD." And they that are born after the flesh, will persecute those that are born after the Spirit. Let not, therefore, a servile fear of being despised by a man that shall die, hinder thy turning unto the living GOD. For what is a little contempt? It is but a vapour which vanisheth away, and cometh not again. Better be derided by a few companions here, than be made ashamed before men and angels hereafter. Better be the song of a few drunkards on earth, than dwell with them, where they will be eternally reproaching and cursing each other in hell. Yet a little while, and they themselves shall praise thy doings; and shall say, We, fools, counted his leaving us to be folly, and his end to be without honour: but how is he numbered among the sons of of GOD, and his lot among the saints!

But I hasten to lay down a

Third means for those who would overcome the sin of drunkenness, to enter upon a life of *strict self-denial* and mortification: for this kind of sin goeth not forth but by prayer and fasting. It is true, this may seem a difficult task; but then, we must thank ourselves for it; for had we begun sooner, our work would have been the easier. And even now, if you will but strive, the yoke of mortification will grow lighter and lighter every day.

And now, by way of conclusion, I cannot but exhort all persons, high and low, rich and poor, to practise a strict self-denial in eating and drinking. For though "the kingdom of GOD consists not in meats and drinks," yet an abstemious use of GOD's good creatures, greatly promotes the spiritual life. And perhaps there are more destroyed by living in a regular sensuality, than even by the very sin I have now been

warning

warning you of. I know indeed, that many, who are only almoſt chriſtians, and who ſeek, but do not ſtrive to enter into the kingdom of God, urge a text of ſcripture to juſtify their indulgence, ſaying, that " it is not what entereth into the man defileth the man." And ſo we grant, when taken moderately; but then they ſhould conſider, that it is poſſible, nay, it is proved by daily experience, that a perſon may eat and drink ſo much as not to hurt his body, and yet do infinite prejudice to his ſoul: for ſelf-indulgence lulls the ſoul into a ſpiritual ſlumber, as well as direct intemperance; and though the latter may expoſe us to more contempt among men, yet the former, if continued in, will as certainly ſhut us out from the preſence of God. St. *Paul* knew this full well; and therefore, though he was the ſpiritual father of thouſands, and was near upon finiſhing his courſe, yet he ſays, it was his daily practice to " keep his body under, and bring it into ſubjection, left after he had preached to others, he himſelf ſhould be a caſt-away," or diſapproved of, or do ſomething that might make him an offence or ſtumbling-block to any of God's children: for of his own, and all other ſaints final perſeverance, he makes no doubt, as is evident from many of his epiſtles; and the word Αδοκιμος bears this ſenſe, 2 *Cor.* xiii. 5. and ſundry other places. But why urge I the apoſtle's example, to excite you to a ſtrict temperance in eating and drinking? Rather let me exhort you only to put in practice the latter part of the text, to labour to " be filled with the Spirit of God," and then you will no longer ſearch the ſcriptures to find arguments for ſelf-indulgence; but you will deal ſincerely with yourſelves, and eat and drink no more at any time, than what is conſiſtent with the ſtricteſt precepts of the goſpel. O beg of God, that you may ſee, how you are fallen in *Adam*, and the neceſſity of being renewed, ere you can be happy, by the Spirit of Jesus Christ! Let us beſeech him to enlighten us to ſee the treachery of our corrupt hearts, and how pure and holy theſe bodies ought to be, that they ought to be living temples of the Holy Ghoſt, and then we ſhall ſhew ourſelves men. And being made temples of the Holy Ghoſt, by his dwelling in our

bodies

bodies here, though after death, worms may deſtroy them, yet ſhall they be raiſed by the ſame Spirit at the general reſurrection of the laſt day, to be faſhioned like unto CHRIST's glorious body hereafter.

Which GOD of his infinite mercy grant, &c.

SERMON LIII.

The Power of CHRIST's Resurrection.

PHILIP. iii. 10.

That I may know Him, and the Power of his Resurrection.

THE apostle, in the verses before the text, had been cautioning the *Philippians* to " beware of the concision," *Judaizing teachers*, who endeavoured to subvert them from the simplicity of the gospel, by telling them, they still ought to be subject to circumcision, and all the other ordinances of *Moses*. And that they might not think he spoke out of prejudice, and condemned their tenets, because he himself was a stranger to the *Jewish* dispensation, he acquaints them, that if any other man thought he had whereof he might trust in the flesh, or seek to be justified by the outward privileges of the *Jews*, he had more: For he was " circumcised the eighth day; of the stock of *Israel* (not a proselyte, but a native *Israelite*); of the tribe of *Benjamin* (the tribe which adhered to *Judah* when the others revolted); an *Hebrew* of the *Hebrews* (a *Jew* both on the father's and mother's side); and as touching the law, a *Pharisee*," the strictest sect amongst all *Israel*. To shew that he was no *Gallio* in religion, through his great, though misguided zeal, he had persecuted the church of CHRIST; and " as touching the righteousness of the law (as far as the *Pharisees* exposition of it went, he was) blameless," and had kept it from his youth. But, when it pleased GOD, who separated him from his mother's womb, to reveal his Son in him, " What things were gain to me," (he *says*) those privileges I boasted myself in, and sought to
be

be juſtified by, "I counted loſs for CHRIST." And that they might not think he repented that he had done ſo, he tells them, he was now more confirmed than ever in his judgment. For, ſays he, "yea doubtleſs (the expreſſion in the original riſes with a holy triumph) and I do count all things but loſs for the excellency of the knowledge of CHRIST JESUS my LORD." And that they might not object that he ſaid, and did not, he acquaints them, he had given proofs of the ſincerity of theſe profeſſions, becauſe for the ſake of them, he had ſuffered the loſs of all his worldly things, and ſtill was willing to do more; for, "I count them but dung (no more than offals thrown out to dogs) ſo that I may win, (or have a ſaving intereſt in) CHRIST, and be found in him (as the manſlayer in the city of refuge) not having my own righteouſneſs which is of the law, (not depending on having *Abraham* for my father, or on any works of righteouſneſs which I have done, either to atone or ſerve as a balance for my evil deeds) but that which is through the faith of CHRIST, the righteouſneſs which is of GOD by faith," a righteouſneſs of GOD's appointing, and which will be imputed to me, if I believe in CHRIST, "that I may know him, and the power of his reſurrection;" that I may have an experimental knowledge of the efficacy of his reſurrection, by feeling the influences of his bleſſed Spirit on my ſoul. In which words two things are implied.

Firſt, That JESUS CHRIST did riſe from the dead.

Secondly, That it highly concerns us to know the power of his riſing again.

Accordingly, in the following diſcourſe I ſhall endeavour to ſhew,

Firſt, That CHRIST is riſen indeed from the dead; and that it was neceſſary for him ſo to do; and,

Secondly, That it highly concerns us to know and experience the power of his reſurrection.

First, CHRIST is indeed risen.

That JESUS should rise from the dead was absolutely necessary;

1. *First*, On his own account. He had often appealed to this as the last and most convincing proof he would give them that he was the true Messiah, "There shall no other sign be given you, than the sign of the prophet *Jonas*." And again, "Destroy this temple of my body, and in three days I will build it up." Which words his enemies remembered, and urged it as an argument, to induce *Pilate* to grant them a watch, to prevent his being stolen out of the grave. "We know that deceiver said, whilst he was yet alive, after three days I will rise again." So that had he not risen again, they might have justly said, we know that this man was an impostor.

2. *Secondly*, It was necessary on our account. "He rose again" (says the apostle) "for our justification;" or that the debt we owed to GOD for our sins, might be fully satisfied and discharged.

It had pleased the Father (for ever adored be his infinite love and free grace) to wound his only Son for our transgressions, and to arrest and confine him in the prison of the grave, as our surety for the guilt we had contracted by setting at nought his commandments. Now had CHRIST continued always in the grave, we could have had no more assurance that our sins were satisfied for, than any common debtor can have of his creditor's being satisfied, whilst his surety is kept confined. But he being released from the power of death, we are thereby assured, that with his sacrifice GOD was well pleased, that our atonement was finished on the cross, and that he hath made a full, perfect, and sufficient sacrifice, oblation, and satisfaction for the sins of the world.

3. *Thirdly*, It was neceffary that our LORD JESUS fhould rife again from the dead, to affure us of the certainty of the refurrection of our own bodies.

The doctrine of the refurrection of the body was entirely exploded and fet at nought among the *Gentiles*, as appears from the *Athenians* mocking at, and calling St. *Paul* " a babbler and a fetter forth of ftrange doctrines," when he preached to them JESUS, and the refurrection. And though it was believed by moft of the *Jews*, as is evident from many paffages of fcripture, yet not by all; the whole fect of the Sadducees denied it. But the refurrection of JESUS CHRIST put it out of difpute. For as he acted as our reprefentative, if he our head be rifen, then muft we alfo, who are his members, rife with him. And as in the firft *Adam* we all died, even fo in him our fecond *Adam* we muft all, in this fenfe, be made alive.

As it was neceffary, upon thefe accounts, that our bleffed LORD fhould rife from the dead; fo it is plain beyond contradiction, that he did. Never was any matter of fact better attefted; never were more precautions made ufe of to prevent a cheat. He was buried in a fepulchre, hewn out of a rock, fo that it could not be faid that any digged under, and conveyed him away. It was a fepulchre alfo wherein never man before was laid; fo that if any body did rife from thence, it muft be the body of JESUS of *Nazareth*. Befides, the fepulchre was fealed; a great ftone rolled over the mouth of it; and a band of foldiers (confifting not of friends, but of his profeffed enemies) was fet to guard it. And as for his difciples coming by night and ftealing him away, it was altogether improbable: For it was not long fince, that they had all forfaken him, and they were the moft backward in believing his refurrection. And fuppofing it was true, that they came whilft the foldiers flept; yet the foldiers muft be caft into a deep fleep indeed, that the rolling away fo great a ftone did not awake fome of them.

And

And our blessed LORD's afterwards appearing at sundry times, and in divers manners, to his disciples, as when they were assembled together, when they were walking to *Emmaus*, when they were fishing; nay, and condescending to shew them his hands and feet, and his appearing to above five hundred brethren at once, put the truth of his resurrection out of all dispute.

Indeed, there is one objection that may be made against what has been said, that the books wherein these facts are recorded were written by his disciples.

And who more proper persons than those who were eye-witnesses of what they related, and eat and drank with him after his resurrection? " But they were illiterate and ignorant men." Yet as good witnesses of a plain matter of fact, as the most learned masters in *Israel*. Nay, this rendered them more proper witnesses. For being plain men, they were therefore less to be suspected of telling or making a lye, particularly, since they laid down their lives for a testimony of the truth of it. We read indeed of *Jacob*'s telling a lie, though he was a plain man, in order to get his father's blessing. But it was never heard since the world began, that any man, much less a whole set of men, died martyrs, for the sake of an untruth, when they themselves were to reap no advantage from it.

No, this single circumstance proves them to be *Israelites* indeed, in whom was no guile. And the wonderful success GOD gave to their ministry afterwards, when three thousand were converted by one sermon; and twelve poor fishermen, in a very short time enabled to be more than conquerors over all the opposition men or devils could make, was as plain a demonstration, that CHRIST was risen, according to their gospel, as that a divine power, at the sound of a few ram's horns, caused the walls of *Jericho* to fall down.

But what need we any farther witnesses? Believe you the resurrection of our blessed LORD? I know that you believe it, it, as your gathering together on this firſt day of the week in the courts of the Lord's houſe abundantly teſtifies.

What concerns us moſt to be aſſured of, and which is the

Second thing I was to ſpeak to, is, Whether we have experimentally known the power of his reſurrection; that is, Whether or not we have received the Holy Ghoſt, and by his powerful operations on our hearts have been raiſed from the death of ſin, to a life of righteouſneſs and true holineſs.

It was this, the great apoſtle was chiefly deſirous to know. The reſurrection of Christ's body he was ſatisfied would avail him nothing, unleſs he experienced the power of it in raiſing his dead ſoul.

For another, and that a chief end of our bleſſed Lord's riſing from the dead, was to enter heaven as our repreſentative, and to ſend down the Holy Ghoſt to apply that redemption he had finiſhed on the croſs, to our hearts, by working an entire change in them.

Without this, Christ would have died in vain. For it would have done us no ſervice to have had his outward righteouſneſs imputed to us, unleſs we had an inward inherent righteouſneſs wrought in us. Becauſe, being altogether conceived and born in ſin, and conſequently unfit to hold communion with an infinitely pure and holy God, we cannot poſſibly be made meet to ſee or enjoy him, till a thorough renovation has paſſed upon our hearts.

Without this, we leave out the Holy Ghoſt in the great work of our redemption. But as we were made by the joint concurrence and conſultation of the bleſſed trinity; and as we were baptized in their name, ſo muſt all of them concur in our ſalvation: As the Father made, and the Son redeemed, so must the Holy Ghost sanctify and seal us, or otherwise we have believed in vain.

This then is what the apostle means by the "Power of CHRIST's resurrection," and this is what we are as much concerned experimentally to know, as that He rose at all.

Without this, though we may be moralists; though we may be civilized, good-natured people, yet we are no christians. For he is not a true christian, who is only one outwardly; nor have we therefore a right, because we daily profess to believe that CHRIST rose again the third day from the dead. But he is a true christian who is one inwardly; and then only can we be stiled true believers, when we not only profess to believe, but have felt the power of our blessed LORD's rising from the dead, by being quickened and raised by his Spirit, when dead in trespasses and sins, to a thorough newness both of heart and life.

The devils themselves cannot but believe the doctrine of the resurrection, and tremble; but yet they continue devils, because the benefits of this resurrection have not been applied to them, nor have they received a renovating power from it, to change and put off their diabolical nature. And so, unless we not only profess to know, but also feel that CHRIST is risen indeed, by being born again from above, we shall be as far from the kingdom of GOD as they: our faith will be as ineffectual as the faith of devils.

Nothing has done more harm to the christian world, nothing has rendered the cross of CHRIST of less effect, than a vain supposition, that religion is something without us. Whereas we should consider, that every thing that CHRIST did outwardly, must be done over again in our souls; or otherwise, the believing there was such a divine person once on earth, who triumphed over hell and the grave, will profit us no more, than believing there was once such a person as *Alexander*, who conquered the world.

As Christ was born of the Virgin's womb, so must he be spiritually formed in our hearts. As he died for sin, so must we die to sin. And as he rose again from the dead, so must we also rise to a divine life.

None but those who have followed him in this regeneration, or new-birth, shall sit on thrones as approvers of his sentence, when he shall come in terrible majesty to judge the twelve tribes of *Israel*.

It is true, as for the outward work of our redemption, it was a transient act, and was certainly finished on the cross. but the application of that redemption to our hearts, is a work that will continue always, even unto the end of the world.

So long as there is an elect man breathing on the earth, who is naturally engendred of the offspring of the first *Adam*, so long must the quickning spirit, which was purchased by the resurrection of the second *Adam*, that Lord from heaven, be breathing upon his soul.

For though we may exist by Christ, yet we cannot be said to exist in him, till we are united to him by one spirit, and enter into a new state of things, as certainly as he entered into a new state of things, after that he rose from the dead.

We may throng and crowd round about Christ, and call him "Lord, Lord," when we come to worship before his footstool; but we have not effectually touched him, till by a lively faith in his resurrection, we perceive a divine virtue coming out of him, to renew and purify our souls.

How greatly then do they err who rest in a bare historical faith of our Saviour's resurrection, and look only for external proofs to evidence it? Whereas were we the most learned disputers of this world, and could speak of the certainty of

this

this fact with the tongue of men and angels, yet without this inward testimony of it in our hearts, though we might convince others, yet we should never be saved by it ourselves.

For we are but dead men, we are like so many carcases wrapt up in grave cloaths, till that same JESUS who called *Lazarus* from his tomb, and at whose own resurrection many that slept arose, doth raise us also by his quickening Spirit from our natural death, in which we have so long lain, to a holy and heavenly life.

We might think ourselves happy, if we had seen the Holy JESUS after He was risen from the dead, and our hands had handled that LORD of life. But more happy are they who have not seen him, and yet having felt the power of his resurrection, therefore believe in him. For many saw our divine master, who were not saved by him; but whosoever has thus felt the power of his resurrection, has the earnest of his inheritance in his heart, he has passed from death to life, and shall never fall into final condemnation.

I am very sensible that this is foolishness to the natural man, as were many such like truths to our LORD's own disciples, when only weak in faith, before he rose again. But when these natural men, like them, have fully felt the power of his resurrection, they will then own that this doctrine is from GOD, and say with the *Samaritans*, " Now we believe not because of thy saying," for we ourselves have experienced it in our hearts.

And O that all unbelievers, all letter-learned masters of *Israel*, who now look upon the doctrine of the power of CHRIST's resurrection, or our new birth, as an idle tale, and condemn the preachers of it as enthusiasts and madmen, did but thus feel the power of it in their souls, they would no longer ask, how this thing could be? But they would be convinced of it, as much as *Thomas* was, when he saw the LORD's CHRIST; and like him, when JESUS bid him reach out his hands and thrust them into his side, in a holy confusion they would cry out, "My Lord and my God!"

But how shall an unbeliever, how shall the formal christian come thus to "know Christ, and the power of his resurrection?" God, who cannot lye, has told us, "I am the resurrection and the life, whosoever liveth and believeth in me, though he were dead, yet shall he live." Again, says the apostle, "By faith we are saved, and that not of ourselves, it is the gift of God."

This, this is the way, walk in it. Believe, and you shall live in Christ, and Christ in you; you shall be one with Christ, and Christ one with you. But without this, your outward goodness and professions will avail you nothing.

But then, by this faith we are not to understand a dead speculative faith, a faith in the head; but a living principle wrought in the heart by the powerful operations of the Holy Ghost, a faith that will enable us to overcome the world, and forsake all in affection for Jesus Christ. For thus speaks our blessed Master, "Unless a man forsake all that he hath, he cannot be my disciple."

And so the apostle, in the words immediately following the text, says, "being made conformable to his death;" thereby implying, that we cannot know the power of Christ's resurrection, unless we are made conformable to him in his death.

If we can reconcile light and darkness, heaven and hell, then we may hope to know the power of Christ's resurrection without dying to ourselves and the world. But till we can do this, we might as well expect that Christ will have concord with *Belial*.

For there is such a contrariety between the spirit of this world, and the Spirit of Jesus Christ, that he who will be at friendship with the one, must be at enmity with the other: "We cannot serve GOD and mammon."

This may, indeed, seem a hard saying; and many, with the young man in the gospel, may be tempted to go away sorrowful: But wherefore should this offend them? For what is all that is in the world, the lust of the eye, the lust of the flesh, and the pride of life, but vanity and vexation of spirit?

GOD is love; and therefore, could our own wills, or the world, have made us happy, he never would have sent his own dear Son JESUS CHRIST to die and rise again, to deliver us from the power of them. But because they only torment, and cannot satisfy, therefore GOD bids us to renounce them.

Had any one persuaded profane *Esau* not to lose so glorious a privilege, merely for the sake of gratifying a present corrupt inclination, when he saw him about to sell his birth-right for a little red pottage, would not one think that man to have been *Esau*'s friend? And just thus stands the case between GOD and us. By the death and resurrection of JESUS CHRIST, we are new-born to an heavenly inheritance amongst all them which are sanctified; but our own corrupt wills, would tempt us to sell this glorious birth-right for the vanities of the world, which, like *Esau*'s red pottage, may please us for a while, but will soon be taken away from us. GOD knows this, and therefore rather bids us renounce them for a season, than for the short enjoyment of them lose the privilege of that glorious birth-right, to which, by knowing the power of the resurrection of JESUS CHRIST, we are entitled.

O the depth of the riches and excellency of christianity! Well might the great St. *Paul* count all things but dung and dross for the excellency of the knowledge of it. Well might he desire so ardently to know JESUS, and the power of his refurrection. For even on this fide eternity it raifes us above the world, and makes us to fit in heavenly places in CHRIST JESUS.

Well might that glorious company of worthies, recorded in the Holy fcriptures, fupported with a deep fenfe of their heavenly calling, defpife the pleafures and profits of this life, and wander about in fheep-fkins, and goat-fkins, in dens and caves of the earth, being deftitute, afflicted, tormented.

And O that we were all like minded! that we felt the power of CHRIST's refurrection as they did! How fhould we then "count all things as dung and drofs for the excellency of the knowledge of CHRIST JESUS our LORD!" How fhould we then recover our primitive dignity, trample the earth under our feet, and with our fouls be continually gafping after GOD?

And what hinders but we may be thus minded? Is JESUS CHRIST, our great High Prieft, altered from what he was? No, " he is the fame yefterday, to-day, and for ever." And though he is exalted to the right-hand of GOD, yet he is not afhamed to call us brethren. The power of his refurrection is as great now as formerly, and the Holy Spirit, which was affured to us by his refurrection, as ready and able to quicken us who are dead in trefpaffes and fins, as any faint that ever lived. Let us but cry, and that inftantly, to Him that is mighty and able to fave; let us, in fincerity and truth, without fecretly keeping back the leaft part, renounce ourfelves and the world; then we fhall be chriftians indeed. And though the world may caft us out, and feparate from our company, yet JESUS CHRIST will walk with, and abide in us. And at the general refurrection of the laft day, when the voice of the archangel and trump of GOD fhall bid the fea and the graves to give up their dead, and all nations fhall appear before him, then will he confefs us before his Father and the holy angels, and we fhall receive that

invitation

invitation which he shall then pronounce to all who love and fear him, " Come, ye bleſſed children of my Father, inherit the kingdom prepared for you from the beginning of the world."

Grant this, O Father, for thy dear Son's ſake, JESUS CHRIST our LORD; to whom, with Thee and the Holy Ghoſt, &c.

SERMON

SERMON LIV.

Intercession every Christian's Duty.

---

1 THESS. v. 25.

Brethren, pray for us.

IF we enquire, why there is so little love to be found amongst christians, why the very characteristic, by which every one should know that we are disciples of the holy JESUS, is almost banished out of the christian world, we shall find it, in a great measure, owing to a neglect or superficial performance of that excellent part of prayer, *intercession*, or imploring the divine grace and mercy in behalf of others.

Some forget this duty of praying for others, because they seldom remember to pray for themselves: and even those who are constant in praying to their Father who is in heaven, are often so selfish in their addresses to the throne of grace, that they do not enlarge their petitions for the welfare of their fellow christians as they ought; and thereby fall short of attaining that christian charity, that unfeigned love to their brethren, which their sacred profession obliges them to aspire after, and without which, though they should bestow all their goods to feed the poor, and even give their bodies to be burned, yet it would profit them nothing.

Since these things are so, I shall from the words of the text (though originally intended to be more confined) endeavour to shew,

I. *First*,

I. *First*, That it is every christian's duty to pray for others, as well as for himself.

II. *Secondly*, Shew, whom we ought to pray for, and in what manner we should do it. And,

III. *Thirdly*, I shall offer some motives to excite all christians to abound in this great duty of intercession.

I. *First*, I shall endeavour to shew, That it is every christian's duty to pray for others, as well as for himself.

Now *prayer* is a duty founded on natural religion; the very heathens never neglected it, though many christian heathens amongst us do: and it is so essential to christianity, that you might as reasonably expect to find a living man without breath, as a true christian without the spirit of prayer and supplication. Thus, no sooner was St. *Paul* converted, but " behold he prayeth," saith the LORD Almighty. And thus will it be with every child of GOD, as soon as he becomes such: prayer being truly called, The natural cry of the new-born soul.

For in the heart of every true believer there is a heavenly tendency, a divine attraction, which as sensibly draws him to converse with GOD, as the load-stone attracts the needle.

A deep sense of their own weakness, and of CHRIST's fulness; a strong conviction of their natural corruption, and of the necessity of renewing grace; will not let them rest from crying day and night to their Almighty Redeemer, that the divine image, which they lost in *Adam*, may through his all-powerful mediation, and the sanctifying operations of his blessed spirit, be begun, carried on, and fully perfected both in their souls and bodies.

Thus earnest, thus importunate, are all sincere christians in praying for themselves: but then, not having so lively,

lasting,

lasting, and deep a sense of the wants of their christian brethren, they are for the most part too remiss and defective in their prayers for them. Whereas, was the love of GOD shed abroad in our hearts, and did we love our neighbour in that manner, in which the Son of GOD our Saviour loved us, and according to his command and example, we could not but be as importunate for their spiritual and temporal welfare, as for our own; and as earnestly desire and endeavour that others should share in the benefits of the death and passion of JESUS CHRIST, as we ourselves.

Let not any one think, that this is an uncommon degree of charity; an high pitch of perfection, to which not every one can attain: for, if we are all commanded to "love our neighbour (that is every man) even as ourselves," nay to "lay down our lives for the brethren;" then, it is the duty of all to pray for their neighbours as much as for themselves, and by all possible acts and expressions of love and affection towards them, at all times, to shew their readiness even to lay down their lives for them, if ever it should please GOD to call them to it.

Our blessed Saviour, as "he hath set us an example, that we should follow his steps" in every thing else, so hath he more especially in this: for in that divine, that perfect and inimitable prayer (recorded in the xviith of St. *John*) which he put up just before his passion, we find but few petitions for his own, though many for his disciples welfare: and in that perfect form which he has been pleased to prescribe us, we are taught to say, not *My*, but "*Our* Father," thereby to put us in mind, that, whenever we approach the throne of grace, we ought to pray not for ourselves alone, but for all our brethren in CHRIST.

Intercession then is certainly a duty incumbent upon all christians.

II. Whom we are to intercede for, and how this duty is to be performed, comes next to be considered.

1. And first, our intercession must be *universal*. "I will, (says the apostle) that prayers, supplications and intercessions be made for all men." For as GOD's mercy is over all his works, as JESUS CHRIST died to redeem a people out of all nations and languages; so we should pray, that " all men may come to the knowledge of the truth, and be saved." Many precious promises are made in holy writ, that the gospel shall be published through the whole world, that " the earth shall be covered with the knowledge of the LORD, as the waters cover the sea:" and therefore it is our duty not to confine our petitions to our own nation, but to pray that all those nations, who now sit in darkness and in the shadow of death, may have the glorious gospel shine out upon them, as well as upon us. But you need not that any man should teach you this, since ye yourselves are taught of GOD, and of JESUS CHRIST himself, to pray, that his kingdom may come; part of the meaning of which petition is, that " GOD's ways may be known upon earth, and his saving health among all nations."

2. Next to the praying for all men, we should, according to St. *Paul's* rule, pray for *Kings*; particularly for our present sovereign King *George*, and all that are put in authority under him: that we may lead quiet lives, in all godliness and honesty. For, if we consider how heavy the burden of government is, and how much the welfare of any people depends on the zeal and godly conversation of those that have the rule over them: if we set before us the many dangers and difficulties, to which governors by their station are exposed, and the continual temptations they lie under to luxury and self-indulgence; we shall not only pity, but pray for them: that he who preserved *Esther*, *David*, and *Josiah*, "unspotted from the world," amidst the grandeur of a court, and gave success to their designs, would also preserve them holy and unblameable, and prosper all the works of their hands upon them. But

3. *Thirdly*, you ought, in a more especial manner, to pray for those, whom "the Holy Ghost hath made *Overseers* over you."

you." This is what St. *Paul* begs, again and again, of the churches to whom he writes: Says he in the text, " Brethren, pray for us;" and again, in his epistle to the *Ephesians*, " praying always, with all manner of supplication; and for me also, that I may open my mouth boldly, to declare the mystery of the gospel." And in another place, to express his earnestness in this request, and the great importance of their prayers for him, he bids the church " strive, (or, as the original word signifies, be in an agony) together with him in their prayers." And surely, if the great St. *Paul*, that chosen vessel, that favourite of heaven, needed the most importunate prayers of his christian converts; much more do the ordinary ministers of the gospel stand in need of the intercession of their respective flocks.

And I cannot but in a more especial manner insist upon this branch of your duty, because it is a matter of such importance: for, no doubt, much good is frequently withheld from many, by reason of their neglecting to pray for their ministers, and which they would have received, had they prayed for them as they ought. Not to mention, that people often complain of the want of diligent and faithful pastors. But how do they deserve good pastors, who will not earnestly pray to GOD for such? If we will not pray to the LORD of the harvest, can it be expected he will send forth labourers into his harvest?

Besides, what ingratitude is it, not to pray for your ministers! For shall they watch and labour in the word and doctrine for you, and your salvation, and shall not you pray for them in return? If any bestow favours on your bodies, you think it right, meet, and your bounden duty, to pray for them; and shall not they be remembered in your prayers, who daily feed and nourish your souls? Add to all this, that praying for your ministers, will be a manifest proof of your believing, that though *Paul* plant, and *Apollos* water, yet it is GOD alone who giveth the increase. And you will also find it the best means you can use, to promote your own welfare; because GOD, in answer to your prayers, may impart a double

portion

portion of his holy fpirit to them, whereby they will be qualified to deal out to you larger meafures of knowledge in fpiritual things, and be enabled more fkilfully to divide the word of truth.

Would men but conftantly obferve this direction, and when their minifters are praying in their name to GOD, humbly befeech him to perform all their petitions: or, when they are fpeaking in GOD's name to them, pray that the Holy Ghoft may fall on all them that hear the word; we fhould find a more vifible good effect of their doctrine, and a greater mutual love between minifters and their people. For minifters hands would then be held up by the people's interceffions, and the people will never dare to villify or traduce thofe who are the conftant fubjects of their prayers.

4. Next to our minifters, *our friends* claim a place in our interceffions; but then we fhould not content ourfelves with praying in general terms for them, but fuit our prayers to their particular circumftances. When *Miriam* was afflicted with a leprofy from GOD, *Mofes* cried and faid, " LORD, heal her." And when the nobleman came to apply to JESUS CHRIST, in behalf of his child, he faid, " LORD, my little daughter lieth at the point of death, I pray thee to come and heal her." In like manner, when our friends are under any afflicting circumftances, we fhould endeavour to pray for them, with a particular regard to thofe circumftances. For inftance, is a friend fick? we fhould pray, that if it be GOD's good pleafure, it may not be unto death; but if otherwife, that he would give him grace fo to take his vifitation, that, after this painful life ended, he may dwell with him in life everlafting. Is a friend in doubt in an important matter? we fhould lay his cafe before GOD, as *Mofes* did that of the daughters of *Zelophehad*, and pray, that GOD's Holy Spirit may lead him into all truth, and give all feafonable direction. Is he in want? we fhould pray, that his faith may never fail, and that in GOD's due time he may be relieved. And in all other cafes, we fhould not pray for our friends only in generals, but fuit our petitions to their particular fufferings and afflictions;

for otherwife, we may never afk perhaps for the things our friends moft want.

It muft be confeffed, that fuch a procedure will oblige fome often to break from the forms they ufe; but if we accuftom ourfelves to it, and have a deep fenfe of what we afk for, the moft illiterate chriftian will not want proper words to exprefs themfelves.

We have many noble inftances in holy fcripture of the fuccefs of this kind of particular interceffion; but none more remarkable than that of *Abraham*'s fervant, in the book of *Genefis*, who being fent to feek a wife for his fon *Ifaac*, prayed in a moft particular manner in his behalf. And the fequel of the ftory informs us, how remarkably his prayer was anfwered. And did chriftians now pray for their friends in the fame particular manner, and with the fame faith as *Abraham*'s fervant did for his mafter; they would, no doubt, in many inftances, receive as vifible anfwers, and have as much reafon to blefs GOD for them, as he had. But

5. As we ought thus to intercede for our friends, fo in like manner muft we alfo pray for *our enemies*. " Blefs them that curfe you, (fays JESUS CHRIST) and pray for them that defpitefully ufe you, and perfecute you." Which commands he enforced in the ftrongeft manner by his own example: in the very agonies and pangs of death, he prayed even for his murderers, " Father, forgive them, for they know not what they do!" This, it muft needs be confeffed, is a difficult duty, yet not impracticable, to thofe who have renounced the things of this prefent life, (from an inordinate love of which all enmities arife) and who knowing the terrible woes denounced againft thofe who offend CHRIST's little ones, can, out of real pity, and a fenfe of their danger, pray for thofe by whom fuch offences come.

6. Laftly, and to conclude this head, we fhould intercede for all that are any ways *afflicted* in mind, body, or eftate; for

all who defire, and ftand in need of our prayers, and for all who do not pray for themfelves.

And Oh! that all who hear me, would fet apart fome time every day for the due performance of this moft neceffary duty! In order to which,

I fhall now proceed,

III. To fhew the advantages, and offer fome confiderations to excite you to the practice of daily interceffion. And

1. *Firft*, It will fill your hearts with love one to another. He that every day heartily intercedes at the throne of grace for all mankind, cannot but in a fhort time be filled with love and charity to all: and the frequent exercife of his love in this manner, will infenfibly enlarge his heart, and make him partaker of that exceeding abundance of it which is in CHRIST JESUS our LORD! Envy, malice, revenge, and fuch like hellifh tempers, can never long harbour in a gracious interceffor's breaft; but he will be filled with joy, peace, meeknefs, long-fuffering, and all other graces of the Holy Spirit. By frequently laying his neighbour's wants before GOD, he will be touched with a fellow-feeling of them; he will rejoice with thofe that do rejoice, and weep with thofe that weep. Every bleffing beftowed on others, inftead of exciting envy in him, will be looked on as an anfwer to his particular interceffion, and fill his foul with joy unfpeakable and full of glory.

Abound therefore in acts of general and particular interceffions; and when you hear of your neighbour's faults, inftead of relating them to, and expofing them before others, lay them in fecret before GOD, and beg of him to correct and amend them. When you hear of a notorious finner, inftead of thinking you do well to be angry, beg of JESUS CHRIST to convert, and make him a monument of his free grace; you cannot imagine what a bleffed alteration this practice will make in your heart, and how much you will increafe day by day in the spirit of love and meekness towards all mankind!

But farther, to excite you to the constant practice of this duty of intercession, consider the many instances in holy scripture, of the power and efficacy of it. Great and excellent things are there recorded as the effects of this divine employ. It has stopped plagues, it has opened and shut heaven; and has frequently turned away GOD's fury from his people. How was *Abimelech*'s house freed from the disease GOD sent amongst them, at the intercession of *Abraham!* When "*Phineas* stood up and prayed;" how soon did the plague cease! When *Daniel* humbled and afflicted his soul, and interceded for the LORD's inheritance, how quickly was an angel dispatched to tell him, " his prayer was heard!". And, to mention but one instance more, how does GOD own himself as it were overcome with the importunity of *Moses*, when he was interceding for his idolatrous people, " Let me alone," says GOD!

This sufficiently shews, I could almost say, the omnipotency of intercession, and how we may, like *Jacob*, wrestle with GOD, and by an holy violence prevail both for ourselves and others. And no doubt it is owing to the secret and prevailing intercessions of the few righteous souls who still remain among us, that GOD has yet spared this miserably sinful nation: for were there not some such faithful ones, like *Moses*, left to stand in the gap, we should soon be destroyed, even as was *Sodom*, and reduced to ashes like unto *Gomorrah*.

But, to stir you up yet farther to this exercise of intercession, consider, that in all probability, it is the frequent employment even of the glorified saints: for though they are delivered from the burden of the flesh, and restored to the glorious liberty of the sons of GOD, yet as their happiness cannot be perfectly consummated 'till the resurrection of the last day, when all their brethren will be glorified with them, we cannot but think they are often importunate in beseeching our heavenly Father, shortly to accomplish the number of his elect, and to hasten his kingdom. And shall not we, who are on earth, be often exercised in this divine employ with the glorious company of the spirits of just men made perfect? Since our happiness is so much to consist in the communion of saints in the church triumphant above, shall we not frequently intercede for the church militant here below; and earnestly beg, that we may all be one, even as the Holy JESUS and his Father are one, that we may also be made perfect in one?

To provoke you to this great work and labour of love, remember, that it is the never ceasing employment of the holy and highly exalted JESUS himself, who sits at the right hand of GOD, to hear all our prayers, and to make continual intercession for us! So that he who is constantly employed in interceding for others, is doing that on earth, which the eternal Son of GOD is always doing in heaven.

Imagine therefore, when you are lifting up holy hands in prayer for one another, that you see the heavens opened, and the Son of GOD in all his glory, as the great high-priest of your salvation, pleading for you the all-sufficient merit of his sacrifice before the throne of his heavenly Father! Join then your intercessions with his, and beseech him, that they may, through him, come up as incense, and be received as a sweet-smelling savour, acceptable in the sight of GOD! This imagination will strengthen your faith, excite a holy earnestness in your prayers, and make you wrestle with GOD, as *Jacob* did, when he saw him face to face, and his life was preserved; as *Abraham*, when he pleaded for *Sodom*; and as JESUS CHRIST himself, when he prayed, being in an agony, so much the more earnestly the night before his bitter passion.

And now, brethren, what shall I say more, since you are taught of JESUS CHRIST himself, to abound in love, and in this good work of praying one for another. Though ever so mean, though as poor as *Lazarus*, you will then become benefactors to all mankind; thousands, and twenty times ten thousands, will then be blessed for your sakes! and after you have employed a few years in this divine exercise here, you will be translated to that happy place, where you have so often wished others might be advanced; and be exalted to sit at the right hand of our All-powerful, All-prevailing Intercessor, in the kingdom of his heavenly Father hereafter.

However, I cannot but in an especial manner press this upon you now, because all ye, amongst whom I have now been preaching, in all probability will see me no more: for I am now going (I trust under the conduct of God's most Holy Spirit) from you, knowing not what shall befal me: I need therefore your most importunate intercessions, that nothing may move me from my duty, and that I may not " count even my life dear unto myself, so that I may finish " my course with joy, and the ministry I have received of " the Lord Jesus, to testify the gospel of the grace of " God!"

Whilst I have been here, to the best of my knowledge, I have not failed to declare unto you the whole will of God: and though my preaching may have been a favour of death unto death to some; yet I trust it has been also a favour of life unto life to others; and therefore I earnestly hope that those will not fail to remember me in their prayers. As for my own part, the many unmerited kindnesses I have received from you, will not suffer me to forget you: out of the deep, therefore, I trust shall my cry come unto God; and whilst the winds and storms are blowing over me, unto the Lord will I make my supplication for you. For it is but a little while, and " we must all appear before the judgment seat of Christ;" where I must give a strict account of the doctrine I have preached, and you of your improvement under it. And O that I may never be called out as a swift witness, against any of those, for whose salvation I have sincerely, though too faintly, longed and laboured!

It is true, I have been censured by some as acting out of sinister and selfish views; " but it is a small matter with me to be judged by man's judgment; I hope my eye is single; but I beseech you, brethren, by the mercies of GOD in CHRIST JESUS, pray that it may be more so! and that I may increase with the increase of grace in the knowledge and love of GOD through JESUS CHRIST our Lord.

And now, brethren, what shall I say more? I could wish to continue my discourse much longer; for I can never fully express the desire of my soul towards you! Finally, therefore, brethren, "whatsoever things are holy, whatsoever things are pure, whatsoever things are honest, whatsoever things are of good report: if there be any consolation in CHRIST, if any fellowship of the spirit," if any hopes of our appearing to the comfort of each other at the awful tribunal of JESUS CHRIST, "think of the things that you have heard," and of those which your pastors have declared, and will yet declare unto you; and continue under their ministry to "work out your own salvation with fear and trembling:" so that whether I should never see you any more, or whether it shall please GOD to bring me back again at any time, I may always have the satisfaction of knowing that your conversation is such "as becometh the gospel of CHRIST."

I almost persuade myself, that I could willingly suffer all things, so that it might any ways promote the salvation of your precious and immortal souls; and I beseech you, as my last request, "obey them that have the rule over you in the LORD; and be always ready to attend on their ministry, as it is your bounden duty. Think not that I desire to have myself exalted at the expence of another's character; but rather think this, not to have any man's person too much in admiration; but esteem all your ministers highly in love, as they justly deserve for their work's sake.

And now, "brethren, I commend you to GOD, and to the word of his grace, which is able to build you up, and give you an inheritance amongst all them that are sanctified." May GOD reward you for all your works of faith, and

labours

labours of love, and make you to abound more and more in every good word and work towards all men. May he truly convert all that have been convinced, and awaken all that are dead in trespasses and sins! May he confirm all that are wavering! And may you all go on from one degree of grace unto another, till you arrive unto the measure of the stature of the fulness of CHRIST; and thereby be made meet to stand before that GOD, " in whose presence is the fulness of joy, and at whose right-hand there are pleasures for evermore!" Amen! Amen!

SERMON LV.

Persecution every Christian's Lot.

---

2 TIM. iii. 12.

Yea, and all that will live godly in CHRIST JESUS, *shall suffer Persecution.*

WHEN our LORD was pleased to take upon himself the form of a servant, and to go about preaching the kingdom of GOD; he took all opportunities in public, and more especially in private, to caution his disciples against seeking great things for themselves, and also to forewarn them of the many distresses, afflictions and persecutions, which they must expect to endure for his name's sake. The great apostle *Paul* therefore, the author of this epistle, in this, as in all other things, following the steps of his blessed Master, takes particular care, among other apostolical admonitions, to warn young *Timothy* of the difficulties he must expect to meet with in the course of his ministry: " This know also, that in the last days perilous times shall come. For men shall be lovers of their ownselves, covetous, proud, blasphemers, disobedient to parents, unthankful, unholy, without natural affection, truce-breakers, false accusers, incontinent, fierce, despisers of those that are good, traitors, heady, high-minded, lovers of pleasure more than lovers of GOD; having a form of godliness, but denying the power thereof: from such turn away. For of this sort are they who creep into houses, and lead captive silly women laden with sins, led away with divers lusts, ever learning, and never able to come to the knowledge of the truth. Now, as *Jannes* and *Jambres* (two of the *Egyptian* magicians) withstood *Moses* (by working sham miracles) so do they also resist the truth; and (notwithstanding they keep up the form of religion) are men of corrupt minds, reprobate concerning the faith." But, in order to keep him from sinking under their opposition, he tells him, that though GOD, for wise ends, permitted these false teachers, as he did the magicians, to oppose for some time, yet they should now proceed no farther: "For their folly (says he) shall be made manifest unto all men, as theirs (the Magicians) also was," when they could not stand before *Moses* because of the boil; for the boil was upon the *Magicians*, as well as upon all the *Egyptians*. And then, to encourage *Timothy* yet the more, he propounds to him his own example; "But thou hast fully known my doctrine, manner of life, purpose, faith, long-suffering, charity, patience, persecutions, afflictions, which came unto me at *Antioch*, at *Iconium*, at *Lystra*; what persecutions I endured; but out of them all the LORD delivered me." And then, lest *Timothy* might think that this was only the particular case of *Paul*, says he, in the words of the text, "Yea, and all that will live godly in CHRIST JESUS, shall suffer persecution."

The words, without considering them as they stand in relation to the context, contain an important truth, that persecution is the common lot of every godly man. This is a hard saying, How few can bear it? I trust GOD, in the following discourse, will enable me to make it good, by shewing,

I. What it is to live godly in CHRIST JESUS.

II. The different kinds of persecution to which they, who live godly, are exposed.

III. Why it is, that godly men must expect to suffer persecution.

Lastly, We shall apply the whole.

1. *First*, Let us consider what it is to live godly in CHRIST JESUS. This supposes, that we are made the righteousness

of God in Christ, that we are born again, and are one with Christ by a living faith, and a vital union, even as Jesus Christ and the Father are One. Unless we are thus converted, and transformed by the renewing of our minds, we cannot properly be said to be in Christ, much less to live godly in him. To be in Christ merely by baptism, and an outward profession, is not to be in Him in the strict sense of the word: no; " They that are in Christ, are new creatures; old things are passed away, and all things are become new" in their hearts. Their life is hid with Christ in God; their souls daily feed on the invisible realities of another world. To " live godly in Christ," is to make the divine will, and not our own, the sole principle of all our thoughts, words, and actions; so that, " whether we eat or drink, or whatsoever we do, we do all to the glory of God." Those who live godly in Christ, may not so much be said to live, as Christ to live in them: He is their Alpha and Omega, their first and last, their beginning and end. They are led by his Spirit, as a child is led by the hand of its father; and are willing to follow the Lamb whithersoever he leads them. They hear, know, and obey his voice. Their affections are set on things above; their hopes are full of immortality; their citizenship is in heaven. Being born again of God, they habitually live to, and daily walk with, God. They are pure in heart; and, from a principle of faith in Christ, are holy in all manner of conversation and godliness.

This is to " live godly in Christ Jesus:" and hence we may easily learn, why so few suffer persecution? Because, so few live godly in Christ Jesus. You may live formally in Christ, you may attend on outward duties; you may live morally in Christ, you may (as they term it) do no one any harm, and avoid persecution: but they " that will live godly in Christ Jesus, shall suffer persecution."

2. *Secondly*, What is the meaning of the word Persecution, and how many kinds there are of it, I come now to consider.

The

The word Persecution, is derived from a *Greek* word signifying *to pursue*, and generally implies pursuing a person for the sake of his goodness, or GOD's good-will to him. The

First kind of it, is that of the *Heart*. We have have an early example of this in that wicked one *Cain*, who, because the LORD had respect to *Abel* and his offering, and not to him and his offering, was very wroth, his countenance fell, and at length he cruelly slew his envied brother. Thus the *Pharisees* hated and persecuted our LORD long before they laid hold on him: and our LORD mentions being inwardly hated of men, as one kind of Persecution his disciples were to undergo. This heart-enmity (if I may so term it) is the root of all other kinds of Persecution, and is, in some degree or other, to be found in the soul of every unregenerated man; and numbers are guilty of this persecution, who never have it in their power to persecute any other way. Nay, numbers would actually put in practice all other degrees of persecution, was not the name of Persecution become odious amongst mankind, and did they not hereby run the hazard of losing their reputation. Alas! how many at the great day, whom we know not now, will be convicted and condemned, that all their life harboured a secret evil-will against *Zion!* They may now screen it before men; but GOD seeth the enmity of their hearts, and will judge them as Persecutors at the great and terrible day of judgment. A

Second degree of Persecution is that of the tongue; "out of the abundance of the heart, the mouth speaketh." Many, I suppose, think it no harm to shoot out arrows, even bitter words, against the disciples of the LORD: they scatter their firebrands, arrows and death, saying, "Are we not in sport?" But, however they may esteem it, in GOD's account evil-speaking is a high degree of Persecution. Thus *Ishmael*'s mocking *Isaac*, is termed persecuting him. "Blessed are ye (says our LORD) when men shall revile you and persecute you, and shall say all manner of evil against you falsely for my name's sake." From whence we may gather, that reviling, and speaking all manner of evil for CHRIST's sake,

is

is a high degree of perfecution. For "a good name, (fays the wife man) is better than precious ointment;" and, to many, is dearer than life itfelf. It is a great breach of the fixth commandment, to flander any one; but to fpeak evil of and flander the difciples of CHRIST, merely becaufe they are his difciples, muft be highly provoking in the fight of GOD; and fuch who are guilty of it (without repentance) will find that JESUS CHRIST will call them to an account, and punifh them for all their ungodly and hard fpeeches in a lake of fire and brimftone. This fhall be their portion to drink. The

Third and *laft* kind of Perfecution, is that which expreffes itfelf in *actions*: as when wicked men feparate the children of GOD from their company; " Bleffed are ye, (fays our LORD) when they fhall feparate you from their company :" or expofe them to church-cenfures. " They fhall put you out of their fynagogues;" threatening and prohibiting them from making an open profeffion of his religion or worfhip; or interdicting minifters for preaching his word, as the high-priefts threatened the apoftles, and " forbad them any more to fpeak in the name of JESUS;" and *Paul* breathed out threatenings and flaughters againft the difciples of the LORD: or when they call them into courts; " You fhall be called before governors," fays our LORD: or when they fine, imprifon, or punifh them, by confifcation of goods, cruel fcourging, and, laftly, death itfelf.

It would be impoffible to enumerate in what various fhapes perfecution has appeared. It is a many-headed monfter, cruel as the grave, infatiable as hell; and, what is worfe, it generallly appears under the cloak of religion. But, cruel, infatiable, and horrid as it is, they that live godly in CHRIST JESUS, muft expect to fuffer and encounter with it in all its forms.

This is what we are to make good under our next general head.

3. *Thirdly*, Why is it that godly men muſt expect to ſuffer perſecution? And,

Firſt, This appears from the whole tenor of our LORD's doctrine. We will begin with his divine ſermon on the mount. "Bleſſed are they who are perſecuted for righteouſneſs ſake; for theirs is the kingdom of heaven." So that, if our LORD ſpoke truth, we are not ſo bleſſed as to have an intereſt in the kingdom of heaven, unleſs we are or have been perſecuted for righteouſneſs ſake. Nay, our LORD (it is remarkable) employs three verſes in this beatitude, and only one in each of the others; not only to ſhew that it was a thing which men (as men) are unwilling to believe, but alſo the neceſſary conſequence of it upon our being chriſtians. This is likewiſe evident from all thoſe paſſages, wherein our LORD informs us, that he came upon the earth, "not to ſend peace, but a ſword;" and that the father-in-law ſhould be againſt the mother-in-law, and a man's foes ſhould be thoſe of his own houſhold. Paſſages, which though confined by falſe prophets to the firſt, I am perſuaded will be verified by the experience of all true chriſtians in this, and every age of the church. It would be endleſs to recount all the places, wherein our LORD forewarns his diſciples, that they ſhould be called before rulers, and thruſt out of ſynagogues, nay, that the time would come, wherein men ſhould think they did GOD ſervice to kill them. For this reaſon he ſo frequently declared, that "unleſs a man forſake all that he had, and even hated life itſelf, he could not be his diſciple." And therefore it is worthy our obſervation, that in the remarkable paſſage, wherein our LORD makes ſuch an extenſive promiſe to thoſe who left all for him, he cautiouſly inſerts perſecution. "And JESUS anſwered and ſaid, Verily I ſay unto you, there is no man that hath left houſe, or brethren, or ſiſters, or father, or mother, or wife, or children, or lands, for my ſake and the goſpel's, but he ſhall receive an hundred-fold now in this time; houſes and brethren, and ſiſters and mothers, and children and lands, with perſecutions; (the word is in the plural number, including all kinds of perſecution) and in the world to come eternal life." He

that

that hath ears to hear, let him hear what CHRIST says in all these passages, and then confess, that all who will live godly in CHRIST JESUS shall suffer persecution.

As this is proved from our LORD's doctrine, so it is no less evident from his life. Follow him from the manger to the cross, and see whether any persecution was like that which the Son of GOD, the LORD of glory, underwent whilst here on earth. How was he hated by wicked men? How often would that hatred have excited them to lay hold of him, had it not been for fear of the people? How was he reviled, counted and called a Blasphemer, a Wine-bibber, a Samaritan, nay, a Devil, and, in one word, had all manner of evil spoken against him falsely? What contradiction of sinners did he endure against himself? How did men separate from his company, and were ashamed to walk with him openly? insomuch that he once said to his own disciples, "Will you also go away?" Again, How was he stoned, thrust out of the synagogues, arraigned as a deceiver of the people, a seditious and pestilent fellow, an enemy to *Cæsar*, and as such scourged, blind-folded, spit upon, and at length condemned, and nailed to an accursed tree? Thus was the Master persecuted, thus did the LORD suffer; and the servant is not above his Master, nor the disciple above his Lord: "If they have persecuted me, they will also persecute you," says the blessed JESUS. And again, "Every man that is perfect (a true christian) must be as his Master," or suffer as he did. For in all these things our LORD has set us an example, that we should follow his steps: and therefore, far be it that any, who live godly in CHRIST JESUS, should henceforward expect to escape suffering persecution.

But farther: not only our LORD's example, but the example of all the saints that ever lived, evidently demonstrates the truth of the apostle's assertion in the text. How soon was *Abel* made a martyr for his religion? How was *Isaac* mocked by the son of the bond-woman? And what a large catalogue of suffering Old Testament saints, have we recorded

corded in the xith chapter of the *Hebrews!* Read the *Acts* of the Apostles, and see how the first christians were threatened, stoned, imprisoned, scourged, and persecuted even unto death. Examine Church History in after-ages, and you will find the murder of the innocents by *Herod*, was but an earnest of the innocent blood which should be shed for the sake of JESUS. Examine the experience of saints now living on earth; and, if it were possible to consult the spirits of just men made perfect, I am persuaded each would concur with the apostle in asserting, that " all who will live godly in CHRIST JESUS, shall suffer persecution."

How can it be otherwise in the very nature of things? Ever since the fall, there has been an irreconcileable enmity between the seed of the woman and the seed of the serpent. Wicked men hate GOD, and therefore cannot but hate those who are like him: they hate to be reformed, and therefore must hate and persecute those, who, by a contrary behaviour, testify of them, that their deeds are evil. Besides, pride of heart leads men to persecute the servants of JESUS CHRIST. If they commend them, they are afraid of being asked, Why do not you follow them? And therefore because they dare not imitate, though they may sometimes be even forced to approve their way, yet pride and envy make them turn persecutors. Hence it is, that as it was formerly, so it is now, and so will it be to the end of time; " He that is born after the flesh, (the natural man, does and) will persecute him that is born after the Spirit," the regenerate man. Because christians are not of the world, but CHRIST hath chosen them out of the world, therefore the world will hate them. If it be objected against this doctrine, that we now live in a christian world, and therefore must not expect such persecution as formerly; I answer, All are not christians that are called so; and, till the heart is changed, the enmity against GOD (which is the root of all persecution) remains: and consequently christians, falsely so called, will persecute as well as others. I observed therefore, in the beginning of this discourse, that *Paul* mentions those that had a form of religion,

as

as persons of whom *Timothy* had need be chiefly aware: for, as our LORD and his apostles were mostly persecuted by their countrymen the *Jews*, so we must expect the like usage from the Formalists of our own nation, the *Pharisees*, who seem to be religious. The most horrid and barbarous persecutions have been carried on by those who have called themselves Christians; witness the days of queen *Mary*; and the fines, banishments and imprisonments of the children of GOD in the last century, and the bitter, irreconcileable hatred that appears in thousands who call themselves Christians, even in the present days wherein we live.

Persons, who argue against persecution, are not sufficiently sensible of the bitter enmity of the heart of every unregenerate man against GOD. For my own part, I am so far from wondering that christians are persecuted, that I wonder our streets do not run with the blood of the saints: was mens power equal to their wills, such a horrid spectacle would soon appear. But,

Persecution is necessary in respect to the godly themselves. If we have not all manner of evil spoken of us, how can we know whether we seek only that honour which cometh from above? If we have no persecutors, how can our passive graces be kept in exercise? How can many christian precepts be put into practice? How can we love, pray for, and do good to, those who despitefully use us? How can we overcome evil with good? In short, how can we know we love GOD better than life itself? *Paul* was sensible of all this, and therefore so positively and peremptorily asserts, that "all who will live godly in CHRIST JESUS, shall suffer persecution."

Not that I affirm, all are persecuted in a like degree: No: this would be contrary both to scripture and experience. But though all christians are not really called to suffer every kind of persecution, yet all christians are liable thereto: and notwithstanding some may live in more peaceful times of the church than others, yet all christians, in all ages, will find by their own experience, that, whether they act in a private or public capacity, they must, in some degree or other, suffer persecution.

Here then I would pause, and, *lastly*, by way of application, exhort all persons,

First, To stand a while and examine themselves. For, by what has been said, you may gather one mark, whereby you may judge whether you are christians or not. Were you ever persecuted for righteousness sake? If not, you never yet lived godly in CHRIST our LORD. Whatever you may say to the contrary, the inspired apostle, in the words of the text (the truth of which, I think, I have sufficiently proved) positively asserts, that all who will live godly in Him, shall suffer persecution. Not that all who are persecuted are real christians; for many sometimes suffer, and are persecuted, on other accounts than for righteousness sake. The great question therefore is, Whether you were ever persecuted for living godly? You may boast of your great prudence and sagacity (and indeed these are excellent things) and glory because you have not run such lengths, and made yourselves so singular, and liable to such contempt, as some others have. But, alas! this is not a mark of your being of a Christian, but of a *Laodicean* spirit, neither hot nor cold, and fit only to be spewed out of the mouth of GOD. That which you call prudence, is often, only cowardice, dreadful hypocrisy, pride of heart, which makes you dread contempt, and afraid to give up your reputation for GOD. You are ashamed of CHRIST and his gospel; and in all probability, was he to appear a second time upon earth, in words, as well as works, you would deny him. Awake therefore, all ye that live only formally in CHRIST JESUS, and no longer seek that honour which cometh of man. I do not desire to court you, but I intreat you to live godly, and fear not contempt for the sake of JESUS CHRIST. Beg of GOD to give you his Holy Spirit, that you may see through, and discover the latent hypocrisy of your hearts, and no longer deceive your own souls. Remember you

cannot

cannot reconcile two irreconcileable differences, GOD and Mammon, the friendship of this world with the favour of GOD. Know you not who hath told you, that " the friendship of this world is enmity with GOD?" If therefore you are in friendship with the world, notwithstanding all your specious pretences to piety, you are at enmity with GOD: you are only heart-hypocrites; and, " What is the hope of the hypocrite, when GOD shall take away his soul?" Let the words of the text sound an alarm in your ears; O let them sink deep into your hearts; " Yea, and all that will live godly in CHRIST JESUS, shall suffer persecution."

Secondly, From the words of the text, I would take occasion to speak to those, who are about to list themselves under the banner of CHRIST's cross. What say you? Are you resolved to live godly in CHRIST JESUS, notwithstanding the consequence will be, that you must suffer persecution? You are beginning to build; but have you taken our LORD's advice, to " sit down first and count the cost?" Have you well weighed with yourselves that weighty declaration, " He that loveth father or mother more than Me, is not worthy of Me;" and again, " Unless a man forsake all that he hath he cannot be my disciple?" Perhaps some of you have great possessions; will not you go away sorrowful, if CHRIST should require you to sell all that you have! Others of you again may be kinsmen, or some way related, or under obligations, to the high-priests, or other great personages, who may be persecuting the church of CHRIST: What say you? Will you, with *Moses*, " rather chuse to suffer affliction with the people of GOD, than enjoy the pleasures of sin for a season?" Perhaps you may say, my friends will not oppose me. That is more than you know: in all probability your chief enemies will be those of your own houshold. If therefore they should oppose you, are you willing naked to follow a naked CHRIST? and to wander about in sheep-skins and goats-skins, in dens and caves of the earth, being afflicted, destitute, tormented, rather than not be CHRIST's disciples? You are now all following with zeal, as *Ruth* and *Orpah* did *Naomi*, and may weep under the word; but are not your tears crocodiles tears? And, when difficulties come, will you not go back from following your LORD, as *Orpah* departed from following *Naomi?* Have you really the root of grace in your hearts? or, are you only stony-ground hearers? You receive the word with joy; but, when persecution arises because of the word, will you not be immediately offended? Be not angry with me for putting these questions to you. I am jealous over you, but it is with a godly jealousy: for, alas! how many have put their hands to the plough, and afterwards have shamefully looked back? I only deal with you, as our LORD did with the person that said, "LORD, I will follow thee whithersoever thou wilt." "The foxes have holes, and the birds of the air have nests, "but the son of man, (says he) hath not where to lay his head." What say you? Are you willing to endure hardness, and thereby approve yourselves good soldiers of JESUS CHRIST? You now come on foot out of the towns and villages to hear the word, and receive me as a messenger of GOD: but will you not by and by cry out, Away with him, away with him; it is not fit such a fellow should live upon the earth? Perhaps some of you, like *Hazael*, may say, "Are we dogs, that we should do this?" But, alas! I have met with many unhappy souls, who have drawn back unto perdition, and have afterwards accounted me their enemy, for dealing faithfully with them; though once, if it were possible, they would have plucked out their own eyes, and have given them unto me. Sit down therefore, I beseech you, and seriously count the cost, and ask yourselves again and again, whether you count all things but dung and dross, and are willing to suffer the loss of all things, so that you may win CHRIST, and be found in him: for you may assure yourselves, the apostle hath not spoken in vain, "All that will live godly in CHRIST JESUS, shall suffer persecution."

Thirdly, The text speaks to you that are patiently suffering for the truth's sake: "Rejoice, and be exceeding glad; great shall be your reward in heaven." For to you it is given, not only to believe, but also to suffer, and perhaps remarkably too, for the sake of JESUS! This is a mark of
your

your discipleship, an evidence that you do live godly in CHRIST JESUS. Fear not, therefore, neither be dismayed. O be not weary and faint in your minds! JESUS, your LORD, your life, cometh, and his reward is with him. Though all men forsake you, yet will not he: no; the Spirit of CHRIST and of glory shall rest upon you. In patience therefore possess your souls. Sanctify the LORD GOD in your hearts. Be in nothing terrified by your adversaries: on their part CHRIST is evil spoken of; on your part he is glorified. Be not ashamed of your glory, since others can glory in their shame. Think it not strange concerning the fiery trial, wherewith you are or may be tried. The Devil rages, knowing that he hath but a short time to reign. He or his emissaries have no more power than what is given them from above: GOD sets them their bounds, which they cannot pass; and the very hairs of your head are all numbered. Fear not; no one shall set upon you to hurt you, without your heavenly Father's knowledge. Do your earthly friends and parents forsake you? Are you cast out of the synagogues? The LORD shall reveal himself to you, as to the man that was born blind? JESUS CHRIST shall take you up. If they carry you to prison, and load you with chains, so that the iron enter into your souls, even there shall CHRIST send an angel from heaven to strengthen you, and enable you, with *Paul* and *Silas*, to " sing praises at midnight." Are you threatened to be thrown into a den of lions, or cast into a burning fiery furnace, because you will not bow down and worship the beast? Fear not; the GOD, whom you serve, is able to deliver you: or, if he should suffer the flames to devour your bodies, they would only serve, as so many fiery chariots, to carry your souls to GOD. Thus it was with the martyrs of old; so that one, when he was burning, cried out, " Come, you Papists, if you want a miracle, here, behold one! This bed of flames is to me a bed of down." Thus it was with almost all that suffered in former times: for JESUS, notwithstanding he withdrew his own divinity from himself, yet has always lifted up the light of his countenance upon the souls of suffering saints. " Fear not therefore those that can kill the body, and after that have no more that they can do; but fear Him only, who is able to destroy both body and soul in hell." Dare, dare to live godly in CHRIST JESUS, though you suffer all manner of persecution. But,

Fourthly, Are there any true ministers of JESUS CHRIST here? You will not be offended if I tell you, that the words of the text are, in an especial manner, applicable to you. *Paul* wrote them to *Timothy*; and we, of all men, that live godly in CHRIST JESUS, must expect to suffer the severest persecution. *Satan* will endeavour to bruise our heels, let who will escape: and it has been the general way of GOD's providence, in times of persecution, to permit the shepherds first to be smitten, before the sheep are scattered. Let us not therefore shew that we are only hirelings, who care not for the sheep; but, like the great Shepherd and Bishop of souls, let us readily lay down our lives for the sheep. Whilst others are boasting of their great preferments, let us rather glory in our great afflictions and persecutions for the sake of CHRIST. *Paul* rejoiced that he suffered afflictions and persecutions at *Iconium* and *Lystra:* out of all, the LORD delivered him; out of all, the LORD will deliver us, and cause us hereafter to sit down with him on thrones, when he comes to judge the twelve tribes of *Israel*.

I could proceed; but I am conscious, in this part of my discourse, I ought more particularly to speak to myself, knowing that *Satan* has desired to have me, that he may sift me as wheat. Without a spirit of prophecy, we may easily discern the signs of the times. Persecution is even at the doors: the tabernacle of the LORD is already driven into the wilderness: the ark of the LORD is fallen into the unhallowed hands of uncircumcised *Philistines*. They have long since put us out of their synagogues, and high-priests have been calling on civil magistrates to exert their authority against the disciples of the LORD. Men in power have been breathing out threatenings: we may easily guess what will follow, imprisonment and slaughter. The storm has been gathering some time; it must break shortly. Perhaps it may fall on me first.

Brethren

Brethren therefore, whether in the ministry or not, I beseech you, "pray for me," that I may never suffer justly, as an evil-doer, but only for righteousness sake. O pray that I may not deny my Lord in any wise, but that I may joyfully follow him, both to prison and to death, if he is pleased to call me to seal his truths with my blood. Be not ashamed of Christ, or of his gospel, though I should become a prisoner of the Lord. Though I am bound, the word of God will not be bound: no; an open, an effectual door is opened for preaching the everlasting gospel, and men or devils shall never be able to prevail against it. Only pray, that, whether it be in life or death, Christ may be glorified in me: then I shall rejoice, yea, and will rejoice.

And now, to whom shall I address myself next?

Fifthly, To those, who persecute their neighbours for living godly in Christ Jesus. But, what shall I say to you? Howl and weep for the miseries that shall come upon you: for a little while the Lord permits you to ride over the heads of his people; but, by and by, death will arrest you, judgment will find you, and Jesus Christ shall put a question to you, which will strike you dumb, *Why persecuted you Me?* You may plead your laws and your canons, and pretend what you do is out of zeal for God; but God shall discover the cursed hypocrisy and serpentine enmity of your hearts, and give you over to the tormentors. It is well, if in this life God does not send some mark upon you. He pleaded the cause of *Naboth*, when innocently condemned for blaspheming God and the king; and our Lord sent forth his armies, and destroyed the city of those who killed the prophets, and stoned them that were sent unto them. If you have a mind therefore to fill up the measure of your iniquities, go on, persecute and despise the disciples of the Lord: but know, "that for all these things, God shall bring you into judgment." Nay, those you now persecute, shall be in part your judges, and sit on the right-hand of the Majesty on high, whilst you are dragged by infernal spirits into a lake that burneth with fire and brimstone, and the smoke of your torment shall be ascending up for ever and ever. Lay down therefore, ye rebels, your arms against the most high GOD, and no longer persecute those who live godly in CHRIST JESUS. The LORD will plead, the LORD will avenge, their cause. You may be permitted to bruise their heels, yet in the end they shall bruise your accursed heads. I speak not this, as though I were afraid of you; for I know in whom I have believed: only out of pure love I warn you, and because I know not but JESUS CHRIST may make some of you vessels of mercy, and snatch you, even you persecutors, as fire-brands out of the fire. JESUS CHRIST came into the world to save sinners, even persecutors, the worst of sinners: his righteousness is sufficient for them; his Spirit is able to purify and change their hearts. He once converted *Saul:* may the same GOD magnify his power, in converting all those who are causing the godly in CHRIST JESUS, as much as in them lies, to suffer persecution! The LORD be with you all. Amen.

SERMON

SERMON LVI.

An Exhortation to the People of GOD not to be discouraged in their Way, by the Scoffs and Contempt of wicked Men.

HEBREWS iv. 9.

There remaineth therefore a Rest to the People of GOD.

WHEN we consider the persecutions they are exposed to, who live righteously and godly in this present world; it is amazing to consider, that the people of this generation should be so fond of a name to live, while they are in effect dead. The people of GOD are to expect little else but troubles and trials while they are in this world; common experience is a contradiction to my text, that there is a rest to the people of GOD; but the author of the *Hebrews*, when speaking of this rest, did not mean that they should have a rest here. No; he too well knew that the people of GOD, all who would seek and serve the LORD JESUS, must be despised, hated, scoffed, slandered, and evil intreated; but the time was hastening when they should have a perfect rest: there is a rest laid up for them, and this is an encouragement for you, my brethren, to hold on, and hold out your way rejoicing; after death there will be a rest for ever; at judgment, you shall be taken up to dwell with the LORD JESUS CHRIST; and there, you shall be for ever exempted from sin; you shall rest from

all

all manner of sorrow, and be no more troubled with the temptations of Satan. Now, you can set about nothing for the glory of GOD, or for your own soul's welfare, but the devil is dissuading you from it, or distracting you in it, or discouraging you after it. Here we are scoffed and derided; as the world hated the LORD JESUS CHRIST, so will it hate you: but be not discouraged, though we are here the scorn and off-scouring of all things; and are as a gazing stock to men and angels. Though they put us out of their synagogues, cast out our name as evil, and look on us as persons unfit for their company; yet, in that rest which is prepared for you, my brethren, we shall then be gazed at for our glory, and they shut out of the assembly of the saints, and separated from us, whether they will or no; unless the LORD JESUS CHRIST, by his free, rich, and sovereign grace, brings them unto himself.

The letter-learned Scribes and Pharisees of this day, look on us as madmen and enthusiasts; but though they make so much noise about the word *enthusiast*, it means no more than this, one in GOD; and what christian can say, he is not in GOD, and GOD in him? And if this is to be an enthusiast, GOD grant I may be more and more so; if we being in CHRIST, and CHRIST in us, makes us enthusiasts, I would to GOD we were all more and more enthusiasts. They now think it strange, that we run not with them into all excess of riot, and because we will not go to the devil's diversions with them, therefore they speak evil of us. We cannot now go along the street, but every one is pointing out his finger with scorn, and cries, Here comes another of his followers; what! you are become one of his disciples too! But there is a rest which will be a complete deliverance for you. Let none of these things move you; for, though you are thus treated here, consider, you shall in heaven have no discouraging company, nor any but what will be an assistance to you; you will have no scoffer there, all will be ready to join with heart and voice in your everlasting joy and praises. You will not be counted enthusiasts, madmen, and rabble, in that rest which remaineth

for

for the people of God. Therefore, poſſeſs your ſouls in patience; account it matter of joy when you fall into tribulation; God, in his own time, will deliver us; let not their hindering us from preaching in the church, be any diſcouragement; do not ſhrink, and draw back, becauſe of oppoſition; be not aſhamed of your work or maſter; but hold faſt your integrity. You muſt expect to go through evil report, and good report; fear not the violence of unreaſonable men; let them hate you, and caſt you out for the Lord's ſake, behold he ſhall appear to your joy, and they ſhall be aſhamed: therefore hold on, and hold out to the end. Be ſtedfaſt and patient, and bear the troubles of the world; if you are the people of God, there is a reſt provided for you, which you ſhall certainly obtain.

I ſhall not ſpeak unto you, Phariſees, this morning, nor to any, except to you who have experienced the pangs of the new-birth, or are at preſent under them, and who know what it is to love the Lord Jesus in ſincerity and truth: do not be diſcouraged, or think hard of the ways of God, my dear brethren, becauſe you are not loved by the men of this world; if you were of the world it would love you; it would then be pleaſed with your company; it would not thruſt you from a tavern, or an alehouſe; it would not diſlike you for ſinging the ſongs of the drunkard, or for going to plays, balls, or other polite and faſhionable entertainments, as they are called; no, theſe the children of the world like; but if you will ſing hymns and pſalms, and go to hear what God hath to ſay unto your ſouls, and ſpend your time in reading, praying, and frequenting religious aſſemblies, then it is that they diſlike you, and thruſt you out of their company, as unworthy thereof; but let none of theſe things move you, for the reſt which Jesus Christ hath prepared for you, is an ample recompence for all you may meet with here.

This reſt is the fruit of the blood of the Lord Jesus Christ: O how will it fill our ſouls with love, to think that through the ſtreams of this blood, we have overcome the

violence

violence of the world, and the snares of the devil. My dear brethren, be not discouraged at the treatment you meet with here, but let it be a means to stir you up to advance in the love of the LORD JESUS CHRIST, who hath prepared a rest for you. Can you consider, what CHRIST has done and suffered for you, and have your hearts stupified with vile and senseless pleasures? Can you hear of a panting, bleeding, dying JESUS, and yet be dull and unaffected? Was there any sorrow like unto his sorrow? and all this, he underwent to save you, who were vile, and polluted, and by nature, since the fall, a motly mixture of the beast and devil. JESUS CHRIST, by dying upon the cross, intended to take away the devil and beast from your heart, and to prepare it for himself to dwell in. Think of the love of this your JESUS, and then, will a little reproach and scorn move you? sure it will not. I hope better things of you, and things that accompany salvation.

O think with what pleasing astonishment you will see the LORD JESUS CHRIST, when he comes to take you to his rest: now his heart is open to us; but our hearts are shut against him; then, then, his heart shall be open, and ours shall be so too. O my brethren, how will your love be increased? With what raptures will you see the LORD JESUS CHRIST? Therefore, undergo a few reproaches here patiently, and revile not again. Let them say what they please of me, the reproaches, scorns, and contempt of this world, will no ways hurt me, but will recoil upon their own heads; leave it to the LORD, who knows what is best for you and me: do not question his love; he will be with you; only do you, who have tasted the LORD to be gracious, follow hard after him.

And now, let me speak a word unto you, who have not yet experienced the love of CHRIST to your souls, but are waiting for his appearance. I shall be but very short, because I would not break in upon the duties of the day.

I shall

I shall speak unto you a word of invitation; even, to wait still on the LORD; do not forsake him, though he may not answer your petitions at once or twice seeking unto him; hold on, do not leave seeking him, and you shall have an answer of peace; remember the poor man who was lame, and had lain at the pool of *Bethesda* thirty-eight years for relief, yet at last he found that it was worth waiting for, he obtained his desire.

And if you are but zealous for the LORD, and seek unto JESUS, if your zeal be according to godliness, and you pray unto him for his Spirit, you shall certainly have an answer of peace; you shall find it is good to seek unto the LORD, you will be adopted into his family, and by his spirit be enabled to cry, " Abba, Father." O then do not leave, but be continually waiting at wisdom's gate, and you shall find all her ways to be ways of pleasantness, and all her paths are peace; then, you shall find that it is worth waiting on the LORD JESUS; and when you have got his Spirit within you, all the power of men or devils cannot make you forsake the ways of the LORD JESUS CHRIST.

If you do but once taste of his pardoning love, it will be so delightful unto you, that you will cry for more and more thereof; you will be as full as you can hold, and still not be satisfied; you will desire more and more of this love of JESUS, you will hunger and thirst, and hunger and thirst again, and never be satisfied till you come to that rest which is prepared for the people of GOD, where all hungering and thirsting will cease, and will be turned into songs and hallelujahs, and that for ever and ever.

As many of you as design to partake of the emblems of the body and blood of our dying LORD, examine well yourselves, lest by eating and drinking unworthily, you eat and drink damnation unto yourselves: remember the dying love of your dying LORD, and eat and drink in commemoration thereof;

thereof; do not let the world keep you from partaking hereof; and when you have eaten and drank, do not go away and run into the world; let the world fee that you have been with JESUS; give them no room to fpeak unfeemly, they do that enough without occafion; but how would they rejoice if they had juft reafon.

Look well then unto your paths, that you do not flip; remember that all your faults are magnified, and that all your little flips are laid upon me; therefore, look well unto your ways, your words, your actions, that they may filence gainfayers; let them fee that we have the prefence of GOD with us, and that there has been good done by field-preaching.

Let me exhort you once more to confider the love of the LORD JESUS CHRIST. O do not forget his love. Confider, I befeech you, how great it has been unto you, and do not flight this his grace, the riches, the love, the kindnefs of your dear Redeemer, the LORD JESUS CHRIST, who hath prepared this eternal reft for you; he alfo laid down his life for your fakes: what great love was here! that while you were enemies to the LORD of glory, he died for you, to redeem you from fin, from hell and wrath, that you might live and reign with him, world without end.

The Lamb that died, and was buried, is now rifen and exalted, and fits on the right-hand of GOD the Father; and when he fhall come to judge all the world, then, my brethren, it will be feen whether we have deferved the ufage the world has given us; then it will be known who are the true followers of the LORD JESUS, and who are madmen and fools; but, may it be determined in this world, that we and our prefent enemies may enter into that reft which GOD hath prepared for thofe that love him.

Which GOD of his infinite mercy grant!

My brethren, let not thefe few words of exhortation be forgotten, but lay them up in your hearts, and remember they muft be called over another day. I fhould have enlarged, but the duties of the day obliged me to forbear.

Now, to GOD the Father, Son, and Holy Ghoft, be all power, &c.

SERMON

SERMON LVII.

Preached before the Governor, and Council, and the House of Assembly, in *Georgia*, on January 28, 1770.

ZECH. iv. 10.

For who hath despised the Day of small Things?

MEN, brethren, and fathers, at sundry times and in divers manners, GOD spake to the fathers by the prophets, before he spoke to us in these last days by his Son. And as GOD is a sovereign agent, and his sacred Spirit bloweth when and where it listeth, surely he may reveal and make known his will to his creatures, when, where, and how he pleaseth; "and who shall say unto him, what doest thou?" Indeed, this seems to be one reason, to display his sovereignty, why he chose, before the canon of scripture was settled, to make known his mind in such various methods, and to such a variety of his servants and messengers.

Hence it is, that we hear, he talked with *Abraham* as " a man talketh with a friend." To *Moses* he spoke " face to face." To others by " dreams in the night," or by " visions" impressed strongly on their imaginations. This seems to be frequently the happy lot of the favourite evangelical prophet *Zechariah*, I call him *evangelical prophet*, because his predictions, however they pointed at some approaching or immediate event, ultimately terminated in Him, who is the Alpha and Omega, the beginning and the end of all the lively oracles of GOD. The chapter from which our text is selected, among many other passages, is a striking proof of this: An angel, that had been more than once sent to him on former occasions, appears again to him, and by way of vision, and " waked him, (to use his own words) as a man that is wakened out of his sleep." Prophets, and the greatest servants of GOD, need waking sometimes out of their drowsy frames.

Methinks I see this man of GOD starting out of his sleep, and being all attention: the angel asked him, " what seest thou?" He answers, " I have looked, and behold, a candle-stick all of gold," an emblem of the church of GOD, " with a bowl upon the top of it, and seven lamps thereon, and seven pipes to the seven lamps, which were upon the top thereof;" implying, that the church, however reduced to the lowest ebb, should be preserved, be kept supplied, and shining, through the invisible, but not less real, because invisible aids and operations of the blessed Spirit of GOD. The occasion of such an extraordinary vision, if we compare this passage with the second chapter of the Prophecy of the prophet *Haggai*, seems to be this: It was now near eighteen years since the *Jewish* people had been delivered from their long and grievous *Babylonish* captivity; and being so long deprived of their temple and its worship, which fabric had been rased even to the ground, one would have imagined, that immediately upon their return, they should have postponed all private works, and with their united strength have first set about rebuilding that once stately and magnificent structure. But they, like too many christians of a like lukewarm stamp, though all acknowledged that this church-work was a necessary work, yet put themselves and others off, with this godly pretence, " The time is not come, the time that the LORD's house should be built:" The time is not come! what, not in eighteen years! for so long had they now been returned from their state of bondage: and pray, why was not the time come? The prophet *Haggai* tells them; their whole time was so taken up in building for themselves cieled houses, that they had no time left to build an habitation for their great and glorious Benefactor, the mighty GOD of *Jacob*.

This ingratitude must not be passed by unpunished. Omniscience observes, Omnipotence resents it! And that they might read their sin in their punishment, as they thought it best to get rich, and secure houses and lands and estates for themselves, before they set about unnecessary church-work, the prophet tells them, " You have sown much, but bring in little : ye eat, but ye have not enough : ye drink, but ye are not filled with drink :' ye clothe you, but there is none warm : and he that earneth wages, earneth wages to put it into a bag with holes." Still he goes on thundering and lightening, " Ye looked for much, and lo it came to little : and when ye brought it home, (pleasing yourselves with your fine crops) I did blow upon it : why ? saith the LORD of Hosts; because of mine house that is waste, and ye run every man unto his own house." A thundering sermon this! delivered not only to the common people, but also unto, and in the presence of " *Zerubbabel*, the son of *Shealtiel*, governor of *Judah*, and to *Joshua*, the son of *Josedech* the high-priest. The prophet's report is believed ; and the arm of the LORD was revealed. *Zerubbabel*, the son of *Shealtiel*, and *Joshua*, the son of *Josedech*, (O happy times when church and state are thus combined) with all the remnant of the people, obeyed the voice of the LORD their GOD, and the words of *Haggai* the prophet."

The spirit of *Zerubbabel*, and of *Joshua*, and the spirits of all the remnant of the people were stirred up, and they immediately came, disregarding, as it were, their own private buildings, " and did work in the house of the LORD of Hosts their GOD." For a while, they proceeded with vigour ; the foundation of the house is laid, and the superstructure raised to some considerable height : but whether this fit of hot zeal soon cooled, as is too common, or the people were discouraged by the false representations of their enemies, which perhaps met with too favourable a reception at the court of *Darius*; it so happened, that the hearts of the magistrates and ministers of the people waxed faint; and an awful chasm intervened, between the finishing and laying the foundation of this promising and glorious work.

Upon this, another prophet, even *Zechariah*, (who with *Haggai* had been joint sufferer in the captivity) is sent to lift up the hands that hang down, to strengthen the feeble knees, and by the foregoing instructive vision, to reanimate *Joshua* and the people in general, and the heart of *Zerubbabel*, the son of *Shealtiel*, in particular, maugre all discouragements, either from inveterate enemies, or from timid unstable friends, or all other obstacles whatsoever. If *Haggai* thunders, *Zechariah's* message is as lightening. "This is the word of the LORD unto *Zerubbabel*, saying, Not by might, nor by power, (not by barely human power or policy) but by my spirit, saith the LORD of Hosts: Who art thou, O great mountain? (thou *Sanballat* and thy associates, who have been so long crying out, what mean these feeble *Jews?* however great, formidable, and seemingly insurmountable) before *Zerubbabel* thou shalt (not only be lowered and rendered more accessible, but) become a plain;" thy very opposition shall, in the end, promote the work, and help to expedite that very building, which thou intendest to put a stop to, and destroy.

And lest *Zerubbabel*, through unbelief and outward opposition, or for want of more bodily strength, should think this would be a work of time, and that he should not live to see it compleated in his days, "The word of the LORD came to *Zechariah*, saying, The hands of *Zerubbabel* have laid the foundation of this house; his hands also shall finish it, and he shall bring forth the headstone thereof with shoutings, crying, Grace, grace unto it." Grace! grace! unto it: a double acclamation, to shew, that out of the abundance of their hearts, their mouth spake; and this with shoutings and crying from all quarters. Even their enemies should see the hand and providence of GOD in the beginning, continuance, and ending of this seemingly improbable and impracticable work; so that they should be constrained to cry, "Grace unto it," and wiſh both the work and the builders much proſperity: But as for its friends, they ſhould be ſo tranſported with heart-felt joy in the reflection upon the ſignal providences which had attended them through the whole proceſs, that they would ſhout and cry, "Grace, grace unto it:" or, This is nothing but the Lord's doing; God proſper and bleſs this work more and more, and make it a place where his free grace and glory may be abundantly diſplayed. Then by a beautiful and pungent ſarcaſm, turning to the inſulting enemies, he utters the ſpirited interrogation in my text, "Who hath deſpiſed the day of ſmall things?" Who are you, that vauntingly ſaid, what can theſe feeble *Jews* do, pretending to lay the foundation of a houſe which they never will have money, or ſtrength, or power to finiſh? Or, who are you, O timorous, ſhort-ſighted, doubting, though well-meaning people, who, through unbelief, were diſcouraged at the ſmall beginnings and feebleneſs of the attempt to build a ſecond temple? And, becauſe you thought it could not come up to the magnificence of the firſt, therefore were diſcouraged from ſo much as beginning to build a ſecond at all?

A cloſe inſtructive queſtion this; a queſtion, implying, that whenever God intends to bring about any great thing, he generally begins with a day of ſmall things.

As a proof of this, I will not lead you ſo far back, as to the beginning of time, when the Everlaſting "I AM" ſpoke all things into exiſtence, by his almighty *fiat*; and out of a confuſed chaos, "without form and void," produced a world worthy of a God to create, and of his favourite creature man, his vicegerent and repreſentative here below, to inhabit, and enjoy in it both himſelf and his God. And yet, though the heavens declare his glory, and the firmament ſheweth his handy work, though there is no ſpeech nor language where their voice is not heard, and their line is gone out through all the earth; and by a dumb, yet perſuaſive language, proves the hand that made them to be divine; yet there have been, and are now, ſuch fools in the world, as to "say in their hearts, There is no God;" or so wise, as by their wisdom, not to know God, or own his divine image to be stamped on that book, wherein these grand things are recorded, and that in such legible characters, that he who runs may read.

Neither will I divert your attention, honoured fathers, to the histories of *Greece* and *Rome*, or any of the great kingdoms and renowned monarchies, which constitute so great a part of ancient history; but whose beginnings were very small, (witness *Romulus*'s ditch) their progress as remarkably great, and their declension and downfal, when arrived at their appointed zenith, as sudden, unexpected, and marvellous. These make the chief subjects of the learning of our schools; though they make but a mean figure in sacred history, and would not perhaps have been mentioned at all, had they not been, in some measure, connected with the history of God's people, which is the grand subject of that much despised book, emphatically called, The Scriptures. Whoever hath a mind to inform himself of the one, may read *Rollin*'s Ancient History, and whoever would see the connection with the other, may consult the learned *Prideaux*'s admirable and judicious connection. Books which, I hope, will be strenuously recommended, and carefully studied, when this present infant institution gathers more strength, and grows up into a seat of learning. I can hardly forbear mentioning the small beginnings of *Great Britain*, now so distinguished for liberty, opulence and renown; and the rise and rapid progress of the *American* colonies, which promises to be one of the most opulent and powerful empires in the world. But my present views, and the honours done this infant institution this day, and the words of my text, as well as the feelings of my own heart, and I trust, of the hearts of all that hear me, lead me to confine your meditations to the history of God's own peculiar people, which for the simplicity and sublimity of its language, the veracity of its author, and the importance and wonders of the facts therein recorded, if weighed in a proper balance, hath not its equal under the sun. And yet, though God himself hath become an author among us, we will not condefcend to give his book one thorough reading. Be aftonifhed, O heavens, at this!

Who would have thought that from one, even from *Abraham*, and from fo fmall a beginning, as the emigration of a fingle private family, called out of a land wholly given to idolatry, to be fojourners and pilgrims in a ftrange land; who would have thought, that from a man, who for a long feafon was written *childlefs*, a man whofe firft poffeffion in this ftrange land, was by purchafing a burying place for his wife, and in whofe grave one might have imagined he would have buried all future expectations; who would have thought, that from this very man and woman, according to the courfe of nature, both as good as dead, fhould defcend a numerous offspring like unto the ftars of heaven for multitude, and as the fand which is upon the fea fhore innumerable? Nay, who would have imagined, that againft all probability, and in all human appearance impoffible, a kingdom fhould arife? Behold a poor captive flave, even *Jofeph*, who was cruelly feparated from his brethren, became fecond in *Pharaoh*'s kingdom: he was fent before to work out a great deliverance, and to introduce a family which fhould take root, deep root downwards and bear fruit upwards, and fill the land. How could it enter into the heart of man to conceive, that when oppreffed by a king, who knew not *Jofeph*, though they were the beft, moft loyal, induftrious fubjects this king had, when an edict was iffued forth as impolitic as cruel, (fince the fafety and glory of all kingdoms chiefly confift in the number of its inhabitants) that an outcaft, helplefs infant fhould be taken, and bred up in all the learning of the *Egyptians*, and in that very court from which, and by that very tyrant from whom the edict came, and that the deliverer fhould be nurtured to be king in *Jefhurun*?

But time as well as ftrength would fail me, was I to give you a detail of all the important particulars refpecting GOD's peculiar people; as their miraculous fupport in the wildernefs, the events which took place while they were under a divine theocracy, and during their fettlement in *Canaan* to the time of their return from *Babylon*, and from thence to the destruction of their second temple, &c. by the *Romans*. Indeed, considering to whom I am speaking, persons conversant in the sacred and profane history, I have mentioned these things only to stir up your minds by way of remembrance.

But if we descend from the *Jewish*, to the Christian æra, we shall find, that its commencement was, in the eyes of the world, a " day of small things" indeed. Our blessed LORD compares the beginning of its progress in the world, to a grain of mustard-seed, which though the smallest of all seeds when sown, soon becomes a great tree, and so spread, that the " birds of the air," or a multitude of every nation, language and tongue, came and lodged in its branches : and its inward progress in the believers heart, CHRIST likens to a little leaven which a woman hid in three measures of meal. How both the *Jewish* and Christian dispensations have been, and even to this day are despised, by the wise disputers of this world, on this very account, is manifest to all who read the lively oracles with a becoming attention. What ridicule, obloquy, and inveterate opposition christianity meets with, in this our day, not only from the open deist, but from formal professors, is too evident to every truly pious soul.

And what opposition the kingdom of grace meets with in the heart, is well known by all those who are experimentally acquainted with their hearts : they know, to their sorrow, what the great apostle of the *Gentiles* means, by " the Spirit striving against the flesh, and the flesh against the Spirit."

But the sacred Oracles, and the histories of all ages acquaint us, that GOD brings about the greatest thing, not only by small and unlikely means, but by ways and means directly opposite to the carnal reasonings of unthinking men : he chuses things that be not, to bring to nought those which are. How did christianity spread and flourish, by one, who was despised and rejected of men, a man of sorrows and acquainted with grief, and who expired on a cross ? he was despised and rejected, not merely by the vulgar and
illiterate,

illiterate, but the Rabbies and Masters of *Israel*, the Scribes and Pharisees, who by the *Jewish* churchmen were held too in so high a reputation for their outward sanctity, that it became a common proverb, "If only two went to heaven, the one would be a Scribe, and the other a Pharisee." Yet there were they who endeavoured to silence the voice of all his miracles and heavenly doctrine with, "Is not this the Carpenter's son?" Nay, "He is mad, why hear you him? he hath a devil, and casteth out devils by *Beelzebub* the prince of the devils." And their despite not only followed him to, but after death, and when in his grave. "We remember (said they) that this deceiver said, after three days I will rise again; command therefore that the sepulchre be made sure;" but, maugre all your impotent precautions, in sealing the stone, and setting a watch, he burst the bars of death asunder, and, according to his repeated predictions, proved himself to be the Son of GOD with power, by rising the third day from the dead. And afterwards, in presence of great multitudes, was he received up into glory; as a proof thereof, he sent down the Holy Ghost, (on the mission of whom he pawned all his credit with his disciples) in such an instantaneous, amazing manner, as one would imagine, should have forced and compelled all who saw it to own, that this was indeed the finger of GOD.

And yet how was this grand transaction treated? with the utmost contempt: when instantaneously the apostles commenced orators and linguists, and with a divine profusion spoke of the wonderful things of GOD; "these men (said some) are full of new wine." And yet by these men, mean fishermen, illiterate men, idiots, in the opinion of the Scribes and Pharisees, and notwithstanding all the opposition of earth and hell, and that too only by the foolishness of preaching, did this grain of mustard-seed grow up, till thousands, ten thousands of thousands, a multitude which no man can number, out of every nation, language and people, came and lodged under the branches of it.

Neither shall it rest here; whatever dark parenthesis may intervene, we are assured, that being still watered by the same

same divine hand, it shall take deeper and deeper root downward, and bear more and more fruit upward, till the whole earth be filled with the knowledge of the LORD, as the waters cover the sea. Who shall live when GOD doth this? Hasten O LORD that blessed time! O let this thy kingdom come! Come, not only by the external preaching of the gospel in the world, but by its renovating, heart-renewing, soul-transforming power, to awakened sinners! For want of this, alas! alas! though we understood all mysteries, could speak with the tongues of men and angels, we should be only like sounding brass, or so many tinkling cymbals.

And yet, what a " day of small things" is the first implantation of the seed of divine life in the soul of man? Well might our LORD, who alone is the author and finisher of our faith, compare it to a little leaven, which a woman took, and hid in three measures of meal, till the whole was leavened. Low similies, mean comparisons these, in the eyes of those, who having eyes, see not; who having ears, hear not; whose heart, being waxed gross, cannot, will not understand! To such, it is despicable, mysterious, and unintelligible in its description; and, if possible, infinitely more so, when made effectual by the power of GOD, to the salvation of any individual soul. For the wisdom of GOD will always be foolishness to natural men. As it was formerly, so it is now; they who are born after the flesh, will persecute those that are born after the spirit: the disciple must be as his master: they that will live godly in him; they that live *most godly* in him, must, shall suffer persecution. This is so interwoven in the very nature and existence of the gospel, that our LORD makes it one part of the beatitudes, in that blessed sermon which he preached, when, to use the words of my old familiar friend the seraphic *Hervey*, a mount was his pulpit, and the heavens his sounding board. A part, which, like others of the same nature, I believe, will be little relished by such who are always clamouring against those few highly favoured souls, who dare stand up and preach the doctrine of *justification by faith alone* in the imputed righteousness of JESUS CHRIST, and are reproached with not preaching, like their master, *Morality*, as they

they term it, in his glorious fermon on the mount: for did we more preach, and more live it, we fhould foon find all manner of evil would be fpoken againft us for CHRIST's fake.

But fhall this hinder the progrefs, the growth, and confummation? and fhall the chriftian therefore be difmayed and difcouraged? GOD forbid! On the contrary, the weakeft believer may, and ought, to rejoice and be exceeding glad. And why? for a very good reafon; becaufe, he that hath begun the good work, hath engaged alfo to finifh it; though CHRIST found him as black as hell, he fhall prefent him, and every individual purchafed with his blood, without fpot or wrinkle, or any fuch thing, before the Divine Prefence. O glorious profpect! how will the faints triumph, and the fons of GOD then fhout for joy? If they fhouted when GOD faid, "Let there be light, and there was light;" and if there is joy in heaven over one finner only that repenteth, how will the heavenly arches echo and rebound with praife, when all the redeemed of the LORD fhall appear together, and the Son of GOD fhall fay, "of all thefe that thou haft given to me, have I loft nothing." On the contrary, what weeping, wailing, and gnafhing of teeth will there be, not only amongft the devil and his angels, but amongft the fearful and unbelieving, when they fee that all the hellifh temptations and devices, inftead of deftroying, were over-ruled to the furtherance of the gofpel in general, and to the increafe and growth of grace in every individual believer in particular. And how will defpifers then behold and wonder and perifh, when they fhall be obliged to fay, "we fools counted their lives madnefs, and their end to be without honour; but how are they numbered among the children of GOD, and how happy is their lot among the faints!"

But whither am I going? Pardon me, my dear hearers, if you think this to be a digreffion from my main point. It is true, whilft I am mufing, the fire begins to kindle: I am flying, but not fo high, I truft, as to lofe fight of my main fubject. And yet, after meditating and talking of the rife

and

and progress of the gospel of the kingdom, I shall find it somewhat difficult to descend so low, as to entertain you with the small beginnings of this infant colony, and of the Orphan-house, in which I am now preaching. But I should judge myself inexcusable on this occasion, if I did not detain you a little longer, in taking a transient view of the traces of divine Providence, in the rise and progress of the colony in general, and the institution of this Orphan-house in particular. Children yet unborn, I trust, will have occasion to bless GOD for both.

The very design of this settlement, as charity inclines us to hope all things, was, that it might be an Asylum, and a place of business, for as many as were in distress; for foreigners, as well as natives; for *Jews* and *Gentiles*. On *February* 1, a day, the memory of which, I think, should still be perpetuated, the first embarkation was made with forty-five *English* families; men, who had once lived well in their native country, and who, with many persecuted *Saltzburghers*, headed by a good old soldier of JESUS lately deceased, the Rev. Mr. *Boltzius*, came to find a refuge here. They came, they saw, they laboured, and endeavoured to settle; but by an essential, though well-meant defect, in the very beginning of the settlement, too well known by some now present, and too long, and too much felt to bear repeating, prohibiting the importation and use of negroes, &c. their numbers gradually diminished, and matters were brought to so low an ebb, that the whole colony became a proverb of reproach.

About this time, in the year 1737, being previously stirred up thereto by a strong impulse, which I could by no means resist, I came here, after the example of my worthy and reverend friends, Messieurs *John* and *Charles Wesley*, and Mr. *Ingham*, who, with the most disinterested views, had come hither to serve the colony, by endeavouring to convert the *Indians*. I came rejoicing to serve the colony also, and to become your willing servant for CHRIST's sake. My friend and father, good Bishop *Benson*, encouraged me, though my brethren and kinsmen after the flesh, as well as

religious

religious friends, opposed it. I came, and I saw (you will not be offended with me to speak the truth) the nakedness of the land. Gladly did I distribute about the four hundred pounds sterling, which I had collected in *England*, among my poor parishioners. The necessity and propriety of erecting an Orphan-house, was mentioned and recommended before my first embarkation. But thinking it a matter of too great importance to be set about unwarily, I deferred the farther prosecution of this laudable design till my return to *England* in the year 1738, for to have priests orders.

Miserable was the condition of many grown persons, as well as children, whom I left behind. Their cause I endeavoured to plead, immediately upon my arrival; but being denied the churches, in which I had the year before collected many hundreds for the *London* charity-schools, I endeavoured to plead their cause in the fields. The people threw in their mites most willingly; once or twice, I think, twenty-two pounds were collected in copper; the alms were accompanied with many prayers, and which, as I told them, laid, I am persuaded, a blessed foundation to the future charitable superstructure. In a short time, though plucked as it were out of the fire, the collections and charitable contributions amounted to more than a one thousand pounds sterling.

With that I reimbarked, taking *Philadelphia* in my way, and upon my second arrival, found the spot fixed upon; but, alas! who can describe the low estate to which it was reduced! the whole country almost was left desolate, and the metropolis *Savannah*, was but like a cottage in a vineyard, or as a lodge in a garden of cucumbers. Many orphans, whose parents had been taken from them by the distresses that naturally attend new settlements, were dispersed here and there in a very forlorn helpless condition; my bowels yearned towards them, and, animated by the example of the great Professor *Franck*, previous to bringing them here, I hired a house, furnished an infirmary, employed all that were capable of employment, and in a few weeks walked to the house of GOD with a large family of above sixty orphans, and others in as bad a condition.

On *March* 25, 1740, in full assurance of faith, I laid the foundation of this house; and in the year following, brought in my orphan family, who, with the workmen, now made up the number of one hundred and fifty: by the money which was expended on these, the remaining few were kept in the colony, and were enabled to pay the debts they owed; so that in a representation made to the House of Commons, by some, who for very good reasons wanted the constitution of the colony altered; they declared, that the very existence of the colony was in a great measure, if not totally, owing to the building and supporting of the Orphan House.

Finding the care of such a family, incompatible with the care due to a parish, upon giving previous warning to the then trustees, I gave up the living of *Savannah*, which without fee or reward I had voluntarily taken upon me: I then ranged through the northern colonies, and afterwards once more returned home. What calumny, what loads of reproach, I for many years was called to undergo, in thus turning beggar for a family, few here present need to be informed; a family, utterly unconnected by any ties of nature; a family, not only to be maintained with food, but cloathed and educated also, and that too in the dearest part of his Majesty's dominions, on a pine barren, and in a colony where the use of negroes was totally denied; this appeared so very improbable, that all beholders looked daily for its decline and annihilation.

But, blessed be GOD, the building advanced and flourished, and the wished-for period is now come; after having supported the family for thirty-two years, by a change of constitution and the smiles of government, with liberal donations from the northern, and especially the adjacent provinces, the same hands that laid the foundation, are now called to finish it, by making an addition of a seat of learning, the whole products and profits of which, are to go towards the increase of the fund, as at the beginning, for destitute orphans, or such youths as may be called of GOD to the sacred ministry of his gospel. I need not call on any here, to cry, " Grace, grace,
unto

unto it." For on the utmost scrutiny of the intention of those employed, and considering the various exercises they have been called to undergo, and the opposition the building hath every where met with, we may justly say, " not by might, " nor by power, but by thy Spirit, O LORD," hath this work been carried on thus far; it is his doing, let it be marvellous in our eyes. With humble gratitude, therefore, would we now set up our *Ebenezer*, and say, " Hitherto thou, LORD, " hast helped us;" and wherefore should we doubt, but that he, who hath thus far helped, will continue to help, when the weary heads of the first founders and present helpers, are laid in the silent grave.

I am very well aware, what an invidious task it must be to a person in my circumstances, thus to speak on an affair in which he hath been so much concerned. Some may perhaps think, I am become a fool in thus glorying. But as I am now, blessed be GOD, in the decline of life, and as, in all probability, I shall never be present to celebrate another anniversary, I thought it best to be a little more explicit, that if I have spoken any thing but truth, I may be confronted; and if not, that future ages, and future successors, may see with what a purity of intention, and what various interpositions of Providence, the work was begun, and hath been carried on to its *present height*.

It was the reading of a like account, written by the late Professor *Franck*, that encouraged me: who knows but hereafter, the reading something of a similar nature, may encourage others to begin and carry on a like work elsewhere? I have said its *present height*, for I would humbly hope, that this is, comparatively speaking, only a " day of small things," only the dawn of brighter scenes. Private genius's and individuals, as well as collective bodies, have, like the human body, the nonage, puerile, juvenile estate, before they arrive at their zenith, and their lives as gradually they decline. But yet I would hope, that both the province and *Bethesda*, are but in their puerile or juvenile state. And long, long may they increase, and make large strides, till they arrive at

a glorious

a glorious zenith! I mean not merely in trade, merchandife, and opulence, (though I would be far from fecluding them from the province, and would be thankful for the advances it hath already made) but a zenith of glorious gofpel bleffings, without which, all outward emoluments are lefs than nothing, or as the fmall duft of the balance: " For what fhall it profit a man, if he fhall gain the whole world and lofe his own foul."

Who can imagine, that the prophet *Zechariah* would be fent to ftrengthen the hands of *Zerubbabel*, in building and laying the foundation of the temple, if that temple was not to be frequented with worfhippers that worfhipped the Father in fpirit and in truth. The moft gaudy fabrics, ftately temples, new moon fabbaths, and folemn affemblies, are only folemn mockeries GOD cannot away with. This GOD hath fhewn by the deftruction of both the firft and fecond temples. What is become of the feven churches of *Afia?* How are all their golden candlefticks overthrown? " GOD is a Spirit, and they who worfhip him muft worfhip him in fpirit and in truth." And no longer do I expect that this houfe will flourifh, than when the power of religion is encouraged and promoted, and the perfons educated here, profecute their ftudies, not only to be great fcholars, but good faints.

Bleffed be GOD! I can fay with Profeffor *Franck*, that it is in a great meafure owing to the difinterefted fpirit of my firft fellow-helpers, as well as thofe who are now employed, that the building hath reached to its prefent height. This I am bound to fpeak, not only in honour to thofe who are now with GOD, but thofe at prefent before me. Nor dare I conclude, without offering to

Your Excellency, our pepper corn of acknowledgment for the countenance you have always fhewn *Bethefda*'s inftitution, and the honour you did us laft year, in laying the firft brick of yonder wings: in thus doing, you have honoured *Bethefda*'s GOD. May he long delight to honour you here

on

on earth! and after a life spent to his glory, and your country's good, may he honour you to all eternity, in placing you at CHRIST's right-hand in the kingdom above!

Next to your Excellency, my dear Mr. President, I must beg your acceptance both of thanks and congratulation on the annual return of this festival. For you was not only my dear familiar friend, and first fellow-traveller in this infant province; but you was directed by Providence to this spot, laid the second brick of this house, watched, prayed, and wrought for the family's good: A witness of innumerable trials, partner of my joys and griefs; you will have now the pleasure of seeing the Orphan-house a fruitful bough, its branches running over the wall. For this, no doubt, GOD hath smiled upon and blessed you, in a manner we could not expect, much less design; and may he continue to bless you with all spiritual blessings in heavenly places in CHRIST JESUS. Look to the rock from whence you have been hewn, and may your children never be ashamed, that their father left his native country, and married a real christian, born again under this roof. May *Bethesda*'s GOD grant this may be the happy portion of your children, and children's children!

Gentlemen of his Majesty's council,

Mr. Speaker, and you members of the General Assembly, many thanks are owing to you, for your late address to his Excellency in favour of *Bethesda*. Your joint recommendation of it, when I was last here, which, though in some measure through the bigotry of some, for the present is rendered abortive, by their wanting to have it confined to a party, yet I trust the event will prove that every thing shall be over-ruled to the furtherance of the work. Here I repeat, what I have often declared, that as far as lies in my power before and after my decease, *Bethesda* shall be always on a *broad bottom*. All denominations have freely given; all denominations, all the continent, GOD being my helper, shall receive benefit from it. May *Bethesda*'s GOD bless you all!

in your private as well as public capacity; and as you are honoured to be the reprefentatives of a now flourifhing increafing people: may you be directed in all your ways! May truth, juftice, religion, and piety be eftablifhed amongft you through all generations!

Laftly, My reverend brethren, and you inhabitants of the colony, accept unfeigned thanks for the honour done me, in letting us fee you at *Bethefda* this day. You, Sir, for the fermon preached here laft year. Tell it in *Germany*, tell my great, good friend, Profeffor *Franck*, that *Bethefda*'s GOD, is a GOD whofe mercy endureth for ever. O let us have your earneft prayers! encourage your people not to " defpife the day of fmall things." What hath GOD wrought? From its infancy, this colony hath been bleffed with many faithful gofpel minifters: O that this may be a nurfery to many more! This hath been the cafe of the *New England* College for almoft a century, and why not the Orphan-houfe Academy at *Georgia*?

Men, brethren, fathers, as many of you, whether inhabitants or ftrangers, who have honoured this day with your prefence, give us the additional bleffings of your prayers. And O that *Bethefda*'s GOD may make this day, though but a day of fmall things, productive of great things to the fouls of all amongft whom I have been now preaching the kingdom of GOD. A great and good day will it be indeed, if JESUS CHRIST, our great *Zerubbabel*, fhould, by the power of the eternal Spirit, blefs any thing that hath now been faid, to caufe every mountain of difficulty, that lies in the way of your converfion, to become a plain. And what art thou, O great mountain, whether the luft of the flefh, the luft of the eye, or the pride of life, fin, or felf-righteoufnefs? Before our *Bethefda*'s GOD, thou fhalt become a plain.

Brethren, my heart is enlarged towards you: it is written, bleffed be GOD that it is written, " In the name of JESUS every knee fhall bow, whether things in heaven, or things in earth, or things under the earth." O that we may be made a willing people in the day of his power! Look, look unto him, all ye that are placed in thefe ends of the earth. This houfe hath often been an houfe of GOD, a gate of heaven, to fome of your fathers. May it be a houfe of GOD, a gate of heaven, to the children alfo! Come unto him, all ye that are weary and heavy laden, he will give you reft; reft from the guilt, reft from the power, reft from the punifhment of fin; reft from the fear of divine judgments here, reft with himfelf eternally hereafter. Fear not, though the beginnings are but fmall, CHRIST will not defpife the day of fmall things. A bruifed reed will he not break, and the fmoaking flax will he not quench, until he bring forth judgment unto victory. His hands that laid the foundation, alfo fhall finifh it: yet a little while and the top-ftone fhall be brought forth with fhouting, and men and angels join in crying " Grace! Grace! unto it." That all prefent may be in this happy number, may GOD of his infinite mercy grant, through JESUS our LORD.

SERMON LVIII.

Peter's Denial of his LORD.

MATTHEW xxvi. 75. *

And Peter remembered the words of Jesus, which said unto him, Before the cock crow twice, thou shalt deny me thrice: and he went out, and wept bitterly.

BIOGRAPHY, as one observes, is the best history; or, in other words, writing or reading the lives of great and good men, is one of the most profitable and delightful kinds of history we can entertain ourselves with. For hereby we are convinced, that Wisdom's ways are indeed ways of pleasantness; and being proved to be practicable by men of like passions with ourselves, we are insensibly allured to follow them as they followed *Christ*, and encouraged to run with patience the race set before us. This, one would hope, is the grand end proposed by all such who undertake to draw the characters, or hand down to posterity the remarkable transactions of persons who have shone as lights in the church of GOD. Many have done worthily in this respect; and for this their labour of love, thousands as yet unborn, shall rise

---

* The two following Sermons came to hand after the others were in the press.

and call them blessed. But without detracting any thing from their due praise, I cannot help observing, that in most of the lives that I have had an opportunity of perusing, there seems to be one deficiency, I could almost say, common to them all. It is this: The writers of them seldom or never mention the blemishes or falls of those whose characters they exhibit. They emblazon their good, without so much as hinting at any of their bad qualities. In short, they paint them blameless, and by not mentioning any of their foibles, or the sins that did most easily beset them, they make them, as it were, equal to the angels of GOD, or rather to the Son of GOD himself, of whom alone it can truly be said, " That he was without sin." Such a method, (however well meant, because we are more prone to imitate others vices than their virtues) to speak in the softest terms, is not according to the pattern shewn us in the mount. The scriptures set us a different copy. In those lively oracles, as in a well-drawn picture, we have both shade and light; and at the same time as they paint out to us, in the most striking manner, the graces for which the holy men of old were most eminent, they also, with an equally impartial hand, expose to public view, not only the common infirmities, but even some of the most dreadful falls, with all their aggravating circumstances, of some of the greatest men of God that ever did, or will live, till time itself shall be no more.

One of these is to be the mournful subject of our present meditation. *Procul ite profani!* Let all profane persons keep at an awful distance: We are going to tread on holy ground. I set an hedge about it in the name of the living GOD. Come not too nigh the mount, lest that which was written for your learning, through your own perverse abuse of it, should prove unto you a further occasion of falling.

If any should enquire, "Why all this caution?" I answer, "We are about to discourse on the Apostle *Peter's* shameful denial of his and our blessed Lord and Saviour JESUS CHRIST." A passage recorded by all the evangelists, St. *Mark* himself not excepted, who is supposed to have been emanuensis to St. *Peter*, and to have taken his gospel from *Peter*'s own mouth. A proof this, not only of the impartiality of the sacred writers, but also that the Holy Ghost intended that this awful story should, in an especial manner, be recorded for our learning, on whom the ends of the world are come. But though all the evangelists are very explicit in relating this perfidious and wicked act, yet we shall chiefly confine ourselves, at present, to the account given us of it in this xxvith chapter of St. *Matthew*, and, for method sake, purpose to consider,

First, The steps that led to this great man's fall.

Secondly, The fall itself. And,

Thirdly, His recovery from it, mentioned in the text: "And *Peter* remembered the words of JESUS, which said unto him, Before the cock crow, thou shalt deny me thrice. And he went out and wept bitterly."

But before we proceed to the prosecution of these points, it may be proper to premise, that we take it for granted the Apostle *Peter*, before his fall, was certainly a converted man. This is controverted by some. For what reason, is best known to themselves. The scriptures evidently leave us no room to dispute it. One passage may suffice for a proof. "Blessed art thou, *Simon Bar Jonah* (said the glorious *Emmanuel* to *Peter*, when he witnessed that good confession, Thou art CHRIST, the Son of the living GOD); for flesh and blood hath not revealed

revealed this unto thee, but my Father which is in heaven." Not content with this, he adds, "Thou art *Peter*, and upon this rock will I build my church, and the gates of hell shall never be able to prevail against it:" Words that carry with them the strongest presumption, not only that *Peter* was a converted man, but that he had some eminent place to be assigned him in the kingdom of grace. For our Lord pronounces him blessed: "Blessed art thou, *Simon Bar Jonah:*" and gives him a reason for it; "For flesh and blood hath not revealed this unto thee, but my heavenly Father." So that *Peter* called CHRIST Lord by the Holy Ghost, which none but a converted person can do. And further, "Upon this rock, says CHRIST, will I build my church;" which, whether it be understood of his confession of CHRIST's divinity, or his being afterwards to be employed in first preaching the gospel to the *Gentiles*, seems to denote some peculiar favour and honour assigned to, and hereafter to be conferred upon him. It is true, indeed, the same all-seeing Redeemer, when afterwards he forewarned him of his fall, subjoined this particular command; "And when thou art converted, strengthen thy brethren." But this only implies, that his fall would be so exceeding great, that his recovery out of it would be, as it were, a second conversion.

The steps that led to this terrible disaster, come now more particularly to be considered. In order to be informed of these, (as I take it for granted you have brought your Bibles with you) I must beg you to look back to the 33d verse of this chapter, where we shall find, that spiritual pride, and a too great dependence on a stock of grace already received, was one of the first steps discernible in this Apostle's denial of his LORD.——The blessed JESUS, knowing all things that should befal him, after the solemn institution and celebration of his last supper, gave his disciples this tremendous warning, backed with a scripture prediction: "All ye (ver. 31.) shall

be

be offended because of me this night; for it is written, I will smite the shepherd, and the sheep shall be scattered." A warning, one would imagine, terrible enough to have struck them all dumb, at least to have filled them with a holy jealousy of their own desperately wicked and deceitful hearts. But what says our Apostle? He (ver. 33.) answered and said, " Though all men shall be offended because of thee, yet will I never be offended." Poor *Peter!* How unlike thy former self, when at thy first calling, thou criedst out, " Depart from me, for I am a sinful man, O LORD." Alas! he now thinks his mountain is so strong, that it never could be moved. " Though all men should be offended because of thee, yet will I never be offended." O these egotisms! How frequently are they used by, but how little do they become such frail creatures as we are! " Yet will I never be offended;" so far from being offended this night, that I will never, at any time, or in any place, be offended because of thee. No wonder, after hearing this, that the holy JESUS said unto him, (ver. 34.) " Verily I say unto thee, that this night, before the cock crow, thou shalt, or will deny me thrice:" (for CHRIST's predicting his fall, laid him under no necessity of falling). Surely *Peter* will now retract! Nothing less. On the contrary, depending too much on the sincerity of his intentions, and his present good frame, he said unto his Master, (ver. 35.) " Though I should die with thee, yet will I not deny thee." As though he should have said, " Die with thee I may; to " die with or for thee, I am ready: but to deny thee, I dare " not. Deny thee in any wise, I cannot, and neither will I. " Is thy servant a dog, a devil, that he should do this?" Stop, *Peter*; whither art thou going? Where is thy present warm zeal carrying thee? What! wilt thou give the GOD of truth the lie? I begin to tremble for thee. Such self-confidence and spiritual pride, generally go before a fall.

But to proceed. Spiritual sloth, as well as spiritual pride, helped to throw this Apostle down." The sun, that glorious Sun of righteousness, was now about to enter into his last eclipse. Satan, who had left him for a season, or, till the season of his passion, is now to be permitted to bruise his heel again. This is his hour, and now the powers of darkness summon and exert their strongest and united efforts. A hymn is a prelude to his dreadful passion. From the communion-table, the Saviour retires to the garden. An horrible dread, and inexpressible load of sorrow begins to overwhelm and weigh down his innocent soul. His body can scarcely sustain it. See how he faulters! See how his hands hang down, and his knees wax feeble under the amazing pressure! He is afflicted and oppressed indeed. See, see, O my soul, how he sweats! But what is that which I see? Blood—drops of blood—great drops of blood falling to the ground. Alas, was ever sorrow like unto this sorrow! Hark! what is that I hear? O dolorous complaint? "Father, if it be possible, let this cup pass from me." Hark! he speaks again. Amazing! the Creator complains to the creature, "My soul is exceeding sorrowful, even unto death: tarry you here and watch with me." And now he retires once more. But see how his agony increases—Hark! how he prays, and that too yet more earnestly: " Father, if it be possible, let this cup pass from me." And will his heavenly Father leave him comfortless? No.—An angel (O happy, highly-favoured angel!) is sent from heaven to strengthen him. But where is *Peter* all this while? We are told that the holy JESUS took him, with *James* and *John*, into the garden. Surely he will not leave his LORD in such deep distress! What is he doing? I blush to answer. Alas! he is sleeping: nay, though awakened once by his agonizing LORD, with a " *Simon Peter*, sleepest thou? what! couldest thou not watch with me one hour?" yet his eyes, notwithstanding

his

his profession of constancy and care, are heavy with sleep. LORD, what is man!

After hearing all this, we need not be surprized at the account given us, (ver. 58.) of another step to his fall, viz. His following JESUS afar off. "But *Peter*, says the Evangelists, followed him afar off." The Redeemer's agony was now over, "and behold the hour is at hand, when he is to be betrayed into the hands of sinners." He warns his sleepy disciples of it, and, acting like himself, goes out to meet the threatening storm. "Arise, said he let us go: behold! he that betrayeth me is at hand." *Judas*, one of the twelve that eat of his bread, performs the hellish task, and lifts up his heel against him. He says, Hail, Master! kisses and then betrays him. For this was the sign agreed on, "Whomsoever I shall kiss, the same is he, hold him fast." They knew the watch-word, and, like so many roaring lions, seize on their unresisting prey. This rouses *Peter*. Out of an honest, but misguided zeal, he draws his sword, and cuts off the High-priest's servant's ear. The blessed JESUS heals the one, reproves the other; and, according to *Isaiah*'s prophecy, is contentedly led as a lamb to the slaughter. *Peter*'s heat is soon cooled, and instead of adhering to his LORD, or saying, as might justly be expected, "Whither "thou goest, I will go; whithersoever they lead thee, they "shall lead me also:" Alas! alas! he followed him afar off. Observe, he does not deny his LORD all at once. No. Satan leads us on by degrees into great sins, and will not suffer us to be very bad immediately. *Peter* at first follows afar off: he skulks behind, and keeps on purpose at a distance, lest he should be accounted one of his followers. O *Peter*, *Peter*, did I not know how prone my own deceitful heart is to go astray from the great Shepherd and Bishop of our souls, I should now begin to say, Fie upon thee, fie upon thee. Hadst thou kept close to thy LORD, thou mightest have been

sheltered

sheltered safely under his almighty wings; but how canst thou avoid falling, and that foully too, when thou beginnest thus to be ashamed of thy glorious master?

But this is not all. For we are not only informed that he followed Jesus afar off, but that " He went into the High Priest's palace (verse 58.) and sat with the servants." So that keeping bad company was another step that led to his great fall. Oh *Peter!* my blood begins now almost to run cold within me. I tremble for thee more than ever. What canst thou propose to thyself, or what bad thing may we not expect to hear of thee, when sitting in such sorry company? I had much rather have heard that thou hadst fled with thy other cowardly brethren. Thou sittest among thy master's professed enemies to see the end. Whatever becomes of him, I dread to hear what the end of all this gradual backsliding will be, in respect to thy own soul.

Well! the blessed Jesus is now at the bar. Omnipotence suffers itself to be arraigned, and he who set bounds to the sea which it cannot pass, is content to be bound, and that as a criminal, by the work of his own hands. False witnesses rise up against him, and lay to his charge things that he knew not. " This fellow, say they, (verse 61.) said, I am able to destroy the temple of God, and to build it in three days." And what reply doth the innocent Jesus make? None at all. Not only because they all knew that it was a malicious slander, but because he stood as our representative. He, therefore, held his peace, and as a sheep before the shearers is dumb, so this immaculate Lamb of God opened not his mouth. At length, being adjured thereto by the High-priest in the name of the living God, he confesses himself to be the Christ, the son of the Blessed; and lets the imperious Sanhedrim know, that however contemptible his appearance might be now, yet they should hereafter see him sitting on

the

the right hand of power, and coming in the clouds of heaven. And does not this strike terror into his accusers and judges? By no means. The haughty High-Priest rises in disdain, hypocritically rends his cloaths, urging this as a reason, "He hath spoken blasphemy; what further need have we of witnesses?" Was ever indignity, like this indignity, put on thee, thou most adorable Mediator! Which shall I marvel at most, the High-Priest's impudence, or thy patience? Both, doubtless, are unparalleled. And yet, alas! a further trial awaits our suffering LORD. For whilst the master is thus arraigned, insulted, and causelesly condemned at the bar within, *Satan* is no less busy in wounding him through *Peter*'s side, who was sitting in the palace without. *Peter*, indeed, thinks to sit there undiscovered; but a damsel comes to him, (verse 69) saying, "Thou also wast with JESUS of Galilee." And what then? Was that high treason? Or rather was it not the highest honour? *Peter*, what sayest thou? Alas, (verse 70) "He denied before them all, saying, I know not what thou sayest." Know not what thou sayest, *Peter?* her words were plain enough, "Thou also was with JESUS of Nazareth." Can any words be plainer? To deny this, in the least, was bad, but to deny this before them all, who could so easily confront thee, proves thee to be falling indeed. Call him now no longer *Peter*, but call him *Ichabod*: for the glory of the LORD is departing from him.

However, as yet there is hope concerning him. For, conscious, as it were, of his guilt (verse 71) "He went out into the porch." *Satan* pursues him. For when a saint begins to fall, his hellish language is, Down with him, down with him, even to the ground. Another damsel, therefore, is put in *Peter*'s way, who, upon seeing him, says, not unto *Peter* himself, but to them that were there, (verse 71) "This fellow was also with JESUS of Nazareth." She speaks the same language with her sister scoffer, and with those

those who accused the blessed JESUS at the bar. Doubtless, our modern scoffers are related to them, for they use the same dialect every day when speaking of CHRIST, or those that, through grace, dare to own and confess him before men. But here would I stop and feign be excused from relating to this great assembly *Peter*'s answer. Oh tell it not in *Gath*, publish it not in the streets of *Askelon!* But we must not be wise above what is written. The Holy Spirit hath left it upon record, and proclaimed it by four Evangelists upon the house-top, and, therefore, I am constrained to tell you, that again (verse 72.) "He denied with an oath, I do not know the man." What! an Apostle swear? Was it not enough barely to deny the damsel's assertion, but he must deny it with an oath? Perhaps, it was a crime he never was guilty of before. Surely, the way of sin is down-hill. One step leads to another. At first he only denied what was said to him, by a kind of equivocation, "I know not what thou sayest." Now he grows bolder, and denies with an oath, "I know not the man." What, *Peter!* Know not the man? That glorious God-man CHRIST JESUS thy LORD? What! not know Him, who called thee from the poor occupation of catching fish, to make thee an Apostle and a fisher of men? What! not know Him, who bad thee come to him upon the waters, and Him who with his own almighty arm saved thee from drowning, when thou wast answering thy name *Cephas*, and sinking like a stone? What! not know Him, with whom thou hast so intimately conversed for three years last past, who, so lately pronounced thee blessed, washed thy feet, gave thee a new name, and took thee to Mount *Tabor*, where he displayed before thee his excellent glory, which made thee cry out, It is good for us to be here? What! hast thou forgot all this, *Peter?*

Surely, it is high time for the cock to crow. Hark! The cock does crow, not only once, but twice; but all in vain.

Fallen as this great man is, he muſt ſtill fall lower. *Satan* is now about to give him the laſt and moſt fatal thruſt. He hath his quiver full of deadly arrows, and hath always inſtruments at hand, the weakeſt of which will foil the ſtrongeſt Apoſtle when left to himſelf, "After a while (verſe 73) came unto him they that ſtood by, and ſaid unto *Peter*, Surely, thou alſo waſt one of them, for thy ſpeech betrayeth thee." As though they had ſaid, "How canſt thou have the "impudence to ſay thou knoweſt not the man, when thy "very language and manner of ſpeaking betrays thy being "even one of his followers?" What ſays *Peter* now? Can he withſtand this glaring evidence? Yes, he not only denies it with a ſingle oath, but (Oh, how ſhall I ſpeak it!) he "began to curſe and to ſwear," and with a whole volly of execrable expreſſions, ſtriving to act the bravado, he perſiſts in ſaying (verſe 74) "I know not the man." And now, *Satan*, thou haſt gained thy point. A great man, through too much ſelf-confidence, ſpiritual pride, ſpiritual ſloth, and too great intimacy with ſome of thy children, is fallen indeed! Thou haſt ſifted him with a witneſs.

But is he fallen, never to riſe again? Is *Peter* ſunk too low for free grace ever to raiſe him up? Will the Redeemer ſuffer his truth to fail; or ſhall the prayer put up for him before he was led into temptation, viz. that his faith ſhould not fail, remain unanſwered? No, all the promiſes in CHRIST JESUS are all yea and all Amen; and having loved his own, he loves them unto the end. The enemy hath broke in upon *Peter* like a flood, but the almighty Redeemer will now lift up his ſtandard againſt him, and deliver his captive ſervant. Immediately, (verſe 74) upon this laſt denial of his LORD, "the cock crew." And what is moſt of all (nay, without which the cock might have crowed ten thouſand times) another Evangeliſt tells us, that "the LORD turned, and looked upon *Peter*." Oh amazing condeſcenſion!

descension! Oh unparalleled instance of endearing love! Our Lord was now upon a trial for his life. Fat bulls of *Bashan* were surrounding him on every side. Yet the same love, that in the night in which he was betrayed, would not permit him to forget his disciples in general, would not, though he was himself now arraigned at the bar, suffer him to forget his poor fallen Apostle in particular. "The LORD, therefore, turned, and looked upon *Peter*." But who besides *Peter*, and souls like him recovering from their backslidings, can tell the language of that look? Doubtless, it carried with it an " *Et tu Peter?* And art thou there *Peter?* " Is it not enough for me to be falsely accused, and con-
" demned by my enemies, but I must be wounded also in
" the house of my friends! Is it not sufficient that *Judas*
" betrays me, but thou must add to my grief by denying
" me? Deny me too with an oath, nay, with oaths and
" curses deny that ever thou knewest me? Is this thy
" kindness to thy friend? Alas! What is become of thy
" boasted professions now? Art thou the man that didst so
" solemnly declare, that though thou shouldst die with
" me, thou wouldst not deny me in any wise? Yes, Thou art
" the man."

This, and much more of the same kind, we may well suppose was the real language of that convincing, heart-piercing look, which the LORD JESUS at this time gave his fallen *Peter*. Amazing! He looks him into contrition; whereas had he rewarded him according to his iniquity, he might have looked him into hell. Rejoice with me, therefore, my dear hearers. This straying sheep, through the tender mercies of the compassionate shepherd and bishop of our souls, by this look is brought back to the fold again. " And *Peter*, says our text, remembered the words of JESUS, which said unto him, Before the cock crow," i. e. at the time emphatically called the cock-crowing, which was about

three

three in the morning, "thou shalt deny me thrice. And he went out." (The word seems to import, that he threw himself out with a holy violence) "and wept bitterly." St. *Mark* only says, "And when he thought thereon, he wept." For being an amanuensis to St. *Peter*, though explicit in the account of his fall, he is very sparing in mentioning his repentance. Unless we suppose that St. *Mark* would insinuate that whenever *Peter* reflected on his fall, he always wept for ever after. However that be, he wept bitterly now. Methinks, I see him wringing his hands, rending his garments, stamping on the ground, and with the self-condemned publican smiting upon his ungrateful breast. See how it heaves! Oh what piteous sighs and groans are those which come from the very bottom of his heart! Alas! It is too big to speak. But his tears, his briny, bitter, repenting tears plainly bespeak this to be the language of his awakened soul. "Alas!
"Where have I been? On the devil's ground. With
"whom have I been conversing? The devil's children.
"What is this that I have done? Denied the LORD of
"glory, with oaths and curses denied that ever I knew him.
"And now whither shall I go? Or where shall I hide my
"guilty head? I have sinned against light. I have sinned
"against repeated tokens of his dear distinguishing and hea-
"venly love. I have sinned against repeated warnings, re-
"solutions, promises and vows. I have sinned openly in
"the face of the sun, in the presence of my master's ene-
"mies, and thereby have caused his name to be blasphemed.
"How can I think of being suffered to behold the face of,
"much less to be employed by, the ever-blessed JESUS any
"more? O *Peter*, thou hast undone thyself. Justly mayst
"thou be thrown aside like a broken vessel. GOD be mer-
"ciful to me a sinner."

And is this the language of thy tears, O *Peter?* Blessed art thou still then, thou *Simon Bar Jonah*. These tears, and this

holy

holy refentment againſt thyſelf, beſpeak thee to be a holy mourner. Yet a little while, and thou ſhalt be comforted with a "Go tell his brethren and *Peter*, that he is riſen;" and with a "*Simon* ſon of *Jonah*, loveſt thou me? Then feed my lambs." And where is now thy boaſting, O *Satan?* Or what haſt thou gained by foiling this favourite of heaven? Thou didſt deſire to have him. Thy requeſt was granted. Thou haſt ſifted him as wheat. But doſt thou imagine the all-prevailing Mediator will ſuffer thee to pluck him out of his hands? No. JESUS hath prayed for him, and therefore *Peter*'s faith ſhall not finally fail. Rejoice not then over him, O thou enemy of ſouls! For though he has fallen, yet ſee how he begins to riſe again. Though at the preſent he ſits in darkneſs, yet, ere long, the glory of the LORD ſhall ſhine around him.

Where then are thoſe Sons of *Belial*, thoſe perverſe diſputers of this world, and yet, if poſſible, more perverſe perverters of the Word of GOD? Dare any of you now go away, ſaying within yourſelves, "Who can blame us for a "little equivocating, or a little innocent lying, curſing, "and ſwearing? Was not *Peter*, the great Apoſtle *Peter*, "guilty of all theſe?" Yes he was, but with this difference, he fell through ſurprize, and but once, you, perhaps, ſin wilfully and habitually. Fall he did, and that dreadfully too; but if his fall was dreadful, his repentence was as ſincere and laſting. Ere long you ſhall ſee this ſame *Peter*, boldly owning his LORD before the whole *Jewiſh* Sanhedrim, and rejoicing that he was counted worthy to ſuffer for his great name's ſake. Ere long you ſhall hear of an angel's being ſent to bring him out of priſon, and at laſt ſealing his bleſſed doctrine with his blood. Go ye then, and entreat the LORD to look you into a godly ſorrow, and ſee that with *Peter* you bring forth fruits meet for repentance; or as the LORD GOD liveth, in whoſe name I ſpeak, and in whoſe preſence

we

we now stand, you, with all your carnal reasonings and wilful wrestings of the word of GOD, shall, ere long, be thrust down to the nethermost hell.

But why should I waste my time in reasoning with men of such perverse minds? To you who do, from your hearts, believe on JESUS of *Nazareth*, and who, in reality, are the children of the most High GOD, the mournful passage we are now upon, does, in a more immediate manner, call me to address myself. You, I am persuaded, on hearing of *Peter*'s fall, and the LORD's turning and looking upon him, will not draw this abominable inference, "Let us sin then, that grace may abound." No. I know you detest it from your inmost souls; and if it was proper to speak, would to a man cry out, "God forbid." Your hearts, I would humbly hope, are rather employed in silent ejaculation to the holy JESUS, saying within yourselves, "Oh, that he "would this day look down from heaven, the habitation of "his holiness, and cause, out of these rocky hearts, floods of "repenting tears to flow." I will readily join with you in this necessary request. For, alas! we are all guilty concerning this thing, viz. Of denying our LORD, as well as *Peter*. Some of us, perhaps, have not so openly with oaths and curses denied that ever we knew him. But then, though we have in words owned, yet in works and practice, it may be, we have habitually denied him. For how often have we been sleeping, when we ought to have been watching? And how often have we been warming and indulging our bodies, when we should have been in our closets warming our hearts in prayer? How often have we needlessly left the communion of saints, and as needlessly put ourselves into the way of, and too intimately conversed with open and unconverted sinners, or at least, with those who we had reason to think were enemies to the cross of CHRIST? How often have we been drowsy when hearing the word of GOD? Nay, how often have we been stupid, and even as dead as stones, at the table of the LORD, when CHISRT has been evidently set forth crucified before us? How often have we been so foolish as to trust our hearts, and instead of trusting the LORD, have leaned on the broken reed of our own understandings? How often have we been puffed up with spiritual pride, and confidently boasted of our graces, as though we had not received them? And oh, how often have we shamefully followed our LORD afar off? And notwithstanding he may have manifested himself to us as he doth not to the world; notwithstanding he may have taken us on the mount of ordinances, given us to see his glory, led us into his banqueting-house, and let his banner over us be love; notwithstanding our repeated vows that we would never leave him, never forsake him; yet how often have we, as it were, been ashamed of him, and his glorious Gospel, and given our LORD occasion, times without number, to complain in that cutting language, " These wounds have I received in the " house of my friends?" And now which of us shall throw the first stone at *Peter?* Behold, he has been placed in the midst of us this day. My brethren, why stand we like statues? I say, let him that is without this sin of denying the LORD JESUS, cast the first stone: But with what face of justice can we do this, being guilty in many respects equally, and in some even more guilty than *Peter* himself? Rather let us turn the edge of our resentment against ourselves, and imitating *Peter* in his repentance, as we have undoubtedly too much imitated him in his crime, let us go out from a wicked, noisy, and deluding world, and weep bitterly. Who knows but the LORD may return and leave a blessing behind him? For this end was this instance of human frailty and divine condescension recorded. In him the Redeemer shewed all this long-suffering, that we, notwithstanding our manifold backslidings, might be kept from despair. True, we have sinned, but though we have sinned

against

against light and love, yet we have still an advocate with the Father, even JESUS CHRIST the righteous, whose precious blood can, and, if applied to our souls by a living faith, will certainly cleanse us both from the guilt and power of all our sins. It was this which washed away the stain of this foul and dreadful fall from *Peter*'s heart. He quickly rose, and was as speedily restored to his blessed master's favour again. " Go tell his brethren and *Peter*," said the angel, " that he goeth before you into *Galilee*. There shall you see him. They did see him. And what said JESUS unto him? He renewed his commission, and bid him " feed his sheep and lambs." Accordingly we hear not only of his preaching, but of his being honoured so to preach, that three thousand were converted in one day. And is not the LORD JESUS the same now as he was yesterday? Yes, he is, and will continue the same for ever. We have his own royal word for it, that he will heal our backslidings, and love us freely. Let us return then unto the LORD, from whom we have revolted. He is long-suffering, slow to anger, and soon repenteth him of the evil which we provoke him to send upon us. But oh let us not return again to folly, but carefully watch and pray against spiritual pride, spiritual sloth, and self-indulgence, from whence all our evils flow.

Young preachers, to you in an especial manner are these words of exhortation sent. Of all people in the world, you had need watch most against spiritual pride. It is a fly that often spoils your whole pot of ointment. This made aged *Paul* so careful to warn *Timothy* not to lay hands upon novices, lest, says he, " being puffed up with pride, they fall into the condemnation of the devil." How many awful instances have we had of this in various places within these few years last past? Young men, therefore, I exhort you to be humble. For CHRIST's sake, for your own souls sake, for the sake of the church of GOD which he hath purchased with his own blood, pray without ceasing that you may be cloathed with humility. Take care of carrying too high sail. Popularity is a dangerous sea, and nothing but the special and almighty grace of GOD can keep you from oversetting in it. Mark the rocks against which others have made shipwreck, and beg of the LORD JESUS night and day, to help you to steer such a course as to avoid and keep clear of them: he alone can preserve you. *Satan* envies the honour put upon you; he has a particular enmity against those whom he sees the Redeemer making use of. He knows your weak sides, and will desire to have you, as he desired to have *Peter*, that he may sift you as wheat. Watch, therefore, and pray always, that you may not fall in an hour of temptation. If *Peter* could not stand when left to himself, what are we?

Have any from among ourselves of late given proofs of this? Nay, have any that once appeared boldly for our LORD, and seemed ready to follow him to prison or to death, have any such, I say, been permitted not only to follow him afar off, but shamefully and openly to disown and deny both him and his people? Let us not marvel as though some strange thing happened unto us, but let us search the scriptures. Many such instances are recorded there; and we know who hath forewarned us to expect them now. "It must needs be, says the unerring, all-seeing JESUS, that offences come. Let us not therefore be high-minded, but fear; and let him that standeth take heed lest he fall." Brethren, pray for them. Who knows but they may yet rise, and the locks at present cut off, grow again? Who knows but the cock may yet crow, JESUS may yet look, and such grievous backsliders, being as it were reconverted, may appear more zealous than ever in strengthening their brethren? When shall this once be? "We wait for thy salvation, O LORD: make no long tarrying, O our GOD!

In the mean while, let none of us be discouraged, God will take care of his own cause. The Redeemer hath declared, that the gates of hell shall never be able to prevail against his church: and, therefore, though the ark may totter, he can keep it from falling; and though driven for a while into the *Philistine's* country, he assuredly can bring it back. He that healed the wound imprudently given by *Peter* to the ear of the High Priest's servant, he can and will heal all wounds, and repair all breaches that have been occasioned either by the backslidings, or unguarded conduct of those whom he vouchsafes to employ. "Out of the eater shall come forth meat, and out of the strong shall come forth sweetness." The wicked, no doubt, rejoiced when they heard of *Peter's* fall, and in all probability frequently vented their spleen in saying, " Here is religion for you! Here is a
" pretty family of reformers, and setters forth of new doc-
" trines. One of them hath betrayed his master with a kiss,
" and another with oaths and curses denied that ever he
" knew him: if this be the beginning, what will the end of
" their boasted reformation be?" What will the end of it be? Ye fools! I have an answer ready: Christ shall be glorified, *Satan* and all his emissaries confounded, and a multitude of souls out of every nation, language, and tongue, redeemed and finally saved. Oh what a Christ have we! Courage then, my brethren, courage! I beat to arms again in the name of the Lord of hosts. Let us not quit the field of battle, but in the strength of our once crucified, but now exalted Jesus, renew the combat. " He is faithful who hath promised not only to make us conquerors, but more than conquerors through his love." Yet a little while, and our warfare shall be accomplished, death will put an end to all. A wicked world, a wicked heart, a wicked devil shall then cease from troubling us, and our weary souls shall never be so much as tempted to deny our blessed Lord any more.

Where is *Peter* now? Yonder he sits, not weeping bitterly, but rejoicing in God his Saviour, on a throne of never-fading glory. To Him, at whose right hand he is now sitting, and who alone is able to keep us from falling, and to present us faultless before the presence of his glory with exceeding joy; to Him the only wise God our Saviour, be glory, majesty, dominion, and power, both now and ever. *Amen.*

SERMON LIX.

The true Way of beholding the LAMB of GOD.

JOHN i. 35, 36.

Again, the next Day after, John stood, and two of his Disciples; and looking upon Jesus as he walked, he saith, Behold the LAMB *of* GOD.

GLORIOUS words these! Before we set about the opening and enforcing them, permit me to introduce myself in the language of *Paul* to King *Agrippa*, "Would to "GOD that both my own heart, and likewise the hearts of "all that hear me this day, may not only be almost, but "altogether in such a divine frame, as I am persuaded the "heart of that man of GOD was who first uttered these "words!" I need not tell you his name; our text tells us, it was *John*; emphatically called *John* the Baptist, because he was sent to baptize with water unto repentance, in order to prepare his hearers for the further baptism of the Holy Ghost. He was a *Boanerges*, a son of thunder. He came in the spirit and power of *Elias*, and thereby soon rendered himself so exceedingly popular, that not only *Jerusalem*, all *Judea*, and all the regions round about *Jordan*, flocked to hear him preach, but even some of the *Jewish Sanhedrim* began to doubt, whether he was not the *Messiah* himself. Accordingly we are told in this chapter, "That they sent priests and levites from *Jerusalem* to ask him, Who art thou? What sayest thou of thyself?" A most commodious opportunity this, had he any thing in view but his master's glory and the good of souls, for *John* to have set up for himself. He might have said, "*Si populus vult decipi, decipiatur*; if "people will be deceived, let them; I will impose on their "credulity, and let them look upon me as the *Messiah*:" But scorning any such sinister and base ends, "He confessed, and denied not, but confessed, I am not the CHRIST." The Evangelist expresses himself in a very peculiar manner, "He confessed, and denied not, but confessed;" implying that he took more than ordinary pains to rectify their mistake, and guard them against thinking more highly of him than they ought to think: nay, impatient, as it were, of the least appearance of any such thing, he speaks of himself in the most diminutive terms, acknowledges that he was unworthy even of carrying his blessed master's shoes, and seizes the very first opportunity that offered itself to point him out in person to the people. The next day (ver. 29.) *John* seeth JESUS coming unto him, and upon seeing him, immediately cries out, "Behold the Lamb of GOD:" "Gaze not on, nor "let your views terminate in me, but look to and behold "the Lamb of GOD which taketh away the sin of the world." Thus *John* spoke in public; and to prove that he acted the same consistent part in private, our text informs us, that, "Again, the next day after, *John* stood, and two of his disciples," who like other newly awakened souls, having their master's person too much in admiration, he labours to divert their views also from himself to CHRIST, and that too in the very same language. "For looking upon JESUS as he walked, he saith, Behold the LAMB of GOD."

Thus

Thus does this difinterefted, honeft-hearted baptift, unweariedly and repeatedly recommend the LORD JESUS, under the fame endearing character of the LAMB of GOD.

It fhall be our bufinefs in the following difcourfe,

Firſt, To fhew you why it is that JESUS CHRIST is ſtiled the LAMB of GOD. And,

Secondly, What we are to underſtand by beholding him. Way will then be made for a word of application.

And firſt, Why is JESUS ſtiled the LAMB of GOD?

I prefume one reafon that may be affigned for it may be drawn from the account we have given us of his moſt amazing and unparalleled meeknefs. A Lamb, you all know, is one of the moſt pacific creatures in the world. When we would defcribe, or point out a perfon of a peaceable difpofition, we fay fuch a one is as quiet as a Lamb. But what is the meeknefs of any perfon, even *Mofes* himſelf, nay, of all the faints that ever lived, put them all together, in comparifon of the meeknefs of the bleffed JESUS? To prove this, I might refer you to his whole life, which was one continued meek and patient enduring of contradiction of finners againſt himſelf; but if you want me to fpecify particular inſtances, only take a walk with me to *Gethfemane*'s garden; there you will fee the traitor *Judas* at the head of a troop of ruffians, accoſting his glorious LORD with a Hail mafter! then kiffing him, and then betraying him. But what fays the Prince of peace? Only, "Friend, wherefore art thou come? *Judas*, betrayeſt thou the fon of man with a kifs?" But how does this fame JESUS behave after he was apprehended? Even in the fame meek manner: for when his warm-hearted difciple *Peter*,

through

through a misguided zeal, had cut off the High Priest's servant's ear, Suffer ye, said the holy JESUS, thus far. In all probability these words were addressed by our LORD to the officers who had tied his hands behind him. As though he had said, "Be pleased to unloose me, whilst I cure that poor man's "ear, which my too forward disciple hath imprudently cut "off, and then you shall bind me again." Was ever reply, was there ever meekness like unto this thy meekness, O thou blessed LAMB of GOD! Well did *Isaiah* prophecy concerning thee, "That thou shouldst be led as a lamb to the slaughter," which goes as willingly to the shambles, as to the pasture: and as justly might thy forerunner call upon sinners to behold thee under the pacific character of the LAMB of GOD. Help us, holy JESUS, to come at thy invitation, and to learn of thee, who gavest such amazing evidences of thy being meek and lowly in heart! then, and not 'till then, shall we find true rest in our souls.

But further, the dear LORD JESUS may properly be called a LAMB, or The LAMB, by way of emphasis, not only in allusion to the Lamb that was offered under the law morning and evening, but more especially because he was typified by the paschal lamb. Hence he is stiled, by that prince of preachers St. *Paul*, CHRIST our passover; and in allusion to the same, the Apostle *Peter* tells us, "That we are not redeemed with corruptible things, as silver and gold, from our vain conversation, but with the precious blood of JESUS CHRIST, as of a Lamb without blemish and without spot." This was an indispensable requisite to be found in the paschal lamb. It was to be a lamb without blemish. A proper type of him who knew no sin, but was spotlessly holy, harmless, and altogether undefiled in heart, lip, and life. Indeed, if we consider him as having the chastisement of our peace, and the iniquities of us all laid upon him by way of imputation, he was, as some divines express it, the greatest

sinner

sinner that ever was: and we should esteem him to be such in reality, were we to judge of his innocence by the abusive and barbarous treatment that he met with whilst tabernacling on earth. But, notwithstanding all this, he was without sin, and therefore could boldly and truly give men and devils the challenge, and say, "Which of you convinceth me of sin? The prince of this world cometh, but shall find nothing in me. There was no corruption in the heart of this immaculate LAMB of GOD for *Satan*'s temptations to lay hold on: But this properly belongeth only to him: for any of his followers, though arrived at the highest pitch of christian perfection, much less for young converts, mere novices in the things of GOD, to presume that they either have, or ever shall, while on this side eternity, arrive at such a sinless state, argues such an ignorance of the spiritual extent of the moral law, of the true interpretation of GOD's word, of the universal experience of GOD's people in all ages, as well as of the remaining unmortified corruptions of their own desperately wicked and deceitful hearts, that I dare venture to tell the preachers and abettors of any such doctrine, however knowing they may be in other respects, that they know not the true nature of gospel-holiness, nor the COMPLEATNESS OF A BELIEVER'S STANDING IN THE UNSPOTTED IMPUTED RIGHTEOUSNESS OF JESUS CHRIST, as they ought to know, or as I trust they themselves, through divine grace, will be made to know before they die. Surely it is high time to awake out of this delusive dream! Pardon this short, (would to GOD there was no occasion of adding) though too necessary a digression.

But to proceed. The paschal lamb was further typical of CHRIST, its great antitype, in that it was to be killed in the evening, and afterwards roasted with fire. So CHRIST, our passover, was sacrificed for us in the evening of the world; only with this material difference, the paschal lamb was first

slain,

slain, and then roasted; whereas the holy JESUS, the spotless LAMB of GOD, was burnt and roasted in the fire of his Father's wrath before he actually expired upon the cross. To satisfy you of this, if you can bear to be spectators of such an awful tragedy, as I desired you just now to go with me to the entrance, so I must now entreat you to venture a little further into the same garden. But—stop—What is that we see? Behold the LAMB of GOD, undergoing the most direful tortures of vindictive wrath! Of the people, even of his disciples, there is none with him. Alas! was ever sorrow like unto that sorrow, wherewith his innocent soul was afflicted in this day of his Father's fierce anger? Before he entered into this bitter passion, out of the fulness of his heart, he said, "Now is my soul troubled." But how is it troubled now! his agony bespeaks it to be exceeding sorrowful, even unto death. It extorts sweat, yea, a bloody sweat. His face, his hands, his garments, are all over stained with blood. It extorts strong cryings and many tears. See how the incarnate deity lies prostrate before his Father, who now laid on him the iniquities of us all. See how he agonizes in prayer! Hark! Again and again he addresses his Father with an "If it be possible, let this cup pass from me!" Tell me, ye blessed angels, tell me, *Gabriel* (or whatsoever thou art called, who wast sent from heaven in this important hour, to strengthen our agonizing LORD) tell me, if ye can, what CHRIST endured in this dark and doleful night; and tell me, tell me what you yourselves felt when you heard this same God-man, whilst expiring on the accursed tree, breaking forth into that dolorous, unheard-of expostulation, " My GOD, my GOD, why, or how hast thou forsaken me? Were you not all struck dumb? And did not an universal awful silence fill heaven itself, when GOD the Father said unto his sword, " Sword, smite thy fellow?" Well might nature put on its sable weeds; well might the rocks rend, to shew their sympathy with a suffering Saviour; and well might the sun

withdraw

withdraw its light, as though it was shocked and confounded to see its maker suffer. But our hearts are harder than rocks, or otherwise they would now break, and our souls more stupid than any part of the inanimate creation, or they would even now, in some degree, at least, sympathize with a crucified Redeemer; who for us men, and for our salvation, was thus roasted, as it were, in the fire of his Father's wrath, and therefore fitly stiled the LAMB of GOD.

But further. The paschal lamb was typical of CHRIST our passover in another respect. For as the blood of the lamb, after it was slain, was sprinkled upon the door-posts of the *Israelites* houses, so the blood of JESUS CHRIST, shed for the sins of the world, is to be applied to, and by faith sprinkled upon the hearts of the true *Israel* of GOD. And as the destroying angel had no power to execute vengeance on, or hurt those whose door-posts were thus sprinkled with the blood of the paschal lamb, so in the great and terrible day of the LORD, he shall be prohibited both from destroying or hurting true believers, who by a living faith in the blood of JESUS, have their hearts sprinkled from an evil conscience. Hence the blood of CHRIST is called "The blood of sprinkling." And lastly, As the lamb under the law was feasted upon by GOD's people, after it was slain, so believers under the gospel by faith feast upon a crucified Redeemer. CHRIST, our passover, says the apostle, is sacrificed for us, therefore let us keep the feast, not barely upon an Easter-day, but all the year round. For the just, i. e. truly justified souls, live by faith, and find, by happy experience, that in a spiritual sense CHRIST's flesh is meat indeed, and his blood drink indeed; and therefore believing on him is stiled "Eating the flesh and drinking the blood of the son of man." Agreeable to this, in our communion office, the minister, when he gives the bread to the communicants, is directed to make use of these affecting words, "Take and eat this in

"remembrance

"remembrance that CHRIST died for thee, and feed on him in thy heart by faith with thankſgiving." May all who give, and all that receive that bread, feel the meaning of this form of ſound words experimentally, and powerfully preſſed home upon their ſouls! Then indeed, but not till then, may they expect to take this holy ſacrament to their comfort. Upon all theſe accounts then, well might the Baptiſt recommend the holy JESUS under the ſignificant character of the Lamb. And with equal propriety might he be called the LAMB of GOD, not only becauſe he was a Lamb of GOD the Father's providing, but becauſe he was co-equal, co-eſſential with the Father: "The Word that was with GOD, the Word that was GOD, even GOD over all, GOD bleſſed for evermore. For ever adored be the triune GOD for this great myſtery of godlineſs, GOD manifeſt in the fleſh! O may it be continually marvellous in our eyes! O make us, thou altogether lovely Redeemer, like-minded with thy bleſſed angels, that with them we may always ſo eagerly, and ſo perſeveringly deſire to look into it, that neither the luſt of the fleſh, the luſt of the eye, or pride of life, may ever in the leaſt divert us from beholding thee!

What this beholding him imports, comes next to be conſidered, under our ſecond general head.

And here I take it for granted, that it cannot imply a beholding the LORD JESUS in perſon with our bodily eyes. It is true, indeed, when *John* called upon the people and his diſciples to behold the LAMB of GOD, they were thus highly favoured: and we are apt to ſay within ourſelves, Bleſſed are the eyes which ſaw what they ſaw; and ſo undoubtedly they were. But had their views terminated only in beholding his perſon, or knowing him barely according to the fleſh, they might notwithſtanding have died in their ſins, and been condemned to depart from him into everlaſting fire, prepared for

the

the devil and his angels.—Our LORD himself hath told us, that there will be many who will plead that they eat and drank in his presence, and heard him preach in their streets, to whom he will say, "Verily I know you not." A true beholding of the LAMB of GOD, must therefore necessarily import something more; and what can that be but a beholding him with an eye of faith? This is what the Old Testament saints were invited to, when the glorious Redeemer called upon them in those emphatic terms, "Behold me, behold me;" and again, "Look unto me, all the ends of the earth." This our LORD in another place terms, believing on him: "Blessed are they which have not seen me, and yet have believed:" not barely as the result of a mere rational conviction, which is no more than an historical faith, but as the consequence of a true spiritual conviction of our being every way undone, and liable to eternal condemnation without him. This is believing on him with the heart, and is sometimes expressed by coming to, receiving, and trusting in him: different expressions, but all importing one and the self same thing. "I wound, and I heal." That is the method the Holy Ghost takes, and that is the pattern gospel ministers must follow in preaching him. From any other, though prescribed to us by an angel from heaven, good LORD, deliver us!

But secondly. By beholding the LAMB of GOD, we are to understand not only looking to him so as to trust him for the pardon of our sins, but beholding him so as to have our hearts broke with a true and godly sorrow for having crucified and slain him by them. For thus speaks the LORD by the mouth of the Prophet *Zechariah*, "They shall look upon him whom they have pierced, and they shall mourn for him, as one that mourneth for an only son, and shall be in bitterness for him, as one that is in bitterness for his first-born." This prediction was in some degree fulfilled immediately after the descent of the Holy Ghost, in the days of Pentecost, when so many being pricked to the heart, were made to look to, believe on, and lament over a pierced JESUS. But it will be continually fulfilling in the experience of every true beholder of the LAMB of GOD, till time shall be no more. True faith, at the same time as it opens the heart to receive CHRIST, melts and dissolves it into tears of godly sorrow, for having betrayed and crucified him. Such were the tears of *Mary*, when she washed the feet of her sin-forgiving LORD. They flowed from a sense of pardoning love. She loved much, having much forgiven her. And though she knew the LORD had forgiven her, yet she could not forgive herself. *Hinc illæ lachrymæ.* Hence those repenting tears: they proceeded from love: sorrow, flowing from any other principle, is not a godly, but a legal sorrow, which the most abandoned wretch may have without the least degree of saving grace. Thus we hear of a *Judas* his repenting, and of an *Esau* crying out with an exceeding bitter cry; but the one all the while was a prophane person, and the other immediately went and hanged himself. And why? Their sorrow was only extorted by a fear of hell, and a despairing sense of impending ruin. It is true, a godly sorrow may, and I believe generally does, begin with something of this nature; but then it does not end there. Through want of a due consideration of this, it is to be feared, many seeming converts have taken up with a few legal convictions, which never ended in savingly and truly beholding the LAMB of GOD. May none here present, by a half-way repentance, and hypocritical sorrow for sin, add to the unhappy number!

But this is not all. A scriptural beholding of the LAMB of GOD, denotes not only such a relying on CHRIST for pardon of sin, as is attended with a truly godly sorrow for it, but such a believing on him, as is productive of a holy life, and a universal chearful observance of all his divine commands.

When

When the two disciples mentioned in our text, heard *John* speak, we are told that they followed him, viz. the LORD JESUS CHRIST. And if GOD hath given us an hearing ear, when called upon to behold the LAMB of GOD, we shall certainly have an obedient heart, and follow him in the way of holy obedience. But then it will be an obedience flowing from love: A working not for, but from life. Not out of a servile fear of being damned, but from a grateful sense of having received the beginning of salvation in our hearts. And this is what the Apostle calls " faith working by love." Many, I know, censure and look upon us as troublers of *Israel*, for preaching up the doctrine of justification by faith alone in the imputed righteousness of JESUS CHRIST. We own the charge. We do preach, and hope shall continue to preach it, till we can preach no more. *Luther* stiles it, *Articulus stantis aut cadentis ecclesiæ*; the article by which the church must stand or fall: and in the ninth article of our own church, it is termed, a most wholesome doctrine. Take away this, and you take away the only solid foundation upon which a truly weary and heavy-laden sinner can possibly build his hopes of pardon and acceptance in the sight of a holy and sin-avenging GOD. But why this outcry against the doctrine of justification by faith alone? They say this doctrine destroys good works. But do we, by preaching this doctrine, make void the law of GOD? No: We thereby establish the law. For, though faith alone justifies, yet, as the good old Puritans used to observe, That faith which is alone, justifieth not. Agreeable to this, speaketh the 12th article of our Church. " Albeit that good works, which are the fruits of faith, and " follow after justification, cannot put away our sins, and " endure the severity of GOD's judgment, yet are they pleas- " ing and acceptable to GOD in CHRIST, and do spring " out necessarily of a true and lively faith, insomuch that by " them a lively faith may be as evidently known as a tree is "discerned by the fruit." They, therefore, who object against our insisting upon justification by faith alone, as destructive of morality, not only betray great ignorance of the articles of our Church, and of GOD's word, but give too great reason to suspect, that they never experienced the blessed influence of a true and lively faith in their own hearts. For true and undefiled religion, is nothing more or less, than a universal morality, founded upon the love of GOD and faith in CHRIST JESUS. And a true beholding him as pierced for our sins, will, in its own nature, sweetly compel us to cry out, "What shall we render unto the LORD?" It was this, that, perhaps, in a quarter of an hour, made that covetous worldling *Zaccheus*, give half of his goods to the poor; it was this, that all of a sudden made the Jailor wash the stripes of those whom he had but a little before thrust into an inward prison; it was this that caused *Lydia*, whose heart the LORD had opened, so freely to open her house to entertain the Apostles; and it was this that excited the Apostles themselves in general, and St. *Paul* in particular, to bid adieu to worldly honours, to glory in nothing but the cross of CHRIST, and to fly like an arch-angel from pole to pole, publishing the blessed and everlasting gospel. "The love of CHRIST, said he, constraineth us." Preaching faith in this manner, seems to me the only scriptural way of preaching CHRIST: and by this means we shall steer a middle course between two dangerous extremes. For to insist only upon morality and good works, and not lay a true lively faith, as a foundation whereon they are to be built, (as it is to be feared too many do) is to act like *Pharaoh*'s task-masters, and bid people make brick without shewing them were to get straw. "My soul, come not thou into their secret!" On the other hand, to call upon people to believe in, and behold the LAMB of GOD, and at the same time not exhort them to maintain good works, as an evidence and fruit of their beholding him, is the way to turn the grace of God into lasciviousness. And therefore, however evangelical such preachers may seem in their own eyes, yet if the writings of *Moses* and the Prophets, of our Lord and his Apostles, are to be our judges, they do not rightly divide the word of truth. " To their assembly, mine honour, be not thou united!"

Once more. A true beholding of the Lamb of God, implies such a beholding him, as will transform us into his divine likeness. This will be the effect of our seeing him as he is in heaven; and this, in its degree, will always be the consequence of our beholding him with an eye of a true and lively faith on earth. When *Moses* came down from mount *Horeb*, where he had been conversing with God, we are told, that his face shone; and if we have been upon the mount of ordinances beholding by faith the blessed Lamb of God, though our faces will not shine, yet our hearts will be moulded into his blessed image. This is what the Apostle *Paul* terms, in one place, " Being transformed by the renewing of our minds;" and in another, " Passing from glory to glory, even by the Spirit of the Lord." All manifestations, of whatever kind or degree, if not attended with this transforming and truly sanctifying influence, are unprofitable, delusive, or merely imaginary. *Balaam* could call himself the man whose eyes were open, and the man who had seen the visions of the Almighty, and yet he was a poor worldling all the while. He loved the wages of unrighteousness, though forced by God not to receive them. Hence we may easily and rationally account for the falling away of some, and it may be the final apostacy of many others, who in the late religious stir, (as some are pleased to call it) seemed to be uncommonly gifted, and to be lifted up, as it were, to the third heaven. Satan being sensible that the Holy Spirit of God was working a great work upon the earth, turns himself into an angel of light, introduces his extraordinaries, and thereby mimics GOD's true work now, as the magicians were once permitted to mimic the real miracles of *Moses* formerly. Such counterfeits, those who are not ignorant of Satan's devices, ought from time to time to add all diligence to search out and detect; but after the utmost caution imaginable, I believe we shall find the saying of a very zealous Reformer (who thought, at his first coming out, that he should convert the whole world) to be too true, viz. " That old Satan will be, in many " cases, too hard for young *Melancthon*." Satan is an old practitioner, and we, comparatively speaking, but novices; and therefore no wonder, that we sometimes mistake his extraordinaries, for the powerful operations of the Holy Spirit; or look upon those, at least for a while, who are only stony-ground hearers, and have received the word with joy, as though they were truly converted to, and had by a living, soul-transforming faith, beheld the LAMB of GOD. Such mistakes may serve to make us more cautious. But to condemn a work in the lump, as merely delusive and diabolical, or roundly to affirm, that all the pretended subjects of it have taken up only with an ideal CHRIST, because some have mistaken imaginations for the true spiritual manifestation of GOD's love to their hearts, discovers such an ignorance of scripture, of Satan's devices, and the accounts given us of past revivals in all ages, that if one did not know the dreadful blindness of a bigotted sectarian zeal, and what a proneness there is in the best of men, to condemn every thing that doth not come just in their own way, we should think it morally impossible that good men should run such lengths as some have done of late, in censuring what I think may be called, amidst all the infirmities and weaknesses that have attended it, A great and glorious work of a GOD.

But it is time for me to draw nearer to a conclusion. We have now then, my dear hearers, done with the doctrinal part of our text; in opening of which, that we might deal with you as rational creatures, we have endeavoured calmly, and in the fear of GOD, to addrefs ourfelves to your underftandings: but the hardeft work is yet behind, namely, to affect and warm your hearts. This I take to be the very life of preaching: for man is a compound creature, made up of affections, as well as underftanding; and, confequently, without addreffing both, we only do our work by halves. It is true, every one hath his proper gift, and fome excel in making ufe of a proper method to inform the judgment, whilft others are more eminent for exciting the paffions. Both are beautiful in their feafon; and both ought and will be ufed by all who have warm hearts, as well as clear heads. *Mofes* and the Prophets, CHRIST and his Apoftles, dealt much in exhortations, as well as in opening and explaining the weighty matters of the law. And if we are taught by the fame Spirit, we fhall, like them, bring light and heat with us, when called to fpeak of, and enforce the things which concern the kingdom of GOD. Without a proper mixture of thefe, however a preacher may acquire the character, in the letter-learned and polite world, of being a calm and cool reafoner; yet he never will be looked upon by thofe whofe fenfes are exercifed to difcern fpiritual things, as a truly evangelical and chriftian orator.—And furely if a minifter's heart is ever warm, it ought to be fo in a more efpecial manner, when calling on a blind and drowfy world, to behold the Lamb of GOD. O! that my tongue was at this time touched with a coal from his altar. O! that my cold and frozen heart (for I muft again repeat the wifh I put up at the beginning of this difcourfe) was in the fame bleffed and divine frame, as we have reafon to believe the holy Baptift was favoured with, when he called upon his difciples and the people, fo repeatedly, to behold the Lamb of GOD. But to whom fhall I apply myfelf firft? Or with what language fhall I addrefs you, when preffing you to the fame important thing?

Will my brethren in the ministry suffer a word of exhortation from one who is less than the least of them all? Does not the practice of this fervent harbinger and fore-runner of the Son of GOD, naturally lead me to it? For did he so unweariedly recommend the LORD JESUS? Did he take such care to preach not himself, but CHRIST JESUS his Lord? And shall not we make this same JESUS the Alpha and Omega, the beginning and end of all our discourses? Did he take such pains to debase himself, exalt his LORD, and evidence to the world that he was disinterested, and sought not his own glory, but the glory of him whose fore-runner he was? And shall we not go and do likewise? To prepare the Redeemer's way before him, by turning the hearts of the disobedient to the wisdom of the just, and to proclaim a coming Saviour, *John* esteemed his highest honour. This is an employ worthy angels. They thought themselves highly favoured, when sent to give notice of the Mediator's birth to some humble shepherds. And I hope I am speaking to some, who had rather be employed in such an errand, than be ambassadors to the greatest monarchs on earth. Go on then, my brethren, or rather fathers, as it becomes such a one as I to call you. Ye angels of the churches, ye stewards of the mysteries of GOD, go on in the name and strength of the everlasting I AM. Preach CHRIST, and him crucified; continue to preach him: be instant in season and out of season; and though you should be called to suffer for so doing, fear not, but rather rejoice, and be exceeding glad: great will be your reward in heaven; for so persecuted they *John* the Baptist, and others that have been employed in calling upon sinners to behold the Lamb of GOD before you.

Are any here present who are entrusted with the care of youth that are intended for the ministry? My text warns me not to leave you out in this address. *John* directed his disciples to behold the Lamb of God: and ought not such, who have the oversight of those who are hereafter to be employed in the same divine work as *John* was, to make it one main part of their daily endeavours, to bring their pupils to a true, experimental, and saving acquaintance with the ever-blessed Lamb of God? This may be done without leaving any one necessary branch of true knowledge and useful learning undone. A neglect of this important point hath been, and it is to be feared even now is, the bane of the christian church. For, if young men's minds are from year to year wholly engaged in studying the heathen mythology, instead of being shewn the beauties of the New Testament; if they are taught to delight more in reading *Cæsar*'s Commentaries, or the exploits of an *Alexander*, than to admire the miracles of *Jesus* of *Nazareth*; if they are directed to employ themselves more in giving an account of *Homer*'s battles, than of the important war between *Michael* and the Dragon; if it is esteemed a greater excellency to be engaged in studying the folds of a *Roman* garment, than to enquire into the various turnings and windings of their own corrupt hearts: if these, and such-like trifling things, are recommended to their daily study, and the glorious doctrines of the gospel, such as regeneration, justification, &c. wholly neglected, or superficially spoken of, is it any wonder, that so many ignorantly strike their heads against the pulpit, or appear when put into it, more like heathen philosophers or *Roman* orators, than gospel preachers, though without half the clearness and sound reasoning of the one, or a thousandth part of the true pathos and unaffected eloquence of the other? The recommending and enforcing the practical study of the doctrines and example of the blessed JESUS, seems to me to be the only remedy for this great, not to say growing evil.

And therefore, I beg leave in the next place to address myself to those who are now actually engaged in the study

study of divinity, and are desirous of being prepared according to the preparation of the sanctuary, for the great and solemn work of calling upon sinners, to behold the Lamb of GOD. When *John* the Baptist was thus employed, he took care to assure the people, that he himself was well acquainted with that CHRIST. " I saw, said he, and bear record, that this is the Son of GOD." And doth not this at least intimate to you, young students, that above all things you should study to get an experimental acquaintance with the LORD JESUS in your own hearts, before you attempt to recommend him to the choice of others? Then, having believed, you will speak; speak not as mere dead, formal, letter-learned scribes, but as men having authority. You will then, like *John* the Baptist, be the voice of one crying; you will lift up your voices like trumpets; you will preach not with the enticing words of man's wisdom, but with the demonstration of the spirit and of power. This, with a moderate share of useful learning, which is quite necessary in its place, will enable you to do wonders. Vallies shall be filled up, mountains shall be brought low, and a highway made, through your instrumentality, into sinners hearts, by the blessed and all-powerful operations of the Spirit of the everliving GOD. Such a method, perhaps, may render your preaching a little unfashionable, but it is the only way to render it useful, and truly evangelical. Take the Apostle *Paul* for your ensample. He was a great scholar, as well as a great saint; and, if called to it, could have fought the learned world with their own weapons; but he chose to fight only with the sword of the Spirit, which is the word of GOD. And even, when preaching at so polite a place as *Corinth*, determined to know nothing among them, but JESUS CHRIST and him crucified. He too, like another *John*, made it his constant, uninterrupted employ to beseech poor sinners to behold the Lamb of GOD. May that mind be in you, which was also in him!

But

But do not the words of our text lead me to addrefs all in general, as well as tutors and their pupils in particular? Yes: to you, even to as many as hear me this day, whether high or low, rich or poor, young or old, one with another, may a word of exhortation naturally be directed. It was to the people, as well as to his difciples, that *John*, when he faw JESUS coming unto him, fpoke thofe endearing words, " Behold the Lamb of GOD." I therefore call upon you all in the fame language, and for the fame reafon; for it is He, and He alone, that taketh away the fins of the world. It is this that you all ftand in need of, whether you know it or not. You are all ftung by that old and crooked ferpent the devil. " Therefore, as *Mofes* lifted up the ferpent in the wildernefs, even fo was the Son of Man lifted up, that whofoever believeth on him fhould not perifh, but have everlafting life." O then behold him, behold him! Look unto him, all ye ends of the earth, even ye upon whom the ends of the world are come, and be ye faved. Some of you, I truft, through grace, have already been enabled to do this. O come, come, I befeech you, and repeat the bleffed look: for this is the chriftian's grand catholicon, the fovereign remedy for all the remaining difeafes of his foul. Are ye tempted? Behold the Lamb of GOD. " He was tempted in all things like as we are," that he might be able experimentally to fympathize with, and fuccour thofe that are tempted. Are ye deferted, and bewailing an abfent GOD? Behold the Lamb of GOD. He once complained, and that too to his own creatures, " My foul is exceeding forrowful, even unto death;" He once cried out, and that to his heavenly Father, " My GOD, my GOD, why haft thou forfaken me." Are ye poor? Behold the LAMB of GOD: He had not where to lay his head. Are ye betrayed and forfaken by friends? Behold the LAMB of GOD: He was betrayed by *Judas*, denied by *Peter*, and when apprehended, all forfook him and fled. Are you

blackened

blackened and maligned by enemies? Behold the LAMB of GOD: He was accounted a mad-man, a deceiver, nay, a Beelzebub, the very chief of the devils. Are ye afraid of death, or dying? Behold the LAMB of GOD: He hath taken away the sting of that king of terrors, and came to deliver those, who through fear of death were all their life-time subject to bondage. Doubt ye whether ye shall hold out to the end? Behold the LAMB of GOD; "He is the Author and finisher of our faith;" and having loved his own, he loved them even unto the end. Do ye want more grace, either to mortify remaining corruption, or to enable you to bring forth more fruit unto GOD? Behold the LAMB of GOD: "Out of his fulness we may all receive, and that too, even grace for grace;" grace upon grace, grace to beget more grace, even till we are filled with all the fulness of GOD. O ye believers, my heart is enlarged towards you; look to, and live much on the blessed JESUS; and then you will live to, and act for him more and more. Be thankful for what you have received, but be looking out continually for fresh discoveries of his love, and fresh incomes of heavenly grace, till you are called to behold this LAMB of GOD in glory: that time, blessed be GOD, will shortly come. Though worms destroy our bodies, yet in our flesh we shall see our GOD; not as we do now, through a glass darkly, but face to face: see him as he is: and what is yet better, be growing up more and more into his divine likeness, through the endless ages of eternity.

But as for ungodly and obstinate unbelievers that die in their sins, it shall not be so with them. Behold him indeed you shall; behold him you must; "For yet a little while, and we must all appear before the judgment-seat of CHRIST." But O! how shall I speak it? You must behold him once, never to behold him any more! Behold him, not so much as the LAMB of GOD, as the Lion of the tribe of *Judah*, and hear him roaring out that dreadful sentence, "Depart, ye curfed, cursed, into everlasting fire, prepared for the devil and his angels." O think of this, all ye that have hitherto neglected to behold this LAMB of GOD by faith, so shall unbelief not prove your final ruin. To you, even to you I once more call. Blessed be GOD, the door of mercy is not yet shut; the day of grace is not yet over; look unto him, and you shall yet be saved: his heart is open, and his arms stretched out ready to receive you. O that he would rend the heavens and come down amongst you; and as he had once compassion upon a poor woman, that was bowed down with the spirit of infirmity, lo eighteen years! O that he would repeat that all-powerful command, " Be ye loosed from your infirmity," and enable every unconverted sinner to look up to, and behold the LAMB of GOD! However, if you will not come to him that you might have life, GOD forbid that I should cease to pray for you. O LORD GOD most holy, O LORD GOD most mighty, O holy and merciful Saviour, thou most worthy Judge eternal, by thine agony and bloody sweat, by thy cross and passion, by thy precious death and burial, by thy glorious resurrection and ascension, and by the coming of the Holy Ghost, we humbly entreat thee to help all such to take the warning that has now been given them! O help them to behold thee by faith here, that so no pains of hell may fall from thee whenever they are summoned to appear before thy awful tribunal hereafter! I am persuaded all that love the LORD JESUS in sincerity, will say, *Amen!* Even so, LORD JESUS! *Amen!* and *Amen!*

www.ingramcontent.com/pod-product-compliance
Lightning Source LLC
Chambersburg PA
CBHW020539300426
44111CB00008B/723